AF240624

DEFEATING JIHADIST TERRORISM

Jacques Baud

DEFEATING JIHADIST TERRORISM

Max Milo

Max Milo, 2022
ISBN : 9782315010790

CONTENTS

FOREWORD

Having lived in New York for several years, it has become a bit «my» city too. September 11 affected me and some of my acquaintances suffered from it. As a New Yorker, I have participated in all the annual commemorations of this terrible event, including the one presided over by Barack Obama at the site of the attacks in 2011. We mourn the innocent victims of these acts of extreme violence.

On 11 September 2021, the world commemorated the 2001 attacks. At no time, in any media, did any journalist mention or try to understand why 19 young Muslims decided to sacrifice their lives on that day. The lack of an answer to this question has, on the one hand, opened the door to a variety of conspiracy theories and, on the other hand, has led to the assumption that terrorism is gratuitous violence perpetrated by individuals, whose aim is simply to 'instil terror'[1].Terrorism has thus been made into an inexplicable phenomenon or, more precisely, one that can only be explained by the very nature of Islam.[2]

Not only is this false, it is idiotic and leads to two main problems. The first is that this lack of reflection makes terrorism an inescapable phenomenon that can only be resolved by the disappearance of Islam or its manifestations. The second is that by attributing to the Muslim religion an inherent project of conquest, a form of conspiracy is created, which feeds on a growing and assumed resentment against immigrant populations, especially in France and Belgium. The result is that no effort is made to deal with terrorism at its roots and the gap between communities is widened.

The real causes of 9/11 were known at the time and still are, as we shall see. But our arrogance has prevented us from admitting them and our hatred of Islam has silenced them.

Thirty years ago, about 500 attacks resulted in 350 deaths per year. Today, after endless wars against terrorism, the number of attacks has increased 30-fold and the number of victims 100-fold. Wherever our forces are engaged, terrorism

---

1   . Sergio Honorez, in the programme C'est vous qui le dites, RTBF, 10 September 2021.
2   . Antoine Hasday, «La pensée djihadiste décryptée», slate.fr, 6 November 2017.

develops: either we unleash communal rivalries (as in Libya and the Sahel), or we end up using jihadists to overthrow governments (as in Afghanistan and Syria) or we generate resistance movements (as in the Sahel). Libya is probably the most blatant example of military engagement without knowing the situation on the ground, without a strategy and without knowing how to get out of the crisis: through political and military incompetence, and - let's say it - through foolishness and ideological blindness, Nicolas Sarkozy's France created the problem of Niger and Mali, encouraged Islamism in Tunisia, while François Hollande's France contributed to the creation of the Islamic State.

No one commits terrorist acts for no reason or «just to scare people» as Tony Blair said[3].No matter how terrible and unacceptable, the terrorist act always has a reason: it may seem futile, exaggerated, inappropriate, but it exists. It is only by dealing with this 'reason' that terrorism will be defeated. But we tend to deal with the problem at the tactical level and ignore its strategic dimension, thus leaving the initiative to it.

The trial of the perpetrators of the 13 November 2015 attacks in Paris opened on 8 September 2021. The victims are waiting for explanations, but this expectation will not be met.

First of all, because we are judging terrorists and not terrorism. The aim is to punish the perpetrators of a criminal act, not to explain a security phenomenon. That said, for many, this trial is more an act of revenge than an attempt to prevent future attacks. For example, the statements of Abdeslam, the main defendant, are not reported by the media for fear of «giving him a platform»[4].As a result, the culprits will logically be punished, but the trial will not shed any light on the terrorist phenomenon. Moreover, at the same time as the trial is taking place, France is acting in such a way as to generate new terrorist acts, as we shall see.

Secondly, because this trial is taking place on the basis of emotion. Since 2015, France has been unable to rationalise the terrorist problem in order to find a lasting solution: exegetes of all stripes have come together in a single vision of the nature of terrorism, obscuring many avenues of reflection and turning their hypotheses into truths. This is why, more than anywhere else, the «experts» maintain a rhetoric that makes terrorism an irrational and inescapable phenomenon.

Finally, because in France, more than in Anglo-Saxon countries, the idea prevails that trying to understand the terrorist approach is a way of excusing and approving it. This is largely due to a certain narcissism that leads one to think that terrorism is rooted in what one is and not in what one does. Symptomatically, no other European country seems to have the same problems with Islamism...

---

3   . Tony Blair, «In full: Blair on bomb blasts», BBC News, 7 July 2005.
4   . Sylvia Falcinelli, «Salah Abdeslam, un 'héros' porté par les médias?», rtbf.be, 10 September 2021.

1. INTRODUCTION

Enriched by the experiences of nearly twenty years of fighting terrorism, this book is a development of my 2003 book, *Asymmetric Warfare or the Defeat of the Winner.* As events since then have shown, the principles I outlined then are even more relevant today. But, like my book, *Governing by Fake News,* it will be rejected by those who work against the interests of France, and favour blind violence over intelligent force against terrorism.

No Western country has succeeded in understanding jihadist terrorism and devising strategies to combat it. This explains the Western failures in Afghanistan, Iraq, Libya and Syria. Terrorism is not inevitable. If it strikes France, but not Switzerland or Iceland, there is a reason. That reason is the key to implementing strategies to prevent terrorism.

In France, more than in any other Western country, reflection on the causes of terrorism has been drowned in national politics. Immigration is confused with communitarianism, Islam with Islamism, Islamism with terrorism. This has resulted in an extremely poor national debate on the nature and origin of the phenomenon, the absence of holistic strategies to solve it and an essentially emotional treatment of terrorism. The consequence is that by fighting it, we feed it. It is therefore a paradoxical situation where the victims of terrorism have contributed to its emergence. This book is for those who have the courage to look terrorism in the face and confront it head on in order to eradicate it, not just to exact revenge. This is not just another book 'about' terrorism. It is a methodological approach to eradicating jihadist terrorism.

In the first part, we will look at our main mistakes in understanding terrorism, which prevent us from acting effectively. Particularly in France, where the integration of the North African immigrant population has never been taken seriously, the confusion between «Islamism» and «Islam» has gradually taken hold in political discourse, to the point of making terrorism unreadable. The lack of consideration for the immigrant population is such that it took France sixty years to recognise the situation of its own allies, the harkis, who had courageously helped it during the Algerian war! A symbol of ignorance and collective incompetence...

But to understand and combat terrorism, it is essential to get rid of prejudice. This is the most difficult part, because prejudice has become so important in our understanding of terrorism that we end up not believing what the terrorists themselves tell us[5].No one is more blind than the one who does not want to see. Understanding does not mean excusing, but it must allow us to explain in order to act.

In the second part, we examine the nature of jihadist terrorism and the implications of its asymmetric nature. These notions have invaded the political vocabulary without the consequences being drawn for dealing with the problem. All attacks look the same and their victims suffer the same pain, but their purpose, their objectives and the doctrine they follow can be very different. To say that terrorism affects us «*for what we are and not for what we do*» is an expression of our arrogance, with serious consequences: we see terrorism as an inevitability against which we can do nothing, and as a monolithic phenomenon.

Particularly in France, the 'experts' remain locked into an obsolete reading of terrorism: we therefore fail to grasp its strategic logic and we only fight it at the tactical level. Thus, its asymmetrical nature is totally ignored. This is why we are always one step behind the terrorists and «*the harder we work, the further we fall*»[6].To understand jihadist terrorism, one must go back to the original texts that explain its principles and mechanics, but which have nothing to do with the Koran.

The third part examines the different ways of effectively fighting terrorism from the strategic to the tactical level. It shows how the differences between communitarian acts (such as the murder of Samuel Paty) and terrorist acts (such as the murder of Father Hamel in Saint-Étienne-du-Rouvray) imply differentiated strategies of struggle. As in medicine, each disease requires an adapted therapy; it is because we do not know how to differentiate treatments that terrorism develops. The reason why we fail to differentiate between different acts of violence is that - particularly in France - the view of this violence is totally passionate. This results in a single explanation, propagated by some authors and journalists[7] , which «de-pluralises» the possible remedies and prevents an effective response against communitarian and terrorist crimes.

---

5   . Aurélie Sarrot, «Procès du 13 novembre : Salah Abdeslam justifie les attentats par l'intervention française en Syrie», lci.fr, 15 September 2021 (updated 16 September 2021).
6   . Donald Rumsfeld, Confidential Report on Iraq to the Joint Chiefs of Staff, October 2003.
7   . Antoine Hasday, «La pensée djihadiste décryptée», slate.fr, 6 November 2017.

16

1.1 Three basic errors

Our main mistake in fighting terrorism is to see it emotionally, not factually. We think we are being «tough» by ruthlessly hitting anything and anyone. We would be tough if we had the courage to look terrorism in the face, in all its complexity. But we do not. If this work had been done, we would not be mourning our dead today.

Thus, '9/11' was seen as the beginning of a new war. This was obviously wrong. The jihadists see it as a battle in a war that the West had started much earlier:

> *9/11 was neither*
>
> *the beginning of a war between Muslims and the West, nor the end. It was simply an episode in a long war [...].*[8]

But the West has adopted a rhetoric based on hatred of the West and its freedoms, which derationalises terrorism and makes it an inescapable phenomenon. The result is a form of denial, the perverse effect of which is to prevent us from dealing with terrorism strategically.

Terrorism is very rational, but the main reason why we cannot control it is that we do not understand or do not want to understand the logic of how it works or why it works... This lack of understanding is based on three fundamental errors.

1.1.1. First mistake: «The purpose of terrorism is just that, to terrorise people». [9]

A common mistake is to see terrorism as a 'self-sustaining' phenomenon, self-satisfied and an end in itself. It is then attributed with the objective of «*creating fear and panic*»[10] and «*dividing us*»[11]. This reading is usually propagated by government institutions seeking to cover up their mistakes that led to the emergence of terrorism. It is frequently evoked in France and raises two essential problems.

Firstly, it makes terrorism a phenomenon independent of the context in which it takes place. But terrorism is *always part* of a dynamic: it seeks to achieve something through the use of violence. Terrorism is not an objective, it is a means.

Secondly, it makes it an inherent inevitability of our society: we are hit for what we are, not for what we do. Originating in Israel, this discourse made

---

8   . Yahya Ibrahim, "Letter from the Editor", Inspire, n° 7, Fall 2011 (1432), p. 3.

9   . Tony Blair, "In full: Blair on bomb blasts", BBC News, 7 July 2005.

10   . Manuel Valls, Prime Minister, 15 July 2015.

11   . President François Hollande, speech on 19 July 2016 in Lisbon, AFP, 19 July 2016.

it possible to dissociate terrorism from Palestinian claims, in order to escape pressure to enter into a negotiation process. In France, it is relayed by «experts» who fill the media with convoluted theories in which the idea of an Islamic project - engineered by Saudi Arabia, Qatar or the Muslim Brotherhood - to fracture French society and thus provoke a civil war dominates[12].Terrorism is therefore the result of the nature of our society and the genetics of Islam. This is not true.

These two problems have two immediate consequences. The first is that we label as «terrorist» those acts that we cannot explain by material causes. This leads us to waste resources and - above all - to strike in the wrong place, with the risk of generating «real» terrorism. But if the violent act is not part of a dynamic or a framework associated with requirements (like «9/11» in the United States and the assassination of Samuel Patty in France), it is probably not terrorism, but a crime (mass, anti-Semitic, etc.).

The second consequence is that it leads us to ignore the 'real' reasons for terrorism and to fight them. By attributing to terrorism a fatalistic explanation (linked to the nature of Islam and/or the nature of our society), we close the door to any strategic and political treatment of the problem: the solution can only exist in the annihilation of one of the two parties. The result is a tactical treatment of terrorism. As in the Middle Ages, the modern security polices reinforce the thickness of protection (video surveillance, increased police presence, systematic searches, extension of the state of emergency, Internet surveillance, etc.), but prove incapable of curbing the terrorist phenomenon. This is why Israel and the West are unable to control the phenomenon.

1.1.2. Second mistake: Jihadist terrorism serves a religious project

In January 2018, France 3 broadcast a documentary entitled *Complotisme, les alibis de la terreur*[13] , in which the philosopher Jacob Rogozinski states:

> *Jihadism is also a movement that aims at sovereignty, at world power. There is a dream behind it, a crazy dream no doubt, but a dream of creating a caliphate, which would be a global caliphate, which will take over Rome, which will take over Europe, which will defeat America, which will establish a global network of true believers, united behind an absolute sovereign power.*[14]

---

12 . Gilles Kepel, Terreur dans l'Hexagone, Gallimard, 2015; France 24, 27 July 2016, http://www.france24.com/fr/20160727-le-debat-france-24-attentats-france-terrorisme-securite-notre-dame-partie1.

13 . Rudy Reichstadt & Georges Benayoun, Complotisme, les alibis de la terreur, YouTube, 24 January 2018, www.youtube.com/watch?v=d8e18NIqWiI.

14 . Jacob Rogozinski in Complotism, the Alibis of Terror, YouTube, January 24, 2018 (31'20"), www.youtube.com/watch?v=d8e18NIqWi.

This is a strictly Western vision that is not found in the jihadist discourse. If Islam has developed in the West, and especially in Europe, it is mainly because of poorly managed and clientelistic immigration policies, which have had the double effect of impoverishing the migrants' countries of origin and lowering the standard of living of the underprivileged in the host countries.

As we shall see, however, jihadist terrorism does not aim to conquer the Western world, but to drive Westerners out of the Muslim world. Terrorism does not serve a religious project: its purpose is secular, more military than political, and religion merely frames its modus operandi. This is exactly the opposite of what many people in France think, especially in far-right circles. In jihadist terrorism, religion only has a unifying and doctrinal role. Moreover, we note that jihadist terrorists generally have only a superficial knowledge of religious texts.

1.1.3. Third mistake: Jihadist terrorism is inherent in Islam

In the documentary *Complotisme, les alibis de la terreur*, made by *France 3* in 2018[15] , the psychiatrist Serge Hefez evokes the concept of «*ancestral jihad*»[16] , thus placing terrorism in a historical fatality linked to Islam. In France, the «Islam - Islamism - terrorism» relationship combines with numerous aversions and cultural biases to dominate security thinking. It takes up a populist ideology that claims that jihadist violence is written in the Koran[17].As Islam has become a part of our societies, one might deduce that jihadist terrorism is an inescapable phenomenon and that confrontation with Islam is therefore inevitable. This is obviously false. The idea that terrorism is linked to Islam is as false as the claim that genocide is inherent to Christianity: these 'prevalences' are not due to religions, but to the geopolitical context that surrounds them.

It is a simplistic reasoning, based only on perceptions and ignorance of the history and nature of the Koran. The problem is that it literally generates a «*fear of Islam*» (in French: *islamophobie*). The proponents of this reasoning make the notion of Islamophobia very concrete and exclude any mutual understanding, since Islam will always be Islam. Initially promoted by the extreme right, this interpretation has become very popular in France in all political circles. It is very dangerous, because it leads to communitarianism.

The confusion maintained between «Islam» and «Islamism» by certain circles has no other effect than to maintain communitarianism and the radicalisation of the immigrant population. The perpetrators should be prosecuted.

---

15 . Georges Benayoun & Rudy Reichstadt, Complotisme : les alibis de la terreur, France 3, 23 January 2018 (47'25").
16 . Ibid (44'40").
17 . Antoine Hasday, «La pensée djihadiste décryptée», slate.fr, 6 November 2017.

1.2 Consequences

1.2.1. The lack of strategies

Nothing resembles a victim more than another victim, and a bomber more than another bomber: seen from below, terrorism looks tragically identical. But seen from above, at the strategic level, its logic and objectives show considerable differences. So much so that it can be said that no two types of terrorism are alike.

The problem is that we fight terrorism with a tactical view, as a uniform phenomenon. This explains why no Western country has a real strategy to combat it. There are documents called «strategy", but a careful analysis shows that they are only a set of tactical and extremely ineffective measures, because they are not holistic.

For example, since the creation of the *US Africa Command* (US AFRICOM) in 2008, the number of violent events in Africa has increased by 960% in ten years, from 288 in 2009 to 3050 in 2018, according to the Pentagon[18].

1.2.2. Misplaced communitarianism

In France, the terrorist attacks of 2015 and 2016 helped to embed in people's minds the existence of causal, or even functional, links between immigration and terrorist violence. The right has found in this a «confirmation» of its intuitions and the left a way of inserting itself into fields it had neglected.

The idea that terrorism is a by-product of Muslim immigration to transform our society by force is simply fantastic. But it finds a fairly large echo in a population that feels «invaded» and is the object of attempts to recuperate it by most political parties. The 2016-2017 presidential campaign has moreover highlighted the shift to the right of public opinion with regard to immigration.

The consequence is that secularism is seen as a way to fight terrorism. The endless discussions around the phenomenon of 'radicalisation', which so disturbs politicians, seem to be limited to *how* individuals become radicalised, not *why*. Prison, the Internet and Salafist mosques have been named as 'causes', depending on the profile of the individuals questioned, whereas research on the subject shows that there is no typical profile of radicalised individuals and that none of these 'causes' can be favoured. In fact, these explanations are only intellectual constructions based on professions of faith. They are often put forward

---

18 . Nick Turse, "Violence Has Spiked in Africa Since the Military Founded AFRICOM, Pentagon Study Finds," The Intercept, 29 July 2019.

by individuals with a Marxist background, where religion is necessarily a factor of tension and where secularism is a criterion for integration.

1.2.3. A poorly exploited experience

Feedback is an important tool in the fight against terrorism, provided that the context of this experience is well understood if it is to be useful. For example, the often-vaunted experience gained in France against terrorism in the 1980s and 1990s is of limited use in the fight against jihadist terrorism: the terrorism of the time was «symmetrical», whereas the jihadist terrorist is «asymmetrical». As a result, the solutions of the time may be counterproductive today. Moreover, it should be noted that groups such as Action directe were neutralised with the tools of organised crime, without any strategic consideration.

In the early 2000s, the Americans turned to the French experiences of the Algerian war to find solutions in Iraq and Afghanistan, but - as usual - they understood nothing and only used torture...

The same is true of the British experience in Northern Ireland in the face of asymmetric Marxist terrorism. Contexts that appear very similar at the tactical level have fundamental differences at the strategic level. Therefore, if misunderstood and misused, RETEX can become a failure factor.

1.3. Drawing the right conclusions

Fighting a phenomenon, whatever its nature, requires an understanding of what generates it and how it develops. Our reading of the terrorist phenomenon today is largely influenced by omnipresent pseudo-experts who do not know anything about terrorism but interpret events in the light of their own perception, their own fantasies or their political affiliation. It is therefore legitimate to ask whether those who try to 'explain' terrorism to us are not part of the problem.

The most difficult thing in the fight against terrorism is to get away from the emotional and to get rid of prejudices. In a complex situation, with actors who are difficult to identify, and with logics and references that defy our Western cultures, rational reading naturally tends to give way to instinctive reactions. In short: the more complex the problem, the more we react 'with our gut'.

The aim of this book is to go back to the facts, to listen to and decipher what terrorists are telling us, so that effective strategies can be put in place to combat jihadist violence. It will challenge many of the preconceived notions, often the result of misinformation produced by democratic governments themselves, which seek to protect themselves from electoral sanction. For the fight against terrorism is more than a tactical problem, as it is being called, it is a problem of strategy. Yet no Western country has a real strategy for fighting terrorism. As is often the case, what is called «strategy» is merely a series of activities of tactical level or scope, but with no real impact on the nature of the threat[19].

This book does not give 'recipes' for defeating terrorism, but examines possible solutions and puts them into perspective with the real nature of jihadist terrorism.

---

19 . See Gregor Mathias, La stratégie française de lutte contre le terrorisme islamiste, Balland, 2018.

2. UNDERSTANDING THE THREAT

Classical' conflicts, where opponents of a similar nature confront each other openly on the same battlefield, are determined by the balance of power. Strategic intelligence, tactical flexibility and daring can compensate for numerical or technological inferiority, but most often victory is determined by quantitative and/or qualitative superiority, because the logic of combat is the same on both sides.

This is what allowed the development of numerical modelling of the battlefield, such as the work of Colonel Dupuy in the 1980s[20].At the same time, in the USSR, a large number of battlefield equation models were developed as decision aids to optimise the engagement of armed forces at the operational level, with the underlying idea of making war a science, and not just an art[21].

Non-conventional conflicts fall outside this field. Called successively - and often indistinctly - «irregular», «indirect», «infra-war", «insurrectionary», «generation 4ᵉ « or «asymmetric» conflicts, they escape a rigid classification. What they have in common is that they avoid open confrontation where the balance of power would be unfavourable to them and instead act in immaterial fields, whether political (for Marxist-inspired movements) or societal (for jihadist movements).

Western military concepts - based on the notion of the balance of power - have found themselves out of step with this type of conflict, pushing military thinking from the strategic to the tactical and legal levels.

2.1. Asymmetric warfare - warfare with different logics

---

20 . Colonel Trevor N. Dupuy, Numbers, Prediction and War, The Book Service Ltd, 1979.

21 . See, for example: Brian Finn and Stephen M. Meyer, Insights from Mathematical Modeling in Soviet Mission Analysis. part 1, Research Report n° 86-5, Department of Political Science, Center for International Studies, Massachusetts Institute of Technology, May 1984.

2.1.1. The notion of asymmetry

A situation is asymmetrical when the response to a problem uses inappropriate logic and causes the opposite effects to those intended.

Asymmetric situations are not exclusively related to military or security issues. There are many examples. In Sweden, the criminalisation of the use of prostitution was based on ideological considerations: on the assumption that the problem is induced by male demand, it was thought that the problem could be eliminated by prohibiting the demand. But a key factor was totally ignored: prostitution probably fulfils - whether we like it or not - a need in society. As a result, rapes increased dramatically in the following years.

Number of rapes in Sweden (1990-2012)

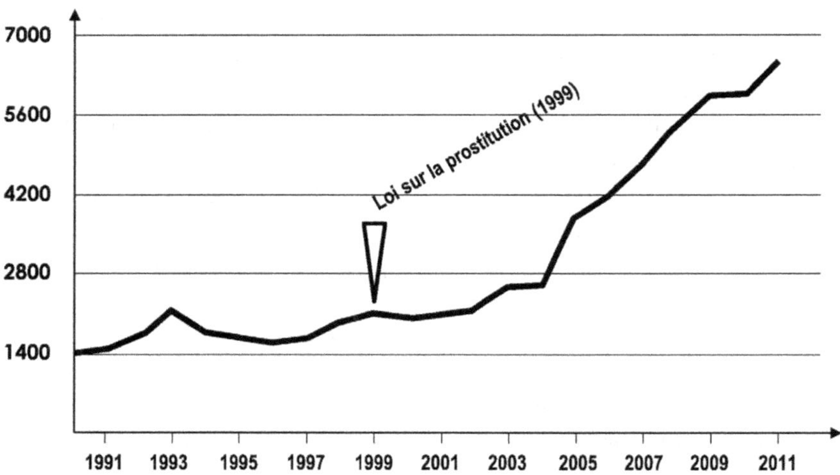

Figure 1. The number of rapes in Sweden - relatively stable since the early 1990s - increased dramatically after the adoption of the Prostitution Act in 1999.

Another example of non-warlike asymmetry is the Road Traffic Act adopted in 1994 in Switzerland to better protect pedestrians. Intended to reduce the number of accidents between pedestrians and vehicles, it gives the former absolute priority over the latter. The results are paradoxical: the pedestrian accident curve, which had been falling since the early 1980s, was suddenly pushed upwards and only resumed its normal downward trend in 2003.

The reason for this paradox is that accidents have been considered to be the result of motorists' behaviour alone. Giving priority to pedestrians did not encourage them to change their behaviour, but instead encouraged their recklessness by shifting the responsibility for the accident onto motorists. In fact, the law was not designed for pedestrians, but against motorists. Hundreds of accidents could probably have been avoided if the new law had been thought through holistically and if pedestrian behaviour had been taken into account.

Pedestrian victims of road accidents in Switzerland (1980-2004)

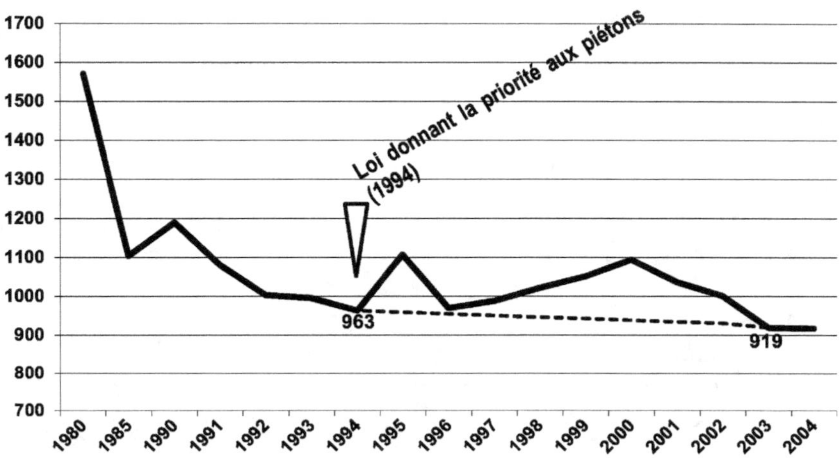

Figure 2: In 1994, the adoption of the law giving priority to pedestrians interrupted the steady decline in accidents observed since the 1980s and was followed by a peak in accidents in 1995, followed by a resurgence of accidents that only stabilised in 2002-2003. The dotted line shows the theoretical line of accidents without the 1994 law. [Source: Swiss Accident Prevention Bureau, 2006]

Another counter-intuitive example is the 1997 gun ban in Britain, which led to an increase in blood crime. There are two reasons for this unexpected effect: the first is the idea that removing guns removes crime; the second is the underestimation of the 'threshold effect' that accompanies the use of a gun to commit a crime. This effect is significantly lower than for the use of knives: there is therefore less hesitation to use them, with a consequent increase in blood crimes.

In Australia, the fight against suicide led to the adoption of a more restrictive law for the acquisition and possession of firearms. This led to a reduction in the firearm suicide rate from 0.009% in 1979 to 0.005% in 1995. However, in the same period, the suicide rate by hanging increased from 0.002% to 0.0105%, and the suicide rate (all methods combined) increased from 0.015% to 0.025%![22]

---

22 . For young men aged 15-24 (Research Centre for Injury Studies, Adelaide, Australia, 1995).

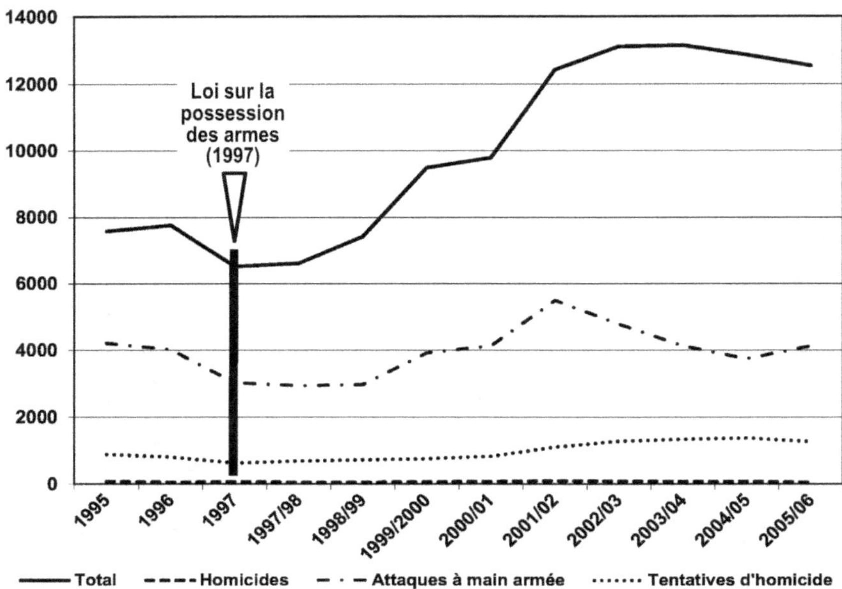

Figure 3: Until 1997, blood crimes tended to decrease. But the ban on gun ownership (vertical line) shows the beginning of a downward trend and an increase in blood crime. Only with the tough anti-terrorism laws passed in 2002 did crime return to a negative slope. (The 'total' line includes all forms of blood crime in addition to the three categories mentioned here). [Source: Home Office Statistical Bulletin, 25 January 2007[23]]

All these asymmetric situations have two things in common: a) a total lack of holistic and multifactorial thinking (they focus on one aspect only); b) they decide on the basis of emotional or ideological criteria (and not on the analysis of facts). This is exactly the same problem that explains the ineffectiveness of our fight against terrorism today.

2.1.2. Symmetric, asymmetric and asymmetric conflicts

Symmetrical conflicts can be associated with 'classical' or 'conventional' conflicts. They oppose adversaries with similar structures, means and training, and fighting according to a similar logic, based on a balance of power. The designation 'symmetrical' does not, however, exclude a *dissymmetry* in the quality (level of technology) and quantity of the means used, or even a difference in the perception of the conflict. Thus, the German offensive against the Netherlands or Belgium in 1940, despite the enormous dissymmetry in the means used on

---

23 . NOA: since 1er April 1998, statistics are established in relation to the fiscal year and not the calendar year.

both sides, falls into the category of symmetrical conflicts. Symmetrical conflict is characterised by the search for superiority, like a zero-sum game: one side's victory is another's defeat.

The notion of 'asymmetric warfare', which appeared in the United States in the 1990s, has gradually entered the Western military vocabulary to designate conflicts that fall outside the conventional warfare framework, without being defined:

> *In military operations, the use of dissimilar strategies, tactics, means and methods to circumvent or render ineffective the strengths of an adversary and to exploit his weaknesses.*[24]

In fact, this definition reflects the inability of Americans to conceptualise conflicts that they cannot control. The exploitation of superiority or vulnerability to achieve success (referred to by some as 'positive asymmetry' and 'negative asymmetry' respectively[25]) takes us back to the very conventional fundamentals of warfare without reflecting the complexity of asymmetric warfare.

The 2014 French Joint Doctrine goes a step further and outlines a more subtle distinction:

> *a. Irregularity. Irregular warfare is not necessarily illegal under international norms, but refers to the presence in the conflict of combatants who are difficult to identify and not subject to state authority. Confronting an irregular adversary requires an appropriate analysis of the use of force to ensure its legitimacy. The existence of a chain of command is sufficient to make a group an irregular adversary;*

> *b. symmetry, which pits comparable adversaries against each other, both in terms of the capabilities they possess and their doctrine of employment;*

> *c. Dissymmetry, which refers to a disparity in power between two entities that are in conflict with each other but share a similar view of conflict;*

---

24 . "In military operations the application of dissimilar strategies, tactics, capabilities, and methods to circumvent or negate an opponent's strengths while exploiting his weaknesses," Joint Publication (JP) 1-02, Department of Defense Dictionary of Military and Associated Terms, 15 February 2016.
25 . Metz Steven, «Strategic Asymmetry», Military Review, July-August 2001.

2. UNDERSTANDING THE THREAT

d. Asymmetry, which is understood as a mode of combat that exploits our weaknesses. This means that our opponent deliberately places himself in a different domain from the one in which we have a clear superiority. This should not be seen as a feature of an irregular conflict, of an irregular opponent, but as a possible option.[26]

However, the reflection remains timid and superficial, because even in a symmetrical (b) or dissymmetrical (c) situation, the opponents will try to exploit the weakness of the other, and thus asymmetry (d) does not express here a situation very different from the first two. However, it has the merit of introducing a qualitative dimension and of highlighting a «gap» between the adversaries, without however managing to conceptualise it. This definition will form the basis of our reflection.

2.1.3. Asymmetry in warfare

Asymmetrical conflicts involve opponents with different rationales. It is the nature of their objectives and the way they are achieved that differ fundamentally. Whereas in 'classical' conflict, military victory (tactical or operational) *must* lead to strategic or political victory, in asymmetric conflict, tactical defeat *can* contribute to strategic success. Conflicts such as the Algerian War (1958-1962), the Vietnam War (1965-1975), the war against drug traffickers, Somalia (1993), Afghanistan (2001-2021), Iraq (2003-2021), the Sahel (2014-2021) and elsewhere are all examples where, despite mastering the terrain at the tactical or even operational level, Western armies have lost strategically because they did not understand the logic of the war they were fighting or are still fighting.

In essence, asymmetric warfare is not new. ᵉIn Russia in the 19th century, the revolutionary group *Narodnaya Volya* (*People's Will*) sought to overthrow the tsar with a strategy of overreacting to the government, which would generate revolutionary momentum. ᵉIn the 20th century, the guerrillas of the 1960s and the Marxist terrorism of the 1970s and 1980s were the most prominent manifestations of asymmetric strategies. But Western strategists - with the probable exception of the British in Malaysia - were unable to understand them outside of a military logic that was symmetrical in nature.

During the Vietnam War, the Americans put considerable effort into sociological and scientific research to try to understand the workings of Viet Cong networks and Vietnamese society. Their studies were exhaustive, thorough and very often remarkable. But, too ethnocentric and oriented on the search for technological and tactical solutions, they did not lead to an 'asymmetric'

---

26 . Doctrine d'emploi des forces, Centre interarmées de concepts, de doctrines et d'expérimentations (CICDE), doctrine interarmées, DIA-01 (A) DEF (2014), n° 128/DEF/CICDE/NP of 12 June 2014, paragraph 127, p. 17.

strategic conceptualisation of counter-insurgency warfare. This is what led to their defeat...

Not all insurrectionary conflicts are asymmetrical. Thus, the fight led by the French Resistance against the German occupier cannot claim to be «asymmetrical», despite methods that today would be described as «terrorist». Indeed, its actions were part of a «symmetrical» logic of the war between the III[e] Reich and the Allied forces. These were essentially unconventional, one-off actions of a dissymmetrical nature (i.e. from the weak to the strong) seeking to materially weaken the adversary. The action of the Resistance was only really effective when its commitments were coordinated in a strategic context set by the Allied Command, mainly from 1944 onwards (sabotage, destruction of logistic axes, etc.). Outside this context, the various assassinations and attacks against the occupier were most often ineffective - and even counter-productive - by unnecessarily exposing the civilian population to reprisals. On the other hand, it could be said that the German occupier provided an asymmetric response to the actions of the Resistance before the letter: by executing civilian hostages for each German soldier killed, the German army tried to turn the successes of the Resistance into failures. This strategy did not neutralise the Resistance, but contributed to depriving it of popular support; indeed, the Allied forces used exactly the same strategy during the occupation of Germany.

Whereas 'symmetrical' warfare is built around power relations, with strategic objectives of a material nature (conquest of territory or destruction of the adversary), asymmetrical warfare is built around strategic objectives of an often intangible nature linked to the legitimacy - real or perceived - of the action. With a «symmetrical» strategy, one seeks to obtain decisive success, whereas an «asymmetrical» actor, often materially incapable of obtaining decisive success, seeks to maintain a determination to exploit the opponent's immaterial weaknesses.

Asymmetric warfare feeds on the logic embedded in the decision-making, political and cultural systems of the adversary. Despite appearances, it exerts its pressure more on decision-making mechanisms than on the forces engaged on the ground, and acts on the adversary as a 'system'.

The Israeli-Palestinian conflict is an example of an asymmetric conflict, which the Israelis have been unable to control for 60 years. Today, Palestinian actions[27] are not about retaking the occupied territories, but exploit the intransigent attitude of the Israeli government to maintain, increase and consolidate the spirit of resistance. The Palestinian rockets that continue to strike southern Israel have

---

27 . This refers to the multiple actions («return marches», firing of rockets and other projectiles, attacks, etc.) carried out by various Palestinian organisations (whether or not associated with Hamas, Fatah and other militant groupings).

no tactical effectiveness: the number of deaths they cause is minimal[28].On the other hand, the approximately 140 times greater losses inflicted by the Israeli retaliation keep the will to resist alive, encourage international support for the Palestinian cause and thus have a strategic effect: they contribute to generating a dynamic that is increasingly less favourable to Israel on the international level. Israel maintains an illusion of victory in Palestine, at the cost of a political legitimacy that is deteriorating day by day, even with its greatest ally: the United States.

On the domestic front, an example of an inappropriate strategy is the destruction of the homes of Palestinian families whose members are suspected of involvement in terrorist activities. According to the *Israeli Committee Against House Demolitions*, 49,707 homes were destroyed between 1967 and December 2019[29].This policy gives the appearance of a virile and dissuasive handling of the terrorist threat. In fact, this is not the case. First of all, there was a significant increase in terrorist acts during this period, with a gradual shift from suicide attacks to the projection of missiles and mortar shells. Secondly, it only strengthened the influence of Hamas. Indeed, the wanted persons (terrorists) often no longer live in their families' homes, and the measure only affects children, women and the elderly. But the Israeli authorities did not foresee that, deprived of a roof over their heads, these families are most often taken in by the Hamas *Family Support Fund (Waqfiat Ria'at al-Usra)* and by the *Union of Good (I'tilaf al-Kheïr)* (which has been coordinating charitable organisations in the occupied territories since October 2000[30]) and are thus pushed into the arms of Hamas, even when they were not necessarily affiliated with it previously. In other words, through this policy, Israel has simply contributed to strengthening the popularity and ranks of Hamas, as well as the hatred of the Israeli occupier, thus undermining its own strategic posture by a tactical measure. Ultimately, these punitive demolitions have damaged its image without deterring terrorist attacks[31] .

---

28 . There were 33 Israeli deaths between 2001 and 2015 (as of 1ᵉʳ June 2015) and at least 4,600 Palestinian casualties due to Israeli strikes.

29 . Figures from the Israeli Committee against of House Demolition (ICAHD), http://icahd.org/ (accessed December 18, 2019). These figures also include destruction through the application of the Dahiya Doctrine and the Hannibal Directive, which will be discussed in the chapter on counter-terrorism.

30 . It is estimated that 75-80% of the Hamas budget is used to fund social and medical assistance, the construction of medical facilities and orphanages. (David H. Gray & Larson John Bennett, "Grass Roots Terrorism: How Hamas' Structure Defines a Policy of Counterterrorism", Research Journal of International Studies, November 2008).

31 . Meir Margalit, "The Truth behind Formal Statistics - Demolition of illegal houses in the West Bank during 2004", Israeli Committee Against House Demolition, April 2005.

Today, the definitions of asymmetry used by Western militaries are based on criteria that are too simple to reflect the complexity of the problem. In fact, there are two main forms of asymmetry:

- asymmetry resulting from a deliberate strategy, based on a systemic analysis of the conflict and the adversary, its decision-making mechanisms and the relationship between its decision-makers and society as a whole. This is the Marxist asymmetric strategy of the revolutionary movements of the 1970s and 1980s;

- asymmetry resulting from the confrontation of different cultural contexts. This is the case with Islamist asymmetry, which results from the opposition between a Western society that values life as such and Islamist groups that value the reason for living. In the West, life is a goal in itself, whereas for an Islamist it is about giving meaning to life, even if one has to sacrifice it to do so.

Strategies that exploit an asymmetrical situation do not necessarily seek to increase the level of violence, but to generate a qualitative multiplier effect:

- In Marxist asymmetry, the asymmetrical strategy is to push the opponent (the state) to engage in violence, so as to be able to exploit this reaction in the political or emotional field. The aim is to inflict 'just enough' pain to provoke an 'over-reaction', playing on image and emotional impact. Here, propaganda plays a key role in accentuating the impact of the security action.

- In Islamist asymmetry, it is essentially a matter of exploiting the determination of fighters in confronting a numerically and/or technologically superior opponent. The manner of response is more important than the final outcome, or more accurately, the outcome is in the determination to fight. Here, the fighter is situated in a perspective that transcends him and places his sacrifice as a personal achievement. His death itself becomes an element of victory.

The fundamental difference between these two asymmetries is that Marxist asymmetry seeks to establish a new socio-political system: it is a strategy of conflict intensification. Islamist asymmetry, on the other hand, essentially seeks to 'keep a flame burning': it may attract followers, but it does not conceptually lead to an intensification of conflict. Moreover, its acceptance of death as an outcome makes it a strategy of last resort, whose logic is 'better to die standing than to live kneeling'.

The essential characteristic of asymmetric warfare is that it is not based on the search for superiority or the exploitation of an opponent's weakness, but - more subtly - on the conversion of his superiority into weakness. Thus, an asymmetric strategy exploits the opponent's superiority to forge its own victory. In a way, it is the application of the principles of Japanese aikido (not judo!) in the strategic field. In such a conflict, not only is firepower - however important it may be - no longer able to bring victory, but it even becomes a weakness if one does not know how to control it.

In the West, despite technological developments, the principles of war remain those of 1914. The war against the Islamic State waged by the Western coalition is not very different from the one waged a hundred years earlier at Verdun: the strikes are strictly tactical and have no strategic ambition. Instead, they have created the myth of an Islamic state as the 'defender of Islam' and encouraged volunteers from all over the world to join its side. The failure of the Western strategy is tacitly acknowledged since, despite having been declared destroyed, the Islamic State remains a sufficient threat to maintain large Western contingents in Afghanistan (where it did not exist), Iraq, Syria and the Sahel.

Even the elimination of Abu Bakr al-Baghdadi (26 October 2019) has not been a deterrent. On the contrary, on social networks, there is a resurgence of willingness to fight around the world. In fact, the movement has only been given publicity by demonstrating the determination of its leader, with a multiplier effect on the audience of the EI[32].Foolish strategists have thus helped to fuel and strengthen the threat they are fighting!

The asymmetrical war waged by Islamists draws most of its effectiveness from the emotional behaviour of our societies. The campaigns against the Islamic veil or the burkini, launched by politicians in search of an audience, have only brought to the surface the fractures in French society caused by the inaction of these same politicians for decades.

In an asymmetric context, our media and politicians thus become, consciously or not, accomplices of terrorism by amplifying the resonance of the attacks for domestic political reasons. The videos produced by the Islamic State show that large demonstrations such as the one held on 11 January 2015 in France or high-profile ceremonies in support of the victims of the attacks, which were intended to express the nation's opposition to terrorism, in fact contribute to the mobilisation and radicalisation of individuals. Indeed, it was during this period that the number of jihadists leaving for Syria began to rise[33].What we saw as a show of strength for the nation has - in fact - shown its vulnerability. The logic of today's wars is no longer that of 1914! We will come back to this.

Although they often talk about the asymmetry of conflicts, Western countries have not realised its nature and have not drawn the consequences in the conduct of the war on terror. Because they shape their strategies more according to their

---

32 . Nicky Harley, 'Surge in pro-ISIS social media posts as group uses Baghdadi's', The National, 29 October 2019; Tim Stickings, 'Terror experts warn of 'surge' in pro-ISIS social media posts after death of leader al-Baghdadi as extremists vow that 'jihad will never stop even if our caliph dies", The Daily Mail, 30 October 2019.

33 . Letter dated 19 May 2015 from the Chair of the Security Council Committee pursuant to re-solutions 1267 (1999) and 1989 (2011) concerning Al-Qaida and associated individuals and entities addressed to the President of the Security Council, S/2015/358, UN, New York, 19 May 2015.

emotions than to the enemy, Western strategists continue to rely on the more easily understood and justified Cold War notion of 'deterrence'.

Here, contrary to the logic of symmetrical conflicts, the use of force does not have a dissuasive effect, but tends to reinforce the posture of the terrorists, in this case the Islamic State:

> *Do you think your coalition and your bombing will weaken us? No by Allah! It strengthens us and makes us even stronger and increases our faith in what Mohammad [...] has brought us!*[34]

The problem is that not only does no one want to listen to the enemy, but researchers are prevented from understanding their logic. For example, the messages of the Islamists are systematically truncated in the mainstream press to support the thesis that terrorism is irrational. The fear of recognising a rational justification for terrorist violence has the effect of creating conditions that favour its perpetuation. Yet, just as a 'normal' combatant is not free to commit any crime on the battlefield, the rationality of the terrorist act does not mean that it is not criminal. Of course, this logic could work if Western countries agreed to judge and punish their own war crimes... which they do not, thus justifying terrorism.

2.1.4. Tactical success versus strategic gain

In order to defeat an opponent, the strategy applied must have a clear objective and be oriented towards his centre of gravity. This is relatively simple in symmetrical conflicts, but much less so in asymmetrical conflicts, where the logic operates 'in a vacuum'. This is the problem of the West in the Middle East, in the Sahel and in Afghanistan, but also of Israel, which is practically a textbook case: of all the countries hit by terrorism in the 20th century, Israel is the only one that has been unable to reduce its importance and - a fortiori - to defeat it.

The key to this inability lies first and foremost in the Israeli strategy towards the occupied territories: it does not aim to solve the problem, but to fight it. Indeed, the Israeli government presents the conflict as a religious confrontation fuelled by anti-Semitism, while the Palestinians regularly repeat that their objective is to recover their land. Paradoxically, the asymmetry is not a direct result of this difference in perspective, but indirectly of the strategies applied as a result of this difference.

In fact, the Palestinians have understood that Israel needs to maintain terrorist activity in order to carry out its plan to take over the entire Palestinian territory. They therefore adopted a strategy of response, avoiding spectacular terrorist

---

34 . Verbatim excerpt from a video addressed to France by the Islamic State in late November 2015.

attacks and putting the burden of the unpopularity of the conflict on Israel alone. This explains their abandonment of international terrorism in the 1970s, and then of suicide attacks in the 2000s. By using rocket attacks - spectacular, but causing very few casualties - in response to Israeli strikes, the Palestinians have clearly won over international opinion. The Israelis, on the other hand, have pursued a deliberately disproportionate policy of repression, contrary to international law, which is supported only by the US government, but which is widely condemned by public opinion around the world, including by American Jews[35].

This is why Israel has been promoting legal provisions in the West to equate anti-Zionism (against Israeli policy) with antisemitism (against the Jewish people), or to prohibit citizens' campaigns to force Israel to respect international law. These initiatives show the strategic weakening of Israel, despite apparent tactical successes.

The effectiveness of an asymmetric strategy is essentially a function of the 'symmetric' (and simplistic) way in which it is responded to. The Israeli interventions in Gaza illustrate this phenomenon perfectly. In Western public opinion, the disproportion of the means engaged provokes a compassion that tends to distance it from the Israeli position and to draw closer to the Palestinians, including Hamas. Palestinian losses fuel their strategic gain in the world.

2.1.5. Gandhi's non-violent strategy

Non-violence - not the militant European pacifism of the 1980s, advocating a naive general disarmament of democracies - but that conceived as a strategy for action is the archetype of an asymmetric strategy.

Conceived and successfully implemented by Gandhi in the late 1940s in India, non-violence is a 'fighting' strategy that transcends the use of violence and literally 'disarms' the opponent. It pits will against arms and is probably the most difficult 'asymmetric form of combat' to counter:

Non-violence does not consist in renouncing any real struggle against evil. On the contrary, non-violence is a more active and real struggle against evil than the law of retaliation, whose very nature has the effect of developing perversity. In order to fight against what is immoral, I envisage a mental and therefore moral opposition. I seek to blunt the tyrant's sword completely, not by striking it with a sharper steel, but by deceiving his expectation that I will offer him physical resistance. He will find in me a resistance of the soul that will escape his embrace. This resistance will first blind him and then force him to bow. And bowing will not humiliate the aggressor, but will elevate him.[36]

---

35 . Jonathan Cook, "Can young Jews in US turn tide against Israel?", The National, 26 June 2017.
36 . Gandhi, Young India, 8 October 1925, in Letters to the Ashram, tr. Herbert, Albin Michel, 1937,

34

This is a typical description of asymmetrical conflict where, with each action, the 'symmetrical' opponent deteriorates his own strategic situation. Much misunderstood in the West, it is not a strategy of impotence, but a deliberate strategy of non-use of force, as Gandhi states:

The precondition for non-violence is the ability to strike.[37]

The strength of non-violence as a method of asymmetrical warfare is that the response to it is complex, because not only is it time-consuming, but it requires that the person who employs it accepts to lose everything:

Just as in the instruction of violence one must learn the art of killing, in the instruction of non-violence one must learn the art of dying.[38]

The asymmetrical essence of non-violence can be summed up very simply as :

There is no defeat in non-violence. [39]

Since it does not seek to conquer, the non-violent strategy offers nothing to lose. It is a 'lose-lose' game that defies the usual Western strategies.

Ghandi was a revolutionary. Our point is not to associate his strategy with terrorism, but to show that at both ends of the spectrum of violence there are strategies of an asymmetric nature against which the state is powerless unless it changes its approach. In other words, it is wrong to automatically associate asymmetry with violence.

2.2. Defining terrorism - squaring the circle

2.2.1. Why a definition?

Our lack of understanding of the phenomenon of terrorism is reflected in the number of definitions used around the world, and in our inability to define coherent strategies for dealing with it. Thus, defining terrorism is not just a stylistic exercise: it determines how we respond to it.

In 1994, there were 212 definitions of terrorism in use worldwide, of which 90 were officially used[40].Today, there are countless definitions, and often institutions in the same country use several different definitions. In fact, work on a universal definition began in 1937, within the League of Nations, with the drafting of the *Convention for the Prevention and Suppression of Terrorism*[41].

---

pp. 86-87.

37 . Gandhi, Young India, 12 August 1926, op. cit, p. 88.

38 . Gandhi, Non-violence in Peace and War, Navajivan Publishing House, Ahmedabad, 1948, vol.

39 . Gandhi, op. cit, p. 111.

40 . Jeffrey D. Simon, The Terrorist Trap, Indiana University Press, Bloomington, 1994.

41 . Convention for the Prevention and Suppression of Terrorism, League of Nations, 16 November 1937, No. C.546.M.383.1937.V.

However, despite endless discussions, the UN has never reached a definition that would allow effective implementation of its resolutions.

In simple terms, the debate is between two main camps: the Western countries, which tend to define terrorism in terms of its modes of action and effects, insisting on its criminal nature, and the rest of the world (mainly developing countries), which prefers a definition in terms of its causes, without defining its criminal nature a priori. This is the case of the member countries of the *Organisation of the Islamic Conference (OIC)*, because of the Israeli-Palestinian conflict, which is considered to be a resistance against an occupation. One could summarise by saying that the Western view allows terrorism to be condemned but not fought, while the view of the rest of the world would allow it to be fought but not condemned.

Westerners fear that including the causes of terrorism in a definition will only serve to justify it:

> *As for the legal definition of «terrorism», the representative of Israel said that some countries still maintain that an act of terrorism - a car bomb in a crowded market, for example - should not be considered terrorism, if it was claimed in the context of national liberation. He said that terrorism was defined by «what you do, not why you do it». To defend an attack on innocent people in the name of the fight for freedom is incomprehensible.*[42]

The rest of the world's position is based on the fact that terrorism is sometimes the last resort in a war against a technologically or numerically superior opponent. Terrorism is then seen as a method of combat, which can serve the most diverse, but also the most legitimate, objectives and causes, and is part of a «weak to strong» strategy:

> *As long as we are unable to distinguish between terrorism and the right to defend one's land, we cannot agree on what terrorism is.*[43]

The problem is that often - particularly in some developing countries - the possibilities for expressing discontent are so limited that the choice of possible strategies tends to focus on terrorism and thus give it legitimacy. This is the case with the Arab-Israeli conflict and Palestinian terrorism, but also with the resistance to foreign interventions in Afghanistan and Iraq, which are legitimate for many countries.

---

42 . Report of the 29ᵉ session of the 6ᵉ Commission of the United Nations, 15 November 2000 (GA/L/3169).

43 . Iran News, reported by AFP, 30 September 2001.

Thus, debates at the UN are systematically blocked by the affirmation of the legitimate struggle or attempts to contain the notion of «state terrorism» as well. The association between terrorism and the revolutionary mechanisms of the 1960s and 1980s led to its being interpreted as an ideology in itself, and thus introduced the antagonism between «freedom fighter» and «terrorist». However, on a semantic level, these are two fundamentally different things: the *«freedom fighter»* is defined in terms of an end, whereas the *«terrorist»* is defined in terms of a mode of action:

> *The adage that one man's terrorist is another man's freedom fighter is a testament to the ineptitude of assumptions about the motivations of terrorists.*[44]

One can «resist» an occupation by «terrorism» and thus be both «resistant» and «terrorist». Technically, the one does not exclude the other, but this analysis is avoided for fear of justifying terrorism or tarnishing the image of a legitimate «resistance» (like the French Resistance, for example). Conversely, the Taliban, who are readily described by the public as terrorists, have never been defined as such by the United States[45].

The confusion between 'causes' and 'means' tends to distort our understanding of terrorism by blurring the distinction between its tactical (requiring police solutions) and strategic (requiring political solutions) dimensions:

> *[...] In reality, a simultaneous study of 'causes' and 'measures' is an impossible condition to sustain. One of the most frequent manifestations of violence is air piracy: here, measures have been found without studying the causes. Moreover, the International Law Commission prepared a provisional draft of the convention on the protection of diplomats without having first elucidated the reasons for the acts of violence directed against them. The demand to consider the issue as a whole is in fact nothing more than a manoeuvre to reduce terrorism to a mere political issue and to prevent concrete measures from being taken.*[46]

---

44 . O'Gorman, R. & Silke, Andrew (2015). "Terrorism as Altruism: An Evolutionary Model for Understanding Terrorist Psychology," in Max Taylor, Jason Roach and Ken Pease (eds.), Evolutionary Psychology and Terrorism, Routledge, London, pp. 149-163.

45 . Jonathan Karl, Taliban Are Not Terrorists, or So Says the White House, ABC News, 29 January 2015, http://abcnews.go.com/Politics/taliban-terrorists-white-house/story?id=28588120.

46 . Quoted in Seymour Finger, 'The United Nations response to terrorism', in Yonah Alexander and Robert A. Kilmarx (eds.), Political Terrorism and Business. The Threat and Response, Praeger, New York, 1979, p. 261.

In other words, we only look at the manifestations of terrorism, without understanding how it works or what drives it. Thus, the fight against terrorism is more about punishing it than fighting it. The definitions used allow for judicial treatment and harsh repression, but are also the main obstacle to preventive action, as they exclude from the outset consideration of the objectives sought and the motivations of terrorists. This is why we limit ourselves to the tactical and police level (anti-terrorism), which leads us to sacrifice our values, our individual freedoms and to place an exaggerated trust in excessive, costly and useless surveillance systems.

Thus, the West is engaged in a war that at best prevents the execution of terrorist acts, but is not able to prevent the intention to commit attacks. In other words, we will always be one step behind the terrorist decision.

2.2.2. Terrorism - method or objective?

Most definitions of terrorism used in the West include three elements: violence, innocent (civilian) victims and the will to terrorise. But they do not include its strategic context or the mechanisms of its genesis. As a result, we tend to see terrorism as an inescapable phenomenon that 'falls from the sky' unexpectedly, simply to satisfy the whims of some 'whacko', as Tony Blair puts it:

The purpose of terrorism is just that, to terrorise people. [47]

This simplistic view is exactly why we die and fail against terrorism. If the purpose of terrorism were only to kill or destroy, then it would exist simply to exist, which is clearly not the case.

Our highly emotional reading of terrorism tends to confuse the notions of «means» and «ends», as journalist Mohammed Sifaoui did on *France 5*[48].This is simply wrong. Not only does this reading make us incapable of dealing with the real causes of terrorism, but it also contributes to widening the gap between communities and needlessly adding fuel to the fire. Rightly or wrongly, killing and destroying are merely means to an end. No one sacrifices themselves «just to scare». Terrorism *always* has a higher purpose (strategic or political), even if we do not see or understand it. Without understanding the nature of that goal, it is impossible to fight terrorism effectively. We will come back to this in more detail.

---

47 . Tony Blair, "In full: Blair on bomb blasts", BBC News, 7 July 2005.
48 . Mohammed Sifaoui in the programme C à vous, « Comment détecter la radicalisation ? - C à vous - 10/10/2019', France 5/YouTube, 10 October 2019 (08'05") and (08'25").

What distinguishes terrorism from other forms of crime is that it is part of a process. It seeks to impose a change in behaviour or decisions to satisfy a higher purpose, and repeats its action until its goal is achieved. This recursive nature is at the heart of the terrorist phenomenon and explains the deep reluctance to make concessions to terrorists.

But it also means that attacks that have the appearance and brutality of terrorist acts are sometimes not. This is the case of the killing of the Jewish Museum of Belgium in Brussels (24 May 2014), which was never claimed by a terrorist organisation, and which was - in all likelihood - revenge for the violence in Gaza. One can also mention the Utoya massacre by Anders Behring Breivik (22 July 2011), which is an act of pure hatred with a messianic character. All of these crimes were subsequently labelled as terrorist. Duly noted. It is important to understand that terrorism is a method of achieving a strategic goal: you strike until you get satisfaction or achieve the goal.

When the crime - however horrific - is not part of a process towards a goal, then it is likely to be something other than terrorism. In the examples above, the more 'clinical' view of the strategist shows that they were generated by hatred, revenge or spite, and are more akin to mass murder: their violence was not part of a strategic process and their 'fight' ended with their actions themselves.

This distinction is essential when seeking to combat terrorism strategically. For example, while the January 2015 attacks (*Charlie Hebdo* and the Hyper Cacher) in Paris were clearly terrorist, the same cannot be said for the crimes of Mohammed Merah in 2012. Yet in both cases the terrorists claimed revenge for Israeli actions in Gaza. Criminally and morally, in both cases, these crimes are unacceptable and must be punished with equal severity. However, the treatment of these two series of killings would have required different strategies. Merah did not make any demands or claims, nor did he place his acts in a political or revolutionary context: the possible strategies for combating them are at the societal and police level. As for the 2015 attacks, the strategies were at the level of foreign policy and communication.

The problem is very different with the attacks committed by, for or in the name of the Islamic State, which are part of a strategy of action and must be countered as part of a broader approach with a strategic and a tactical component. Thus, seen from a strategic perspective, Merah's crimes were virtually unpreventable, whereas the attacks of 2015-2016 were.

2.2.3. Defining terrorism to defeat it

The existing definitions of terrorism have been established in order to punish the perpetrators. This is good, but it is not enough, because it does not understand the nature of the problem. Our definitions allow us to punish terrorists, but not to fight against terrorism. These two things are regularly confused in France, where thinking on the subject is limited to its police aspect.

A «good» definition of terrorism should be based on its strategic dimension. A possible solution, universal and objective, could be :

The use or threat of force to achieve political change.[49]

But it does not sufficiently reflect the strategic context in which terrorism operates. Thus, we will adopt the following definition here, free of any moral or legal considerations:

Terrorism is a method based on intimidation, which seeks to achieve strategic goals by tactical means.[50]

Its merit is to make a difference between tactical and strategic levels, which escapes traditional definitions, but which is nevertheless indispensable.

Some will object - and rightly so - that the use of tactical means to achieve strategic objectives is not unique to terrorism, but can also be applied to the air strikes carried out by Western air forces in Libya, Iraq, Pakistan, Afghanistan or Syria. However, these strikes are not always innocent and aim - like sanctions - to put the civilian population in such a situation that they seek to overthrow their government. In this context, Western strikes in Iraq or Syria can also be a terrorist strategy. We will come back to this.

Thus, without addressing here the question of the legitimacy of the objectives of terrorism - which we will see below - this definition already makes it possible to establish that the fight against terrorism must be articulated along three axes: a first axis at the level of its objectives, a second axis at the level of its implementation and the third to reduce its impact. The first is strategic in nature and seeks to act on the motivation of terrorists and is part of a preventive approach (counter-terrorism), while the second and third are tactical in nature and aim to act pre-emptively[51] or reactively on the means used by terrorists, as well as on reducing the impact of attacks (counter-terrorism). We will discuss these issues in more detail below. The important point is that the fight against terrorism must include a strategic component, which no country is currently doing.

---

49 . Biran Jenkins, advisor to the RAND Corporation, in Charles-Philippe David & Benoît Gagnon, Repenser le Terrorisme, éditions PUL, Université de Laval (Canada), 2007, p. 35.

50 . Jacques Baud, Le Renseignement et la Lutte contre le Terrorisme, Lavauzelle, 2009.

51 . In the absence of equivalent expressions in the French military vocabulary, we will use the terms 'pre-emptive' or 'pre-emption' in their Anglo-Saxon sense, which will be defined in more detail in this book. In essence, it is a matter of acting after the adversary has made his decision and before he does so: an intermediate window between prevention and reaction.

Terrorism is neither an end nor a doctrine. It is a method of action. It may serve a philosophy, but it is not a philosophy in itself. This distinction is more than an academic exercise, because it determines the possibility (and the will) to fight it:

> *Fascism is a doctrine, communism is a doctrine, but terrorism is only a method: it does not imply a world view.*[52]

Indeed, this is how jihad theorists understand and use terrorism, i.e. as a technique, in a very neutral sense, whose moral value is given by the context in which it is used or by the objective it pursues:

> *We refuse to understand the term in terms of its American definition. «Terrorism» is an abstract word, and like many abstract words, it can carry good or bad meanings depending on the context, what one attaches to it and what one associates with it. The word is an abstract term, which has neither a positive nor a negative meaning.*[53]

For those seeking to combat terrorism, this much cooler and more technical approach has the advantage of distinguishing between a freedom fighter and a terrorist, which the Western reading tends to place on the same level, as we have seen above. Moreover, it offers the possibility of integrating its action into a greater strategic coherence.

2.2.4. The political definition of terrorism

As we have seen, terrorism is a method of coercing individuals or a population by threatening them with the use of force (physical, economic or otherwise). But beyond this technical definition, some countries use the label «terrorist» for strictly political purposes, to put pressure on a state or an organisation. This also allows the rules of international law not to apply to entities defined as «terrorist». This is why, at the end of 2014, Ukraine labelled its operation against the Donbass autonomists as an *Anti-Terrorist Operation* (ATO).

While it likes to wrap the fight against terrorism in morality and law, the West is not really consistent in this area and applies international humanitarian law (IHL) only when it suits it, thus helping to blur the message it conveys about the legitimacy and sincerity of its action.

Armed groups are put on - or taken off - terrorist lists according to the political expediency of the moment, not a rigorous analysis of how they act. Thus,

---

52 . Régis Debray, interview with the Journal de la Télévision Suisse Romande, 14 June 2004.
53 . Inspire, n° 5, Spring 2011 (1431), p. 29.

in Libya, when France supported the *Islamic Group Fighting in Libya* (GICL) (*Al-Jama'ah al-Islamiyyah al-Muqatilah bi-Libya*) and Bernard-Henri Lévy (BHL) or the American ambassador Chris Stevens plotted with this group against the government of Colonel Muammar Gaddafi, did they support jihadist terrorism? Formally yes, as the ICLG was defined as a terrorist by the United Nations since 6 October 2001 (and retains this status in 2017). The US State Department had listed it as a terrorist group on 17 December 2004 and removed it from the list on 9 December 2015, in gratitude for «services rendered» in the overthrow of Gaddafi and in the war in Syria.

The same applies to the Iranian *Mujahedin-e-Khalq* (MeK) (or *People's Mujahedin*), designated as a terrorist on 8 October 1997. It was delisted on 28 September 2012 in order to «legalise» US assistance to it in carrying out attacks in Iran with Israeli support.

The *East Turkestan Islamic Movement* (ETIM), an Islamist movement with a strong presence in China among the Uighur minority, which collaborates with the Taliban. On 3 September 2002, the United States designated it as a terrorist movement. This was the reason for China's support for the US and NATO in Afghanistan[54].Yet in 2020, the US, then in the midst of an economic war with China, decided to remove MITO from the list of terrorist movements, allowing the funding and training of its militants... Was this removal due to a change in MITO policy? No. The US has finished its war in Afghanistan and is embarking on an economic and influence war with China, and it is now a matter of «legalising» its aid to groups fighting the Beijing government.

After the 18 July 2012 attack in Bourgas (Bulgaria), which targeted Israeli tourists, Hezbollah was immediately accused, without any proof. France, through its Minister of Foreign Affairs, Laurent Fabius, then declared the armed wing of Hezbollah as terrorist and asked for its inclusion on the EU list of terrorist organisations[55] , which was done in July 2013[56].But in 2018, the investigation conducted by the Bulgarian prosecutor's office was unable to reveal any involvement of Hezbollah, and removed it from the indictment[57].This does not prevent the *Arte* channel in a documentary broadcast in 2019, entitled *Lebanon, hostage of the Middle East,* from affirming that it is responsible for the attack[58] !

---

54 . Haleigh Morgus, 'Tracing China's Engagement in Afghanistan: History and Motivations', South Asian Voices, 24 March 2019.

55 . «Pour Paris, la branche armée du Hezbollah est un groupe terroriste», AFP/France 24, 23 May 2013

56 . Benjamin Barthe and Philippe Ricard, «Le Hezbollah classé organisation terroriste par l'UE», Le Monde, 23 July 2013

57 . Yonah Jeremy Bob, "Hezbollah role unmentioned in charges for 2012 Bulgaria terrorist attack", The Jerusalem Post, 31 January 2018

58 . Michael Richter, «Le Liban, otage du Moyen-Orient», www.arte.tv, (12'50") (broadcast on Arte on 24 September at 10:25 pm) (withdrawn on 22 December 2019)

One acts on the basis of rumours, without proof and without integrity, in order to justify policies that are too closely aligned with that of Israel...

During the battle for East Aleppo in late 2016, the official line from Western countries, including France, was that they were supporting the 'moderate' rebels. In September 2016, ceasefire agreements provided for the separation of 'moderate' rebels from jihadists. Finally, in early 2017, of the 32 rebel factions in East Aleppo, 18 joined *Hayat Tahrir al-Sham (HTS)* (formerly *Jabhat al-Nosra*) and 14 joined *Ahrar al-Sham* (from the 'al-Qaeda' movement). None attempted to form a «moderate» group. Gathered in the Idlib pocket, these groups will continue to be supported and protected by the West, before allying with Turkey to attack the Kurds, and before Abu Bakr al-Baghdadi, leader of the Islamic State, is shot dead in his residence in October 2019...

The lists of groups and movements, considered as terrorists, and of countries that support terrorism should contribute to the implementation of coherent policies and strategies at the international level. But this is not the case. In fact, they are more of a pressure tool than a reflection of reality. For example, in Syria, *Ahrar al-Sham* and *Jaish al-Islam* are referred to by John Kerry as being affiliated with *Jabhat al-Nosra* and the *Islamic State*[59] (and committing the same atrocities, as we shall see below). Yet the US, Britain and France will refuse to put them on the UN list of terrorist organisations[60] , because they support them militarily.

Since 31 May 2018, the HTS has been on the US State Department's list of terrorist movements[61] , which does not prevent its militants from fighting alongside the Ukrainians[62] , in the name of Western values!...

In other words, the qualification of an entity as «terrorist» by Western countries is not always based on factual elements, but very often on opportunistic and political criteria. Beyond the issues of substance, this way of applying the qualification «terrorist» contributes to the misunderstanding of the phenomenon. The result is that it is almost impossible to have a coherent approach to the fight against terrorism: the Western countries themselves create the problems and scuttle the solutions!

In the United States, after the Capitol Hill riots on 6 January 2021, Joe Biden, the new president-elect, declared the rioters to be 'domestic terrorists'. Whatever one thinks of this event, calling it 'terrorist' (as was done in France with regard to the 'Gilets jaunes') is a passionate decision that makes no sense. Confusing a

---

59 . Juan Cole, "Is Kerry Right? Are Freemen of Syria and Army of Islam Radical Terrorists?", Informed Comment, 13 July 2016.

60 . "U.S., Britain, France block Russia bid to blacklist Syria rebels", Reuters, 11 May 2016.

61 . https://www.state.gov/executive-order-13224/

62 . «Terrorism, Violent Extremism, and the War in Ukraine, gwu.edu, 25 May 2022 (https://extremism.gwu.edu/terrorism-violent-extremism-and-war-ukraine-nexus)

riot with an act of terrorism rules out any strategic treatment of the problem (as riots and acts of terrorism can only be stages in a process of subversion).

As early as 2014, this was also the case with Ukraine, which labelled the Donbass separatists as «terrorists» and waged a war against them called «*Anti-Terrorist Operation*» (ATO). The result is that it has dealt with the problem with an incoherent mix of anti-terrorist measures and tactical actions, without having an adequate operational doctrine. This explains - to a large extent - its inability to defeat the autonomists, despite superior means. Under the pretext of refusing to finance terrorism, the Kiev government has stopped the payment of salaries and pensions to the citizens of Donbass, as well as banking services. In the same spirit, rail links and water supplies were physically interrupted. As a result, the government has cut itself off from its citizens (whom it is also bombing relentlessly), forcing them to seek help from neighbouring Russia. Today, Donbass has become functionally linked to Russia, whereas it was only seeking autonomous status in order to keep Russian as its main language. So Ukraine has already lost the war...

Under the guidance of NATO officers, Ukraine has been unable to control the situation in the Donbass and has had to resort to brutal methods by hiring extremist militias and death squads. The Ukrainian example illustrates the inability of Westerners to conceptualise counter-insurgency strategies.

The same applies to the lists of countries that support terrorism, which were justified during the Cold War, when ideologies clashed and revolutionary processes were tools of influence, especially for Eastern countries such as the USSR, Czechoslovakia or Poland. Today, the only countries that seek to change governments through subversion are the United States, aided by Britain and France... But it is tempting to use these lists as a means of pressure. So it is with Cuba, which the Obama administration removed from the list in 2015, but which the Trump administration put back on on January 11, 2021, for no reason...In fact, we are not trying to understand terrorism to make it go away, but to punish it. Researcher Andrew Silke correctly notes that the majority of authors on terrorism tend to adopt a 'firefighter' posture rather than studying the 'burning phenomena'[63] .

2.3 **Typology of terrorism**

In every country, history has shaped the way we understand terrorism. In the West, we irrevocably associate terrorism with the destabilisation - or even

---

63 . Andrew Silke, "The Devil You Know: Continuing Problems with Research on Terrorism", Terrorism and Political Violence, Winter 2001, vol. 13, n° 4, pp. 1-14.

destruction - of the rule of law and democracy. This is a consequence of the 1960s-1970s, when Western countries put in place the tools to fight Marxist terrorism supported by Eastern countries. The problem is that this is still our framework for 'understanding' Islamist terrorism.

Terrorism is the use of tactical violence to achieve a strategic objective. Although this definition is debatable, it highlights a key fact: terrorism is not only defined by the way it is carried out, but also, and more importantly, by its objectives. For example, some of the methods used by the French Resistance in 1941-1945 are identical to those used by 'caliphate fighters' in 2017, but in a different context and with different objectives.

Thus, the various classifications of terrorism based on its modus operandi or on the structures used are of no use in combating terrorism. To be effective, it is necessary to approach the problem by the objectives it seeks to achieve.

The problem with countries like France, Britain or the United States is that they treat terrorism as a single phenomenon, as in totalitarian countries. There is a tendency to apply the label 'terrorist' to any heinous act for the sole purpose of placing it under a harsher legal regime. Although the tactical responses are often the same, each type of terrorism requires a different strategy. France generated its own inability to respond effectively to terrorism before 2015.

2.3.1. Terrorism under ordinary law

Common law terrorism is the use of terror to achieve criminal objectives of a villainous or obsessive nature. It can be carried out by isolated individuals or criminal groups. In both cases, it is an essentially symmetrical form of terrorism.

2.3.1.1. Individual common law terrorism

When carried out by isolated individuals who feel they have a mission in or for society, it can easily be confused with criminal acts of a communitarian nature. It generally uses the techniques of terrorism in the means it employs, but its motivations are most often obsessive in nature and similar to those of serial crime. However, the individual terrorist does not seek personal pleasure, but uses the visibility of the terrorist act to accomplish what he or she perceives as a «mission». In this context, he meets the Western definitions of a «lone wolf».

The best known cases are in the United States, such as Theodore Kaczynski[64] , known as the «*Unabomber*"[65] , who carried out 16 bombings between 1978 and 1996. On 19 September 1995, he had a manifesto published simultaneously in the *New York Times* and the *Washington Post*, setting out his philosophy. Another

---

64 . Born on 22 May 1942, Theodore Kaczynski had a doctorate in mathematics from the University of Michigan and was an assistant professor at Berkeley from 1967 to 1969.

65 . Unabomber = University and Airline Bomber. His attacks killed 3 people and seriously injured 29.

similar example is Lucas J. Helder, a philosophy student who was arrested in May 2002 for planting 18 pipe bombs in five Midwestern states to raise Americans' consciousness about the importance of life and death (!).

In Europe, this type of terrorism is more rare. A recent example was the bombing of the Dortmund football team on 11 April 2017, the sole purpose of which was to influence the stock market value of the team in order to enable speculative activities[66].Another example is the attempted extortion by a German citizen in September 2017, who threatened to poison food products if a ransom of 10 million euros was not paid.

This form of terrorism is often difficult to distinguish from serial crime or mass murder. There is a desire to manifest one's existence, one's role and one's difference in a society which, through its complexity, tends to blur the importance of the individual. The link between the action and its purpose is often difficult to identify, as it is often irrational. Detecting the disorders that trigger the murderous enterprise requires a granularity of information that is almost impossible for the state to assume. The role of local communities, but also and above all of the family nucleus, is decisive in preventing such acts.

2.3.1.2. Mafia terrorism

When carried out by criminal organisations, common law terrorism generally has objectives of a rational and material nature, aimed at promoting or facilitating lucrative criminal activity. Examples include the *Mafia* bombing campaign in Italy[67] , *narco-terrorism* in South America in the 1990s, or kidnapping campaigns in some Philippine islands. The drift of some nationalist terrorist movements in Northern Ireland and Corsica in the 1990s could also fall into this category.

Common law terrorism is not part of a revolutionary process. On the contrary, its 'ideological' credo is often conservative. It seeks to put pressure on the state in order to maintain the status quo and freedom of action vis-à-vis political power. It may also have a purely internal purpose within the criminal organisation: to re-establish or maintain the cohesion of the organisation. It is rarely indiscriminate, as it tends to avoid police intervention, and its actions are mainly directed against members of the group or rival groups. It is essentially symmetrical in nature and uses brutality - not to say sometimes horror - to encourage loyalty among members of the organisation and to serve the law of silence, known in the Italian mafia as *omertà*. In some ways, it is similar to the 'state terrorism' discussed below.

---

66 . Philip Oltermann, "Dortmund attack: man arrested on suspicion of share-dealing plot", The Guardian, 21 April 2017.

67 . Notably the bombing of the Galleria degli Uffizi in Florence on 27 May 1993.

Popular support for ordinary terrorism varies greatly. Most often, as in southern Italy, it is weak, and terrorist action is aimed at encouraging passive support through intimidation in order to weaken its willingness to cooperate with law enforcement. Often, terrorist techniques are used more for tactical purposes (eliminating individuals) than for strategic purposes (terrorising). The assassinations of General Dalla Chiesa (3 September 1982), Judge Giovanni Falcone (23 May 1992) and Prosecutor Paolo Borsellino (19 July 1992) were primarily intended to «lock down» investigations and paralyse anti-Mafia action.

2.3.1.3. Narcoterrorism

The case of *narcoterrorism* in Latin America is particular because it is based on an economic activity (coca cultivation) that generates a certain social welfare in disadvantaged regions, and where alternative crops are not always competitive. Thus, popular support for the drug cartels can be relatively strong at the local or even regional level. In the 1980s, Pablo Escobar, leader of the Medellín cartel, made a significant contribution to improving the living conditions of the under-privileged classes with, among other things, his *'Medellín without slums'* project[68] , which brought hundreds of decent housing units, street lighting, asphalt streets, football fields and a zoo to the slums. Moreover, the income generated by coca cultivation for a peasant is ten times higher than that generated by potatoes. As a result, the interests of the criminals are aligned with those of the small peasantry.

Indeed, it was this same convergence of interests that was exploited by the US CIA in the 1960s to block the spread of Marxist revolutionary movements in the Latin American countryside. This strategy was not new and had already been implemented in Burma, Thailand and Laos to fight communist guerrillas. It was the French SDECE special services that encouraged and participated in the opium trade, thus favouring the local warlords who constituted a 'natural' protection against the spread of communism. This strategy led to the rise of the «Golden Triangle» and was taken up by the American CIA in the early 1960s.

Common law terrorism defines its legitimisation by the «social» role of criminal action, which constitutes a very concrete motivation, often perceived as existential. The stakes here are material and therefore the struggle is conducted on a symmetrical basis. Nevertheless, mafias are difficult to combat because they are often the result of deficient social or integration policies and are embedded in the economic and social environment of dependent populations. The difficulty of depriving narcoterrorism of its popular support is linked to the difficulty of establishing alternative sources of income for the peasants in the areas concerned.

---

68 . See Vincent Gouëset, «L'impact du 'narcotrafic' à Medellín», Cahiers des Amériques latines, Université Paris 3, Institut des Hautes Études de l'Amérique latine (IHEAL / Université Paris 3), 1992, pp. 27-52.

2.3.2. Marginal terrorism

Marginal terrorism is on the borderline between ordinary terrorism and political terrorism. It is carried out by a handful of enlightened people who are trying to start a revolutionary process, but without any popular support.

This category includes many terrorist groups from the 1970s and 1980s, such as the *Baader Gang/Rote Armee Fraktion (RAF)* in Germany, *Action Direct (AD)* in France or the Belgian *Cellules Communistes Combattantes (CCC)*. In Greece, the *17 November Movement*, dismantled in the early 2000s, also belonged to this category: despite its revolutionary discourse, it was never able to crystallise a broad opposition and its attacks remained 'punitive' actions without political impact.

These movements generally claim Che Guevara's «*foco*» theory, which advocates terrorist action «*to mobilise the masses*». However, their political action often takes the form of behaviour similar to that of criminal gangs: lacking a political base and financial support, they generally have to ensure their economic survival through exactions. The latter - often referred to as «*proletarian expropriations*» or «*proletarian taxes*» - can take the form of attacks on the property of the proletariat.- can take the form of bank robberies, kidnapping for ransom and blackmail. Their ideological basis is usually tenuous and they lack the popular anchorage necessary for a revolutionary process. This form of terrorism is essentially symmetrical in nature: the action of the security forces has no multiplier effect on the virulence of the group.

Marginal terrorism is the easiest form of terrorism to combat, without requiring a complex strategy, as is the case for political terrorism. In Belgium, Germany and France, it has been possible to combat this terrorism effectively with the tools of the fight against organised crime. This may explain why these three countries have failed to develop a strategic approach to the fight against terrorism, and their fight is almost totally based on a tactical/police approach. This is the reason for their failure in the current fight against jihadist terrorism.

2.3.3. Political terrorism

Political terrorism is part of a process that aims to establish a new authority. It can be revolutionary in character and is usually aimed at provoking upheavals that lead to the emergence of new political forces. In this context, political terrorism, whether left or right wing, frequently has an asymmetric dimension.

The Italian *Red Brigades* of the 1960s-1970s are an example of terrorism that straddled the line between the fringe and the political, and never came to maturity. With a relatively broad base of sympathy in intellectual and working-class circles at the beginning of its existence, the movement could have evolved into a revolutionary process, but with the arrest of its historical leaders, it lost its ideological substance at the beginning of the 1980s and became marginal terrorism. It then broke up into several ephemeral movements with sporadic demonstrations and no popular support.

Political terrorism is sometimes difficult to distinguish from fringe terrorism, as many terrorist groups claim a revolutionary process, even if they do not have the popular base to sustain it in the long term. This is the case of the *Rote Armee Fraktion (RAF)*, which often claimed a revolutionary process, but in fact never had a sufficient base to achieve its goals and thus remained marginal. In Spain, the Basque ETA's revolutionary process was interrupted by the advent of democracy in 1982, and was never able to mobilise a sufficient base to resume it. But it has enjoyed the passive support of the Basque population for many years. This explains its «flight forward» with the adoption of Carlos Marighella's urban guerrilla strategy. The aim was to push Spain to adopt extreme repressive measures that would have favoured the resumption of a popular revolutionary mechanism. The difference between these two forms of terrorism is therefore linked to the potential to create a popular base that can sustain and support a revolutionary process over time.

The peculiarity of political terrorism is that it must judiciously balance the use of violence in order not to alienate the popular support it needs to build a new society. The Basque ETA, for example, targeted members of the forces of law and order and certain individuals who might have jeopardised its authority or existence, but rarely carried out completely 'indiscriminate' attacks. Spain never really understood ETA's strategy, and instead of fighting it effectively, it became its unwitting accomplice.

2.3.3.1. Right-wing terrorism

In general, far-right ideologies are driven by a nationalist reading of politics and aim to strengthen the role of the state. Their doctrine most often combines the idea of socialism with that of national preference, hence the term 'national socialism'. It thus differs from socialism and its derivatives, which are internationalist in outlook. Contrary to a widespread and carefully maintained opinion, antisemitism is not a fundamental aspect of these doctrines.

However, in reality, this form of terrorism has often lost all political content and its supporters have turned it into a «catch-all» doctrine, which focuses all frustrations without any real coherence. This is why we find in these movements symbols and behaviours that resemble the IIIᵉ Reich, without seeing a coherent political project.

Right-wing terrorism has several dimensions, which may or may not overlap:

- Intimidation of a particular community (immigrants, foreigners in general, people of colour, people of a particular ethnicity or religion, etc.) in order to drive them out or discourage their settlement in a particular area or country. It is a form of terrorism that is essentially symmetrical in nature, without multiplier effects. Groups such as the Ku Klux Klan are involved in this type of terrorism, although they are not considered terrorist movements in the United States. In Europe, this type of violence has been developing since the late 1970s, in the wake of poorly managed and often instrumentalised immigration policies.

- The exacerbation of a sense of identity, which may be based on nationalism or the preservation of moral values. In the United States, this type of movement has taken the form of a struggle against the federal government - dubbed *the Zionist Occupation Government (ZOG)* - and members of non-white communities. It is often linked to a religious and/or political ideology akin to 'single cause terrorism'. It is essentially symmetrical in nature.

- Terrorism that seeks to push the state to harden its authority, or even to establish a dictatorship. Even if its actors are different, it is similar to «state terrorism» in that it is not part of a logic of weakening the state, but, on the contrary, aims to strengthen its power. It was this strategy that fuelled «black terrorism» in Italy during the 1980s, the most violent and deadly manifestation of which was the attack on the Bologna railway station (2 August 1980). This form of terrorism tends to be asymmetric, as the way the state responds to it fuels the terrorist action.

2.3.3.2. Extreme left-wing terrorism

Far-left terrorism is one of the phases of the Marxist revolutionary process and is part of a very precise logic which envisages the «iterative» use of violence, until the open confrontation between the bourgeoisie and the working class. It doesn't strike randomly and seeks to provoke a violent reaction from the forces of order, in an escalation that must generate a popular mobilisation and lead to the victory of the working class. It seeks to undermine the foundations of liberal society in order to replace it with a new form of society. Seen as a process that goes with the grain of history, it leaves no room for negotiation. It is a terrorism that is difficult to combat, because political solutions based on compromise that directly affect the revolutionary process are rejected out of hand. This is why Italian Prime Minister Aldo Moro, who was about to conclude a historic agreement between the Communist Party and the Christian Democracy, was kidnapped and then executed by the Red Brigades in March 1978.

The particularity of Marxist terrorism is that it relies on the government's reaction to mobilise the masses: each action of the government corresponds to a deterioration of its strategic situation. This is an asymmetric mechanism.

The practice of not negotiating and not granting concessions to terrorists dates from this period, since the conflict is precisely about the foundation of society.

Marxist revolutionary process		
Phases	**Action by revolutionary forces**	**Reaction of the police**
Crystallization	Selection and political education of grassroots activists. The first step is to create a popular base for the movement. Propaganda, information - and disinformation - are then the central elements of this phase, which also makes it possible to widen the circle of active militants who will constitute the core of the revolutionary action.	Police cordon and penetration.
	Corrosion of the social order, strike, agitation, sabotage, beginning of terrorist action («selective» terrorism). Revolutionary forces and the forces of law and order clash in an increasingly violent manner. Demonstrations are the starting point and are followed by phases of rioting. The aim is to demonstrate the presence of the movement, its strength and its determination towards the state. This combination of agitation and propaganda constitutes 'agitprop'. It also feeds on state repression which stimulates the mobilising effect of the action.	Intervention of law enforcement brigades, special police units.
Location	Popular education, psychological impregnation of the masses, military training of militants. It is about stimulating the mobilisation of the masses through targeted actions against the property and people of the ruling class. These punctual and violent actions aim to demonstrate objective successes, and thus the effectiveness of the movement. It constitutes «armed propaganda», which is often difficult to distinguish from terrorism proper.	Establishment of exceptional jurisdictions and definition of a state 'doctrine'.
	Systematic and repeated destruction of opposing forces, establishment of parallel hierarchies, elimination of diehards. Terrorism is the next phase of the process. It aims to achieve operational objectives that are of two kinds: material and immaterial objectives that weaken the forces of order and/or the ruling class. Here the distinction with armed propaganda is subtle and sometimes merely rhetorical.	Army intervention, protection of axes and sensitive points (defensive activity) - first military operations (offensive activity), local actions, patrol, ambush.
	Creation of guerrilla support bases. The extension of terrorism and the broadening of the popular base of action give rise to guerrilla warfare which is the expression of a people in arms against the ruling class.	Surface control, creation of no-go zones (systematic strafing and bombing without warning), regrouping of populations.

Edification	Expansion of support bases in liberated areas, establishment of new structures, self-management, councils, people's cooperative.	Large-scale operations, cordon and sweep operations, staggered in area and time.
	Transformation of guerrilla groups into a popular army. The ultimate stage of the revolution is the establishment of the new social system, which involves the transformation of the guerrilla war into a conventional conflict, a 'civil war' supported by friendly foreign powers.	Conventional warfare operations, but conditioned by factors inherent in the tactics of popular warfare and by international factors.
	Establishment of popular power	Defeat, elimination (independent state), partition or negotiated grant of independence.

Table 1 - The Marxist revolutionary process. Each new stage depends on the government's response and plays with its reactions to develop its revolutionary mechanism.

Theorists of insurgent warfare, including Che Guevara and Carlos Marighella, used the same principles, but adapted them to local conditions.

2.3.3.2.1. Che Guevara's Foco theory

Adapted to the revolutionary action of the peasant classes, the «*foco theory*» was developed by Che Guevara. It advocates the creation of guerrilla centres *(focos)* based in the countryside, which rely on their operational successes («*armed propaganda*») to win the support of the rural and then the urban populations until they gradually incorporate the whole population.

Applied by 'Che' in Bolivia, the *foco* theory proved to be a failure: the exponential development of urban centres in Latin America in the early 1960s progressively emptied the countryside, leaving the *focos* without the necessary popular support and depriving tactical successes of the resonance that should have encouraged the revolutionary process. Moreover, in large countries with a topography that tends to partition space, the *foco* theory favoured the development of more or less autonomous and uncoordinated factions, as in Colombia. This fragmentation facilitated the work of counter-subversion forces and encouraged struggles between revolutionary movements.

The *foco* model inspired many other movements, Marxist or not, including some Islamic revolutionary movements in Algeria, Egypt and Tunisia, and in Palestine in the 1960s-1980s. From its appearance in 1987, Hamas tried to counter the influence of Fatah by seeking limited but spectacular successes, allowing it to crystallise its presence. It thus acquired significant popularity among the Palestinian population and quickly became a political force in the occupied territories. Then, as it could only exist through armed struggle, it adopted a strategy very similar to Carlos Marighella's urban guerrilla warfare: it was to provoke ever more virulent Israeli responses, and thus to generate a dynamic that discredited Israel. This strategy led to the tragic interventions of spring 2002, which cost the Palestinians dearly in tactical terms, but which changed the perception of Israel in the world and thus affected its strategic posture in a lasting way.

Better adapted to the evolution of Latin American society and large metropolises, Carlos Marighella's urban guerrilla strategy in Argentina gradually eclipsed the *foco* theory.

2.3.3.2.2. Carlos Marighella's theory of urban guerrilla warfare

In June 1969, Carlos Marighella wrote his *Small Manual of Urban Guerrilla Warfare*[69] , which explains the strategy of political and guerrilla terrorism even more precisely and adapts it to the growing urbanisation of Latin American society. It is essentially a matter of pushing the state into a logic of repression, and taking anti-democratic measures, so as to decouple the population from the state and thus legitimise the armed struggle:

> *A political crisis must be transformed into an armed crisis by carrying out violent actions that will force those in power to transform a military situation into a political one. This will alienate the masses, who will then revolt against the army and the police and blame them for this state of affairs.*

> *The government has no alternative but to intensify its repression. Police networks, house searches, arrests of suspects and innocent people, and roadblocks make life unbearable. The military dictatorship engages in massive political persecution. Political assassination and police terror become routine.*

> *Despite this, the police fail. The armed forces, navy and air force are mobilised to carry out routine police operations. [...]*

> *The population refuses to collaborate with the government, and there is a general feeling that the government is unjust, unable to solve problems, and forced to physically liquidate its opponents. The political situation in the country is turning into a military situation in which the 'gorillas' are*

---

69 . See: https://www.marxists.org/archive/marighella-carlos/1969/06/minimanual-urban-guerrilla/

increasingly seen to be responsible for the violence, while the lives of the people are deteriorating.[70]

This type of terrorism does not lend itself well to political or peaceful solutions. Political action - as envisaged here - can only exist through armed confrontation. This is why some revolutionary movements systematically seek to undermine peace efforts through perpetual provocation. In Europe, this was the strategy of the *Irish Republican Army* (IRA) until the early 1990s, the Basque *Euskadi ta Akasatuna* (ETA), and the first generation Corsican independence movements.

This strategy, which has as its goal the seizure of power through a revolutionary mechanism, can only work through the radicalisation of the state response. This is why the IRA or ETA have systematically fought against all attempts at political compromise.

ETA, which had killed 45 people during the Franco dictatorship, killed almost 800 after the advent of democracy. This increase is not due to the Spanish repressive apparatus, but to the fact that the revolutionaries had to increase their pressure to provoke the government's reaction. After Franco's death in 1975, the government relaxed considerably. But in 1978, terrorism intensified. The new constitution established a semi-federal system based on autonomous regions, each with a parliament and a regional government. The Basque Country, Catalonia and Galicia were granted a status of «*great autonomy*», and their languages became official languages. The revolutionary process of ETA then lost its legitimacy. In order to restore it, the terrorists sought to create the conditions for the restoration of a dictatorship:

> *We have achieved one of our essential objectives: to force the enemy to commit a thousand injustices and a thousand atrocities. [...] The population, which until then had been more or less passive, became angry at the colonialist tyrant, reacted and came over entirely to our side. We could not have wished for a better result.*[71]

This strategy almost succeeded with the attempted military coup of 23 February 1981, which could have installed a dictatorship and thus set in motion a real revolutionary process. But the king managed to maintain the democratic process, and thus contain the terrorist phenomenon, which remained without managing to develop. In the end, it was the end of the Cold War and the advent of Islamic terrorism that condemned Basque terrorism in Spain. This is an

---

70 . Carlos Marighella, Mini-Manual of the Urban Guerrilla, 1969.
71 . José Maria Portell, Euskadi: Amnistia Arrancada, Dopesa, Barcelona, 1977, p. 251.

example of victory against an asymmetric phenomenon by maintaining the use of force at a tactical level.

By early 1969, the death toll in Northern Ireland had risen to 13. On 14 August 1969, the British Army was deployed to help restore order. It was warmly welcomed by both Protestants and Catholics as an impartial entity capable of restoring security: it successfully intervened and established a 'peace line' between the two communities. The revolutionary action lost momentum, creating tensions within the IRA between the supporters of social stability[72] and the supporters of Irish reunification. As a result, on 28 December 1969, the IRA split into its 'Provisional' and 'Official' wings. The *Provisional IRA* (PIRA) then initiated an unprecedented campaign of violence that began on Easter Tuesday 1970 with the first Catholic attack on the army and culminated in 1972 with 468 deaths. It had two objectives: to demonstrate the army's inability to ensure the security of the population in order to undermine the confidence it enjoyed, and to provoke reprisals from the forces of law and order. This strategy worked and very quickly the army was discredited among all Irish communities and the revolutionary process could continue.

The IRA and ETA apply the Marxist asymmetry: provoking repression to fuel the revolutionary process. The response to such terrorism requires a careful mix of firmness and flexibility, deep work in society and the ability to strike at the centre of gravity of the terrorist movement. While Spain and Britain ultimately benefited from the end of the Cold War, they were able to control the use of force skilfully, avoiding a slide into uncontrolled violence. Spain, more than Britain, dealt with terrorism strategically - as Italy had done - by combining the use of force with political measures.

2.3.3.3. Single-cause terrorism

Single-issue terrorism, which is very similar to religious terrorism in terms of its content, but different in terms of its targeting, has developed mainly in Anglo-Saxon countries. In this respect, it can be seen that the leaders of so-called «patriotic» movements, whose behaviour is similar to terrorism, such as the *Michigan Militia*, the *Aryan Nation* and the *Ku Klux Klan* in the United States, have religious titles such as «Reverend» or «Pastor». Human life has only a relative value and is no longer an obstacle to violence justified by 'moral' criteria.

It includes the terrorism of the vegan, environmentalist, anti-abortion and anti-speciesist movements. Often very similar to far-right terrorism, it seeks to promote an idea, often in a very narrow niche, but does not present a broader

---

72 . Bernadette Devlin, «We did not build our barricades for the reunification of Ireland, but to restore justice». Le Nouvel Observateur, 25 August 1969.

political project and is often difficult to place on the 'traditional' political spectrum.

Its credo is often moral:

> *We, the undersigned, declare the rightness of taking all divine measures*[73] *necessary, including the use of force, to defend human life (born or embryonic). We proclaim that all force is legitimate to defend the life of a born child, and is legitimate to defend the life of an embryo child.*[74]

And :

> *You have a responsibility to protect the life of your neighbour, and to use force if necessary. If you want to erase this truth, you can mix my blood with the blood of an embryo*[75] *, and of those who have fought to defend the oppressed. However, truth and righteousness will prevail. May God help you to protect the embryos as you would like to be protected.*[76]

Relatively violent during the 1980s and early 1990s, the virulence of this type of terrorism has diminished somewhat (largely due to measures taken in the fight against Islamist terrorism), but it remains deadly in the United States.

2.3.3.4. The black bloc, a non-terrorist asymmetry

It is important to stress here that the *black bloc* is a form of asymmetric combat that is not terrorism. It is not originally a structure, organisation, network or ideology, but a functionality within a demonstration. This functionality is associated with a specific action strategy and is carried out by a group of people temporarily gathered for the occasion.

Situated on the borderline between «incivility», urban guerrilla warfare and terrorism, the *black bloc* strategy has its origins in the demonstrations of autonomous groups in Germany in the 1980s. The demonstration against the *World Trade Organisation (WTO)* summit in Seattle (30 November 1999) marked the beginning of its existence. The *black blocs* then developed and accompanied all the major meetings of the world economy, in particular the G8 summit in Genoa (21 July 2001), which gave them worldwide notoriety.

---

73 . In the text: godly.

74 . http://www.armyofgod.com/defense2.html.

75 . In the text: unborn.

76 . Statement by Reverend Paul J. Hill, sentenced to death for murdering an abortion doctor, http://www.armyofgod.com/Paulhillindex.html.

The fact that some of its theorists belong to the *«Eugene»* movement, created in the United States by Colin Clyde and John Zerzan[77] , tends to associate the *black bloc with an* anarchist phenomenon. However, its supporters are recruited from various extreme left, autonomous, environmentalist or anarchist movements, and they do not claim to represent a particular ideology. In fact, they are more a collection of «mercenaries» from the various anti-globalisation movements ready to function as a «shock» group for the benefit of the whole demonstration.

The real asymmetrical dimension of the *black bloc* is that it mainly serves the political interests of other movements that claim pacifist methods, and that thus exploit the «police brutality» provoked by the black bloc «mercenaries». These «mercenaries» - often referred to as *commandos* or *brigadistas* - «sacrifice» themselves in order to disrupt the police apparatus and provoke indiscriminate police brutality. Peaceful» demonstrators can thus be victimised. Brutality and globalisation can then be combined to discredit government action. This explains why even the 'pacifist' components of the anti-globalisation movement accept and support the role of the *black bloc.*

During demonstrations, such as those of the «Gilets jaunes» in France or Belgium, the media and some «experts» have described the rioters as «*black blocs*». This is an abuse of language. Even if their appearance is similar and their profiles are often similar to those of the *black blocs,* they are simply «casseurs» who act for themselves, unlike the «real» *black blocs.* They are just «copies» of a movement created 30 years earlier, which functions without doctrine or real tactics. This confusion contributes to the misunderstanding of the phenomenon and the inability to fight it.

To put it simply, the *black blocs* have an asymmetrical approach, while the rioters have a symmetrical one: instruments that are effective against the one will have an opposite effect on the other. The problem is that the police forces in France and Belgium are very weak in understanding insurrectionary movements. This is why they do not achieve lasting effects.

2.3.3.4.1. Strategy

The essence of the *black bloc* strategy is to push the police into a process of escalating violence, in order to demonstrate the incapacity of the powers that be and the authorities in place to manage a crisis situation.

The forms of action of the *black bloc* change from case to case, but follow a general strategy focused on creating a spirit of solidarity, against police repression, by creating a chaotic situation that serves as a springboard for the protest.

---

77 . John Zerzan, with degrees in political science and history, is an American anarchist living in Eugene, Oregon, a friend of Theodore Kaczynski, better known by the pseudonym «Unabomber».

Through provocation and great tactical mobility, they seek to break the cohesion of the police forces and to draw them into confrontations that allow the «main body of the demonstration» to develop. Sometimes - and even often - using violence, destruction and ransacking, sometimes verbal violence and the threat of violence, the strategy changes depending on the location and the participants.

This mechanism starts from peaceful/pacifist demonstrations which should give legitimacy to the demonstrators. The *black bloc* then intervenes in a second phase to reveal the incapacity and oppressive violence of the authorities.

2.3.3.4.2. Operations

The planning and strategic management of the *black blocks* is carried out via online messaging. The grouping of the teams and the strategy are discussed and decided only a few hours before the action. During the G8 summit in Genoa (2001), the Italian police's attempts to intercept the *black bloc* plans were quickly identified and immediately published on the Net, with false information intended to mislead them.

Black bloc operations are generally conceived on the principle of «*swarming*». The idea is to use individuals or very small groups scattered in a crowd or in a given sector to quickly create ephemeral concentrations capable of generating poles of violence with a temporary superiority over the forces of order.

A more developed variant of *swarming* has been developed in '*rhizome*' operations, which have the capacity to generate several clusters of violence spread over several sites, but within the same operation. The '*rhizome*' is composed of small, independent *nodes* that are linked together in a non-hierarchical manner.

Black bloc operations have no material or territorial objectives other than the deployment of violence. In order to symbolise its success, the black bloc establishes «*Temporary Autonomous Zones*» (ZATs), which simply materialise the achievement of an objective, even if its value is more symbolic than territorial. The simple destruction or ransacking of a shop can constitute a ZAT.

The four principles of rhizome combat are clearly defined:

- *Independence of* the nuclei from each other, on the one hand, for operational reasons (the actions of each nucleus do not involve or endanger a central structure) and, on the other hand, for philosophical reasons (hierarchy is inherently violent).

- *Interaction*: hierarchical structures waste too much energy filtering and channelling information, which slows down the flow. Hierarchy is therefore replaced by interaction where action takes precedence over information flow, with the idea that informal information exchange through action allows for a faster reaction than in structured systems.

- *Open source*: the exchange of information in a rhizomic network takes place horizontally and indiscriminately, as a consequence of the principle of interaction.

- *No dependence on* space and time, which is seen as a characteristic of 'hierarchical' combat.

2.3.3.4.3. Tactics

On the ground, the *Black Block* doctrine advocates the engagement of small cells of 5-20 people who generally know each other and coordinate their presence and operational strategy before the action. The tactical action is decided on the spot a few minutes before the demonstration starts. Masked and dressed in black, the «members» of the *Black Block* march with (black) flags and drums, reminiscent of armies from another time. Their presence in the main demonstration is organised in a theatrical and methodical way. In Genoa, the *Black Block* was inserted into the main demonstration and surrounded by members of the *Pink Bloc*, who provided a «*tactical frivolity*» group for the occasion, whose function was to create a diversion and encourage the exit and entry of the *Black Block* into the procession. The latter only initiated the chaos, then quickly withdrew as soon as the situation degenerated, leaving the other members of the demonstration to grapple with the police. Their actions are recorded on video, in order to study and improve tactics.

Police violence finally «gave the victory» to the clients of the *Black Block*: shortly after the violent demonstrations in Genoa, the photo of the young Carlo Giuliani, killed by a carabiniere, was immediately put on the Net, and contributed greatly to denigrating the action of the police.

2.3.4. Guerrilla terrorism

By *guerrilla terrorism* we mean mainly terrorism carried out in the context of a war of liberation or resistance to an occupier, which has broad popular support but is not necessarily part of a revolutionary process. However, some forms of guerrilla terrorism may occur at an advanced stage of a revolutionary process of a political nature.

It is generally distinguished from other forms of terrorism in that it focuses its actions on the military or occupying forces. It carries out actions, like the Resistance in 1944-1945, targeted at the occupier, with «operational» objectives. It is not totally «blind» and aims to discourage the invader or occupier. The use of the term «terrorism» is often contested to designate this form of combat. Indeed, some Western definitions define terrorism as actions directed against civilians, as in the United States:

2. UNDERSTANDING THE THREAT

*[premeditated; perpetrated by a sub-national or clandestine actor; poli-
tically motivated, which may include religious, philosophical or culturally
symbolic motivations; violent; and perpetrated against non-combatant
targets[78] , by sub-national groups or clandestine agents, usually intended to
influence an audience.[79]*

In other words, when this form of violence is used against an armed force, it is not systematically considered as terrorism. For example, attacks on US forces in Iraq are not considered terrorism. This definition partly explains the (too) low figures reported in the State Department's *Patterns of Global Terrorism*, 2003 edition[80].However, it should be noted that this distinction remains highly theoretical: virtually all armed groups that emerged in Iraq in resistance to the US intervention were considered to be «al-Qaeda» offshoots, and thus terrorist organisations.

In non-communist and/or non-revolutionary conflicts, this form of terrorism is often only a form of military action that aims to weaken the adversary and raise the cost of its occupation or presence. When not part of a jihadist or Marxist revolutionary process, the approach often remains 'symmetrical' in substance. Both sides fight in the same space, with the same logic, but with different tactics. The aim is to paralyse logistics, reduce the occupier's freedom of movement, prevent him from living a 'normal' life in the country and affect his morale. This form of terrorism is generally relatively easy to combat with «unconventional warfare» tactics, and has no real multiplier effect.

Examples include the «*small war*" (Spanish: *guerrilla*) against Napoleon's troops in Spain, the Resistance against the Nazi occupiers in the Second World War, the resistance against Western forces in Afghanistan or Iraq. The NATO-supported guerrilla movements in Ukraine and the Baltic States in the 1950s and 1960s are examples of «symmetrical» wars in the aftermath of the Second World War, which Western countries were never willing or

---

78 . The term non-combatant includes, in addition to civilians, military personnel who were unarmed or off duty at the time of the incident, such as Colonel James Rowe, killed in Manila in April 1989, Captain William Nordeen, a military attaché killed in Athens in June 1988, the two military personnel killed in the LaBelle discotheque in Berlin in April 1986, and four Marines on guard duty at the US Embassy in San Salvador in June 1985. Attacks on military installations or personnel in countries where there are no hostilities are also considered terrorist acts.

79 . United States Code, Title 22, Section 2656f(d). This definition has been used by the US government for statistical or analytical products since 1983.

80 . The report released on 29 April 2004 presented terrorism figures showing the lowest level of terrorist activity in 2003 since 1969! Accused by Democratic members of the House of Representatives of falsifying the data in order to present a more favourable presidential record in an election year, the State Department announced in June the publication of a corrected edition. Data for the report was compiled by the Terrorist Threat Integration Center (TTIC), CNN, 10 June 2004.

able to give political and strategic resonance to. Thus, they were easily and bloodily crushed by the Soviets. The same phenomenon can be observed in the insurgency of Russian-speaking minorities in Ukraine from 2014: it is a purely symmetrical phenomenon, whose effectiveness is essentially due to the inability of the Ukrainian government - and NATO - to combat it.

Theorists of jihadist terrorism see this form of terrorism as part of the *open front jihad* (OFJ), which we discuss in detail below. The Islamic State, for example, developed in the wake of Western action against the Syrian government (and in the Sahel). Its attacks in the West are clearly an extension of its resistance to Western interventions in Iraq and Syria.

2.3.5. Religiously inspired terrorism

Contrary to a widely held view in the West, terrorism based on religious fundamentalism (with religious objectives) is very rare and mostly present in Asia, such as Sikh and Buddhist terrorism in India. In most cases, religion is not the objective of the terrorist act, but it provides a doctrinal framework and operating 'software'. It would therefore be more accurate to speak of *religiously inspired terrorism*.

It is mainly observed in two contexts: millenarian movements and religious nationalism.

Millenarian movements, for which violent action is part of a perspective in which they would constitute the vanguard of a new society resulting from the apocalypse. It is generally not a question of provoking this apocalypse - which remains God's work and is inescapable - but of opposing, even by violence, anything that might threaten the 'good course' of the divine decision. They often develop a «besieged» mentality and see the outside world as a threat to the very existence of this «chosen people». The proximity or closeness of the fateful date of the apocalypse increases the risk of the community being destroyed or neutralised by the government, and violent action becomes legitimate. This position is not far removed from that of Christian Zionists (who form a significant part of Donald Trump's support) who support the state of Israel, with the prospect of its destruction and the return of the Messiah[81].Millenarian movements are similar to the idea of political nihilism, which advocates the destruction of a society before proposing a new one. As Bakunin said, «*the passion for destruction is also a creative passion*!

These are the main lines of thought of sects such as *Aum ShinriKyō*, which saw the apocalypse as the starting point for a New Man and a purer world. While such movements are often murderous, the use of the word 'terrorist' could be debated. Terrorism implies that the effect of terror is exploited to achieve

---

81 . Pascal Riché, «Why the American religious right supports Israel», L'Obs, 14 May 2018.

something. But if the aim is 'simply' to kill, without any particular behaviour being expected from this violence, then the term is - in theory at least - inappropriate and should instead be called mass crime.

Religious nationalism is the use of religion as a support for a nationalist or identity-based approach. Religion constitutes the unifying element and the reference around which violent action is built, whether it be revolutionary, insurrectionary or legalistic. ᶜThus, from the beginning of the 20th century, Islamism constituted a platform for counter-revolutionary movements in the Soviet republics of Central Asia (Basmatchis) and Judaism became the support of Zionist terrorism in Palestine at the beginning of the 20th centuryᶜ.

Unlike millenarianism, religious nationalism is not emotional or irrational, and its objectives are very secular. The religious dimension has an effect on the strategic parameters (e.g. the notion of victory), tactical parameters (e.g. the role of civilian populations) and in the modus operandi (e.g. the notion of sacrifice), but does not provide the objectives. The link to religious objectives is the combined result of Western discourse and the use of religion as a unifying element.

Religious nationalism manifests itself in three main ways:

- The struggle against corrupt secular governments (or those deemed to be corrupt)[82]. This was essentially the approach of the mujahideen who returned to their respective countries after the war against the Soviets ('Afghans'). In the early 1990s, they formed the backbone of a rebellion in countries such as Algeria, Tunisia, Morocco and Libya. In this context, religion provided a moral reference to fight against the abuses of power. The ambition of the fighters was national in nature and had no reason to go beyond the national framework.

- A resistance struggle against an occupying power, in the same way as the European resistance movements during the Second World War. The objective is to maintain or gain authority over a territory (Palestine, Afghanistan, Iraq, Syria, Libya, etc.) or to respond to foreign intervention and occupation (Palestine, Iraq, Afghanistan, Sahel, etc.). Its most virulent forms are justified by the various Western interventions, whether by air or land, in the Near and Middle East, all of which were based on lies. They have led to the creation of independent territories under Islamist governance. This is the approach of the Islamic State, derived from the resistance against the American occupation.

It should be noted that terrorism is only a method and not a doctrine; not all resistance movements are therefore terrorist movements. This is the case, for

---

82 . «The Wandering Mujahidin: Armed and Dangerous", Bureau of Intelligence and Research (INR), 21-22 August 1993 (SECRET/NOFORN/NOCONTRACR/ORCON - Declassified 23 November 2007).

example, of *Hezbollah*, which is not recognised as a terrorist by a majority of countries. We will examine its case in more detail below.

In the Middle East, the countries as we see them on the map are recent and the idea of 'nation' is often caught between a sense of belonging to a tribal community and a religious community. Contrary to the Western perception, it is therefore not defined simply in terms of political boundaries. This is why religion (in this region: Islam) often makes it possible to crystallise an identity beyond the tribal level, to federate wills and to articulate a political project.

The 'Westphalian' Western mindset has been overtaken by this community dimension. Thus, prior to their involvement in Iraq and Syria, France and Belgium totally neglected communication with their large national Muslim communities. The assumption was that living in France, or even having a French passport, was enough to be integrated into the French nation and to adhere to the government's decisions. This was a strategic mistake.

Explaining Islamist terrorism in terms of a religious project avoids a critical examination of irrational military interventions and excludes any dialogue. This is the Israeli approach, which maintains the idea that Hamas' struggle is strictly religious: confrontation is therefore inevitable and there is no possible compromise. In fact, Islamism has taken over from Marxism as a support for the struggle against the Israeli occupation: the Palestinians have not changed their objective of recovering their land occupied by Israel, but since Marxism has disappeared, Islamism has become a kind of cement for the political project. After the end of the Gulf War (1991), the American refusal to leave the Arabian Peninsula triggered a wider anti-Western resistance movement (a form of anti-imperialism) with a religious cement, which the West would call 'Al-Qaeda'.

A peculiarity of conflicts based on religious software is that they are generally 'harder'. For the jihadists, Westerners are crusaders who intervene in the Middle East to attack the community of believers. From then on, we are in an 'absolute' frame of reference, where the stakes are existential and exceed the economic calculations (loss/gain) that prevail in secular conflicts, and where the human dimension becomes secondary. In such a context, the 'economic' balance sheet- In such a context, the «economic» balance sheet - insofar as such a calculation is relevant - is always positive, regardless of the losses suffered, since they are accepted for the survival of the community and the faith. From then on, all sacrifices and all extremes are permitted...

But there is nothing really new in this; Christianity itself has also justified war, torture and even genocide to spread the faith. The Inquisition, the repression of the Cathars, the Camisards and other religious factions used some of the most extreme and inhumane measures. This is not to mention the extermination of Amerindian populations in the name of Catholicism, for the sole purpose of seizing their wealth...

This principle is not so different from the Western acceptance of placing 'reason of state', 'Western values' and the like above life. Thus, the wars started by the US and France in defiance of international law, their use of torture or even the bombing of Christians in Syria find justifications that nobody in the West questions. A report by the *United Nations Assistance Mission in Afghanistan* shows that in 2019, Western coalition forces are killing more civilians than the Islamic State[83] ! In the Sahel, people are more afraid of the blunders of the military fighting terrorists than of jihadist attacks[84] !

2.3.6. State terrorism

State terrorism is beyond the scope of this book and is mentioned here only for the sake of completeness, as it differs fundamentally from other forms of terrorism. Whereas other forms of terrorism are generally a 'weak to strong' method of action, state terrorism is a 'strong to weak' strategy. Its principle is as old as the hills, but it was during the French Revolution, with the *Terror* regime (1793-1794), that state terrorism was first formalised. The Terror is therefore not the origin of modern terrorism, as some claim. Indeed, while other forms of terrorism seek to influence or overthrow state authority, state terrorism, on the contrary, results from an excessive application of that authority.

By extension, during the Cold War, the term 'state terrorism' was regularly used by Eastern countries to describe the policies of 'imperialist' states, which imposed power on the working class. In particular, it referred to the counter-insurgency strategy of some countries, including the use of «death squads» organised by certain police forces (in El Salvador, Chile, Argentina and Brazil), as well as the Spanish *Anti-Terrorist Liberation Group (GAL)*, etc.

The West, which has always favoured respect for the rule of law, is now tending to move away from it and dangerously close to practices akin to state terrorism. This is the case in the United States and France. The principle of «terrorising terrorists» is often used as a cover. The problem is that this violence tends to go beyond the fight against terrorism, and is applied against anything that might threaten the state. This is the case with the excessive violence applied against the Yellow Vests[85].

---

83 . Midyear Update on the Protection of Civilians in Armed Conflict: 1 January to 30 June 2019, United Nations Assistance Mission in Afghanistan (UNAMA), 30 July 2019, p. 12; Amy Woodyatt & Arnaud Siad, "More civilians are being killed by Afghan and international forces than by the Taliban and other militants", CNN, 31 July 2019.

84 . Daniel Fontaine, 'Sahel: les populations craignent plus les bavures des forces de protection que les attaques djihadistes', rtbf.be, 14 April 2021; Nathanaël Charbonnier, 'Les armées régulières seraient tout aussi meurtrières (voire plus) que les terroristes au Sahel', franceinter.fr, 3 May 2021.

85 . Envoyé spécial, «Violence, la surenchère», 13 December 2018 (France 2), France2/YouTube, 18 December 2018 (18'45").

In November 2018, in an interview with the BBC, Mike Pompeo presented the US sanctions and announced that the Iranian government would have to do the right thing «*if it wants its people to* eat»[86]. This way of threatening the civilian population in order to force the government to act as the United States wishes corresponds to the definition of... terrorism!

2.4. Special forms of terrorism

2.4.1. Superterrorism

Superterrorism[87] is a term that emerged after 11 September 2001. It does not correspond to any internationally recognised definition and tends to refer to a form of terrorism that aims at mass destruction of human life or property. By extension, it is associated with forms of terrorism involving *weapons of mass destruction (WMD)*.

9/11» promoted the idea that terrorism seeks to maximise the number of deaths and encouraged the development of catastrophic scenarios, widely relayed by the cinema, but totally disconnected from reality[88]. Because in the real world, attacks always respond to relatively precise and concrete objectives.

It can be seen that terrorist movements rarely use their destructive capacity 'for free'. It is most often a matter of conveying a message to an audience, not destroying it. An attack that wipes out part of humanity would immediately remove any popular or political support for the movement. In most cases, the terrorist group derives its strength from the legitimacy granted to it by its audience. It must therefore strike a fine balance between the benefit of violence and the rejection it provokes. This is what the Palestinians understood when they abandoned international terrorism in the 1970s and concentrated on actions against the Israeli occupier, even though the death toll was clearly against them.

Thus, guerrilla terrorists, whether in liberation or separatist movements, do not seek the total destruction of the country or territory they want to liberate. By analogy, if the Islamic State is said to intend to extend its caliphate to Europe, it would seem rather contradictory that it would be bent on «nuclearising» it. In addition, despite a great capacity to learn from past mistakes in order to adapt and improve their methods, the terrorists remain very conservative in their

---

86 . "Secretary of State Mike Pompeo's Interview with Hadi Nili of BBC Persian", Washington DC, 7 November 2018; Brendan Cole, "Mike Pompeo Says Iran Must Listen To U.S. 'If They Want Their People To Eat'", Newsweek, 9 November 2018.
87 . There is also the term «hyperterrorism», which covers the same issue.
88 . Darren Boyle, "Isis planning 'nuclear holocaust' to wipe hundreds of millions from face of the earth', claims reporter who embedded with the extremists", Daily Mail, 29 September 2015.

methods. Indeed, it is above all a question of demonstrating success through their determination. They therefore generally use the simple, tried and tested tactics and methods that work and that they are able - and not afraid - to carry out.

It is different for millenarian movements, which seek to 'purify' humanity through an apocalyptic situation, such as the *Aum ShinriKyō* sect in Japan, which had sought to exploit uranium mines in Australia and to buy nuclear warheads in Russia, before going down the road of chemical weapons. But in this case, we are no longer really in the situation of terrorism, where the objective is to obtain something by repeatedly putting pressure on the state, an authority or a community.

Islamic terrorism, despite its brutality, is not apocalyptic in nature: it seeks neither the purification of humanity nor the destruction of Christianity.

Moreover, the spectacular nature of a terrorist act is probably more the result of the evolution of our society than of the destructive will of the terrorists: the general trivialisation of violence and disasters pushes terrorists to outdo each other to make their message visible. Timothy McVeigh, one of the perpetrators of the Oklahoma City bombing (1995), said: «[...] *We needed a number of dead bodies to get our point across».* [89]

The shock of 9/11 quickly led to the idea that the next step must be the use of «weapons of mass destruction» (WMD), and one «expert» after another developed complex and fanciful scenarios.

Initially, WMD were defined as nuclear, biological and chemical weapons. In recent years, the definition has gradually been «enriched». For example, in order to justify a harsher sentence against the perpetrators of the attempted attack on the *World Trade Center* in New York in 1993, the US judiciary included in the definition of WMD high explosives (e.g., explosive charges reinforced with gas cylinders) that seek to increase the number of victims.

In 1995, the Oklahoma City bombing shook up American opinion: its power opportunely provided a bridge between the threats of the Cold War and contemporary terrorism:

Mass casualties and widespread physical destruction are the hallmarks of weapons of mass destruction, making their detection, prevention and destruction a priority for the FBI. A weapon of mass destruction (WMD), although traditionally associated with nuclear/radiological, chemical or biological agents, can also take the form of explosives, as in the 1995 bombing of the

---

89 . Original text: "[...] We needed a body count to make our point", New York Times, 1ᵉʳ March 1997.

Alfred P. Murrah Building in Oklahoma City. A weapon crosses the threshold of a WMD when its consequences exceed local response capabilities.[90]

The United States responded to the 9/11 attacks in a totally emotional, disproportionate and ill-considered manner: the terrorists were portrayed as bloodthirsty psychopaths acting for the sole purpose of killing. In the months that followed, the psychosis of further attacks led legislators to expand the definition of WMD:

> *The term «weapon of death and mass destruction» includes bombs; or grenades; or rockets with a propellant charge of more than 4 ounces (100 g); or missiles with an explosive or incendiary charge of more than ¼ ounce (8 g); or mines; or devices similar to those described above; or [...]*

> *Any type of weapon (other than a shotgun, or a sporting cartridge) that will be, or can rapidly be, converted to project a projectile by the action of an explosive [...].*

> *Any firearm capable of rapid fire [...].*[91]

In this race to the extreme and absurd, some US military personnel have also proposed to include in WMD computer weapons and personal computers, which could create disasters (air or otherwise) and thus threaten thousands of human lives. Apart from the fact that such a proposal would be virtually unfeasible without broad restrictions on individual freedom, it would condemn an entire industrial and economic sector to extinction and would significantly damage Western technological development.

For example, in the case against the perpetrators of the Boston bombing in April 2013, the FBI described an improvised pressure cooker device as a weapon of mass destruction![92]

As can be seen, even concepts that seemed relatively unambiguous become inextricable interpretations that can paralyse any security action.

---

90 . «The FBI and Weapons of Mass Destruction,» U.S. Federal Bureau of Investigation (FBI), August 4, 1999, http://norfolk.fbi.gov.wmd.htm.

91 . «House Bill 1468, North Carolina General Assembly, 2001 session, 28 November 2001.

92 . «Criminal Complaint United States vs Dzhokhar Tsarnaev, Department of Justice (www.justice.gov), https://www.justice.gov/iso/opa/resources/363201342213441988148.pdf.

2.4.4.1. Bioterrorism and chemical terrorism

Bioterrorism is a form of terrorism using biological or bacteriological means as weapons. Often referred to as the «poor man's nuclear weapon», chemical weapons have been part of the arsenal attributed to terrorist movements since the chemical weapon attack carried out by the *Aum ShinriKyō* cult in 1995.

The most publicised manifestation of 'bioterrorism' was the mailing of anthrax spores to various political and media figures in the United States in October 2001. Quickly dubbed «Amerithrax», this campaign created a totally artificial psychosis, as the Americans know how to do. As soon as it appeared, the proximity of Amerithrax to the September 2001 attacks led the «experts» to point the finger at Iraq: the «bad jihadists" could only be allied with a state actor, and therefore the «bad Iraqis»[93] ... thus directing the FBI's research in the wrong direction. However, the nature of the targets and the sequence of attacks over time, as well as the strains of anthrax, tended to rule out Iraqi involvement in this action from the outset[94].Indeed, on 28 October, the FBI officially announced that Amerithrax was linked to criminal activity in the United States itself, and that the Bureau was halting its investigations in relation to the jihadists. In essence, this incident demonstrated that the «mass destruction» capability of a biological weapon is very relative, that its impact is low without a sophisticated dissemination capability, and thus it is not suitable for terrorist use.

In fact, the less spectacular and equally random letter release was a novelty, as releases in the form of large-scale 'spore clouds' were more likely to be envisaged in order to cause mass casualties. But such a method requires a particular technology: the spores must be light enough to remain suspended in the air for a long time in order to be inhaled, but heavy enough to remain clustered and in sufficient concentration; they must be resistant to variations in humidity and temperature; the cloud must be large enough to be significant; and the spores must be able to be dispersed without being damaged by explosion or combustion, etc. Clearly, weaponising biological agents is a complex task, beyond the reach of terrorist groups.

Furthermore, while the focus is always on the «modus operandi», the key to understanding the terrorist act is the identification of its political purpose. The profile of the Amerithrax attack seemed closer to a serial crime of an antisemitic nature than to a political act. Indeed, terrorism is generally a message, and it rarely hides behind other criminal acts, because then its rationality would disappear, which explains why we generally observe an «over-claiming» of the

---

93 . Olivier Lepick, Télévision Suisse Romande, 26 October 2001, https://www.rts.ch/play/tv/19h30/video/peur-de-lanthrax-explications-scientifiques-et-politiques?id=1613745.

94 . Ibid. On 26 October 2001, the author announced on the Télévision Suisse Romande news channel the involvement of American extreme right-wing movements in the anthrax attacks, while the intelligence services were still recommending an action by al-Qaeda.

attacks, rather than an «under-claiming». In many cases, the claim comes before the attack itself, which allows the message to be conveyed at a lower human cost. In the case of Amerithrax, however, the opposite was true: a criminal act, hiding behind the 9/11 attacks.

The attacks carried out by the *Aum ShinriKyō* cult in the early 1990s are a special case. *Aum* was a millenarian-type group whose goal is the redemption of humanity through its rebirth after an apocalyptic demise. The aim of the cult was therefore not to obtain something from a government through blackmail or intimidation, but was 'simply' to generate an apocalypse. Unlike terrorism, which 'exchanges' violence for policy change, for example, the cult made no demands. The cult was therefore not a terrorist group in the strict sense, even if its attacks had the appearance of one. Indeed, the chemical and - perhaps - biological attacks in the Tokyo underground were merely 'tests', but were not intended to fuel a political process[95].They were thus more 'mass murder' than terrorism per se. While the nuance is imperceptible in terms of damage and loss of life, it is important for understanding the strategy of the group or movement. It does not change the way criminals are punished, but it is essential for designing strategies to combat and prevent them.

2.4.1.2. *Nuclear terrorism*

It is a form of terrorism that uses the nuclear threat to achieve its objectives. *Nuclear terrorism* could come from a nuclear-armed country or it could be carried out by groups with nuclear weapons. It could take the following forms:

- Conventional attack on nuclear infrastructure to create a catastrophe: destruction of facilities or disruption of their operation, such as preventing the cooling of a reactor: a kind of deliberate Chernobyl. In July-August 2022, the Ukrainian drone, artillery and missile attacks on the Zaporozhie nuclear power plant belong to this type of terrorism. The aim was to threaten the European population with nuclear disaster, in order to push the West to demand the establishment of a demilitarised zone in southern Ukraine. It should be noted that in this case, no Western country or the International Atomic Energy Agency (IAEA) protested against Ukraine, although the projectiles fired were unquestionably of Western origin.

- Dispersal of radioactive material in various forms: use of a conventional explosive to disperse radioactive material («dirty bomb»). In this case, materials that cannot be used for nuclear bombs, but are radioactive enough to cause death (e.g. residues of materials used in X-ray laboratories) could be used. Technically

---

95 . Philip C. Bleek, "Revisiting Aum Shinrikyo: New Insights into the Most Extensive Non-State Biological Weapons Program to Date," Center for Nonproliferation Studies, 11 December 2011, http://www.nti.org/analysis/articles/revisiting-aum-shinrikyo-new-insights-most-extensive-non-state-biological-weapons-program-date-1/.

feasible, the effects of such a bomb would be relatively random, but could create a panic effect. In Russia, two such attempts have been made by Chechen fighters. On 23 November 1995, Shamil Basayev, a Chechen guerrilla leader, announced on Russian television that four suitcases containing caesium had been hidden in Moscow[96].One of them containing 32 kilos of caesium 137, which was 310 times more radioactive than normal, was found buried in Izmailovsky Park[97].In 1998, another attempt was made in the Argun region of Chechnya with a caesium container attached to a mine[98].This is the explosive version of caesium-137 or cobalt-60 poisoning that was widely used by the Russian mafia in the mid-1990s.

- The explosion of a homemade or stolen nuclear bomb. In the chaos that reigned in Russia after the collapse of communism in the early 1990s, the fear that nuclear weapons or engineers could be used by terrorist or criminal groups for blackmail operations stimulated the imagination. Given that the average salary of a Russian nuclear scientist at that time was around $67 per month[99] , it would have been easy for clandestine organisations to acquire the services of unscrupulous scientists. This is what the Japanese *Aum ShinriKyō* sect tried to do - unsuccessfully. In fact, such a project has never been carried out by terrorist groups before.

- Blackmail by a country with nuclear weapons. However, this would be a form of state terrorism, probably not part of a revolutionary process, and is beyond the scope of this book.

2.4.2. Cyberterrorism

The concept of cyberterrorism is often unclear as to its substance and is not universally accepted. Without going into the technical details, it can be seen that in practice the notions of «cyberterrorism» and «cybercrime» are often confused. It is generally accepted that cyberterrorism is the use of computer networks to disrupt or damage critical infrastructure in order to paralyse a country or cause loss of life by, for example, disrupting air traffic control systems. What differentiates cybercrime from cyberterrorism is the strategic objectives. For example, Dorothy Denning, professor of computer science and director of the Georgetown Institute for Information Assurance, defines cyberterrorism as: «an attack or attempted attack that uses computers to intimidate or terrorise a government or society for religious or ideological political purposes.[100]

---

96 . Jeffrey Bale, "The Chechen Resistance and Radiological Terrorism", Center for Nonproliferation Studies, 1er April 2004.

97 . Rob Edwards, "Risk of radioactive 'dirty bomb' growing", New Scientist, 2 June 2004.

98 . Ibid.

99 . Russian American Nuclear Security Advisory Council (RANSAC), Washington DC, October 1999.

100. Dorothy Denning, Professor of Computer Science and Director of the Georgetown Institute for Information Assurance, "Is Cyber Terror Next?", www.ssrc.org/sept11/essays/denning.htm.

In theory, attacks on computer networks could cause considerable damage. Air traffic control, nuclear power plant management, electricity distribution management, currency trading and financial markets are just a few examples of the crucial role that IT plays in managing a country's security and vital economic activity. This dependence is simultaneously a vulnerability, as network failures are inevitable, no matter how sophisticated. In addition, these «conventional» attacks could be complemented by the takeover of nuclear missiles or missile defence systems, etc. There is no shortage of scenarios and they are a constant preoccupation of Western intelligence services.

In reality, however, there are several obstacles to these extreme forms of cyberterrorism. Firstly, there is a tendency to view networks in a rigid manner. However, they must be seen in a dynamic way. Indeed, the primary property of networks is their ability to adapt and their «elasticity» to frontal shocks. Thus, an attack against a computer network does not behave like the collapse of a line of dominoes, but the individual resistance capacities of the network elements add up and absorb the «shock» with great stability. In other words, the sum of the vulnerabilities of individual systems is greater than the vulnerability of a network as a whole.

Secondly, contrary to the image given by some disaster films, not everything is interconnected in a «linear» way. As we saw during the Y2K crisis in most countries, the sensitive computer systems of aviation security or banking and financial systems are generally managed independently of the major computer networks: the inventory of risks carried out on a global scale before 31 December 1999 showed that the interdependence of systems was much less than some experts had predicted, thus limiting the possibility of generating major disasters through actions in cyberspace. Today, interconnections are more important, especially for individual users, but at the level of critical or sensitive infrastructures, lessons have been learned.

Third, terrorist movements face the same dilemma as security agencies: everyone is using the same platform, so any network paralysis can quickly backfire. Today's terrorist groups - such as the Islamic State - exploit computer networks for strategic and operational communication, propaganda, donations and recruitment. Moreover, as we shall see, its concept of «open jihad» is closely dependent on computer networks: it would be the first to be affected by malfunctions.

The use of cyberspace by terrorists can take many different forms: Information and Propaganda, Leadership and Mobilisation, Funding and Logistics, and Direct Action. Proselytising, propaganda, e-mail exchanges, dissemination of «technical» information (bomb-making, etc.), mobilisation of activists are only peripheral activities to the actual terrorist action.

Cyberterrorism must be distinguished from the use of the Internet in support of terrorism. While the former substitutes destructive or paralysing computer action for physical violence, the latter uses computer networks to inform, communicate and influence. The concept of «*open jihad*», which we will see below, shows that the Internet is a privileged tool for sharing know-how and feedback, recruiting militants and publicising the movement's cause. In particular, the Internet provides tutorials on how to make improvised explosives, bombs or use small arms. However, these manuals are often «rehashes» of commercially available Marxist terrorist manuals from the 1960s-1970s.

It is important to analyse the purpose of the use of the Internet by insurrectionary or even terrorist movements. Indeed, it can be seen that cyberspace sometimes supports the action of terrorist groups by offering them an additional communication channel to publicise and justify their action, but does not necessarily constitute a weapon as such. From this perspective, and bearing in mind that terrorism is in itself a way of disseminating or giving credibility to a message, the use of the Internet for communication purposes could - in theory - reduce the need for violence to make one's cause known. This was identified by the *Zapatista Army of National Liberation* (EZLN) in Mexico:

> *The Net will allow armed actors to make themselves known without alienating the support of international opinion. This is something that some guerrillas have understood very well. The traditionally most violent groups have always had problems exporting their propaganda on the Net. [...] On the other hand, the less violent groups, such as the EZLN, have had great success on the Internet. They have won the sympathy of Internet users by managing to impose on the world the image of freedom fighters, not terrorists. It is possible that some groups may become aware of this phenomenon, integrate it into their communication strategy and soften their stance.*[101]

Thus, in a strategic approach to the fight against terrorism, it should be assessed whether the use of the Net can provide a substitute for terrorist action or whether it is an accelerator of it.

Moreover, excluding users whose speech might be radical is a double-edged sword: as one US FBI profiler notes, excluding them drives them underground and off the radar[102].Censorship by states and social networks - often at their request - is therefore not necessarily an effective solution in the long term.

---

101. Grégory Destouches, Menace sur Internet, éditions Michalon, Paris, 1999, p. 222.
102. Rich Schapiro, "Off the grid, heavily armed and radicalised: He's a law enforcement nightmare", NBC News, 17 January 2021.

The various forms of possible conflict in cyberspace, whose vocabulary is developing day by day (*cyberpiracy*, cyberstalking, *cybersquatting*, «electronic Pearl Harbor", etc.) often boil down to common cybercrime. Experience shows that it affects private companies more than states and that it often consists of blackmail for the disclosure of databases, credit card numbers or the paralysis of a digital activity, etc., and thus often takes the form of a «racket». It can also be manifested in a more superficial way by the modification of a site («*defacing*»).

Data theft and network disruption are definite risks for companies and the state. But the purpose of such actions is probably generally more criminal than «terrorist». A distinction must be made here between the threat in an industrial context and in a state context. The risks incurred by a company in a context of heightened competition, or in a political context because of its activity, are considerably higher than for a state.

Security advisors and «experts» are fond of complex scenarios, inspired by American cinema, but which do not seem to resonate with «real» terrorists. Real' cases of cyberterrorism are little observed. In essence, (Islamist) terrorism is not geared towards the destruction of society, but is essentially about communication. It must therefore be visible, be fuelled by essential fears and have predictable effects.

2.4.3. International terrorism

International terrorism is a form of terrorism resulting from the international collaboration of various terrorist movements to achieve a common goal. It was at its most successful during the Cold War in the service of a Marxist revolutionary ideal. Described by Claire Sterling[103] , the Marxist terrorist international was the expression of a central will, which aimed to exploit the use of violence for strategic purposes. In the Marxist dialectic, Western capitalism and imperialism were forms of 'state terrorism', as they oppressed the working class. Revolution was therefore part of an inescapable historical process, which legitimised aid to revolutionary movements.

From the early 1960s, active collaboration between terrorist and liberation movements developed under the aegis of the Soviet Union, with the help of allied countries such as Cuba, Libya, Czechoslovakia, Poland and the German Democratic Republic. This collaboration took the form of financial aid, logistical support, training, etc. It was an expression of a common commitment to the cause. It was the expression of a global strategy, bringing together a wide variety of actors in a vast process of destabilisation, even if their objectives were contrary to the principles of Marxism-Leninism. Thus, the communist bloc actively supported extremist environmentalist, far-left or even far-right movements.

---

103. Claire Sterling, The Network of Terror, J.-C. Lattès, Paris, 1981.

The aim was to support anything that could contribute to the destabilisation of Western countries. The aim was to maintain a permanent «correlation of forces», as the Soviet military doctrine called it, favourable to the Eastern bloc.

Interactions between terrorist movements often took the form of «conferences», the most famous of which was the *Tricontinental Conference* in Havana in 1966, which brought together 83 terrorist movements from around the world. The Cold War was in full swing and the anti-colonial revolutionary dynamic served the interests of the USSR, which was thus able to practice a form of «ideological encirclement» of the West. These collaborations continued into the 1990s, in transatlantic associations between Latin American movements with the Salvadoran *Popular Liberation Forces*, the Basque *Euskadi ta Askatasuna (ETA)* and other revolutionary organisations in Chile and Uruguay.

At the European level, conferences of a more regional scope, such as the one held in Porto on 9 September 1981 between members of *Direct Action*, the Italian *Prima Linea*, the Spanish *GRAPO* and the Portuguese *Popular Forces,* also took place. Given the very different objectives of the participants, the function of these conferences was more to establish mechanisms for logistical or technical co-operation than to elaborate common strategies of action.

The most successful example of strategic coordination between two terrorist groups was between *Direct Action* and the German *Rote Armee Fraktion* in the mid-1980s.

Collaboration between Direct Action (DA) and the Rote Armee Fraktion (RAF) (1985-1986)		
Type of lens	**Purpose and date of the attack**	
	AD	**RAF**
Arms industry	Assassination of General Audran (21 January 1985)	Assassination of Dr Zimmermann (1 February 1985)
International counter-terrorism bodies	Attack on Interpol (9 July 1986)	Attack on the Bundesgrenzschutz (11 August 1986)
Industry	Attempted assassination of Mr. Brana (15 April 1986)	Murder of Dr Beckurts (9 July 1986)
Industry	Assassination of Mr Besse (17 November 1986)	Assassination of Dr von Braunmühl (10 October 1986)
Economic cooperation with the Third World	Attack on the Organisation for Economic Cooperation and Development (21 July 1986)	Announcement of an attack on the Federal Ministry for Economic Cooperation (not carried out)

Table 2 - An example of international coordination between terrorist movements, the attacks by Direct Action (DA) and the Rote Armee Fraktion (RAF) in the mid-1980s.

However, international terrorism takes many forms:

- The exchange of 'services' such as training or logistical support between movements, but not necessarily associated with a convergence of political or operational objectives. This is the case of the cooperation between the *ETA* and the *Provisional IRA* for the supply of weapons and techniques for the use of explosives. This collaboration continued until the early 2000s. In August 2001, the arrest of three members of the *Irish Republican Army (IRA)* in Colombia revealed the existence of regular links[104] between the *Revolutionary Armed Forces of Colombia (FARC)* and the IRA, notably for training in the use of explosives[105].

- Sponsorship and coordination of terrorist actions by a third country, which seeks to achieve political objectives in a target country[106].Such sponsorship may involve terrorist movements, which may have divergent tendencies and objectives, but serve the interests of the sponsoring state. For example, during the Cold War, the Warsaw Treaty countries, in particular the USSR, the German Democratic Republic, Czechoslovakia and Bulgaria, supported a wide range of terrorist movements (including right-wing extremists) with the sole aim of destabilising NATO countries. More recently, Israel has supported *Jabhat al-Nosra* and the Islamic State in areas near the Golan Heights.

- The «multinationalisation» of terrorist action by a movement that has front organisations that carry out violent actions in other countries, in order to accompany the main action in the target country. This is the example of Armenian terrorism *(Armenian Secret Liberation Army)* in the early 1980s in France and Switzerland (target country: Turkey), and the *Kurdistan Workers' Party (PKK) in the* late 1990s (target country: Turkey).

- Cross-services, such as the request for the release of prisoners. This was the case with the attack on the Lufthansa plane in October 1977, carried out by a Palestinian Fatah commando, whose aim was to have ten members of the *Rote Armee Fraktion* (RAF) imprisoned in Germany released.

2.4.4. Transnational terrorism

Transnational terrorism is a mobile terrorism, which has its objectives in a given country or region, but uses channels outside this area, thus maintaining a border between its sanctuaries and its operational areas.

Terrorists benefit from the ignorance, complacency and even complicity of host countries and thus escape the justice of the target country. This was the case with the Basque *Euskadi ta Askatasuna (ETA)* and the *Provisional IRA*, which maintained rear bases in France and Ireland. In some cases, terrorist groups

---

104. An estimated 15 IRA members have visited Colombia since 1997, BBC News, 24 April 2002.
105. All three men were specialists in violent action: David Bracken (34), IRA liaison man in Cuba; Edward J. Campbell (55), explosives specialist; John J. Kelly (37), weapons and explosives specialist, The Observer, 19 August 2001.
106. This is known as «state-sponsored terrorism».

unknowingly use neighbouring countries as «resting zones» to escape the police after an operation, as was the case with the *Rote Armee Fraktion (RAF)* and the *Red Brigades,* which in the 1970s used Switzerland as a temporary fallback zone[107].

For the Marxist terrorist movements of the 1960s-1980s, which sought above all to promote a revolution in a particular country, the border offered a refuge.

For the jihadist movements, which have also developed this form of terrorism, the concept is significantly different: their objective is not to overthrow a state, but to fight against the countries that are waging wars against them in the Near and Middle East. It is therefore a question of striking at the strategic depths of their enemies, just as the Allies did in 1943-1945 by bombing German civilians. The objective here is to push the Western populations to demand the withdrawal of their respective countries from the international coalitions engaged in the Middle East.

Whereas Marxist terrorists used 'transnationality' to protect their networks, Islamists, on the contrary, use it as an extension of their war zone. The Muslim diasporas spread across the West constitute a real instrument of 'force projection'. Thanks to social networks and modern means of communication, transnational terrorism can 'project' its action selectively by activating individuals who are ready to act, but who are not necessarily violent at the base, to carry out murderous actions.

It is essential to understand that jihadist terrorism in Europe does not have global ambitions, but is an attempt to influence what is happening in the Middle East (Iraq or Syria). Believing that it is the manifestation of an «octopus» that seeks to spread its tentacles across the world only leads us to the wrong strategies. For example, the Americans understood that the emergence of an Islamic State in Syria could only harm the Syrian government, which is why they favoured its emergence[108].The problem came when France started to strike at the EI: the latter then retaliated in France, but its ambitions remained in Iraq-Syria.

Location of the end state sought by the terrorists		
	Marxist terrorism	**Jihadist terrorism**
Tactical objectives	In the target country	In the target country
Strategic objectives	In the target country	In the target country
Desired end state	In the target country	In the Middle East

Table 3 - Example of the location of the strategic objectives of terrorism according to its nature

The transnational nature of Islamist terrorism is a consequence of Western interventions in the Middle East. While the *Islamic State* (IS) has been responsible

---

107. Claire Sterling, The Network of Terror, J.-C. Lattès, Paris, 1981.
108. Brad Hoff, "West will facilitate rise of Islamic State 'in order to isolate the Syrian regime'", 2012 DIA document, Foreign Policy Journal, 21 May 2015; see also: http://www.judicialwatch.org/wp-content/uploads/2015/05/Pg.-291-Pgs.-287-293-JW-v-DOD-and-State-14-812-DOD-Release-2015-04-10-final-version11.pdf.

for numerous attacks in the West since a coalition was formed to fight it in Iraq and then in Syria, its predecessor, the *Islamic State in Iraq and the Levant* (ISIL or DAECH), was only an organisation of resistance to the American presence in Iraq and had not committed any terrorist attacks in the West before the appearance of the IS in 2014!

2.5. Jihad - A culture, more than a military doctrine

Our inability to deal with terrorism stems largely from our prejudices when it comes to understanding the notion of 'jihad': we tend to attribute to the Islamists *our* reading of terrorism and not the one they are trying to communicate to us. This has led to a form of conspiracy, which lends the Islamists a global project of conquest:

> *[...] The message of fundamentalist ideologues is that the betterment of our situation requires the destruction of others.*

> *[The Iranian revolution was the first great uprising against the Western model with the aim of destroying it.*[109]

It is too often forgotten that we went to war in their countries before they came to commit attacks in ours. In fact, Westerners are somewhat naive in admitting that we can go and fight wars in other countries without suffering the consequences. This can be explained by the fact that they take little interest in the foreign policies of their governments. The attacks are then superimposed on the feeling of «invasion» created by clientelist migration policies that are poorly controlled by these same governments. They are fuelled by readings - most often uninformed - of the Koran, which is seen as the driving force behind terrorist action. This is not true.

A strategic reading of Islamist thought and the observation of jihadist actions since the early 1990s allows us to identify four basic principles, which emanate from Muslim culture and explain the way in which 'military' jihad is conducted:
- its fundamentally defensive nature;
- its community dimension;
- the pre-eminence of intention over result ;
- the notion of victory, directed more at oneself than at one's opponent.

---

109. Professor Kurt R. Spillmann, interview in «Terrorisme islamiste: causes et conséquences», Bulletin SIT, 2/2002, Bern.

These four principles do not carry violence per se, but provide the key to the use of violence, which is only one of the many expressions of jihad. Although jihadist rhetoric and propaganda show great brutality, the destruction of the West is not an objective for either Islam or Islamists. Various studies of the psychology of Islamist terrorists show that they have a very rational reading of things and that their blindness is not such that they envisage «destroying» the West by terrorist means.

2.5.1 Islam and Islamism

With the Western defeat in Afghanistan and the Taliban's takeover of Kabul, our media is raising the threat of renewed international terrorism. Yet, although the Taliban are sometimes included in the literature on terrorism, they are not officially considered a terrorist movement. The problem is that they seek to establish an Islamic state. Yet in our media, 'Islamic' becomes 'Islamist', 'Islamist' becomes synonymous with 'jihadist', and 'jihadist' is considered 'terrorist'.

Islam» is differentiated from «Islamism» by referring to the latter as «political Islam», a vague and ill-defined notion that commentators avoid defining. In fact, the term «Islamism» appeared in the West in the 1970s and refers to a form of nationalism based on Islam, in the same way that Zionism refers to Judaism. It differs from the Arab nationalism of the 1950s and 1960s (which was secular and socialist-based) in that it uses Islam as a unifying element. It may be linked to anti-imperialism or anti-colonialism (e.g. the Muslim Brotherhood), to a resistance movement (e.g. Palestinian Hamas), or to movements that fight foreign intervention (e.g. 'Al Qaeda' or the Islamic State), but it is not a philosophy in itself.

In the West, religion in general, and Islam in particular, is often seen as a brake on development and democracy. But in other parts of the world, where the idea of 'nation' is more linked to ethnic, cultural or religious criteria than to the political borders of states, religion allows tribal rivalries and social divisions to be overcome. Thus, Islamism is not based on the idea of a 'nation' in the Western sense of the term, but rather on a community of belief (*Ummah*[110]).

Just as Zionism developed in the wake of the nationalisms of the early 20th century, Islamism developed with the collapse of the great empires, mainly after the First World War. At that time, Middle Eastern societies largely followed a tribal model, and there was not yet a unifying ideology for independence movements. Islam would play this role. This political exploitation of Islam, which would much later be called 'Islamism', became the vehicle for a militant doctrine of a religion that had become a marker of identity.

---

110. Ummah: community of believers.

78

In 1928, this was illustrated by the emergence of the *Muslim Brotherhood Association* in Egypt, which fought against both the Franco-British occupation of the former Ottoman Empire and the corruption of Arab elites by Westerners[111]. To achieve its objectives, the movement had to overcome factional and ethnic rivalries by uniting them under the banner of Islam; the result was an Islamic nationalism in which religion only had a unifying character. This is why today the movement is mainly present in the Middle East, but very little in the Maghreb and North Africa. During the Cold War, under the impetus of the Soviet Union, Marxism was the driving force behind many revolutionary or anti-colonialist movements, competing with pan-Arabism. In the early 1980s in Syria, the Muslim Brotherhood was ruthlessly hunted down by Hafez al-Assad and found refuge in Turkey. In 2012, they will provide the backbone of the *Free Syrian Army* (FSA), formed and supported by the US, Britain and France to overthrow the government of Bashar al-Assad.

From 1990, with the fall of communism, Islamic nationalism took over from anti-Western movements in the Middle East. In Palestine, the socialist resistance movements, supported by the USSR and its allies, took on a more nationalist colour... or disappeared. In the Gaza Strip, with the help of Israel, which sought to light a counter-fire against Yasser Arafat's *Palestine Liberation Organisation* (PLO), Hamas emerged as a «derivative» of the Muslim Brotherhood[112]. But instead of the expected fratricidal struggle, the Israeli initiative results in a radicalisation of the Palestinian struggle. Indeed, Israel's intransigence in its negotiations with the PLO pushed the Palestinians towards Hamas, which was more combative. The latter does not obtain more results through violence, but it gives the impression of holding its head high. This is the jihad, which the Israelis cannot understand: it is their weakness. The result is that the more they fight terrorism, the more it develops until it peaks in 2002-2004.

After the Oslo Accords in 1993, world opinion shifted in favour of the Palestinians and Israeli policy was criticised. To combat the growing influence of Hamas, Israel tries to exploit the wave of indignation that follows «9/11». Israel seeks to legitimise its doctrine by trying to equate Hamas with the global jihadist movement. Paradoxically, this discourse does not «take hold» across the Atlantic, but takes root in France, where a myth is developing that takes up the Israeli discourse on the Muslim Brotherhood, which is out of step with Western realities.

---

111. ''Muslim Brotherhood Marks 100-Year Sykes-Picot, Vowing Victory Despite Wounds, Sacrifices'', ikhwanweb.com, 18 May 2016 (accessed 13 November 2020).
112. Ishaan Tharoor, ''How Israel helped create Hamas'', The Washington Post, 30 July 2014; «Tzipi Livni's grave accusation: Netanyahu's government supports Hamas in order not to solve the Palestinian problem», Infos-Israel.news, 2 September 2018; «Hamas Israel's own creation», The Times of Israel, 3 December 2018.

In France, more than in other Western countries, the perception of the link between 'Islam' and 'Islamism' is of the same nature as the very official confusion between 'Zionism' and 'Judaism' (respectively, between 'anti-Zionism' and 'anti-semitism'). In both cases, a political movement is confused with a confession (or a religious community). Moreover, there is a parallel in the interpretation of the terms «antisemitism» and «Islamophobia».

The problem is that in France, immigration has been so poorly managed and has taken such a large place in society that it has created a fear of cultural and ethnic submersion that affects its perception of Islam. The result has been a persistent tendency to establish a linear relationship between Islam and Islamism, and to define the latter as an extension of the former. Carried by politicians like Manuel Valls :

> [To say that it has nothing to do with Islam is to take away the responsibility of Islam[113] .

... or certain journalists, such as Mohammed Sifaoui:

> The veil [NDA: hijab] is not Islamic, [...] the veil is Islamist.[114]

The 'Arab - delinquency' relationship that predominated in the 1980s and 1990s shifted to the 'Islam - Islamism - Jihadism/terrorism' relationship at the turn of the 21st century[e].The focus shifted from 'fear of Arabs' to 'fear of Islam' (literally: Islamophobia). Even if the term 'Islamophobia' is sometimes used improperly, it reflects - rightly or wrongly - a growing anxiety among the population about the Islamisation of society and immigration. This leads to a confusion between communitarian issues (a societal phenomenon, linked to internal politics) and jihadist or terrorist issues (linked to external politics).

Another frequent confusion is between «Islamism» and «fundamentalism». Fundamentalism is an essentially religious and spiritual approach, which advocates a return to the «foundations» of religion in order to recover its original «purity». The term comes from the Christian vocabulary and can be found in the three great «religions of the Book» (Judaism, Christianity and Islam)[115].In Islam, its most controversial form is Salafism, which some equate with Wahhabism. While official French media tend to promote the idea that Salafism is inherently

---

113. Manuel Valls, Grand Jury programme, RTL, LCI and Le Figaro, 26 November 2017.
114. Mohammed Sifaoui in the programme On a tellement de choses à se dire, «'Le voile n'est pas islamique' mais 'islamiste' selon Mohamed Sifaoui», RTL/YouTube, 25 September 2019 (06'30").
115. See Jean-François Mayer, Les Fondamentalismes, Georg, 2001.

violent[116] , this is not the view of the US intelligence community, which defines it as «*a largely non-violent stream within* Islam»[117].

Discussions of Islamism invariably involve a quotation or verse from the Qur'an to demonstrate the warlike nature of the Muslim religion. In reality, very few have read the Koran, which allows Islamists and Islamophobes alike to use its quotations in a totally fanciful way. They even go as far as unfounded exaggerations that encourage this fear, such as Éric Zemmour on iTV:

> *You open the Koran on any page and it says: « You must kill the Jews, you must kill the Christians. God curses them, you have to kill the infidels».*[118]

This is simply not true. Not only does the Qur'an have only a marginal connection with Islamism, it is not a book of war. Instead, it was written in a social, economic, political and military environment in which nascent Islam had to struggle to flourish, especially against the dominant religions of the time; this is reflected in the text, just as our Old Testament[119].Logically enough, it speaks of the lessons learned from the struggles that the early Muslims had to face in order to exist. This is the case with the notion of jihad, which is not a military term in essence, but which expresses a cultural and societal 'mechanics', which is *also* found at the military level.

You have to listen to Lesley Hazleton, who is neither Arab nor Muslim, but an Anglo-American Jew, to understand the true meaning of the verse that «commands» Muslims to «kill Jews and Christians»:

> *Take the infamous verse about slaughtering the infidels. Yes, it does say that, but in a very specific context: the planning of the conquest of the holy city of Mecca, where fighting was normally forbidden. And permission is given with a whole bunch of restrictions. Not « You must kill the infidels in Mecca», but « You may, you have the right to, ...but only after the end of a period of grace, ...and only if there is no other pact going on, ...and only if they try to prevent you from reaching the Ka'bah, ...and only if they attack you first... And even then, God is merciful, forgiveness is supreme, and therefore, first of all, better not to do it!*[120]

---

116. Mohammed Sifaoui in the programme C à vous, « Comment détecter la radicalisation ? - C à vous - 10/10/2019', France 5/YouTube, 10 October 2019 (05'45").
117. «Trends in Global Terrorism: Implications for the United States, Office of the Director of National Intelligence (ODNI), National Intelligence Estimate (NIE) NIE 2006-02R, April 2006 (SECRET-NOFORN), p. 11 (declassified September 2011).
118. «Mehdi Nemmouche : les ratés du renseignement ?», CNews/YouTube, 11 June 2014.
119. Samuel Osborne, 'Violence more common' in Bible than Quran, text analysis reveals', The Independent.uk, 10 February 2016; Christine Talos, 'The Bible is far more violent than the Quran', Tribune de Genève, 11 February 2016.
120. Lesley Hazleton, «About Reading the Qur'an,» www.youtube.com/watch?v=Si4Ep6DjDUo.

The confusion between Islam and Islamism has led to endless debates about whether Islam is a religion of war or peace. People compare the frequency of appearance of the words 'war' or 'love' between the Koran and the Bible and try to distinguish 'good Islam' from 'bad Islam'. This simplistic discourse inspires extreme right-wing theorists, who try to explain jihadist thought by associating concepts of different natures, as does the freelancer Antoine Hasday[121] , who clearly has not understood anything about the issue. With little intellectual honesty, they assimilate the different types of terrorism into a single phenomenon, mixing the discourses and terminology of various schools of thought. The result is pseudo-theories that obscure our understanding of the terrorist phenomenon, become an obstacle to solving the problem and ultimately encourage violence.

These interpretations are popular in France, but are specious, as religion does not play a central role in jihadist terrorism. In fact, most terrorists have only a limited knowledge of Islam[122] , which is confirmed by the findings of the British *Security Service* (MI5) in 2008 already[123].

In France, since the end of the 1970s, North African immigration and rising unemployment have led to the development of 'banlieues' and petty crime, which have provoked a form of 'Arabophobia'. In the early 2000s, with the emergence of jihadist terrorism, the fear of a brutal and conquering Islam (Islamophobia) gradually replaced this 'ordinary racism'. The result has been a tightening of Muslims around what unites them: Islam. It is wrong to see this as a political objective: it is much more a question of cementing a community that is generally divided along ethnic lines and that feels - rightly or wrongly - the victim of stigmatisation.

For the Islamists, Islam allows them to back up a mode of action with a higher interest. Islam thus becomes the equivalent of what Westerners call 'raison d'État': a frame of reference that allows 'the end to justify the means'. By analogy with Carl von Clausewitz's three components of strategy (objectives, manner and resources), religion is only a resource, but not an objective. The direct link between Islam and Islamism, which some make by claiming that terrorism has its roots in Islam itself, is simply not true.

---

121. Antoine Hasday, «La pensée djihadiste décryptée», slate.fr, 6 November 2017.
122. Aya Batrawy, Paisley Dodds & Lori Hinnant, "Islamic State gets know-nothing recruits and rejoices", Associated Press, 15 August 2016; Martin Planques, "3000 documents reveal poor religious knowledge of Daech recruits", lefigaro.fr, 18 August 2016.
123. Behavioural Science Unit Operational Briefing Note: Understanding radicalisation and violent extremism in the UK, Security Service - MI5 (UK RESTRICTED), Report BSU 02/2008, 12 June 2008; Sarah Knapton and Duncan Gardham, "MI5: Terrorists not frustrated religious loners", The Telegraph, 21 August 2008.

2.5.2. The nature of jihad

Translated in the West by the expression «holy war» (which - ironically - comes from the Christian vocabulary of the crusades!) the concept of jihad is often simplistically associated with the idea of a conquering Islam, fuelled by imagery that comes directly from the Middle Ages.

In Arabic, the word 'jihad' comes etymologically from the notion of striving (*djahada*), effort (*djouhd*) or resistance, and expresses a refusal to give up and surrender to temptation. To express 'war', in its physical and military sense, Arabic uses the words *'harb'* (war) or *'qital'* (fight). Although it is interpreted in many different ways in Islam, it finds its essence and strength in a defensive posture, where the notion of resistance and the will not to bow down to an external force - even a superior one - predominates. Beyond the fact of war, jihad is therefore the refusal to give up a fight and to give in to defeatism.

At the individual level, jihad expresses first of all an inner discipline, through which the Muslim assumes the responsibility of keeping to the path of God. Secondly, it refers to the will to defend Islam, individually or collectively, against external aggression, whether moral or physical. Jihad is thus essentially an attitude of mind, which seeks to preserve a set of values in accordance with the faith and which implies a certain number of sacrifices to achieve this. The one who performs jihad is the *mujahid* ('the one who strives' or 'the one who resists')[124] .

For Muslims, 'jihad in the way of God' *(jihad fi Sabil Allah* or *jihad fi sabili-llah)* has two dimensions:

- *Jihad al-Akbar* («great jihad»), which is an individual, peaceful and permanent process, practiced by each Muslim in order to maintain a line of conduct in harmony with his or her faith and aims to elevate his or her spirit in spite of the temptations of the material world, through a search for God;

- *Jihad al-Asghar* ('little jihad')[125] - the 'easiest' according to Mohammed - which is part of a collective approach and aims to protect Islam against external aggression.

The concrete forms of these two dimensions of jihad have been the subject of many interpretations by Islamic exegetes. The four most frequently mentioned are[126] :

---

124. Algerian fighters who confronted the French army during the Algerian War (1954-1963) were also referred to as «moudjahid» or «moudjahidoun» (Schmidt Jean-Jacques, Vers une approche du monde arabe, éditions du Dauphin, Paris, 2000), despite the obviously secular character of their revolt. In fact, in Algeria, this more appropriate terminology appeared as early as the mid-1990s, in order to give a more Islamic colour to the regime and to «take the wind out of the sails» of the jihadists.
125. Literally 'major jihad' and 'minor jihad'.
126. Jon MC, "Jihad - The Four Forms and the West", Counterjihadreport.com, 3 November 2013.

- *bil-Nafs jihad ('jihad with the soul'), which is* an individual and inner struggle against evil. It also forms the backbone of the higher form of jihad *(jihad al-akbar)*;

- *Jihad bil-Lisan ('jihad with the tongue')*, which is the defence and dissemination of Islam through the word *(da'awah)*, sermons and writing. It also includes fighting lies, vanity and hypocrisy;

- *Jihad bil-Yad ('Jihad with hands')*, which is the defence of Islam through one's actions, by practising charity, caring for the disinherited, widows and orphans, among others by paying the Islamic tax *(zakat)*[127] , as well as by performing the pilgrimage to Mecca *(Hajj)*;

- *Jihad bis-Sayf ('jihad with the sword'),* which is the defence of the Islamic community when it is attacked by an external enemy. Fighting in defence of the faith is also called 'fighting in the way of God' *(qital fi sibil Allah)*. It is the main component of minor jihad *(jihad al-asghar)*.

When it leads to war *(harb)*, jihad has above all a defensive connotation. But, as in any conception of war, the notion of 'defence' is not limited to passively awaiting the action of the adversary, but can also have an offensive form (in modern operational terms, one would speak of 'pre-emptive' war). It then constitutes a collective obligation *(fard kifaya)* for the *Ummah, for* which the warlord is responsible. In theory, believers can therefore evade it individually, but various interpretations of this obligation exist. Thus, for some - such as the Islamic State - when Muslim populations are threatened, there is an individual obligation *(fard ay'n)* to take up arms.

Unlike the Catholic religion, which has a guardian of dogma in the person of the Pope, Islam is subject to diverse interpretations and is not a monolith. Thus, there are very offensive interpretations of jihad, but they are more the expression of fiery rhetoric than a doctrinal reality. For the concept of jihad does not *a priori* express the intention *to impose* Islam, but simply to defend it against aggression:

> *If thy Lord had willed, all the inhabitants of the earth would have believed. Is it for thee to compel men to believe?*[128]

Indeed, in the Christian areas they occupied (notably in the Ottoman Empire), Muslims generally did not attempt to convert other *'peoples of the*

---

127. At the time of the emergence of Islam, there were no social security systems, the desert populations, often nomadic and in a territory without borders (caliphate), did not benefit from the protection and assistance of a suzerain - as was the case in Europe at the same time - so social welfare often depended on individual actions. Marriage to several wives was thus permitted, so that the widows and children of those who fought for Islam would not sink into poverty.
128. Q'uran, Sura 10, verse 99.

84

book'[129] , but granted them 'protected' (*dhimmi*) status. They were not subject to the Muslim tax (*zakat*[130]), but had to pay a special tax *(jizyah)* and other taxes like other citizens. In its 'caliphate', the Islamic State had established the same rules... but with a very low tolerance threshold for offenders[131] !

It is important to understand here that Islam is a real 'system', affecting all aspects of society: daily life, the family, gender relations, the exercise of political power and, of course, the relationship with God. While Westerners have relegated religion to the realm of spirituality, Islam is a real socio-cultural glue that gives coherence to the whole society. For example, in many Muslim countries, welfare and social security mechanisms are (or were) run by religious and non-governmental bodies. Thus, our tendency to want to change their society sounds like an attack on their religion. Even with the best of intentions, we create the conditions for a 'military jihad' when we try to impose change.

2.5.2.1. Jihad and jihadism

The concept of 'jihadism' is Western in origin, and its definition varies from author to author. Globally, it is associated with religious radicalism and refers to the use of violence in the service of jihad. For the purposes of this book, we will consider 'jihadism' as the combatant form of Islamism. In other words, it is the use of violence in the service of a form of religious nationalism, and not the other way around, as is commonly suggested.

Unable to deal with terrorism preventively as part of a political process, or having no intention of doing so (as in Israel), Western governments (as well as intelligence services, 'experts' and other so-called security specialists) have made jihadism an irrational phenomenon. Thus the notion of 'global jihad' was born, which aims to falsely establish the idea of a conquering Islam with global ambitions.

In January 2018, in a documentary, made by *Conspiracy Watch*, entitled *Complotisme, les alibis de la terreur*[132] and broadcast on *France 3*, the philosopher Jacob Rogozinski states:

> *Jihadism is also a movement that aims at sovereignty, at world power. There is a dream behind it, a crazy dream no doubt, but a dream of creating a caliphate, which would be a global caliphate, which will take over Rome,*

---

129. For Muslims, Jews, Christians and Muslims belong to the same «family» of «peoples of the book» (the Bible), who share the same religious roots.
130. See the chapter on 'The financing of jihad'.
131. See «The Status of Christian Belligerents», Rumiyah, n° 9, p. 4.
132. Rudy Reichstadt & Georges Benayoun, Complotisme, les alibis de la terreur, YouTube, 24 January 2018, www.youtube.com/watch?v=d8e18NIqWiI.

which will take over Europe, which will defeat America, which will establish a global network of true believers, united behind an absolute sovereign power.[133]

This reading is in line with that of Bat Ye'or (Gisèle Littman) who states:

Jihad aims to abolish all non-Islamic law and government in order to establish sharia, the government of Allah over all of humanity.[134]

... a totally fanciful idea, developed in the wake of his book *Eurabia*[135], which describes a Muslim plot to dominate the Western world. In fact, it is more a kind of revenge for the expulsion of his family from Egypt in 1956 as a result of the 'Lavon Affair'[136].It has inspired other books, such as *Conquest of the West* by Swiss journalist Sylvain Besson[137], referenced by Norwegian right-wing extremist Anders Behring Breivik[138] (perpetrator of the Utoya massacre on 22 July 2011), and their scenario is taken up by all major far-right movements in Europe[139].

In fact, an examination of the 'after action' claims and analyses of the jihadists themselves shows us a much more rational discourse in terms of their ambitions. For example, the study of the terrorist attacks during the «*Intifada of the Knives*» in Israel tends to show that Palestinian jihadists are essentially driven by nationalist sentiment and secondarily by religion[140].Thus, if the religious dimension is present, it is not at the centre of the action: it is only a doctrinal tool to define behaviour or principles of action.

Armed jihad takes two main forms:

---

133. Jacob Rogozinski in Complotism, the alibis of terror, YouTube, 24 January 2018, www.youtube.com/watch?v=d8e18NIqWi, (31'20").

134. «Interview with Bat Ye'or on jihad', Dreuz Info, 15 November 2020.

135. Bat Ye'or, Eurabia, published by Jean-Cyrille Godefroy, Paris, 2006.

136. This is the Susannah operation conceived and executed by the Israeli military intelligence service (Agaf Modiin or AMAN) in 1954. It aimed to carry out terrorist attacks against British, American and Egyptian targets in order to blame the Muslim Brotherhood and provoke an Anglo-American intervention. The operation ended in a fiasco, leading to the resignation of Pinhas Lavon, Israeli Minister of Defence. This was followed by the expulsion of Jews from Egypt and several Arab countries who feared that Israel would carry out similar actions there. See Wikipedia, article «Lavon affair».

137. Sylvain Besson, La Conquête de L'Occident. Le Projet secret des islamistes, éditions du Seuil, Paris, 7 October 2005.

138. Mattias Gardell, "Crusader Dreams: Oslo 22/7, Islamophobia, and the Quest for a Monocultural Europe", Terrorism and Political Violence, 26:129-155, 2014.

139. Raphaël Liogier, «Le mythe de l'invasion arabo-musulmane», Le Monde diplomatique, May 2014, pp. 8-9.

140. "Initial findings of the studies of the profile of Palestinian terrorists who carried out attacks in Israel, [...] during the current wave of terrorism" (Updated to October 25, 2015), Meir Amit Intelligence and Terrorism Information Center, 2 November 2015.

- *Military resistance* to an occupation, as in Iraq, Afghanistan, Palestine or South Lebanon. Most often, it limits its scope of action to a given country or region, where the occupying power is directly confronted. In Iraq, for example, the resistance was initially organised around the regime's loyalists (*Feddayin Saddam*) and tribal organisations. However, in some cases, especially when the foreign force conducts long-distance strikes, jihadists can extend their war zone to the home country of the foreign forces.

- *Political-military resistance* within a country, against the government or local authorities whose policies are perceived as corrupt or in the pay of Western countries (as in Algeria, Egypt or Tunisia). This form of jihad has similar characteristics to the revolutionary movements of the 1960s-1980s, relying on the protection of traditional cultures and structures. It tends to remain confined to its region or country of origin and not to leave it, but it has to spend a lot of energy to mobilise supporters.

Terrorism that results from an expansion of the war zone of resistance movements in the Middle East and strikes the West is therefore not religiously motivated. However, it may seek to gain support within Muslim communities in the West; not for religious purposes, but because religion is the medium for a form of nationalism.

2.5.2.2 'Al Qaeda' and the global jihad

Global jihad» is an ill-defined concept, which the West tends to understand as a globalised «holy war» to impose Islam. Historically, the West initially associated it with 'Al Qaeda', an ill-defined entity (which is why it is called a 'nebula') whose spirit was evident from the end of the first Gulf War.

From 1991, the stationing of American forces in Saudi Arabia worried the authorities, as it fuelled an ultra-nationalist radical opposition that threatened the kingdom's existence. This opposition, which had already tried to overthrow the government by seizing the Great Mosque of Mecca in 1979, considered, rightly or wrongly, the Saudi territory as sacred and saw the Western presence as a provocation. But the United States turned a deaf ear to repeated requests to withdraw its troops from the Dhahran base[141].A series of attacks then hit the American presence in the Arabian Peninsula.

Osama bin Laden (OBL) is the most publicised figure in this ultra-nationalist movement. Considered responsible for these attacks, he took refuge in Sudan. But after the June 1996 attack on the Khobar Towers in Saudi Arabia, he was expelled from Sudan under pressure from the United States. He then took refuge in Afghanistan, in the Kandahar region, where he organised training camps for Jammu and Kashmir fighters.

---

141. Gresh Alain, «Les grands écarts de l'Arabie saoudite», Le Monde diplomatique, June 2003.

However, it did not give up its fight against the US presence in Saudi Arabia, which it considered illegitimate. Thus, in August 1996, OBL issued a *'Declaration of War'* against the United States:

> *It is no longer current and acceptable to claim that the presence of the crusaders is a necessity and only a temporary measure to protect [Saudi Arabia], especially if Iraq's civilian and military infrastructure has been savagely destroyed [...].*[142]

It was this declaration that led him to be considered responsible for the attacks of 11 September 2001. However, this 'declaration of war' and the '9/11' attacks had different causes and nothing in common: the first was aimed at pushing the Americans to leave Saudi soil, while the second was a 'simple' act of revenge, as we shall see.

At the beginning of 1998, he created a movement called the *World Islamic Front for the Fight against Jews and Crusaders* (*Al-Jabhah al-Islamiya al-'Alamiyah li-Qital al-Yahud wal-Salibiyyin*), which brought together several jihadist groups. In a declaration ('fatwa') of 23 February 1998, which forms the doctrinal basis of what later became known as 'al-Qaeda', he set out three demands:

- the withdrawal of the American presence from the territory of Saudi Arabia (because non-believers cannot occupy all or part of the sacred land of Arabia);

- the lifting of the embargo against Iraq, which was seen as a manifestation of Western arrogance against a Muslim country (although Saddam Hussein was then generally considered by fundamentalists as a 'traitor' because of his secular regime);

- the cessation of support for the State of Israel, as it is seen as a tool to divide the Arab nation. This demand is not a coincidence and refers to the «Yinon plan», elaborated by an American *think tank* for Benjamin Netanyahu, published in 1996 under the title *A Clean Break*[143] , which calls for the fragmentation of the Middle East.

Thus, contrary to the fanciful claims that followed '9/11', and that have persisted since, there was no global Islamic ambition, no caliphate, no holy war against Christianity around the world, and no holy war against the Western world, but only resistance against a US presence in the Middle East that was perceived as invasive, arrogant and destabilising. OBL's message was simple, clear and consistent, but the West refused to understand it.

---

142. Osama bin Laden, «Declaration of War Against the Americans Occupying the Land of the Two Holy Places», 23 August 1996 (published in Al-Quds al-Arabi).
143. A Clean Break: A New Strategy for Securing the Realm', The Institute for Advanced Strategic and Political Studies, July 1996, http://www.informationclearinghouse.info/article1438.htm.

9/11» was nothing more than a retaliation operation, carried out by a score of young Islamists. Bill Clinton's unfounded decision to bomb Afghanistan and Sudan on 20 August 1998 was the sole cause of '9/11'. The incident is conveniently forgotten by the history books, but on 6 August 2001, a CIA memo to President Bush[144] entitled «*Bin Laden Determined to Strike in the United States*" indicated that an attack was being prepared in response to the bombings[145].Since 2001, it has been known that '9/11' was the result of an unfortunate decision by Bill Clinton to distract the American public from the sex scandal in which he had embroiled himself, and for which he had to appear before a grand jury on 17 August 1998.

The name 'Al Qaeda' (which OBL himself has never claimed) to describe this nascent jihadist movement was created by the American authorities[146]. There is no plot or Machiavellian calculation here, but a simple legal artifice. In January 2001, when the United States was preparing to try the perpetrators of the February 1993 attack on the *World Trade Center* (WTC), it had no anti-terrorism legislation. The only legal instrument available was the RICO Act ([147]), which allowed for the indictment of those who sponsored criminal acts abroad, but only if their organisation had a name[148].However, the protagonists of the February 1993 attack had not acted within the framework of a known organisation[149] , but they were said to have links - which were never subsequently proven - with OBL. American lawyers therefore simply assumed that OBL was running an organisation[150] , which they arbitrarily named after its former Afghan base (*al qa'ida al'askariyya*): 'Al Qaeda'[151].

In 1996, the CIA created a special unit to track down OBL, the «*Bin Laden Issue Station*» (note that it was not named „*Al-Qaeda Issue Station*»!) which was dismantled at the end of 2005[152].Its leader, Michael Scheuer, confirms that «Al-Qaeda» never existed, but that it is a simple and easily understandable way to designate Islamic terrorists[153].Some 'conspiracy theorists' have interpreted this

---

144. This is a daily briefing note called the Presidential Daily Brief (PDB).
145. Translation: "Bin Laden determined to strike in US", CNN.com, 10 April 2004.
146. Jason Burke, Al-Qaeda - The True Story of Radical Islam, Cahiers libres, March 2005, p. 324.
147. Racketeer Influenced and Corrupt Organizations Act (RICO Act), 15 October 1970.
148. The RICO Act will be complemented by the PATRIOT Act, adopted just after the 9/11 attacks.
149. Indeed, Islamists see this attack as a precursor to 'individual terrorism'. See Abu Mu'sab al-Suri, "The Jihadi Experience: The Schools of Jihad", Inspire, n° 1, (1431), Summer 2010.
150. Jason Curtis, The Power of Nightmares (part 3), BBC/YouTube, 2004.
151. The Power of Nightmare, (series of three films), BBC, Autumn 2004.
152. Mark Mazzetti, "C.I.A. Closes Unit Focused on Capture of bin Laden", The New York Times, 4 July 2006.
153. CIA Agent Exposes How Al-Qaeda Doesn't Exist, YouTube, 16 November 2011, https://www.youtube.com/watch?v=-8CqUJoEWBs.

statement as proof that 'Al Qaeda' was a CIA creation for some obscure plot. This is obviously not true.

The name «Al-Qaeda» has been used so much in the West that it has become the symbol of jihadism and a real «label", which has been claimed little by little by certain terrorist groups, more for reasons of *branding* than structural membership. Thus, from 2005 onwards, the expression «*Qaidat al-Jihad*» (*Base of Jihad*) became widely used in various countries to designate a core of armed resistance. Names such as «*Al Qaeda in the Islamic Maghreb*» (AQIM) or «*Al Qaeda in the Arabian Peninsula*» (AQAP) are inaccurate translations, used by Western countries to accredit the existence of a multinational terror organisation with its «subsidiaries». Their respective real names are «*Qaidat al-Jihad fi'l-Maghrib al-Islamiy*» (*Base of Jihad in the Islamic Maghreb*) and «*Qaidat al-Jihad fi'l-Jazirah al-Arrabiyyah*» (*Base of Jihad in the Arabian Peninsula), and do* not imply any functional relationship with a hypothetical central structure[154] , as the documents captured in Abbottabad in 2011 will demonstrate[155] .

Military interventions are the main driving force behind the internationalisation of terrorism, carried out since the end of the Cold War to support or provoke regime change and the spread of Western values. Their concentration in Muslim space reinforces the perception of a continuation of the medieval crusades and explains the recurrent use of the terms 'crusader' or 'Roman' to describe Westerners. Although Europeans do not emphasise the religious dimension of these interventions, this is not the case for Americans, as we shall see. Moreover, the correlation between these interventions and support for Israel is fuelled by a Christian Zionism that is more present in the United States[156] than in Europe, where it tends to be denied by labelling it as conspiratorial.

The problem is that the West did not want to understand the nature of the terrorism that was hitting them. The war in Afghanistan, then in Iraq, will only be a passage from «Charybdis to Scylla»:

> *[Ironically, an invasion and occupation of Iraq in the name of fighting terrorism will likely cause an increase in anti-American attacks from fundamentalist Islamic sources. The Bush administration has simply replaced a military presence in one nation that is home to the Holy Places of Islam*

---

154. Kangil Lee, "Does Al Qaeda Central Still Matter?", UNISCI Journal, n° 37, International Center for Political Violence and Terrorism Research, January2015.

155. Nelly Lahoud et al, Letters from Abbottabad: Bin Ladin Sidelined? The Combating Terrorism Center, West Point, www.ctc.usma.edu, 3 May 2012.

156. Mark T. Finney, "Christian Zionism, the US and the Middle East: A Sketch and Brief Analysis", quoted in Sandford, M., (ed.) The Bible, Zionism and Palestine: The Bible's Role in Conflict and Liberation in Israel-Palestine, Bible in Effect, 1 Relegere Academic Press, Dunedin, New Zealand, 2016, pp. 20-31, ISBN 978-0-473-33279-2.

with an armed occupation in another. Iraq also has holy places, and is the cradle and academic and spiritual centre of Shiite Islam. The administration should remember that the «infidel» Soviet occupation of the Islamic nation of Afghanistan during the 1980s drew fanatical fighters from around the world into the opposition. [...] The Islamic world perceives the US war on terror as a war on faith.[157]

What we call *global jihad* - with which the terms 'jihadism' and 'jihadist' are associated- is simply the extension of the battlefield into the rear of Western countries that intervene militarily in a country. We will come back to this in more detail.

2.5.2.3. The Muslim perception of the war jihad

In order to understand the Muslim - and not only the «Islamist» - reading of the «warlike» jihad, it is necessary to recall that the West has initiated wars without reason, with lies and manipulations, only to satisfy political objectives and overthrow governments.- of the «warlike» jihad, it is necessary to recall that the West initiated wars without reason, with lies and manipulations, for the sole purpose of satisfying political objectives and overthrowing governments, causing the loss of some 4 million people[158].We have forgotten this, but not the Muslims. Moreover, these repeated aggressions, which systematically affect Middle Eastern or North African populations, are accompanied by increasingly aggressive rhetoric towards Islam, and give the image of a crusade.

Thus, when France went into Iraq in September 2014, it had never been threatened by the Islamic State before. Its reasons then were probably more political than religious. But this is not the case with its American ally, which went to war in Afghanistan and Iraq with a very clumsy but clearly expressed religious motivation. It goes beyond the word 'crusade' uttered by George W. Bush, in which the *Wall Street* Journal had perceived the risk of a religious war developing[159].In June 2003, in Sharm el-Sheikh, George W. Bush declared to a Palestinian delegation:

---

157. Eland Ivan, "Is Withdrawal of US Forces from Saudi Arabia Enough?", The Independent Institute, 30 April 2003, www.independent.org.

158. Nafeez Ahmed, "Unworthy victims: Western wars have killed four million Muslims since 1990", Middle East Eye, 18 April 2016.

159. Peter Waldman & Hugh Pope, "'Crusade' Reference Reinforces Fears War on Terrorism Is against Muslims", The Wall Street Journal, 21 September 2001. See also: 9/11 George Bush - This Crusade Is Gonna Take A While, YouTube, 17 September 2001.

I am guided by a mission from God. God told me George, go and fight those terrorists in Afghanistan. And I did. Then God told me George, go and end that tyranny in Iraq. And I did.

In 2009, it was learned that Donald Rumsfeld, Secretary of Defense, regularly peppered his messages to the troops in Iraq with biblical quotations; a practice that had been instigated by Major General Glen D. Shaffer, then Director of Military Intelligence (J2). Shaffer, then *Director of Military Intelligence (J2)*[160].

The phenomenon is not only American. John Burton, who worked with Tony Blair for 24 years, revealed:

Tony's Christian faith is part of him, right down to his cotton socks. At the time, he was firmly convinced that intervention in Kosovo, Sierra Leone and also Iraq was part of a Christian struggle. Good must overcome evil and make life better.[161]

Erik Prince, founder and director of the private security company Blackwater, which was responsible for the US military's dirty work in Iraq, and who was indicted - but never convicted - for the murders caused by his employees, declared himself a «*Christian crusader charged with wiping Muslims and the Muslim faith off the face of the* earth»[162].

In the US forces, reference to a '*crusade*' is common[163].The *Special Operations Command* recruited personnel under the slogan '*On a mission for God and country*'[164].In addition, a high proportion of officers are members of Christian fellowship organisations, such as the *Officer's Christian Fellowship* (OCF), whose leader, Lieutenant General Bruce Fister, defines US military personnel as '*ambassadors for Christ in* uniform'[165].At the highest levels of command, this idea is carried by officers such as Lieutenant General William G. Boykin, Deputy Undersecretary of Defense under George W. Bush, who believed that the President was chosen by God and should say about terrorism:

---

160. Alex Spillius, 'Donald Rumsfeld covered Iraq briefing papers with Biblical texts', The Telegraph, 17 May 2009.

161. Jonathan Wynne-Jones, "Tony Blair believed God wanted him to go to war to fight evil, claims his mentor", The Telegraph, 23 May 2009.

162. «Erik Prince and the last crusade", The Economist, 6 August 2009.

163. "Erasmus, 'One army under God?", The Economist, 9 September 2014.

164. Although after some time, the Department of Defense removed the posters (Kellan Howell, The Washington Times, 17 January 2015).

165. Alan Cooperman, "Marching as to War", The Washington Post, 16 July 2006.

Some seemingly insignificant details have not escaped the notice of Islamists.
For example, *Trijicon*, which supplies sights for assault rifles, has engraved references to the Gospels on its ACOG sights, so much so that in Afghanistan the
rifles so equipped have been dubbed «*Jesus rifles*»![167]

In France, the idea of a «crusade» or «Islamophobic war» provokes vehement
reactions from intellectuals like Alain Finkielkraut:

> *If the term Islamophobia is used, it is to terrorise and to prohibit any
> criticism of Islam. We are not waging an Islamophobic war against DAECH!
> This is absurd!*[168]

While the term «*Islamophobia*» is often misused and he is right in saying
that we are not waging an «*Islamophobic war against DAECH*», his comment is
irrelevant because we have created the legend of a conquering Islam, of which
DAECH is the armed wing. Our interventions in the Middle East are not guided
by Islamophobia (which we will define below), but they are nevertheless permeated
by it. By burying the issue under the label of «conspiracy», we evacuate it without
making the effort to modify a perception that is far from irrational. Moreover, the
feeling of Islamophobia is provoked by a whole series of behaviours and political
interpretations, such as equating Islam in a 'linear' way with immigration, with
delinquency, with terrorism, with unemployment and with humanitarian refugees.
We will come back to this.

We also tend to ignore the fact that the way we fight helps to encourage
jihadism. For example, Western interventions are mostly conducted «from a
distance», by drones or through proxy armed groups. This is obviously to spare
the lives of our soldiers - and that's fine - but it removes the stakes - and the
credibility - from our engagements. If we were risking our lives in these wars,
we would probably be more careful about how they were fought, and public
opinion would probably be more attentive to government decisions. But with
strikes beyond the reach of enemy weapons, we are fighting wars where we risk
nothing, thus validating the adage «*victory without peril is triumph without glory*».

---

166. William M. Arkin, "The Pentagon Unleashes a Holy Warrior", Los Angeles Times, 16 October
2003.
167. Deliberate references to «John 8:12» and «2 Corinthians 4:6» on Trijicon ACOG rifle scopes have
caused a stir in the United States, where secularism is the rule in the military. (Joseph Rhee, Tahman
Bradley & Brian Ross, "U.S. Military Weapons Inscribed with Secret 'Jesus' Bible Codes", ABC News,
18 January 2010).
168. Alain Finkielkraut, programme C à vous, France 5, 23 November 2015.

This way of waging war, where drone operators sit comfortably thousands of miles away from the battlefield and conduct strikes based on algorithms, without even necessarily seeing the targets, is seen as a cowardly practice. The civilian casualties that result from the modus operandi itself become a justification in itself for conducting terrorist acts:

> *Don't be cowards by attacking us with drones. Send us your troops instead, the ones we humiliated in Iraq!* [169]

Indeed, the use of cruise missiles by the United States in 1998 in response to the Dar-es-Salam and Nairobi bombings (Operation INFINITE REACH) was considered particularly 'cowardly' in Arab nations. Not only because these bombings hit innocent people, who had nothing to do with terrorism, but also and above all because the Americans 'risked nothing' in this case.

> *The [1998] attacks did not improve America's image among the muja-hideen I interviewed, who describe Tomahawk missiles as cowardly weapons, too afraid to risk their lives in battle or look their enemy in the eye.* [170]

Thus, in trying to show its strength, America has shown its weakness in the eyes of the Islamists. This contempt for American fighters who fight from a distance but lack the courage to face their adversary head on is underlined in the Islamic State's *No Respite* video, released in 2015. It points out that these soldiers are running on 'Prozac'[171] and committing suicide at a rate of 6,500 a year back home. In fact, between 7 October 2001 and 28 July 2015, the US armed forces were engaged in five major operations, with a total of 6,855 deaths[172] plus nearly 6,000 veterans of the wars in Iraq and Afghanistan who kill themselves each year after returning to the United States (i.e. about 18 per day)[173].In total, America loses almost as many military personnel to suicide each year as it has in 14 years on all battlefields.

---

169. Islamic State spokesperson, http://dailycaller.com/2014/08/08/isis-threatens-america-we-will-raise-the-flag-of-allah-in-the-white-house/#ixzz3n1ziZgJ5.

170. Jessica Stern, "Being Feared Is Not Enough to Keep Us Safe", Washington Post, 15 September 2001.

171. NOA: an antidepressant.

172. Hannah Fischer, A Guide to U.S. Military Casualty Statistics: Operation Freedom's Sentinel, Operation Inherent Resolve, Operation New Dawn, Operation Iraqi Freedom, and Operation Enduring Freedom, Congressional Research Service (www.crs.gov), RS22452, 7 August 2015.

173. Janet Kemp, RN PhD & Robert Bossarte, PhD, Suicide Data Report, 2012, Department of Veterans Affairs, Mental Health Services, Suicide Prevention Program; 2019 National Veteran Suicide Prevention Annual Report, Office of Mental Health and Suicide Prevention, US Department of Veterans Affairs.

The Islamists see the weakness of the society that the West is trying to impose on them. Jihadists feel totally at the service of their cause. Their self-sacrifice is fuelled by imagery that is very present in EI propaganda, recalling the sacrifice of the mythical heroes of the struggle against the Crusaders.

2.5.3. The war space

Because we project our own patterns onto the opponent, we attribute to them behaviours derived from our own understanding of things. Thus, terrorist acts are always perceived as an attack on the state where they were perpetrated. This is obvious for Marxist terrorism, since its credo is revolution, i.e. the destruction of the national social order in order to replace it with new institutions. But this is not the case for jihadist terrorism, which does not fight against institutions, but against their decisions.

Moreover, unlike Western thinking, which tends to see things in terms of a vertical and linear rationality, the Middle Eastern mind combines a horizontal and non-linear reading of problems. Thus, we think in terms of left/right, country X/country Y, etc., whereas in the East - as in Africa, moreover - transversal notions such as ethnicity or religion come into play. The result is a much more complex reading of human and political relations: just because an opponent of the Syrian regime accepts Western weapons does not mean that he respects the countries that bomb Arabs or Muslims, even if they are sympathetic to the regime. Thus, Osama bin Laden's fatwa of 23 February 1998 criticised the American embargo against Iraq, even though the latter was secular at the time. The same logic explains the opportunistic and temporary alliances between rival rebel factions in Iraq and Syria, which the West understands so poorly.

The notion of jihad must be understood in terms of these complex logics that give the space of war a considerably wider dimension than in the West. It is this same logic that explains why, rightly or wrongly, a fairly large proportion of Muslims feel solidarity with the victims of our wars in the Middle East, even if they do not adhere to radical ideologies and do not approve of their methods.

2.5.3.1 Geography and Islam

Geographically, Islam sees the world in terms of the 'land of Islam' *(dar al-islam)* and the 'land of ungodliness' *(dar al-kufr)*. The 'land of ungodliness' is the area where Muslim and infidel *(kafir)* communities face each other. In the 'land of Islam', Sharia law is applicable and there is no need for jihad. For example, in the early 1990s, this is what would have kept Osama bin Laden from undertaking a jihad against the Saudi regime, which had accepted the American presence on its territory[174].

---

174. Upon his return to Afghanistan in 1996, Osama bin Laden is said to have consulted Younis Kha-

Western 'experts' tend to confuse the 'land of ungodliness' *(dar al-kufr)* with an area of confrontation or war *(dar al-harb),* where people are at war *(ahl al-harb* or *harbis).* This reading corresponds to the situation at the birth of Islam, when it was surrounded by enemies and still had to fight its way through animist, Jewish and Christian tribes. Today, the reality is more complex and Islam is surrounded by countries with friendly and/or strongly Muslim populations, which are no longer (necessarily) enemies. In these areas there is a contractual peace *(dar al-ahd)* where both communities decide to live in peace *(ahl al-ahd).*

According to Islamic jurisprudence, the 'peoples of contractual peace' *(ahl al-ahd)* are non-Muslim populations, which are divided into three categories: populations living on Muslim soil with the status of 'protected people' *(ahl al-dhimma* or *dhimmis);* peoples with whom there is a peace agreement *(ahl al-hudna);* and individuals (travellers, diplomats, etc.) who benefit from temporary protection *(ahl al-aman).*

As many Muslim exegetes point out, the notions of 'land of ungodliness' and 'land of war' are neither mutually exclusive nor incompatible, and to confuse them is a sham.

And yet, the confusion is common on social networks, but is also propagated by intellectuals, such as Alain Finkielkraut, who presents the image of an Islam whose vision of the world would be divided into only two zones: the «land of Islam» and the «land of war»; thus suggesting that the only alternative to Islam is war, carried out by armed jihad which - according to him - would be a religious obligation[175].Not only is the statement false... but it is also dangerous, because it excludes any compromise within a society that we have wanted - rightly or wrongly - to be multicultural. In their defence, it should be noted that Western interventions have had the effect of erasing intermediate positions. The Islamic State magazine *Dabiq, for* example, emphasises the disappearance of the *'grey zone'* (which broadly covers the notion of *'ahl al-ahd'*) and quotes Osama bin Laden:

> *The world today is divided into two camps. Bush is telling the truth when he says, «You are either with us or you are with the terrorists.» That means you are either with the crusade or with Islam.*[176]

---

lis, leader of the Afghan Hezb-i-Islami, on several occasions in order to determine the legitimacy of a jihad against the Saudi regime. Alex Linschoten and Felix Kuehn, An Enemy We Created: the Myth of the Taliban/al-Qaeda Merger in Afghanistan, 1970-2010, Oxford University Press, London, 2012.

175. http://www.lepoint.fr/societe/finkielkraut-le-djihad-est-une-obligation-leguee-par-mahomet-a-tous-les-musulmans-11-12-2015-1989225_23.php.

176. Interview 21 October 2001, quoted in 'The Extinction Of The Grayzone', Dabiq Magazine, n° 7, Rabi al-Akhir 1436, February 2015, p. 54.

Thus, Western interventions tend to polarise Muslim perceptions of the world. Although the vast majority of Muslims clearly disapprove of Islamist violence, they often have sympathy for their cause. The shift in opinion in favour of the Islamists is an issue that no Western country (unlike Russia) really realised before committing militarily: none undertook societal groundwork to win the minds of their own Muslim nationals.

2.5.3.2. Borders and strategic depth

It is often said that jihadists - and the Islamic State in particular - do not recognise the principle of national borders and are trying to extend the domain of Islam into our countries. This is not true, because they are mixing up several things. The Islamic State does not challenge the national borders we have in the West. On the contrary, it challenges the territorial divisions inherited from colonisation or the dismantling of the Ottoman Empire, imposed by the colonial powers in the Levant, according to their geostrategic interests at the time, without regard for the populations concerned.

It is also wrong to draw the conclusion that jihadists are attacking the West in order to recreate the Abbasid caliphate: their attacks mainly affect northern European countries, which were never part of the caliphate (such as Germany or France), and very few southern European countries, some of which were part of the caliphate (such as Portugal).

Theorists of armed jihad have understood the asymmetric nature of the battlefield where Westerners and Muslims clash: military operations take place in direct contact with Muslim civilian populations, while on the Western side, populations remain outside the battlefield. They have therefore simply turned the principles of the «five circles» of the American colonel John A. Warden, at the heart of the concept of the strikes carried out in Iraq and Syria, which target the civilian populations in order to push them to rebel against their leaders (Syrian government, leaders of the Islamic State, etc.) We will talk about this below.

Clearly, they have re-established a form of (geographical) symmetry by extending the notion of the battlefield to the national territory of the countries that are attacking them:

> *Any country that goes to war against Muslims, or participates in the invasion of a Muslim country, has become a de facto War Zone (Dar al-Harb). This is why all Western countries that have an active participation in the occupation of Afghanistan, Iraq or some Muslim countries are considered as war zones.[177]*

---

177. Sheikh Anwar al-Awlaki, «The Rules for Dispossessing Believers of Their Wealth in a War Zone»,

Thus, theories involving *the 'distant enemy'* (*al-Add al-Baid*) or *the 'near enemy'* (*al-Add al-Qarib*) have lost all meaning with Western interventions. Although located in discontinuous geographical spaces, the national territory of the countries intervening in the Near and Middle East is part of the battlefield. Thus, the United States has become a *close enemy*[178].This is why the United States has not suffered any terrorist attacks on its soil since 2001, not because of the security measures adopted, but because Americans have gone to 'get killed on the spot'. Jihad can just as easily be invoked against Americans in Iraq and Afghanistan! It does not matter where you fight your opponent: the important thing is to fight him.

This extension of war zones beyond the physical battlefield (Afghan, Iraqi or Syrian) is all the more legitimate in the eyes of the Islamists since the United States and other Western countries (such as France or Great Britain) do not respect national borders either (as in Pakistan, Syria and Yemen, for example) when conducting their wars. But in order not to be held responsible for unfortunate decisions without taking the necessary precautionary measures to protect their populations, Western states have preferred to turn a blind eye to this doctrinal development. Thus, the report of the *Foreign Affairs Committee* of the National Assembly testifies to the doctrinal confinement in which France has engaged in the war in the Middle East:

> *Daesh also differs from al-Qaeda Central in that its strategic priorities have been reversed. These are no longer against the 'distant enemy', i.e. the United States and its 'crusader' allies, the Western countries, but against the 'near enemy', i.e. the local Arab regimes, which are considered corrupt and unworthy of Islam.*[179]

2.5.3.3. *The notion of a «Community of believers*

We do not understand those who go into battle, ready to die and carry out actions that are geographically discontinuous. Military action in the context of Islamic jihad does not necessarily follow a territorial logic, but rather that of a community of thought or values, which is covered by the notion of «*community of believers*» (*Ummah*).

According to Islamic jurisprudence, war jihad can be declared when the *Ummah* is threatened. The Ummah refers to a community bound by a common

---

Inspire, n° 4, (1431), Winter 2010.

178. "Inspire Interview with Sheikh Abu Mus'ab Abdul-Wadood", Inspire, n° 17, Summer 2017, p. 46.

179. Information report on the Near and Middle East, Foreign Affairs Committee, National Assembly, Document n° 2666, 18 March 2015, p. 63.

faith, but not necessarily within a continuous geographical space. Furthermore, an attack on the faith can be interpreted, in fact, as an attack on the entire Islamic community.

In operational terms, this approach is not far removed from the 'proletarian solidarity' that fuelled the international revolutionary communist movement in the 1920s in Europe and was invoked to create the *International Brigades* in Spain[180].It is one of the reasons for the flow of foreign fighters to fight the Soviet occupation in Afghanistan (1979-1989), for the creation of the International Islamic Units in Bosnia, for the aid provided by Muslim countries to the KLA[181] (1999), and for the jihadist volunteers in Afghanistan and Iraq, then in Syria (2001-).

This explains a crucial factor in the radicalisation process, but one that has been largely underestimated by French and Belgian intelligence services (and their political authorities): the deep emotional closeness that exists between European Muslim populations and their counterparts in the Near and Middle East. Muslims living in Europe are certainly not terrorists, and they all aspire to live in peace. But when their brothers are bombed, when civilian populations, women and children die (collateral damage) for obscure and never explained reasons, then a feeling of solidarity is awakened which can go as far as terrorism. This is exactly what the Kouachi brothers, Ahmedi Coulibaly, Abballa Larossi, Mohamed Lahouaiej Bouhlel, and many others have told us in a consistent and systematic way.

It is also symptomatic to note that a large proportion of jihadists in the West are very recent converts, with no particular knowledge of Islam, but who joined the jihad in solidarity with the populations attacked by the West. The images showing the civilian victims - especially children - of Western strikes have certainly played an essential role in the genesis of solidarity with the victims. The phenomenon is undoubtedly exacerbated by the deafening silence of the Western media on these 'collateral' civilian victims, who are the result of interventions triggered by lies that they themselves have spread.

In addition to «functional» attacks, there are isolated acts of «solidarity» with the populations that are victims of military interventions and actions against the Muslim community. This is the case of Mohammed Merah's crimes in March 2012, which can be broken down into two «sub-attacks»: one directed against the French government, because «*he was against the law on the veil and fighting*

---

180. Nicolas Lépine, International Socialism and the Spanish Civil War, Department of History, Faculty of Arts, Laval University, Quebec, 2013.
181. Ushtria Çlirimtare e Kosoves: Kosovo Liberation Army.

2. UNDERSTANDING THE THREAT

against the French operations in Afghanistan»[182] and the other directed against Israel, because «*the Jews killed our brothers and sisters in Palestine!*» [183]

2.5.4. The pre-eminence of intention over result

The notion of 'conquering Islam' (or 'conquering jihad') comes to us from the Middle Ages, when the then nascent Islam (between 632 and 750 AD) developed rapidly. It should be remembered here that Islam was not born in a religious vacuum, but in the midst of Jewish, Christian and animist communities, which tried to crush it from the outset. In North Africa and much of the Middle East, however, it spread largely peacefully in the wake of trade. It was only when it came into contact with the 'established' empires, notably in Europe and Iran, that it took an armed form. The Muslims, who were numerically inferior at the time, had only their faith and an operative art[184] based on movement as tools for success. The conceptualisation of the 'military jihad', based more on the effort made than on the result obtained, dates from this period:

> *Acts are only as good as their intent. And to each man comes what he intended.*[185]

A reading that we will find below in the notion of victory. To simplify and use Western terminology, the action does not have an obligation of result, but an obligation of effort. We find here the notion of effort intrinsically present in that of jihad.

This partly explains why Islamist terror suspects claim credit for countless - and often unrealistic - attacks. This has been the case in the cases of Khalid Sheikh Mohammed (nicknamed 'KSM'), Zacarias Moussaoui and José Padilla in the United States. KSM 'confessed' (under torture) to involvement in over 30 terrorist attacks worldwide (including 9/11, the Reid shoe bombs, the Bali bombing and many others). His confession was so implausible that he was dubbed the «*One-Stop Shopping Terrorist Super* Store»[186] .

Beyond the fact that these confessions were obtained under torture, the refusal of legal counsel (in the absence of a lawyer) by the «guilty» underlines the jihadist character of their «confessions». Although they are undoubtedly innocent of most

---

182. «The killer contacted France 24: «This is only the beginning», he said», France 24, 21 March 2012.

183. Ibid.

184. The term «operative» is taken here in its Clausewitzian sense («relating to operations»), as an intermediate level of action between tactics and strategy.

185. Hadith attributed to Muhammad, reported by Al-Bukhari, Imam, 41. Quoted in The Book of Stops, Abd Al-Qadir Al-Djazairi, translated by Michel Lagarde, Brill, 2000, ISBN 9004115676.

186. http://mayday.blogsome.com/2007/03/19/khalid-sheikh-mohammed-the-wally-world-of-wickedness/

of the crimes of which they accuse themselves, they assume responsibility for their intentions. Thus, the American judicial system gives them the opportunity to continue their jihad and serve as a model for new generations of terrorists! Here too, this approach illuminates an asymmetric dimension. The system of «military commissions» set up by the United States in 2006 to try suspected terrorists does not allow for the production of witnesses or discussions that contradict the charges against the accused. There is thus no way to determine the veracity of the crimes of which the detainees are accused, and these trials do not allow the full light to be shed on the real facts. These «tribunals», which are intended to be tougher, thus allow the accused to attribute success to themselves and, in this asymmetrical logic, contribute to giving meaning to jihadism.

The pre-eminence of intention over action, which is widely found in the culture of Muslim countries, tends to encourage a form of resilience that makes Muslims generally more 'philosophical' about political or military events. This gap between intention and action - often translated as '*irja*- tends to spill over into religious practice, which is often interpreted in a flexible manner. Recently, however, there has been an increased emphasis on a more rigid consistency between intention and action in Islamic State literature. In other words, it is no longer just a matter of agreeing with the jihad, but of actually practising it in all its aspects. The reason for this refocusing is twofold: on the one hand, to fight against those Islamists who prefer to join neighbouring Islamist factions - to avoid being bombed by the Western coalition - and, on the other hand, to push the militants to a more concrete and radical commitment.

In the United States and France, since 2015, based on the violence of the attacks, a discourse has developed linking jihadist terrorism to nihilism[187] (!) This is false and dangerous. False, because this discourse distracts us from the real objectives of terrorism, and dangerous, because it inspires us with inappropriate strategies and solutions. Moreover, the Vatican, which should - by this logic - be the main target of the jihadists, does not seem to be in the jihadists' sights. A good understanding of the reasons that drive terrorism allows us to identify the objectives it seeks and, consequently, the capabilities it needs.

The attacks are certainly deadly, but they are often not 'optimised' for maximum casualties. For example, on 17 August 2005, the simultaneous detonation of more than 500 bombs in 63 out of 64 districts of Bangladesh resulted in only two deaths! The media give an overestimated picture of the «effectiveness» of attacks: for the period 1996-2006, terrorist attacks caused an average of 1.6 deaths per year worldwide. In fact, terrorism is not effective because of the number of deaths it causes, but because of the determination it shows: this is the basis of jihadist terrorism.

---

187. France 24, Special News Bulletin, 23 March 2018.

This is a fairly literal application of the notion of jihad, where victory is not associated with what one does to the opponent, but with the effort one has made not to give up the fight. For example, the magazine *Inspire*, produced by the *Jihad Base in the Arabian Peninsula* (also known as '*Al Qaeda in Yemen*') and which is the doctrinal reference for jihadists - including the Islamic State - makes it very clear:

> *I would also like to say to my brothers that we have to understand what the objective of our operations is: the primary objective is not to achieve a maximum number of deaths, but to achieve a maximum impact and leverage. So an operation like a parcel bomb that doesn't kill anybody can have an effect that surpasses an operation where dozens of people are killed.*[188]

This can be compared to the Basque ETA 'attacks', which mainly targeted police targets and - more often than not - informed the police about 30 minutes before the bomb was detonated in order to allow it to be defused[189]. The operative objective here is to demonstrate the ability to strike, but without causing casualties and without losing the support of sympathisers.

With ARIG, it is not the number of victims that counts, but the determination of its supporters who are ready to die. The logic is asymmetrical: even when cells are dismantled, they are a manifestation of this determination and contribute to the jihadists' victory. As can be seen, in this situation, a success for the state does not automatically mean a defeat for the jihadists, but can, on the contrary, strengthen their position. The mere fact that the terrorist will exists demonstrates the determination of the terrorists and is in itself formidable propaganda.

Thus, based on the idea that «*terrorism seeks to divide us*», remembrance ceremonies and other events designed to show the unity of the nation are intended to bring people together. This makes sense to us. The problem is that the aim of terrorism is not to divide us, but to get governments to stop intervening abroad. This goal has rarely been achieved, but the emphasis on terrorism in these ceremonies has done much to fuel the flow of foreign fighters to where the Islamic State needs them: Iraq and Syria.

This is what happened after the January 2015 attacks in Paris. An examination of social network activity showed that the French government's high-profile response only positioned the Islamic State as the main organisation fighting against Western interventions. Thus, paradoxically, the French government has been the main propagandist for the Islamic State...

---

188. "Q & A with Sheikh Anwar Al-'Awlaki", Inspire, n° 12, Spring 2014, p. 17.
189. For example, the 9 August 2009 attack in Palma de Mallorca was the latest in a long list of attacks in which ETA has systematically announced its attacks, demonstrating its capabilities, without causing any victims.

The effectiveness of terrorism stems from our inability to think in the terrorists' logic.

2.5.5. The notion of victory

The very definition of jihad, and the primacy of intention over action, gives rise to a notion of victory that is fundamentally different from that generally understood in the West. Whereas in the West victory is associated with the destruction of the adversary, in Islam it is associated with the determination not to give up the fight.

Thus, on 17 March 2004, after the Madrid attack, the text of the Abu Hafs al-Masri brigades' claim thanked George Bush:

> *[...] a major operation [in the United States] will destroy your administration. We don't want you to lose the election [...] we want you to win, Bush the criminal.*[190]

This is perfectly in line with the logic of jihad, where our action feeds the terrorist act. This claim can be compared to Mullah Omar's statement in Afghanistan:

> *We are truly blessed. Never in our wildest dreams did we hope for a gift as precious as Bush. He is the poster boy for our international movement.*[191]

We are in a different logic. After the Westminster attack on 22 March 2017, the jihadists' analysis of the attack published in *Inspire Guide* states:

> *One of the most important messages of the operation is the determination of its implementer and the fact that he was not deterred by his lack of resources.*[192]

No one can defeat a stronger opponent than himself, but it is his duty to try to do so. Thus, in the greater jihad as in the lesser jihad, the notion of victory is similar: it is essentially a victory over oneself, a victory over apparent ease and discouragement. In the greater jihad, victory is associated with the essential: the defence of the faith, while in the lesser jihad, it is more about self-sacrifice in relation to a higher cause.

In other words, victory in Islam is not absolute, but relative: it is enough to show a willingness to fight in order to be victorious. In practical terms, victory

---

190. «Un texte attribué à Al-Qaïda menace d'attentats «les valets de l'Amérique», lemonde.fr, 18 March 2004.
191. Tom Goeller, "Playing Devil's Advocate", Egypt Today, October 2004.
192. Inspire Guide - The British Parliament Operation in London, issue 5, 23 March 2017, p. 3.

is often about 'having the last word', even if it is not decisive. For example, the Islamic State does not need to hide its failures or 'small' victories: the mere fact that it is able to strike unexpectedly is already a success[193].

This reading of victory is not unique to Islamists, but is found more widely in Muslim thought. It explains, for example, why the Egyptians celebrate their crossing of the Suez Canal in October 1973 and the breaking of the Bar-Lev line as a victory[194] ... even though they were subsequently defeated. This also explains Saddam Hussein's proclaimed victory in Baghdad in 1991 despite the destruction of much of his military capability; the victory cries and parades of Ayatollah Moqtada al-Sadr's militias in the Ali Mosque in Najaf, after the end of the fighting negotiated by Ayatollah Sistani in August 2004[195] , and Hassan Nasrallah's victory in Lebanon, despite the massive destruction caused by the Israeli army in 2006[196].Perceived in the West as 'blowhards', they had achieved their victories not by destroying their opponents, but by refusing to give in to the pressure of considerably stronger forces and despite major losses and destruction. Their victory - in the spirit of jihad - is thus to have held their heads high, regardless of the outcome of the battle. This is the heart of the asymmetrical phenomenon: the victory of one brings the victory of the other!

This principle was perfectly explained in a speech by Mohammed al-Adnani, spokesman for the Islamic State:

> *Do you think, America, that you are victorious in killing one leader or another? Were you victorious when you killed Abu Musab, Abu Hamza, Abu Omar or Osama? Would you be victorious if you killed Al-Shishani, Abu Bakr, Abu Zayd or Abu 'Amr? No. Indeed, victory is the defeat of one's opponent... were we defeated when we lost the cities in Iraq and were in the desert without a city or land? And would we be defeated and would you be victorious if you took Mosul or Sirte or Raqqa or even if you had taken all the cities and we had to return to our original condition? Certainly not! The real defeat is the loss of will and the desire to fight. America will be victorious and the Mujahideen will be defeated in one situation... if you were able to remove the Qur'an from the hearts of Muslims.[197]*

For example, after the Bali bombing in October 2002 and the arrest of its main leaders, the *Jemaah Islamiyya (JI)*, which had organised the attack, saw a massive increase in its membership and a rejuvenation of its numbers with

---

193. Charlie Winter, "Why ISIS Is So Good at Branding Its Failures as Successes", www.theatlantic.com, 19 September 2017.

194. A museum in Cairo («Panorama of the October War») is specially dedicated to this operation.

195. Report by Grégoire Deniau, «La Bataille de Najjaf», France 2, 2 September 2004.

196. «Nasrallah wins the war", The Economist, 17 August 2006.

197. Speech by Abu Mohammed al-Adnani, June 2015.

the appearance of new leaders[198].Contrary to Western military principles, victory does not have a material or territorial dimension, but a moral and ethical dimension: it essentially marks the refusal to bow one's head and the determination to fight whatever the cost.

The asymmetric nature of this notion of victory is clearly illustrated by Palestinian rocket fire from the Gaza Strip. Since the erection of the «Wall» between Israel and the occupied territories in 2000, the possibility of carrying out attacks on Israeli soil has been considerably reduced. Initially, the number of planned attacks against Israel increased sharply to compensate for the difficulty of carrying them out, but as the number of prevented attacks also increased, the Palestinians chose another mode of action: firing rockets.

Palestinian actions since the construction of the wall

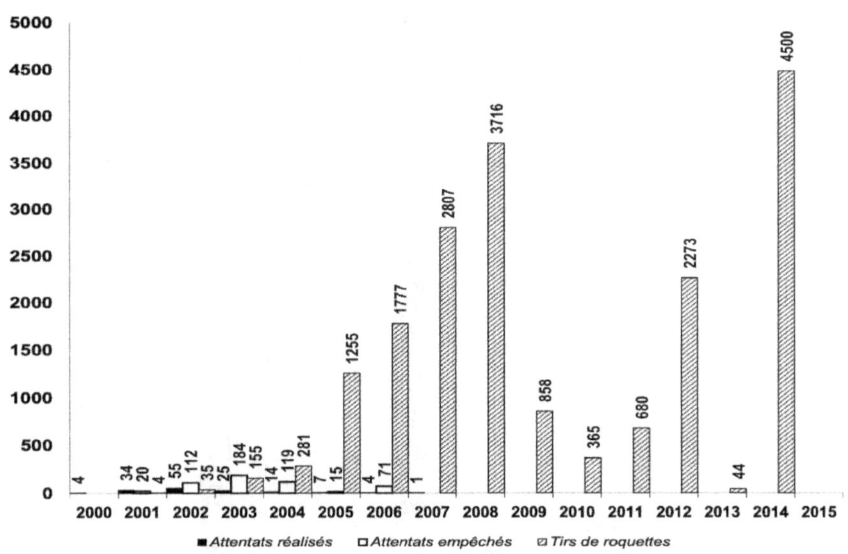

Figure 4: After the construction of the wall, the number of planned attacks increased considerably in 2002-2003. However, faced with the effectiveness of the Israeli security services in preventing their execution, the Palestinian movements switched to other methods: rockets. The «barrier» did not «break» the Palestinians' determination. In asymmetrical and jihadist terms, this is already a Palestinian victory. In more than 60 years of war, the Israelis have never managed to understand the logic of their adversary: it is the only country in the world that has not found a solution to its terrorist problem. [Figures: Israeli Ministry of Foreign Affairs]

The number of projectiles fired from the Gaza Strip into Israel between 2001 and 2015 is estimated at 18,928[199] , with peaks during the Israeli operations HARD LEAD (2007-2008), CLOUD COLUMN (2012) and PROTECTIVE

---

198. Jane's Intelligence Review, August 2004.
199. "Palestinian rocket attacks on Israel", Wikipedia (accessed 20 March 2018).

EDGE (2014), causing 44 casualties, almost all of which occurred *during* Israeli military operations (resulting in 4, 6 and 17 casualties respectively)[200]. Thus, rocket attacks - even if they constitute a permanent threat for the populations concerned - are considerably less deadly than suicide attacks. Without wishing to justify these shootings, it must be noted that with one killed for every 280 shootings (most of them during combat), the number of deaths is not the objective here. Moreover, it is important to note that the vast majority of Palestinian rocket and mortar fire is in response to Israeli air strikes - but that the international press does not report. The objective of the Palestinians is to keep the confidence of the population by showing that they are not giving up the fight.

There is therefore clearly a tactical gain for the Israelis. On the other hand, strategically, the gain is in favour of the Palestinians, who can mark their refusal to 'give up' the struggle. In line with the idea of jihad, the act of fighting back is more important than the effect (the number of victims) caused. In reality, the actions of the Israeli army contribute to strengthening the Palestinians' will to resist. In the logic of asymmetric warfare, the victory is clearly Palestinian.

Victims of rocket attacks from the Gaza Strip (2000-2015)

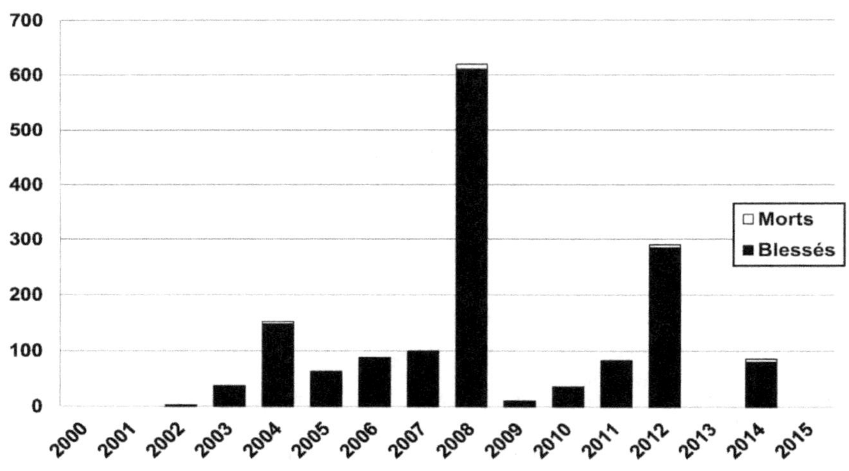

Figure 5. The effectiveness rate of Palestinian rocket fire is minimal and the number of fatalities is 1 for every 200 rockets fired. The important thing for the Palestinian Islamists is not the number of deaths, but to show their will to resist. [Figures: Israeli Ministry of Foreign Affairs]

Thus, the simple fact of resisting, whatever the methods or weapons used, gives the Palestinians the satisfaction of a «victory». This explains the dazzling success of Hamas in the occupied territories: its attacks feed - in small steps - a

---

200. Phan Nguyen, "How many people have died from Gaza rockets into Israel?", Mondoweiss, 29 August 2014, http://mondoweiss.net/2014/07/rocket-deaths-israel (accessed 20 March 2015).

feeling of victory by refusing to give up the fight, while Fatah, oriented on a negotiation process, gives the impression of «giving ground».

This also explains the fact that - militarily - the Palestinian Islamists do not seek what the West calls «a decisive victory», but limit themselves to punctual attack campaigns without decisive scope in operational terms, but which are enough to show that they are not giving up and thus constitute a strategic victory. Thus, Hamas keeps a large popular support, even if its actions directly and indirectly cause many Palestinian losses, because the fact of showing its determination to continue the struggle is a kind of pledge of hope for the Palestinian opinion.

The fact that these rocket attacks cause very few casualties does not make them more legitimate, but it does indicate that Hamas's sense of victory and popular success is not linked to the number of casualties it causes. It derives its success from its determination to resist with concrete actions.

Since the terrorist act is the expression of a refusal to give up the fight against numerically superior powers, it is already a victory in itself. Thus, the air strikes in Iraq, Syria or Palestine are certainly tactical victories, but each response to these strikes in the form of an attack *or attempted attack* will constitute a strategic victory for the jihadists.

After the ceasefire between Hamas and Israel on 21 May 2021, the Palestinians claim victory. A resident of Gaza exclaims[201] :

Even if they destroy all of Gaza, they cannot destroy our spirit of resistance!

What appears to be an Israeli success is a strategic defeat. The Palestinians were able to highlight the expropriations in East Jerusalem and the differences in status between Arab and Jewish Israeli citizens, as well as the disproportionate means committed by both sides.

2.6. Jihadist terrorism

2.6.1. The nature of jihadist terrorism
Unlike the West, which tries to attach a moral notion to the word 'terrorism', jihadists understand it simply as a method. Free of moral prejudices, their approach is fundamentally more rational and coherent:

---

201. 13 h, RTBF, 21 May 2021.

> *We refuse to understand this term [terrorism] according to the American definition. «Terrorism» is an abstract word, and like many abstract words, it can mean good or bad things depending on its context, on what is added to it and what is attached to it. The word is an abstract term with no positive or negative meaning.* [202]

This is why Islamic State jihadists claim the term 'terrorists':

> *Even if you can't find any way to kill these people (sic) who are fighting Allah and His Messenger, find any way: poison them, kill them with knives, take their weapons, enter their houses, slit their throats, terrorise them [...] Allah has told us that you must terrorise the enemy of Allah and ours. We are terrorists. Whatever they say about us, we are terrorists!* [203]

While the West tends to see terrorism as an amoral attack on an established order (as the occupiers did with the Resistance during World War II), jihadists see it as a term that applies indiscriminately to any attempt to terrorise:

Whoever terrorizes others is a «terrorist», without exception, so there is :

1. A bad terrorist attacker
2. A just terrorist who defends himself or an oppressed people

> *Thus, we do not find any negative meaning in the word terrorist when it is used to define resistance fighters or mujahideen... They are, in fact, terrorists towards their enemies, the enemies of Allah and their miserable servants. So where is the ambiguity and blame?* [204]

This approach is an extension of the principle of the pre-eminence of intention over result and is more doctrinally coherent than the Western approach:

> *Terrorism can be commendable, and perhaps reprehensible. Terrifying an innocent person and terrorising him or her is unacceptable and unjust, and terrorising people without reason is unjust. On the other hand, terrorising muggers and criminals and thieves and bandits is necessary for the safety of people and for the protection of their property. There is no doubt about that. Every state and every civilisation and culture must resort to terrorism in certain circumstances in order to abolish tyranny and corruption.*

---

202. Abu Musab al-Suri, "The Jihadi Experiences: Individual Terrorism Jihad and the Global Islamic Resistance Units", Inspire, n° 5, Spring 2011, p. 29.

203. Verbatim excerpt from the video Explode France - 3, Islamic State, November 2015.

204. Abu Musab al-Suri, "The Jihadi Experiences: Individual Terrorism Jihad and the Global Islamic Resistance Units", Inspire, n° 5, Spring 2011, p. 30.

> *In today's wars, there is no morality, and it is clear that humanity has descended to the lowest level of decadence and oppression. They are stripping us of our wealth, our resources and our oil. Our religion is under attack. They kill and murder our brothers. They compromise our honour and dignity and if we dare to utter a single word of protest against this injustice, we are called terrorists. This is a grave injustice. And the insistence of the United Nations on indicting the victims and supporting the aggressors is a serious precedent that shows the extent of the injustice that has been established in this land ...* [205]

From this pragmatic reading, jihadists distinguish between two basic types of terrorism[206] :

Blameable terrorism (*irhab madhmum*), which is the *terrorism of lies* (*irhab al-batil*) and the use of the *force of lies* (*quwwat al-batil*). It refers to actions, speeches or behaviours that aim to hurt or terrorise the innocent without a just cause. This type of terrorism includes terrorism associated with robbery, brigandage, invaders, attackers, oppressors and illegitimate rulers of peoples. The perpetrator of an act of terrorism of this kind must be punished according to his or her actions and their effects. (Note: this definition, which is close to the notion of «state terrorism» often evoked in the West, refers more specifically to Western strikes by drones or cruise missiles, which cannot be guarded against and which strike in a «very poorly discriminated» way at combatants and non-combatants and are seen as particularly cowardly in the Islamic world).

Commendable terrorism (*irhab mahmud*) is the terrorism of the righteous who have been unjustly treated. It is aimed at combating the injustice done to the oppressed and is practised so as to terrorise and repel the oppressor. The terrorism of security personnel fighting thieves and robbers is of the same nature as the terrorism of those resisting occupation, and the terrorism of peoples «*defending themselves against the servants of Satan*». (Note: This reading of terrorism is consistent with the position of some developing countries in discussions on the definition of terrorism in international fora such as the UN, with a focus on resistance to foreign occupation.)

There is no inescapable desire in the jihadists' approach to attack Western democracies in order to 'impose' a system or belief on them. After the attacks of 2015-2017, there were no claims of a «will to impose» Islam or anything else in France. In fact, a rational analysis shows that as early as 2015, the Islamic State sought to consolidate its presence in the Middle East, not to expand to other continents. Besides, why would it seek it when it is already fighting local

---

205. Interview with Osama bin Laden by John Miller of the American TV channel ABC, May 1998 (https ://www.pbs.org/wgbh/pages/frontline/shows/binladen/who/interview.html)
206. Abu Musab al-Suri, "The Jihadi Experiences: Individual Terrorism Jihad and the Global Islamic Resistance Units", Inspire, n° 5, Spring 2011, p. 29.

governments, rival factions and ethnic groups with their own regional ambitions, such as the Kurds?

Modern jihadism emerged after the first Gulf War. Westerners will identify it with «Al Qaeda», but - as we will see later - it is an idea or movement rather than an organisation. Between 1990 and 2003, one cannot really speak of a «strategy», but rather of a «guiding idea» that can be summarised as: «*The aim was to push the United States to disengage from the Middle and Near East, as Osama bin Laden's «Declaration of the World Islamic Front» of 23 February 1998 clearly explains. This is why the Americans were hit during this period. The fact that European countries felt affected by 9/11 - beyond a natural compassion - was absurd. The Old Continent was thus drawn into a conflict that was not its own, contributing greatly to the development of international terrorism afterwards.

With the successive interventions in Afghanistan, Iraq, Libya and Syria, jihadism found a second wind, which led to the emergence of the Islamic State. It has evolved into a form of identity-based resistance to Western hegemonic temptations. The names of *'crusaders'* or *'Romans'* in jihadist discourse thus make explicit reference to what is perceived as a Western expansionist drive.

Some Islamists and Western 'experts' explain terrorist acts by 'revenge'. This is misleading. The reality is a bit more complex: revenge is a static concept, which is a goal in itself. Terrorism is a dynamic phenomenon: it seeks to achieve a goal. This does not mean that there is no taste of revenge in terrorist acts, but to explain it solely by it is both reductive and sterile. For example, we now know that 9/11 was a revenge attack, which is why it was not accompanied by any claims: it was an act intended to remain unique and all its protagonists died. On the other hand, the attacks that followed (from 2003 onwards) are part of a terrorist mechanism clearly explained by the jihadists themselves.

The increase in the number of attacks on France has often been explained as a flip-flop effect due to the poor performance of the EI in Syria and Iraq. This too is a misleading simplification. The objective of terrorism, it should be remembered, is to provoke the withdrawal of the participants in the international coalition. As the pressure on the battlefield increases, terrorists feel a greater need to act in order to have that pressure reduced. We will come back to this.

The idea that jihadist terrorism is aimed at overthrowing our governments, generating civil wars and the like is baseless rhetoric. Jihad theorists have always been clear and consistent:

1. Our religion and our Prophet are red lines. Let anyone who crosses these lines beware of what happened to Charlie Hebdo.

2. Palestine is a cause of our Islamic Ummah. And whoever supports the Jewish occupiers should never dream of peace, with Allah's permission.

3. The Levant is a cause of our Islamic Ummah. Our people in the Levant are facing genocide. And all those who participate in their torment with bombing or by supporting Bashar and his allies will not escape punishment.

4. Our lands are occupied. The land of the two Holy Places is occupied. We will continue to target you until you withdraw your forces from the Arabian Peninsula and every piece of land of Islam.

5. Our airspace is violated by your planes dropping their deadly load on our children. Our wealth and resources are stolen every day.[207]

As we can see, the aim here is not to impose Islam or to divide our society, but to defend theirs. This is a nationalist jihad, where the 'nationalist' dimension is based on a system of societal values, not on borders as in the West.

Terrorism is clearly a method, not an end. For Islamists, it is situated in a context in which particular interests must take a back seat to the general interest, which explains the acceptance of individual sacrifice. Our inability to understand their way of acting is linked to the fact that terrorism is placed in a wider societal frame of reference than that in which the Western mentality places war. This also explains why terrorism has become more deadly.

Our inability to give strategic coherence to our interventions, and our repeated lies to justify them, have reinforced the idea of a «clash of civilisations». Even to stop our wars in Iraq and Afghanistan, we are unable to keep our word. The result is a mobilising effect and an encouragement to communitarianism, which affects our own societies.

2.6.2. The West's weakness: its perception of jihadist terrorism

The West tends to see terrorism as an exogenous phenomenon over which states have no upstream control, and which can only be defeated by eliminating all combatants one by one. This is how France, Germany and Belgium solved their terrorism problem in the 1980s: without really needing to understand the underlying mechanisms.

---

207. Hamza Usama bin Laden, 'Advice for Martyrdom Seekers in the West', Inspire, n° 17, Summer 2017, p. 17.

As victims of their own history, Western countries have never really imagined that terrorism could be a response to their own actions. Thus, despite the fact that Islamists try to use violence to stop Western aggression in the Middle East, Western countries turn a deaf ear and continue to see it as an attempt to overthrow their democracies, systematically excluding their responsibility for the spiral of violence.

The explanations provided by the jihadist literature are very clear, but we refuse to listen to it. Our perception of Islamist terrorism has become a cacophony, with 'experts' giving free rein to their fantasies. They thus blur the message of the jihadists, preventing an objective reading of the problem that could allow the implementation of a real strategy against terrorism.

Symptomatically, the terrorists have realised that these 'experts' are a threat: not because they understand the rationality of Islamists, but precisely because they *fail to* understand it, and their 'analyses' only lead to fueling the fire and encouraging interventions in Iraq and Syria:

> *This is typical of Western arrogance. You prefer to ask self-proclaimed experts what the «barbarians» want rather than listen to them directly.*[208]

This explains why Aballa Larossi names some of these «experts» in the claim to his attack on 13 June 2016 in Magnanville and calls for their killing.

In fact, our perception of jihadist terrorism oscillates between incoherence and intellectual dishonesty. We tend to see it as a form of conquering «revanchism», based on hearsay and historical approximations, which surf on resentments about poorly controlled immigration:

> *Islamists have a certain capacity for initiative and they have something to do with Islam, because Islam has been a conquering religion from the beginning. The conquest has stopped, it has had its ebbs and flows, but for a certain number of Islamists the time has come for expansion, for conquest once again; and jihadism is a declaration of war against the entire West and not a response to France's occasional interventions in Syria and Iraq.*[209]

Such statements, which combine perceptions without causal links, inevitably lead to Islam being seen as the cause of the problem. This creates a fear of Islam (Islamophobia), which feeds communitarian reflexes and the non-resolution of the problem.

---

208. Dar al-Islam, n° 9, Rajab 1437, April 2016, p. 4.
209. Alain Finkielkraut, programme C à vous, France 5, 23 November 2015.

This approach ignores the effect of the absurd wars that the West has unleashed without serious reason in Afghanistan, Iraq and Syria. For a quarter of a century, the West has brought bloodshed to the Middle East, causing hundreds of thousands of deaths, with no clear objective and without providing any viable alternative to the regimes that have been overthrown. Can we really imagine that these populations - whatever their political or religious leanings - can accept these interventions without reacting?

In Britain, on 10 February 2003, a month before the start of the war in Iraq, the *Joint Intelligence Committee (JIC)* - responsible for synthesising the products of the intelligence community - sent a memo to Tony Blair, the then Prime Minister, which stated:

> *I. The threat from Al Qaeda will increase from the outset of any military action against Iraq. They will target coalition forces and other Western interests in the Middle East. Attacks on Western interests elsewhere in the world are also likely, particularly in the US and UK, for maximum impact. The global threat from other terrorist groups and Islamist individuals will increase significantly.*

> *[...]*

> *18. Al Qaeda and associated groups will continue to pose by far the greatest terrorist threat to Western interests, and this threat will be enhanced by military action against Iraq. The wider threat from Islamist terrorists will also increase in the event of war, reflecting growing anti-American and anti-Western sentiment in the Muslim world, including among Muslim communities in the West.* [210]

Thus, it was known that engaging in this war would generate a terrorist surge in Europe. On 13 April 2005, in a TOP SECRET classified report entitled *International Terrorism: Impact of Iraq*, the JIC noted:

> *I. The conflict in Iraq has exacerbated the threat of international terrorism and will continue to have a long-term impact. It has strengthened the conviction of extremists that Islam is under attack and must be defended by force.*

---

210. International Terrorism: War With Iraq, JIC Assessment, 10 February 2003 (TOP SECRET - Declassified), paragraphs 1 and 18, http://www.iraqinquiry.org.uk/media/230918/2003-02-10-jic-assessment-international-terrorism-war-with-iraq.pdf.

It has strengthened the resolve of terrorists already prepared to attack the West and motivated those who were not yet ready.

[...]

V. Iraq is likely to be an important motivating factor for the radicalisation of British Muslims and for extremists who see attacking the UK as legitimate for some time to come.[211]

These findings were confirmed again in April 2006 in a secret report on the July 2005 London bombings by the *JIC*:

[The war in] Iraq is likely to remain an important factor in the radicalisation of British Muslims and for extremists who see attacks on the UK as legitimate for some time to come.

And concludes:

We believe that the conflict in Iraq has exacerbated the threat of international terrorism and will continue to have a long-term impact.[212]

Clearly, the British services have found and admitted that there is a clear causal relationship between interventions in the Middle East and the development of terrorism in the West.

The Madrid attack of 11 March 2004 (M-11) was the pivotal event for the jihadists. Spain was in the middle of an election period and the majority of the population was opposed to participating in the war in Iraq. A few weeks after the attack, the elections brought the socialist opposition to power, which decided to withdraw Spanish forces from Iraq, prompting Honduras to take the same decision.

Jihadists see this decision as the effect of terrorism in getting Western countries to withdraw from a conflict: from 'punitive' (like '9/11'), terrorism becomes 'deterrent'.

In fact, the jihadists have misread the events: the Spanish withdrawal is not intended to satisfy the terrorists (whose motives are not understood at this

---

211. International Terrorism: Impact of Iraq, JIC Assessment, Joint Intelligence Committee, 13 April 2005, TOP SECRET (declassified January 2011).
212. Richard Norton-Taylor, "Iraq war 'motivated London bombers'", The Guardian, 3 April 2006.

114

stage), but public opinion, which was opposed to the war *before* the attacks. The problem is that the Spanish did not realise this problem and did not know how to dissociate the attacks from their decision to withdraw in their strategic communication. Unintentionally, they made the 'M-11' a source of inspiration for the jihadists, who saw it as a strategic success, later conceptualised as a *'deterrence operation'*[213]. It is this logic that will lead to the London attacks (7 and 21 July 2005)[214] and the Paris attacks in 2015-2016.

In the West, since 2001, the lack of rational and factual explanations for the motives of the attacks has created a 'conspiracy', which proliferates along two axes: a) the idea that the attacks are the work of obscure powers in search of power, and b) the idea that the attacks are the expression of a global project[215] to *'conquer the West'*.

Both axes are fanciful, but if the first is rather folkloric, the second is false and very dangerous, even deadly, for two reasons.

The first is that it fosters the fear of a warlike Islam which - combined with the perception of invasion due to poorly managed immigration policies - creates a fear of Islam, literally: Islamophobia. This idea feeds the radical far right and conspiracy mongers of all stripes[216] , as we have seen. But the media and the authorities turn a blind eye, preferring to let the myth of a conquering Islam, which seeks to destroy America, the West, Western civilisation or Christianity, develop.

The second is that it hides the real causes of terrorism and leads us to take inappropriate and even counterproductive measures. Since the early 2000s, intelligence agencies have been warning us that our interventions in the Middle East are generating terrorism and a threat on home soil. In April 2006, a *National Intelligence Estimate* (NIE) by the US intelligence community, classified as SECRET, found that the war in Iraq is directly contributing to the spread of jihadism around the world and has created a new generation of Islamic radicalism[217].

The same phenomenon is repeated in France after 2015, reflecting a serious ignorance of the strategic context and a denial of reality. There is a refusal to

---

213. Abu Mu'sab al-Suri, 'The Jihadi Experience - The Strategy of Deterring with Terrorism', Inspire, n° 10, Spring 2013, p. 29.

214. Op. cit. , p. 23.

215. Georges Benayoun & Rudy Reichstadt, «Complotisme : les alibis de la terreur», France 3, 23 January 2018 (47'25").

216. Antoine Hasday, «La pensée djihadiste décryptée», slate.fr, 6 November 2017.

217. «Trends in Global Terrorism: Implications for the United States", National Intelligence Estimate (NIE) NIE 2006-02R, Office of the Director of National Intelligence (ODNI), April 2006; Mark Mazzetti, "Spy Agencies Say Iraq War Worsens Terrorism Threat", The New York Times, 24 September 2006.

learn from the past, as the Islamic State jihadists themselves noted after the Paris attacks in November 2015:

> *The many benefits of these [Paris] operations will only be fully understood in the months to come and, more particularly, as a result of France's position and its inevitably stupid reaction. Indeed, if there is one thing that history has shown, it is that the crusaders do not learn from their failures against the mujahideen.*[218]

So the terrorists have understood very well that we do not learn from our mistakes and they use this loophole. Jihad is clearly understood as resistance. It is the incompetence of our services and the bad faith of our leaders that are responsible for the deaths in our countries. In two ways: by taking wrong, often illegal decisions without clear justification, and (at the very least) by engaging in these conflicts without having taken the basic measures to protect their own populations, knowing that a terrorist risk could result.

It goes even further by distorting the facts to maintain the idea that the EI began its operations in Europe before the Western strikes in the Middle East. For example, a joint report by the French DGSE and the *Canadian Security Intelligence Service* (CSIS), published in May 2017, attributes Mehdi Nemmouche's attack on the Jewish Museum in Belgium in May 2014 to the EI, stating that it «*well predates the US-led coalition's bombing of Daech, starting in August 2014 in Iraq, and September in* Syria»[219].Although its imprimatur states that it is not an «*analytical document and does not represent the official position of any of the participating agencies*», this report is a perfect example of the misinformation that aims to exonerate policymakers from their decisions. This attribution is simply based on the fact that an EI flag was found at his home. However, not only is this flag identical to the flag previously attributed to «al-Qaeda» (and therefore does not allow an attribution to the EI), but his act was never claimed by the EI and is not mentioned in any of its publications[220], which are used to glorify its fighters. It seems that during his trial in Brussels in February 2019, his links with the EI and his terrorist project were fabricated, mainly to justify Belgium's participation in the international coalition in Syria. In fact, the attack on the Jewish Museum in Belgium follows the same logic as

---

218. Dar al-Islam, n° 7, safar 1437, November 2015, p. 4.

219. Understanding Post-Daech, Publication No.° 2017-05-01, CSIS, May 2017.

220. To be perfectly accurate, there is a mention of this attack in issue 8 of Dar al-Islam magazine (January-February 2016), under the heading «In the words of the enemy», where the way in which Westerners view terrorism is presented. Mehdi Nemmouche is not presented as a terrorist linked to the Islamic State.

the attacks of Mohammed Merah: crimes with a vengeful character, but outside a terrorist logic.

Furthermore, it shows that Western services have not understood the way jihadist terrorism is articulated. By focusing on the EI, we tend to forget that it is only one of the multiple expressions of jihadism generated by the West and that the various groups fighting are not separated by hermetic partitions. Moreover, we can see, according to the Western strikes, transfers of fighters to less targeted groups... but whose modes of action are identical! The strategy of getting rid of the EI through air strikes is simplistic, not to say childish. As everywhere, Western interventions are not dimensioned and organised to fight populations in resistance. It seems that we are beginning (!) to realise that they only reinforce the will to defend and support - even passively - the jihadists, as in Afghanistan[221].

By ruling out from the outset that jihad could be a response to Western operations in the Middle East, the West is reduced to using its fantasies to explain terrorism, drawing on its historical perception of conflicts:

Jihad is a declaration of war on the entire West.[222]

Assuming this to be true, it is difficult to understand why the jihadists would seek to declare war on the whole world when they are already at war - and in a precarious military situation - on their own territory. Moreover, it would not explain why the EI would have set its sights on France, and not on Italy, which is the seat of Christianity.

As we will see below, the *Call for Global Islamic Resistance* has established a priority for operations that begins with the Levant and Arabian Peninsula region and extends into Muslim countries, while European countries are only listed in sixth place, and only insofar as they are engaged in an armed conflict with Islam.

After the 22 March 2016 attacks in Brussels, the claim of the EI clearly stated the reason for the attacks:

[...] We promise the crusader states that have allied themselves against the Islamic State dark days in response to their aggression against our state [...][223]

In its video released after the attack, the EI claims:

---

221. Julien Licourt, «Afghanistan: «The Taliban are much stronger than before the American intervention», lefigaro.fr, 11 March 2018.
222. Alain Finkielkraut, in the programme C à vous, «Finkielkraut face aux terroristes - C à vous - 23/11/2015», France5/YouTube, 23 November 2015 (03'20").
223. Official Islamic State claim, 12 Jumada al-Akhira 1437 (21 March 2016).

O Europeans, it was not the Islamic State that started fighting you. It was you who attacked us first, and the one who is starting is certainly more unjust. [You will pay the price when your present crusade breaks down and we attack you in the heart of your land. After that, you will never attack anyone again [...][224]

The same thing happened in Great Britain after the attack in Westminster (22 March 2017). Prime Minister Theresa May states:

The terrorist chose to strike in the heart of our capital, where people of all nationalities, religions and cultures gather to celebrate the values of freedom, democracy and freedom of expression.[225]

The French and Belgian press relayed the same message[226] , stressing the symbolic significance of the parliament. But they fail to explain the reason for the choice of this objective, which is clearly stated in an «after-action analysis», entitled *Message of the Operation*, published by the Islamic State on 23 March:

[...] This is certainly an important message to Britain: no matter how much you fortify and barricade yourselves, we will not stop fighting you, until you stop your aggression against us and leave the Muslims and their business alone.

[...] Just as the location of the operation «Parliament» carries a major meaning and allusion. Indeed, the British Parliament that approved the war against Iraq, in which thousands of Muslims were killed, is also the one that today approves the global war against the Mujahideen, among America's cursed servants. As a result, the place has been a political and military target par excellence. [227]

Thus, the Western press explained exactly the opposite of the reason given by the EI: it was not for its symbolic image that the parliament was targeted, but

---

224. Eye for an Eye video, Wilaya al-Furat, 27 March 2016.
225. «What is known about the attack on the outskirts of the London Parliament», lemonde.fr, 22 March 2017 (updated 23 March 2017).
226. See, for example: Philippe Bernard, 'À Londres, une attaque touche un symbole de la démocratie britannique', Le Monde, 23 March 2017; 'Attentat de Londres : Ayrault à la session du Parlement britannique', La Libre.be/AFP, 23 March 2017.
227. «The Individual Jihad Guidance Team», Inspire Guide - The British Parliament Operation in London, Global Islamic Media Front, 23 March 2017.

because it had not played its role of relaying the popular will and controlling the executive, and had not prevented an illegal and illegitimate war. Under the pretext of not spreading the terrorists' message, it was blurred and rendered illegible. If we are unable to curb terrorism, it is because we refuse to understand what it is.

2.6.3. France's Achilles heel: its reading of jihadist terrorism

The specificity of the French reading of jihadist terrorism in 2021 is explained by three factors:

- The presence of a large Muslim minority resulting from 60 years of poorly managed immigration, which has gathered in certain areas where delinquency has developed into a form of parallel economy. Sometimes called «lost territories of the Republic» or «lawless areas», some of these areas are poorly controlled and have become real hotbeds of identity. The deplorable treatment of this situation has generated a societal fracture that is now a facilitating factor for terrorism. It is the result of the lack of interest of the population and of politicians who preferred to let the situation deteriorate rather than give the impression of giving ground to the National Front. Today, the size of this Muslim minority gives the impression of a slow disappearance of the «native» French identity, which is part of the idea of a conquering Islam.

- There have been several series of attacks over the past 25 years, mostly by individuals of immigrant origin, which have no connection between them, but which give the impression of a common objective directed against France. We will come back to this.

- A sudden influx of refugees from the southern Mediterranean, simultaneously with the wave of jihadist attacks that hit France hard between 2015 and 2017.

These three elements are combined in various forms in the official reading of jihadist terrorism, maintaining the feeling of a kind of fatality that strikes the country in an unpredictable way. In fact, having not «prepared» its involvement in the Middle East in advance, France was forced to adopt a discourse based on the idea that terrorism is an exogenous and inevitable phenomenon against which nothing can be done:

The objective of the Islamic State? To start a civil war in France. [228]

---

228. Marie Lombard-Latune, «Gilles Kepel: 'The objective of the Islamic State? Déclencher une guerre civile en France», Le Figaro.fr, 14 December 2015 (updated 18 December 2015).

Assuming that the jihadists seek to divide France, what would be their purpose? Create a civil war? But with whom and to what end? There are no structures or organisations or even a revolutionary will capable of taking over from terrorist acts and exploiting them in a civil war mechanism, or even in a political dynamic. Even the social inequalities and cleavages that affect immigrant Muslim populations do not seem to have a sufficient mobilising effect to trigger a civil war. Thus, they did not exploit the 'Yellow Vests' movement of 2018-2019 in this sense. In fact, the jihadists have a very consistent discourse that never mentions the social dimension as a cause or motivation, which could serve as a catalyst for a mass movement. So there is something else.

The idea, propagated by Gilles Kepel, of a jihadism seeking to generate a civil war in France for the purpose of conquest is simply absurd, and is only an extrapolation of the principle of Marxist revolution, rearranged in the «Islamist sauce». Thus, his notion of «*Europe, the soft underbelly of the West*», which is the basis of this catastrophist - not to say «conspiracy» - interpretation- is wrong. The notion of 'soft underbelly' is not wrong, but its logic is very different from what Kepel asserts.

Wrongly - as we have seen - jihadists are inspired by the example of Madrid in 2004. They start from the (not false) idea that wars in the Middle East are waged against the will of Western populations. But they also understand that these wars do not arouse interest, compassion or reaction from the North American population. They consider the European populations to be more «receptive» («soft underbelly»), and that attacks can create sufficient pressure for them to demand the withdrawal of their troops. They see two factors for success: a) the presence of large Muslim minorities in the country and b) the unpopularity of the government. In 2015-2016, France met these criteria. This is why, despite contributing only 4.7% to the strikes in Iraq and Syria, it was hit harder than the US. So the idea of the «soft underbelly» has nothing to do with a global revolution!

In France, in the same vein, the book entitled *Gestion de la barbarie (Management of barbarism)*[230] , published in 2004 on the Internet, then translated into English in the United States and into French in 2007, is often cited, the title of which evokes sinister designs. The identity of its author, who uses the

---

229. Bérénice Dubuc, 'Attentats à Paris : diviser la société française, l'objectif ultime de Daesh', 20 minutes, 18 November 2015; Cédric Mas, president of the Institut Action Résilience in 'Terrorists seek to divide society, to create cleavages' according to Cédric Mas', Franceinfo/YouTube, 17 August 2017.
230. Abu Bakr Naji, Managing Barbarity - The Stage Islam Will Have to Pass Through to Restore the Caliphate, Paris Publishing, 2007, p. 250 (ISBN 978-2-85162-221-1).

pseudonym Abu Bakr Naji, is unknown. At first, it had only limited circulation, but from January 2015, its sales exploded in France, thanks to the «publicity» given by some «experts»[231] , who saw in it a plan to conquer the West.

In fact, published three years after the intervention in Afghanistan and one year after the beginning of the war in Iraq, it expresses the determination to resist the Western occupation, considered as a phase of «barbarism» from which the Iraqi population must be saved. There is no question of conquering the West, but of reconstituting *the Levant (Al-Sham)* that the West had divided by the Sykes-Picot agreements of 1916. That said, it probably inspired the architects of the EI, as it advocates the establishment of a caliphate and the carrying out of attacks against Western countries in order to make them renounce their interventions. Thus, these 'experts' have extrapolated a guide to resistance against the US-British occupier in Iraq into a manual for global conquest. This is a conspiracy theory that is widespread in France and follows on from Bat Ye'or's theories[232] about a «global caliphate».

Moreover, if we accept the existence of a hypothetical global project to transform Western society into a Muslim society, it is not clear what role the terrorist attacks would play in this process. The progression of Islam in Europe has been achieved through immigration largely consented to by the European countries themselves, and the contribution of bombs to this process would seem to go rather in the opposite direction...

The idea that France is being targeted for what it is, not what it does, is the result of the inability to question the policies of various governments and is fuelled by the perception of ever more invasive immigration. Even the «professionals» see it as the expression of a long-term project whose aim is to destroy France methodically:

There has been a [terrorist] continuum between 1995 and today.[233]

However, a closer look at the main 'waves' of attacks that have affected France shows that there is no continuum.

2.6.3.1. The 1995 attacks

The 1995 attacks had only vague claims in the name of the *Armed Islamic Group* (GIA) that were never really authenticated, condemning France's support for the Algerian regime. One of the claims even demanded the conversion

---

231. «We read for you the bedside book of jihadists», Les Inrocks, 29 November 2015, http://www.lesinrocks.com/2015/11/29/actualite/on-a-lu-pour-vous-le-livre-de-chevet-des-jihadistes-11790634/#.VlsO-WQ4DGI.twitter.
232. «Interview with Bat Ye'or on jihad', Dreuz Info, 15 November 2020.
233. Jean-Louis Bruguière, Le Grand Référendum, Sud-Radio, 19 April 2017.

of President Jacques Chirac to Islam within three weeks. In other words, the motives of these attacks were never clearly explained by their authors and their objectives remain a mystery to this day.

In French (and European) intelligence circles, it was suspected that the attacks were a 'false flag' operation designed to draw France into the civil war raging in Algeria, as President Jacques Chirac suggested in his memoirs:

> *Was this first transposition of the internal Algerian conflict onto our territory the work of the GIA, the victim having condemned the acts of violence committed against foreigners, notably French? Or was it the work of the Military Security, at a time when attempts to resume dialogue between the FIS and the government are far from being unanimously supported by the ranks of the Algerian army? The first possibility is the most likely. But it is difficult to rule out the second, insofar as the armed groups are often infiltrated and manipulated by the same Military Security in order to discredit the Islamists in the eyes of the population and the international community.*[234]

This cautious formulation reflects the desire not to poison the sometimes complicated relations between France and Algeria. But the testimony of Abdelkader Tigha, a former agent of the Algerian *Department of Intelligence and Security* (DRS), in his book *Françalgérie, crimes et mensonges d'Etats*, is clearer:

> *The anti-terrorist cooperation with the French did not work, reveals today the ex-adjudant Abdelkader Tigha. At the beginning of 1995, there were a few meetings in Lyon with my brother, a senior member of the judicial police in Blida, and Colonel Achour Boukachabia, head of the SDCI, the counter-intelligence, but the information we had, which came from simple interrogations, did not carry much weight. As a result, the French services did not want to help us. They told us that our information was «salad». They explained that they had to take into account public opinion, political parties, the justice system, that they couldn't do just anything, arrest just anyone. The Algerians came back angry and disappointed. Smaïl Lamari was looking for a way to encourage French politicians to help us. We needed intelligence, weapons, technical means, bomb detectors. That's when we decided to export some actions to France.*[235]

---

234. Jacques Chirac, Mémoires - Le temps présidentiel (tome 2), Nil, Paris, 2011.
235. Lounis Aggoun & Jean-Baptiste Rivoire, Françalgérie, crimes et mensonges d'Etats, La Découverte, Paris, 2005, p. 442.

Today, although the French government has decided to close the case for political reasons, it is quite clear that the attacks in France in the mid-1990s were a set-up and have nothing in common with the Islamist attacks of the 2000s, except that innocent people paid the price[236].

Whatever the instigators, the idea of a continuity between the attacks of 1995 and those of 2015-2016 in order to make people believe in a Muslim «plot» against the republic is irrelevant. As twenty years later, we are trying to explain the terrorist acts, but we are unable to identify coherent objectives. You cannot destroy a society with a few bombs if there are no powerful political structures behind these terrorist acts that are capable of taking over, even if only in terms of communication. But there is nothing like that in France.

In 1995, Algeria probably played on the inability of French services to understand the mechanisms of Islamist terrorism in an attempt to involve France in the Algerian conflict.

2.6.3.2. The Roubaix gang

We open a parenthesis here to mention the actions of the 'Roubaix gang'. They are often associated with a «continuum» of Islamist terrorism, particularly because of the bombing of a G7 meeting in Lille on 28 March 1996, but the reality is more prosaic. It is true that the protagonists were Muslims, ex-combatants in Bosnia and had had contacts with individuals linked to terrorism. But from that point on, one must remain cautious.

First of all, the attack did not target the meeting itself, but a police station in Lille on the eve of the event. No strategic objective could be identified: the Islamists were not anti-globalisationists.

Then, until then, the group had specialised in armed attacks on cash in transit and other crimes of a villainous nature. The Lille attack is therefore most likely an example of common law terrorism, aimed not at destroying French society and establishing Sharia law, but at intimidating the local police force, much like the Italian mafia did in the early 1980s.

Moreover, Jean-Louis Debré, the Minister of the Interior at the time, said:

> *It has nothing to do with Islamism, terrorism or the G7. So let's leave it at that!*[237]

The absence of a claim, a stated or identifiable political objective, or an organisation capable of taking over terrorist action, seems to confirm the Minister's

---

236. Guy Pervillé, 'Vingt ans après 1995 : les attentats de Paris, Lyon et Lille reconsidérés', figaro.fr, 24 July 2015.
237. Georges Moréas, Dans les coulisses de la lutte contreterroriste, Paris, First, 2016.

statements. The extent to which this case was sought to be «inflated» to a terrorist enterprise for political or corporate interests is an open question.

2.6.3.3. Mohammed Merah's attacks in 2012

According to Europol[238] , between 1997 and March 2012, many individuals suspected of belonging to (foreign) terrorist networks were arrested, but no jihadist terrorist attacks were prepared, prevented or carried out in France. Have the jihadists taken a break from their «fight against democracy» and their conquest of the West? In fact, at this stage, France is not in the jihadists' sights.

In March 2012, the crimes of Mohammed Merah seemed to mark a break, and the official discourse saw it as the starting point for the attacks that would strike France in 2015-2017 with the aim of fracturing French society. In fact, they opened a period in which two distinct phenomena manifested themselves in parallel in France: communitarian violence and terrorist attacks. These two phenomena have different origins and purposes, but draw their perpetrators from the same social pool. Thus, Merah's acts have the appearance and brutality of terrorist attacks, but they are not. Here is why...

According to Merah himself, these attacks had two targets: France and Israel. The assassination of three French soldiers (11 and 15 March 2012) is clearly motivated by the war the French army is waging in Afghanistan. Merah filmed these attacks and launched[239] :

You kill my brothers, I kill you!

The reasons for the attack on the Ozar Hatorah Jewish school in Toulouse (19 March 2012) were never really detailed in the media and were immediately labelled as antisemitic. In fact, a rhetoric that satisfies Jewish (or, more accurately, Zionist) organisations was simply adopted. But there is a danger that it hides the real reasons and prevents adequate preventive solutions.

Merah was undoubtedly antisemitic, but it was probably not antisemitism that was at the heart of his approach. The reasons that drove him to the crime are more specific. In fact, they are to be found in Gaza at the beginning of the month, as he himself explained by phone to Ebba Kalondo, editor-in-chief of *France 24*:

The Jews killed our brothers and sisters in Palestine![240]

---

238. See TESAT reports 2007-2017, Europol (www.europol.europa.eu/newsroom).

239. Maxime de Valensart, «Merah filmed the murders: 'You kill my brothers, I kill you'», 7sur7.be, 22 March 2012.

240. «The killer contacted France 24: «This is only the beginning», he said», France 24, 21 March 2012.

It refers to the Israeli strike on 9 March 2012 (Operation ECHO BACK) against Zohair al-Qaisi, Secretary General of the *Popular Resistance Committees (PRC)*, killing some 15 innocent civilians[241].It triggers Palestinian rocket fire, to which new air strikes respond. In total, 23 Palestinians were killed and 74 injured, and 23 Israelis were wounded[242].

The event seems quite 'banal' and - as usual - the French media have remained quiet about it. One may therefore wonder why they triggered such a desire for revenge in Merah. In fact, we don't know and we are reduced to hypotheses. The answer probably lies in the reaction of the French government, which did not go unnoticed. The Foreign Affairs communiqué of 10 March 2012 does not mention or condemn the initial Israeli strike, but only the Palestinian rocket fire that followed[243] :

> *We condemn the firing of rockets and the humanitarian consequences of this violence and deplore the civilian victims. France urges a return to calm and restraint in order to avoid an escalation that could again affect civilians. Our Consul General in Tel Aviv will visit Ashdod and Ashkelon on Sunday morning to express his solidarity.* [244]

Given the sensitivities of a part of the French population, one could have imagined a more measured and balanced reaction, if any at all.

Two years later, on 9 July 2014, during Operation PROTECTIVE BORDER, François Hollande repeated the same mistake with a message to Benjamin Netanyahu stressing that «it *is up to the Israeli government to take all measures to protect its population in the face of* threats»[245] thus showing his support for the application of the *Dahiya doctrine*, which we will see below. Despite a timid correction from the Élysée a few days later, this initial «cry from the heart» will remain in the memory of a large part of the French population[246].

To what extent this partisan position helped trigger Merah's criminal madness by provoking his outrage will remain a mystery, and emotion will label

---

241. The Guardian and The Washington Post, 10 March 2012.

242. See Article «March 2012 Gaza-Israel clashes», Wikipedia.

243. «Press release - Israel and the occupied Palestinian territories. All parties must protect civilians in Gaza and Israel following ceasefire announcement», Amnesty International, 13 March 2012.

244. Alain Gresh, «Gaza, Palestine et apartheid», Le Monde diplomatique, 11 March 2012 (http:// blog.mondediplo.net/2012-03-11-Gaza-Palestine-et-apartheid) (Original link to Foreign Affairs release: http://www.diplomatie.gouv.fr/fr/pays-zones-geo/israel-territoires-palestiniens/la-france-et-les-territoires/situation-dans-la-bande-de-gaza/article/nouvel-episode-de-violence-a-gaza.

245. Libération, 22 July 2014.

246. Grégoire Biseau and Jonathan Bouchet-Petersen, 'Soutien à Israël : Hollande ou le péché originel', Libération, 22 July 2014; 'Le soutien de Hollande à Israël agace une partie de la gauche', Le JDD, 11 July 2014.

his crimes as 'terrorist'. Yet, technically, they are not associated with a process of recurrent violence aimed at exerting pressure to achieve something, nor are they part of a political process with concrete and expressed objectives. In fact, they are essentially vengeful and communitarian in nature. While this does not make much difference in terms of horror and guilt, it does make a major difference in terms of how the problem is dealt with at the strategic level, as we shall see below.

Seen through the eyes of the intelligence community, Merah's crimes herald several problems that remain unresolved in France ten years later. First, this case shows that there has been little reflection at the head of the French state on the integration of Muslim sensitivities into its foreign policy decisions. Merah was just the tip of the iceberg of a population that feels - rightly or wrongly - an enemy in its own country, and which will provide the perpetrators of the 2015-2019 attacks. Secondly, it was a testimony to the depth of the societal fracture that affects France.

However, the Hollande government did not learn from this. By restricting its field of vision to anti-Semitism, it missed the real problems and opened the door to the attacks of 2015-2016. An objective and dispassionate understanding of the reasons why Merah and others committed their crimes does not excuse them, but could have allowed for a better preparation of the strategic context of the intervention in Iraq, and then in Syria, in order to guard against the attacks of 2015-2016 and the communitarian crimes of 2019-2020. By communicating better on the reasons and objectives of its external commitments, by better targeting the messages, by articulating operations around punctual missions rather than long-term missions with no end in sight and no strategy, by adapting the language concerning Israel, etc., the French government could have mitigated the exacerbation of the feeling of solidarity of certain radical French Muslim elements.

The inability to 'read' Merah's crimes is the result of the convergence of three phenomena: an exclusively police treatment of the case, the absence of strategic intelligence and authorities who lead ideologically, ignoring the opinion and sensitivities of a part of their own population. These same errors are at the root of the events of 2015-2016 (and later)...

2.6.3.4. The attacks of 2015 and beyond

2.6.3.4.1. The «official» explanations

In France, after the 2015 attacks, the reaction was one of blanket condemnation, rather than a search for rational explanations. At no time was the hypothesis raised that the attacks could be a response to Western interventions. The official rhetoric was a flight to the front, like the Americans in 2001: the finger was pointed at a conquering Islamism, which seeks to impose a model of society or an ideology against democracy, and therefore totalitarian. As in 2001, they tried to convince the international community that it was concerned, and to mobilise it. The United States had invoked Article 5 of the *NATO Charter*, France invoked - and thus activated for the first time - Article 42(7) of the *Treaty on European Union*[247].

In France, attributing an external cause to one's own mistakes seems to be a cultural trait, which can be found in other crises (such as the COVID crisis, for example). Thus, Manuel Valls immediately dismisses the responsibility of the government:

> *Make no mistake: a totalitarianism has struck France not for what it does, but for what it is.* [248]

A discourse relayed by researchers:

> *It is wrong to see Western military interventions as the main reason for jihadist terrorism.* [249]

To this fatalistic reading are added the reminiscences of the Marxist ideologies of the 1960s and 1980s, which see terrorism in a 'post-anticolonial' dynamic:

> *The strategy of global jihad was part of the genetics of all EI fighters [...]. They all dreamed of carrying out attacks in France [...]. We must therefore not link everything to France's external operations. [...] Historically, it is a former colonial power, particularly in the Maghreb [...] France is perceived as the enemy of Islam, with secularism and the law on the veil. Finally, it is an easier country to hit than Great Britain, which has a natural barrier with the English Channel.*[250]

---

247. «Activation of Article 42(7) of the Treaty on European Union: request for assistance by France and replies by Member States», European Parliament, 11 April 2016 (PDF).
248. Manuel Valls, 19 November 2015.
249. Bruno Tertrais, «Les interventions militaires, cause de terrorisme?», Foundation for Strategic Research, n°06/2016, 15 February 2016.
250. David Thomson, 'On the commandos who carried out the attacks on the evening of 13 November', Against, 15 November 2015.

Official explanations quickly focus on a revolutionary will, stemming from the social condition of the immigrant population[251] , to divide French society[252] , to fight against secularism[253] , or to abolish its freedoms:

«Charlie Hebdo»: terrorists wanted to kill freedom of expression. [254]

For others, it is a larger project of world conquest[255] , where the imagery of the crusades[256] is not far away. Thus, for the journalist Jean-Dominique Merchet:

We are faced with what could be called a revolutionary movement [...] which has chosen terrorism in a number of countries and armed struggle on its own territory. It is a revolutionary movement that mobilises thousands or even tens of thousands of young men throughout the world [...] These are people who have decided to attack the established order, the established international order, in the primary sense of the word, to overthrow it in the name of religious ideas. [257]

... and for Gilles Kepel, the EI seeks to :

[...] to create a civil war in Europe, now perceived as the soft underbelly of the West, by promoting a war of enclaves. Between the Islamised enclaves in the working class suburbs and the rest of the population to blow up the system from within. And establish the caliphate of Daech on the ruins of Europe. [258]

An argument taken up by the academician Alain Finkielkraut, on *France 5*:

---

251. Numerous articles. See in particular: «La sociologie de la radicalisation: entretien avec Farhad Khosrokhavar», Ressources en Sciences économiques et sociales, 10 January 2016, http://ses.ens-lyon. fr/articles/la-sociologie-de-la-radicalisation-entretien-avec-farhad-khosrokhavar-291659.
252. Bérénice Dubuc, «Attentats à Paris : Diviser la société française, l'objectif ultime de Daesh,» 20 minutes, November 18, 2015; Cédric Mas, President of the Action Resilience Institute, Franceinfo, August 17, 2017, https://www.youtube.com/watch?v=UzkKAJw52pY.
253. «Why France is the preferred target of jihadists», Europe 1, 17 November 2015.
254. Florence Gabay, «'Charlie Hebdo': the terrorists wanted to kill freedom of expression. Ils la renforcent «, L'Obs, 13 January 2015, http://leplus.nouvelobs.com/contribution/1303800-charlie-hebdo-les-terroristes-voulaient-tuer-la-liberte-d-expression-ils-la-renforcent.html.
255. Thierry de Montbrial, programme C dans l'air, France 5, 15 September 2017.
256. Numerous articles. See in particular: Michel Garrot, «Le califat - But ultime des djihadistes», LesObservateurs.ch, 30 March 2017.
257. Jean-Dominique Merchet, C dans l'air, France 5, 22 April 2017.
258. «Gilles Kepel: Daech wants to provoke a civil war in Europe», Ouest-France, 28 December 2015; Gilles Kepel, Terreur dans l'Hexagone, Gallimard, 2015.

One of the goals of the jihadists is to provoke a civil war, by putting the French population in a terrible state of nerves; and so they would like to provoke attacks on mosques, attacks on veiled women, even lynchings, so that there is a civil war.[259]

Not without a certain arrogance prevails the idea that Islamists target France because of its exemplary lifestyle and democracy. The philosopher and academic Alain Finkielkraut did not even hesitate to claim that on 13 November 2015, Islamists targeted café terraces because in France women can sit there and thus symbolise a model of society (!)[260]. There is no basis for this and it is simply silly.

The obsession with a Muslim plot against France has led some journalists to link the November 2015 attacks to the 22 February 2009 attack in Khan el-Khalili, Cairo, because some actors were involved in both events[261]. This is an example of the difference between strategic and tactical analysis. On the tactical level, we can find common points through certain people or the mention of the Bataclan as a possible objective. But at the strategic level, no similarities appear. Considered as «anti-French» by France[262] , the motives of the Cairo attack remain - in reality - unknown to this day and are more similar to an «anti-tourist» operation, directed against the Egyptian government, which had given in to American and Israeli pressure for its policy towards the Gaza Strip. This attack has the same characteristics as the one of 17 November 1997 in Luxor, which killed 36 Swiss citizens, but which was never considered «anti-Swiss».

In contrast, the November 2015 attacks in Paris were clearly 'anti-French' with clearly expressed motives: the strikes in Syria and Iraq. The fact that the Bataclan is mentioned in both cases at most lends credence to the idea that the jihadists have a sort of informal 'catalogue' of possible targets, peddled by rumour and hearsay. We will come back to this when dealing with the issue of civilian targeting.

Generally accepted as truths, these hypotheses correspond to an imagination based more on opinions and prejudices than on facts, without explaining the causes of the problem. For example, they do not explain the fact that Islamist terrorism suddenly and quite systematically hit Europe in 2014, after a lull of almost ten years!

---

259. Alain Finkielkraut in the programme C à vous («Finkielkraut face aux terroristes - C à vous - 23/11/2015»), France5/YouTube, 23 November 2015 (05'50").
260. Ibid.
261. In short, it is Farouk Ben Abbes, associated with the events of 2009, who is said to be close to an Islamic State jihadist, Fabien Clain ('Terrorisme: Des menaces d'attentats contre le Bataclan dès 2010', France-Soir, 16 December 2015).
262. Tangi Sala, «Un an après la mort d'une jeune Française, l'enquête n'est toujours bouclée», Le Figaro, 23 February 2010.

In reality, the wave of attacks that began in January 2015 was directly linked to poorly thought-out, poorly communicated and poorly prepared government decisions.

2.6.3.4.2. Locking in alternative explanations

In parallel to the official discourse, explanations that could have revealed clumsy political decisions were immediately blocked. Thus, at the ceremony commemorating the 9 January 2015 attack on the Hyper Cacher in Paris, Prime Minister Manuel Valls declared:

> *For these enemies who attack their compatriots, who tear up the contract that unites us, there can be no valid explanation. For to explain is already to want to excuse a little!* [263]

This has resulted in the ostracism of researchers and critics of French foreign policy. Government and media have thus discouraged an objective understanding of the terrorist and jihadist phenomenon, contributing 'hollowly' to its spread and leading to the failure of anti-radicalisation campaigns in France[264] and Belgium[265].

For example, in 2016, the French justice system sentenced a French citizen to six months in prison for having *consulted*[266] the website *«jihadology.net"*, which it considered a *«jihadist site»*[267].This site, linked to the *Washington Institute for Near East Policy*, is not considered to be an extremist or radical site and provides researchers with original documents from various jihadist movements. Its objective is precisely to facilitate the understanding of radical Islamist doctrines and it has quickly become an indispensable tool for the study of the jihadist phenomenon. It is managed by a researcher (of Jewish faith, and therefore - a priori - unlikely to be a jihadist...) who is also active in a number of academic and research media.

---

263. «For Valls, there can be no possible 'explanation' for the acts of jihadists», Le Figaro.fr, 9 January 2016.

264. Achraf Ben Brahim, 'Why de-radicalisation policies are a fiasco', The Huffington Post, 26 November 2016.

265. «Salafistische Islam en Wahhabitisch Proselytisme - Factoren en Vectoren van Radicalisering en Extremisme», OCAM, 24 October 2016.

266. Note here that in February 2017, the Constitutional Council decriminalised the consultation of jihadist sites (Martin Untersinger, «Le délit de consultation de sites terroristes censuré par le Conseil constitutionnel», Le Monde, 10 February 2017).

267. Pierre Alonso, 'Six mois ferme pour avoir consulté le site d'un chercheur sur le jihadisme', Liberation.fr, 18 November 2016.

Moreover, the viewing of videos published by the Islamic State, in which their motivations and claims are explained, are punishable in France[268].Everything possible has been done to ensure that the explanations - and therefore the possible solutions - for terrorist acts are beyond the reach of researchers. This has encouraged the stigmatisation of Muslims.

The philosopher Michel Onfray, whose statements critical of the French government's foreign policy on *BFM TV*[269] have been repeated in several EI videos, has also been the subject of virulent attacks from political and intellectual circles. Thus, Alain Finkielkraut takes his exact opposite view and vehemently denies any causal link between the attacks in France and Western interventions, castigating the slogan «*Your bombs, our dead*» which he assimilates to «*integral pacifism*», unscrupulously mixing the notions of «Islam» and «Islamism» and invoking the existence of Israel as a motive[270] .

In fact, we adapt the claims of terrorists to fit our perceptions. For example, after the *Charlie Hebdo* attack, the official French discourse totally obscured the fact that it had been supported by the *Arabian Peninsula Jihad Base* (APJB), as Chérif Kouachi had declared[271].It is then necessary to define a single enemy and justify the military engagement in Syria: the Islamic State is highlighted[272] , but this is not true. The difference is important and if we had had real strategists at the head of the state, the course of events could probably have been better managed. But with a government that worked in an ideological way, we went in a straight line towards disaster. The victims of 13 November 2015 will testify to this...

The press and media *never* report the full text of the claims of terrorist acts, which explain their motives precisely. As a result, the attacks are explained on the basis of interpretations that are sometimes byzantine, that confuse the facilitating factors and the causes, and whose sole purpose is to exonerate the West from its responsibilities.

2.6.3.4.3. The reality

After the attack of 13 November 2015, Stéphane T., one of the survivors of the Bataclan, reported the words of one of the terrorists, which very few media reported:

---

268. Andréa Fradin, «You thought you were watching Daesh videos incognito? Faites gaffe», L'Obs - Rue89, 24 July 2015.

269. Interview 24 May 2016, https://www.youtube.com/watch?v=BaELn7AJUvA.

270. Alain Finkielkraut in the programme C à vous («Finkielkraut face aux terroristes - C à vous - 23/11/2015», France5/YouTube, 23 November 2015 (02'15").

271. Audio message from the Kouachi brothers, YouTube, 9 January 2015, https://www.youtube.com/watch?v=KNFbfnPBKdY.

272. Jean-Pierre Filiu, 'Ten years after the death of Bin Laden, Al-Qaeda still mobilised against France', Le Monde, 2 May 2021.

You can thank President Hollande, because it is thanks to him that you are suffering this. We left our wives and children in Syria, under the bombs. We are part of the «Islamic State» and we are there to avenge our families and our loved ones for the French intervention in Syria.[273]

After the 14 July 2016 attack in Nice, the Islamic State published a small after-action analysis booklet, with the stated aim of inspiring other mujahideen and helping them to design their action. It confirms, once again, the strategic objective of the terrorist attacks:

Finally, we say that it is up to the French people to decide whether they want to continue to wage war against us or whether they will decide to stop their government's aggression against us? [...] We will continue to fight France until it stops meddling in the affairs of Muslims and plundering their wealth directly or indirectly.[274]

Thus, our politicians, our intellectuals and our media have made up a story: the reason for the 2015 and 2016 attacks in France was neither Islam, nor the desire to create a civil war in France, nor an obscure revolutionary project, but simply to stop the French intervention in Iraq and Syria. As we have seen, British intelligence services - with whom French services have regular contacts - had clearly established a causal relationship between Western interventions in the Middle East and jihadist terrorism. Despite this, French 'intellectuals' show an incomprehensible determination to deny the evidence.

Apart from its participation in the international coalition, the three reasons why France has been hit more by the EI than other countries are very clear, and largely explained by the terrorists themselves. The first is that France has been much more 'loudly' engaged than other coalition countries. The second is the unpopularity of the Hollande/Valls government, which the jihadists thought they could exploit to provoke a withdrawal from the coalition, as in Spain after the Madrid attack. The third is that the jihadists discerned a deep rift in France between the Muslim community and the rest of society, which favoured the recruitment of militants.

Thus, if the French government had really wanted to protect its population and acted strategically, it would have accompanied its intervention with greater discretion, it would have sought to «win the hearts and *minds*» of its Muslim minority, it would have avoided confusing peripheral struggles (burkini,

---

273. Interview by Alexandre Fache, «Deux heures trente avec les terroristes du Bataclan», humanite.fr, 17 November 2015.
274. «Nice Operation, France», Inspire Guide, 17 July 2016.

headscarves, Dieudonné, etc.) with the fight against terrorism, and above all, it would have taken measures to protect the population before the interventions. None of this was done: the government acted out of touch with reality, out of blind ideology, without any reflection...

Indeed, it is significant that the multiple attack of 13 November 2015, which shook French politics to the point of prompting the government to request military assistance from the European Union[275] , made only a few lines in *Dabiq* (the 'official' organ of the Islamic State) at number thirteen, after twelve other operations in Syria, Sinai and elsewhere[276].

2.6.3.4.4 Explanation

The inability to fight terrorism effectively is linked to the inability to understand its true nature. The intellectual incapacity of the French political, parliamentary and judicial authorities is illustrated by the multiple interpretations of the phenomenon of radicalisation and its link with terrorism: prisons, Salafist mosques, poverty, criminality, unemployment, Islam and madness are all mentioned in turn. Yet none of these 'causes' appears systematically and decisively in the various attacks.

This inability to understand the nature of terrorism leads us to perceive the fundamentalists, the Salafists[277] , the Muslim Brotherhood, and even Iran[278] (!), as guilty and to lump them together in a common project of Islamisation of France.

These 'explanations' echo a very 'Israeli' reading of terrorism, which excludes any political or 'negotiable' cause: its causes are said to lie in the nature of Islam itself[279].Terrorism is thus seen as inescapable, destined to conquer the West and destroy its 'values' by relying on structured organisations such as the Muslim Brotherhood. The latter seem to crystallise the fantasies of French 'experts'. But these accusations are not based on any concrete facts. Moreover, even the «experts» heard by the members of the Senate contradict themselves[280]. In Germany, where the perception of the problem is less emotional and more analytical, the intelligence services note that the Muslim Brotherhood numbers

---

275. «Mutual defence clause invoked by France: what is it about?», European Parliament, 20 January 2016.

276. Dabiq Magazine, n° 12, p. 28.

277. «Valls: a Salafist 'minority' 'winning the battle' of Islam in France», LEXPRESS.fr/AFP, 4 April 2016.

278. François Colcombet (President of the Foundation for Middle East Studies), «La 'terreur noire' et sa racine historique en Iran», Huffingtonpost.fr, 5 October 2016.

279. Antoine Hasday, «La pensée djihadiste décryptée», slate.fr, 6 November 2017.

280. Report of the Commission of Inquiry into the responses of the public authorities to the development of Islamic radicalisation and the means of combating it, Senate, 7 July 2020, Document No. 595.

only 1,040 individuals out of a total Muslim population of some 4.4 million. Furthermore, they note that :

> *The supporters of the Muslim Brotherhood in Germany act in a non-violent way. They try to spread their understanding of Islam through the work of da'awah.*[281]

In France, the contribution of «experts» and other «intellectuals» seems to be guided more by a desire for revenge than by a concern that this not be repeated. This is why the various trials carried out against terrorists and radicalised individuals have not helped to solve the problem, quite the contrary: the problem is not so much the rigour of the sentences imposed as the ideological reading given by a justice system that is more myopic than blind.

As in many European countries, the French approach is explained by an overly police culture, which understands terrorism through its modus operandi and not through its causes. Yet even when they have similar characteristics and modus operandi, terrorist attacks have their own logic.

Thus, in the 1980s, terrorism could be fought as a criminal phenomenon, without having to understand its deep mechanisms, because there were none. In 2017, Judge Jean-Louis Bruguière, who had successfully investigated many cases of terrorism in the 1980s and 2000s, is totally out of step with the Islamist terrorism of today:

> *Fundamentally, what is the cause of all this [...] I think there are other elements that are much more fundamental than the rather circumstantial element of the commitment of France and other countries against Daech in Syria and Iraq. [...] I have made an in-depth study of these causes. We have to go back to the basics. We are faced with organisations that for thirty years, practically since Abdul Azzam, have had a fundamental political agenda, which is to destroy the West and our values. It's a fight against our values. That's what's important, because they want to substitute their values for ours. [...] Today, what they want to destroy is democracy. There is no doubt about it. Because they cannot accept it. The only acceptable, legitimate law is Sharia law.*[282]

---

281. Antwort der Bundesregierung auf die Kleine Anfrage der Abgeordneten Martin Hess, Dr. Bernd Baumann, Dr. Gottfried Curio, weiterer Abgeordneter und der Fraktion der AfD (Drucksache 19/7182), Gefährdung der Bundesrepublik Deutschland durch die Muslimbruderschaft (Drucksache 19/7570), Deutscher Bundestag, February 7, 2019 (question 17).
282. Jean-Louis Bruguière in the programme Le Grand Référendum, Sud Radio, 19 April 2017.

Other experts continue to understand terrorism through the experiences of the 1960s and 1980s. But the Marxist terrorism of that time had a revolutionary vocation: it sought to replace one system with another, with the support of the population. So there was a process that is not found in any form in jihadist terrorism, simply because it does not seek to replace a system, but to stop an intervention. The problem for Westerners is that by admitting this reality, we also admit that we are the aggressor!

In France, since 2015, the same recipe as Israel has been applied and attempts have been made to present Islamist terrorism in the context of a societal conflict that would be the expression of an inescapable conflict between Islam and French society, and which can only be resolved by violence. This *deliberate* attempt to confuse the two forms of terrorism is at the root of most of the French victims of terrorism.

An attack always seeks to achieve an objective, according to a «logic», which is the *strategy of* the terrorist group. Everything must be coherent. How could an attack divide France to the point of creating the conditions for a civil war? How could the same attack destroy our values? If the objective of the jihadists is to bring down democracy, why don't they take advantage of the Yellow Vests crisis to achieve it? Assuming that an attack could trigger an insurrectionary mechanism, which forces could take over from the terrorists? Finally, if the objective is to recreate the caliphate, why attack France which has never been part of it?

2.6.3.4.5. Consequences of ignorance

The obsession with associating terrorism with religion has led France to use the lever of secularism. This has resulted in sterile discussions (on the Islamic veil, the burqa or, even more absurdly, the burkini) which have only had a counter-productive effect on terrorism by deepening the divide between communities. The fact that after the attacks of 2015, the immigrant population in France, even though they largely disapproved of the terrorists' method, had a fairly broad sympathy for their cause[283] was totally ignored.

The politicians who have initiated - and fanned - this debate have understood nothing about the asymmetric nature of terrorism. In fact, this attempt at societal smoothing tends to reinforce a «nationalistic» dimension, which - in the Muslim community - tends to generate «Islamism».

The lack of serious analysis of the causes and objectives of terrorism has led to the exploitation of the widespread fear of cultural and ethnic submergence into a form of Arabism or Islamophobia, which cuts across all political tendencies. In the run-up to the 2017 presidential elections, the debate on terrorism took a political turn that did not allow for a calm analysis and treatment of the issue.

---

283. "Paris through the eyes of IS supporters", religionfactor.net, 24 November 2015.

Practically all the candidates took up the discourse of the former National Front in different forms, with the perverse effect of increasing tensions between the Muslim population and «native France».

Many commentators were then shocked by President Hollande's use of the word «war». However, whatever the reasons, it was the West that declared war on the Islamic State back in September 2014 - giving it a status it should not have had. *Le Figaro* online headlined *«In Paris, the allies declare war on the Islamic State»*[284].A few days later, François Hollande recalled this declaration of war before the United Nations General Assembly in New York:

> *Our best response to this threat, to this aggression, is national unity in this war, for it is a war, against terrorism.*[285]

However, at this stage, France had not yet been hit by the EI, which did not constitute a threat to the West (since the Americans had to 'invent' the Khorasan group). The reason for this declaration of war, whose objective was never really defined and which varied over the months, was never really questioned either in parliament or among the population.

On social networks, the terrorists' supporters did not rely on religious arguments, but on geostrategic considerations. More precisely, the religious argument supported the geostrategic reasoning, not the other way around. The 2015 Paris attacks were frequently referred to as *«ghazawat»* (razzias), a military term that refers to the raids conducted by the followers of Mohammed in the seventh century[e] [286] , and which continues to designate the inter-tribal operations that can be observed in North Africa or Darfur, for example. Thus, we have a violence that finds its justification throughout the history of Islam, but which does not have a religious objective in itself. This reasoning is not very different from that of certain Western countries (United States, Great Britain, France, Germany), which accept and exploit the use of torture in the name of human rights and Western values[287].The collateral victims of Western bombing in Afghanistan, Pakistan, Iraq, Syria, Yemen, etc., are recurrent topics in the messages and claims of Islamist organisations, not the spread of the faith.

In France, there is not only a denial of the relationship between Western interventions and terrorism, but even a total denial of the reality of French strikes as early as 2014, prior to the 2015-2016 attacks[288].The result is an image

---

284. Isabelle Lasserre, «À Paris, les alliés déclarent la guerre à l'État islamique», lefigaro.fr, 15 September 2014.

285. Cordélia Bonal, «Is France really at 'war'?», Libération, 26 September 2014.

286. "Paris through the eyes of IS supporters", religionfactor.net, 24 November 2015.

287. No Questions Asked, Human Rights Watch, June 29, 2010.

288. See Jean-Louis Filiu, programme C à dire, France 5, 1er December 2016.

of terrorism that strikes for no reason, with the only justification being that we exist.

This is, moreover, the same interpretation that is needed to explain other terrorist attacks: after the Barcelona attack in August 2017, speaking of Islamist terrorism, the journalist François Clémenceau said:

> *Few people know that between 2004 and 2017 there have been dozens of foiled attacks in Spain and that hardly a week or month goes by without cells being dismantled, people being arrested, people being expelled.* [289]

It implies that jihadist terrorism has been part of the Spanish environment since the Madrid bombing in 2004. While it is true that during this period the Spanish government arrested dozens of individuals suspected of being associated with jihadist movements, Europol reports confirm that during the same period Spain was not the object of any Islamist attack or attempted attack. In fact, these were mainly arrests, in the framework of international cooperation against terrorism, of individuals seeking to leave for Iraq or Syria[290]. This is just one example of a manipulation that aims to decouple attacks from Western military interventions.

This refusal to accept terrorism as it is - such as calling the Islamic State «DAECH» - and the reality of its causes, in fact reflects our fear of facing it head-on.- and the reality of its causes actually reflects our fear of facing up to it. Moreover, the refusal of a causality between Western military action and terrorism implies the search for other explanations, which are ultimately found in the very nature of Islam, thus constituting a real conspiracy against Muslims[291] , by lending them the project to subjugate the West. The responsibility of Russia in this enterprise is even added in a fallacious and primitive way[292] !

The problem of the misreading of Islam and Islamism in France leads to polarisation of positions: it encourages aggressiveness and a discourse - widely relayed in the mainstream media - against Islam that is confused with anger against terrorism. This aggressiveness in turn generates identity and community reflexes that are sometimes violent. The first measure against these phenomena would be to have more objective and factual information on Islam, and not approximations. The fact that violent discourse is associated with the Koran is contradicted by anyone who has lived in Muslim countries. This is the famous case of a young French Internet user, who would probably not have uttered the insults against Islam if she had received more

---

289. See François Clémenceau, programme C dans l'air, France 5, 18 August 2017.
290. See TESAT reports 2007-2017, Europol (www.europol.europa.eu/newsroom).
291. Antoine Hasday, «La pensée djihadiste décryptée», slate.fr, 6 November 2017.
292. See Jean-Michel Carré, Putin, le Nouvel Empire (documentary), La Une, RTBF, 30 November 2016.

objective information about it. The fact that these insults are received with a certain complacency pushes some weak minds to a violent reaction, as we will see below.

2.6.3.5. *The attacks of 2020-2021*

On 25 September 2020, while the trial of the «helpers» of the 2015 attacks was taking place - referred to in the press as the «*Charlie Hebdo* trial» - and after the republication of the Mohammed cartoons on 2 September, two employees of a TV production agency were attacked with a knife near the former Charlie Hebdo premises.- and after the republication of the Mohammed cartoons on 2 September, two employees of a TV production agency were attacked with knives near the former premises of *Charlie Hebdo*. The perpetrator, an 18-year-old Pakistani, had arrived in France in August 2018 and had shown «*no signs of radicalisation» while in the care of* child *welfare»*[293].

On 16 October 2020, in Conflans-Sainte-Honorine, Samuel Paty, a teacher who had shown the *Charlie Hebdo* cartoons to his pupils during a lesson on freedom of expression, was beheaded by Abdouallakh A. Anzorov, a young Chechen, who had arrived as a refugee in France in March 2020 and was «*totally unknown to the anti-terrorist services»*[294].In his tribute speech to Paty on 21 October, President Emmanuel Macron stated that «*we will not give up on caricatures, on* drawings»[295] , while he published a series of tweets that unleashed the anger of crowds in the Muslim world[296].

On 29 October 2020, a young Tunisian man aged 21 killed three people in the Basilica of Notre-Dame de l'Assomption in Nice. Having arrived on the island of Lampedusa in September 2020 thanks to the services of an NGO, then entered France illegally and arrived in Nice on 27 October, the killer was «*unknown to the* intelligence *services»*[297].

In addition to these three attacks on French soil, there was a knife attack in Morges (Switzerland) on 24 September by an individual of Turkish origin and a gun attack in Vienna on 2 November by Kujtim Fejzulai, of Macedonian origin.

This accumulation of violence gives the image of a terrorist wave. However, none of these acts have been claimed by a terrorist organisation. Shortly before

---

293. «Charlie Hebdo: The main suspect «accepts his act»», www.lecho.be/economie-politique/europe/general/charlie-hedbo-le-principal-suspect-assume-son-acte/10253947.html.

294. «Teacher beheaded in Conflans-Sainte-Honorine: 'he was murdered because he was teaching students about freedom of expression', says Emmanuel Macron», francetvinfo.fr (live - no date); Jean-Michel Décugis & Jérémie Pham-Lê with Timothée Boutry & Ronan Folgoas, 'Enseignant décapité à Conflans : l'assaillant n'était pas sur le radar de l'antiterrorisme', leparisien.fr, 16 October 2020 (updated 17 October 2020).

295. Speech by the President of the Republic, national tribute to the memory of Samuel Paty, 21 October 2020, www.diplomatie.gouv.fr.

296. Justine Daniel, «Caricatures : Paris affiche sa fermeté face aux appels au boycott», liberation.fr, 26 October 2020.

297. «Nice attack: what we know about the knife attack», France24.com, 30 October 2020.

he was shot, Anzorov explained his act on Twitter by «insulting» the prophet Mohammed. The Morges attack appears to be the work of an unbalanced person. As for the Vienna attack, it appears to be an individual act, even if the perpetrator declared himself a member of the Islamic State before being shot; **moreover**, the Amaq press agency only reported the attack, but without claiming a link with the terrorist organisation.

Even if these crimes have a clear similarity with previous attacks (such as the one in Saint-Étienne-du-Rouvray on 26 July 2016, for example), or even commonalities (the publication of the *Charlie Hebdo* cartoons), they are not terrorism. As we have seen, terrorism is the juxtaposition of attacks, the repetition of which must lead to the achievement of an objective. However, the 2020 attacks are essentially punitive and vengeful, without being associated with a strategic objective. In fact, these attacks are more similar to the crimes of Mohammed Merah in 2012, they are more about «mass murder» or «communal crime» than terrorism.

The beheading of a contractor in Saint-Quentin-Fallavier, in June 2015, or the killing of the police headquarters (PP) in Paris, in October 2019, have - also - the appearances and the staging of terrorist crimes. But in the first case, Yassin Sahli, the perpetrator of the crime, will claim that it is a personal matter[298] ; and the second shows no link between the killings and an Islamist objective[299]. Moreover, the report by Françoise Bilancini, director of intelligence at the PP[300] tends to indicate an outburst of violence, as is regularly seen in the United States, probably linked here to a form of harassment by colleagues. In this case, the crimes are neither terrorist nor communitarian, but the perpetrators wanted to give them a terrorist appearance. Their reasons are unclear, but it is probably a question, in their minds, of giving a more «noble» character to their crime by creating the illusion that they are obeying a higher objective.

The distinction between these different forms of crime is far from academic, as the treatment of each requires different tools. As we shall see, terrorism can also be dealt with through its objectives and foreign policy measures, while communal crime requires a societal response. The former can be dealt with in the short to medium term, while the latter can only be tackled in the long term.

That said, we note that the crime of Saint-Quentin-Fallavier received only modest media coverage, whereas that of Samuel Paty was covered in a loop in our media. Yet, it is the same horror, which has not been claimed by any terrorist movement. One can discern in this differentiated treatment the evil

---

298. Caroline Politi, «Attentat en Isère : «Le motif personnel n'exclut pas l'action terroriste»», Lexpress.fr, 30 June 2015.
299. «Attack at the police headquarters: the EI evokes the facts but does not claim responsibility», lexpress.fr, 11 October 2019.
300. https://drive.google.com/file/d/16BTR1r6mRQ8SLnu--NCb6B_DVOOjYPm5/view.

that affects French society: an emotional approach that does not focus on the facts, but on their perception. This is why France is condemned to live with increasing violence in its midst, which will continue to manifest itself in terrorist or communitarian acts...

The problem is that the French intelligence and security services - guided by an ideological perception of the problem, largely conveyed by the media - have understood absolutely nothing about the nature of the threat. There is no systematic and methodical approach to the fight against the various forms of violence, including terrorism.

Differentiation of individual acts of violence

	Individual crime	Communal crime	Jihadist terrorist act
Nature of the objective	Punishment, revenge	Punishment, revenge	Strategic
Recurrence	Single Act	Single Act	Recursive act
Nature of the problem	Staff	Societal	Strategic/political
Solutions field	Psychiatric, criminal	Society, social	Foreign policy
Solution Horizon	Medium to long term	Medium to long term	Short to medium term

Table 4 - Strategic criteria for comparing different types of jihadist-looking violence

2.6.4. Radicalisation - a poorly understood phenomenon

Understanding the nature of jihadist terrorism is the key to deciphering the mechanism of radicalisation. Yet, having become one of the pillars of the fight against terrorism, the fight against radicalisation seems to almost systematically turn into a failure, as shown by the adventure of the only 'de-radicalisation' centre in France, which opened in September 2016 and closed in February 2017, after taking in nine residents, none of whom completed their 'treatment'[301].

The main reason is that we are fighting a problem defined by our prejudices and not by reality. Radicalisation is often *de facto* seen as a phenomenon that stands on its own, without reason and without purpose. The problem is described in a fanciful way, without any intellectual rigour, as if we wanted to perpetuate it:

Radicalisation is not just about challenging or rejecting the established order. Jihadist radicalisation is driven by the desire to replace democracy with a theocracy based on Islamic law (Sharia) using violence and weapons. It

---

301. «Closure of France's only 'deradicalisation' centre», Le Monde.fr/AFP, 28 July 2017.

therefore implies the adoption of an ideology that provides a framework for life and benchmarks to guide all behaviour. Radicalised people divide men and women into two categories: those who share their cause and those who do not and are, as such, called to die.[302]

This is a false, imbecilic reading, which is not found in the messages of jihadist groups and which is in flagrant contradiction with the less religious character observed in captured terrorists. A major weakness of the system put in place in France after the 2015 attacks is that it tends to confuse the causes of terrorism with the factors that facilitate the act. Thus, the *National Plan for the Prevention of Radicalisation (PNPR)*[303] , presented by Prime Minister Édouard Philippe in February 2018, shows a simplistic and backward-looking reading of the problem. Not only are its measures shaped from a Marxist analysis of the problem, but it limits itself to a multidisciplinary, not holistic, approach. Clearly, it proposes to act *after* individuals have been radicalised and does not see this mechanism as a process that can be influenced.

As a prelude, it should be recalled that an insurgent and/or terrorist process involves three circles of individuals:

- *sympathisers*, who are not formally affiliated to an organisation, but are aware of its cause and share its motivations, without necessarily approving its objectives or methods. They form the recruitment base of the movement;

- *Activists*, who belong to the close circle of active terrorists and provide them with concrete support without being directly involved in the action;

- *Activists*, who are the terrorists who are active or ready to take action, and sacrifice their lives for the cause.

In the European Marxist revolutionary movements of the Cold War years, the proportion of sympathisers could be estimated at 60-80%, that of militants at 10-30% and activists at 1-3% depending on the group and its cause. Obviously, these proportions varied according to the movements and their geostrategic context.

For Islamist movements, however, it must be taken into account that their popular base goes far beyond national borders. With the doctrine of «*jihad by individual terrorism*" (JIT), based on information gathered through social networks, the following proportions can be estimated: about 97-99% sympathisers, 1-2% militants and 1% activists. The particularity of the «open jihad» (which the EI claims to be and which we will see below) is that it has made

---

302. http://www.stop-djihadisme.gouv.fr (quoted in Rapport d'information, de la Commission des lois constitutionnelles, de la législation et de l'administration générale de la République sur les services publics face à la radicalisation, Éric Diard and Éric Poulliat, Assemblée nationale, 27 June 2019, p. 10).
303. «Prévenir Pour Protéger» - Plan national de prévention de la radicalisation, Matignon press service, 23 February 2018.

the limits between the three circles permeable, with a progressive erasure of the notion of «militant».

Beyond the figures, the important thing here is to note that there are basically three «publics», with different degrees of propensity to act. The problem is that in the hysteria that followed the Paris attacks, all of them were lumped together, including «antisemites». We didn't understand anything. Emotion and the desire for revenge - clearly more present in France than elsewhere - guided the action, without strategy, without a clear line, thus paving the way for the following attacks. The fight against terrorism must be cold, but not blind.

In the 1950s, during the communist insurgency in Malaya, the psychological warfare expert F.H. Lakin studied the interrogation of 430 prisoners and over 2,800 young men across the country. He found that only 8 per cent were convinced communists, 24 per cent generally adhered to the aims of communism, 47 per cent had been lured by promises of material benefits and 21 per cent had virtually no political awareness. Moreover, Lakin found that the bulk of the terrorists joined the movement for fear of being considered traitors and of being subjected to violence by the communists[304].In subsequent conflicts, such as Vietnam, no extensive and wide-ranging studies of the psychology of terrorists have been carried out and Lakin's work remains valuable, despite the obvious changes in the nature of insurgent warfare.

The main challenge in the fight against radicalisation is therefore to stop the process of sympathisers sliding into activism. However, Westerners have been more interested in how individuals join the EI than in their reasons and degree of commitment. The Israeli view was adopted, which postulates that anything remotely related to a terrorist is considered terrorist: this satisfies feelings of revenge, but does not lead very far - as we saw in the trials of Abdelkader Merah and Jawad Bendaoud - and does not allow for the implementation of effective strategies.

At this point, two mechanisms must be distinguished: the expansion of the EI in the Middle East (2014-2016) and the development of terrorism in the West. The former is an 'open' confrontational dynamic, the latter is a clandestine struggle in support of the former.

Operationally, as with the expansion of the Taliban (1994-1996), we can see that the EI has spread by 'contagion'. In Syria, *Jabhat al-Nosra* developed in the wake of the *Free Syrian Army* supported by the United States and France, and then the EI spread in exactly the same areas by gradually «phagocytising» *Jabhat al-Nosra*. This would tend to show an evolution similar to what Lakin observed

---

304. F.H. Lakin, Psychological Warfare research in Malaya 1952-55, Army Operational Research Establishment, UK Ministry of Defence, Paper to the 11th Annual UA Army Human Factors Research and development Conference, October 1965, report in Peter Watson, War on the Mind, Hutchinson & Co Publishers, London, 1978, p. 349.

in Malaysia: it is not ideological adherence that determines the development of the movement, but a kind of societal pressure that somehow places the «truth» on the side of the stronger.

The lack of a credible alternative and the determination of the movement are often enough to attract militants. In movements that conduct an open insurgency (*'open-front jihad'* or OFJ), supporters and a large proportion of militants do not fully adhere to the organisation's objectives, but are drawn into its wake by the pressure of their environment. This mechanism can be compared with the remark of the author's driver in Kabul in 2008:

> *We don't like the Taliban, but if we have to choose between the West and them, we will choose the Taliban.*

This explains the rapid expansion of the movement, virtually without fighting. In conflicts where a movement's centre of gravity is associated with its legitimacy (real or perceived), this is a critical vulnerability. In Syria, the Russians have understood this subtle mechanic and are attempting to exploit this critical vulnerability of the IE with a *Centre for Reconciliation of Warring Parties on the Territory of the Syrian Arab Republic* (CRPB) that has allowed cities to be 'dropped' without significant fighting.

2.6.4.1. The mechanism of radicalisation

The phenomenon of radicalisation has been the subject of much more serious and critical studies in the United States and Britain than in continental Europe, which have identified a fairly consistent process of radicalisation that includes several components:

- A *driving force*: indignation. In essence, it is irrevocably associated with Western action in the Middle East, which is often understood as action against the Muslim population. This indignation is fuelled first and foremost by the 'collateral damage' of Western interventions since 1990, but also 'benefits' from the bickering of everyday life, police abuses and violence, and the 'double standards' felt in relation to other communities (especially the Jewish community)[305] .

- An *element of strategic cohesion*: nationalism[306] , where the word 'nationalism' should not be understood in a Western sense, but as belonging to a community

---

305. Behavioural Science Unit Operational Briefing Note: Understanding radicalisation and violent extremism in the UK, Security Service - MI5 (UK RESTRICTED), Report BSU 02/2008, 12 June 2008.
306. Rausch C. Cassandra, "Fundamentalism and Terrorism", Journal of Terrorism Research 6(2); DOI: http://doi.org/10.15664/jtr.1153, 2015; Report of the Defense Science Board Task Force on Strategic Communication, Office of the Under Secretary of Defense For Acquisition, Technology, and Logistics, Department of Defense, Washington, D.C. 20301-3140, September 2004.

of thought (community of believers). It generates a feeling of solidarity between those fighting on the battlefield and their 'brothers' in the rest of the world. Just as the 2015-2016 attacks in France strengthened national cohesion and stimulated nationalistic - even extremist - behaviour across the political spectrum, Western interventions in the Middle East have strengthened ties within the Muslim community and encouraged extreme positions. At the end of 2014, Italian researchers analysed the flow of messages (in Arabic) on social networks and showed that support for the Islamic State was then stronger in Europe than in Syria itself! The proportion of positive messages towards the EI was distributed as follows: Belgium: 31%; Great Britain: 23.8%; USA: 21.4%; France: 20.8%; Canada: 15.3%; Italy: 9.8%. On the other hand, the same study showed that negative feelings towards the Islamic State after the attacks were only 4.7 per cent, while positive feelings were 37.5 per cent, mainly because the EI was seen as a defender of Islam in the face of foreign intervention[307].

- An *element of doctrinal cohesion*, which legitimises the nature of the action: religion. This is more of an 'operating software' than a deep religious aspiration. Doctrinal elements that derive from this include the higher reason for accepting collateral casualties, the value of self-sacrifice, the importance of intention over outcome, and the notion of victory.

- One *objective*, which has remained constant, identical and clearly expressed on the occasion of each jihadist attack since 1990: to put an end to Western interventions and bombings in the Middle and Near East[308].

It is also important to understand that the combination of these various elements does not occur in a linear fashion, as a Western mind would. Paradoxically, to put it simply, even opponents of the Syrian or Iraqi regime will have an antipathy towards Western strikes. This explains the sympathy that the EI enjoys overall, even though the vast majority of Muslims disapprove of its methods.

After the attack of 7 July 2005, concerned about his political future, Prime Minister Tony Blair denied any link between the war in Iraq and terrorism[309]. But on 2 April 2006, the British *Security Service* (MI5) explained in a classified SECRET report:

---

307. Shiv Malik, "Support for Isis stronger in Arabic social media in Europe than in Syria"', The Guardian, 28 November 2014.
308. Report of the Defense Science Board Task Force on Strategic Communication, Office of the Under Secretary of Defense For Acquisition, Technology, and Logistics, Department of Defense, Washington, D.C. 20301-3140, September 2004.
309. Matt Dathan, "Iraq war not to blame for 7/7 bombings, insists Tony Blair", The Independent UK, 7 July 2015.

Iraq is likely to be an important factor in the radicalisation of British Muslims for some time to come, and for extremists who see attacks on the UK as legitimate.[310]

This analysis was taken up ten years later by the report of the parliamentary commission of enquiry into the conditions of Britain's entry into the Iraq war (Chilcot Commission)[311].But it was totally ignored by the French government, which entered the Middle East conflict without any accompanying measures to protect its own population.

Thus, the Western deployment in the Middle East and Afghanistan between 2001 and 2014 not only had no deterrent effect on the willingness of Islamists to engage in terrorism, but on the contrary had a multiplier effect on the willingness to fight the West. And the phenomenon was further accentuated with the announcement of the US and French bombing of Iraq and Syria from summer 2014: according to a UN Security Council report published in May 2015, the number of foreign volunteer fighters in these countries increased by 71% between summer 2014 and March 2015[312].In summer 2014, there were an estimated 15,000 foreign fighters from 80 countries. By the summer of 2015, 30,000 fighters from 100 countries were in Syria[313] , underlining the ineffectiveness of the Western strategy, as highlighted by the official Islamic State body:

By taking the path of war, governments have set themselves on a deadly path. Every bomb dropped in Syria or Iraq is a recruitment tool for the Islamic State. This is an unwise choice when there are millions of Muslims living in these same countries who could quickly answer the call of the jihad, leading irreparably to the situation that is now blowing up in their faces at home and abroad.[314]

While terrorism, which affects innocent people and whose brutal effects shock the mind, appears to be profoundly at odds with the principles of our societies, it is possible to reconstruct the path that leads the terrorist to override human principles to achieve his or her goals. Thomas E. Hill, professor of philosophy at the University of North Carolina, imagines the following dialogue:

---

310. Richard Norton-Taylor, "Iraq war 'motivated London bombers'", The Guardian, 3 April 2006.
311. Glenn Greenwald, "Chilcot Report and 7/7 London Bombing Anniversary Converge to Highlight Terrorism's Causes", The Intercept, 7 July 2016.
312. Letter dated 19 May 2015 from the Chair of the Security Council Committee pursuant to resolutions 1267 (1999) and 1989 (2011) concerning Al-Qaida and associated individuals and entities addressed to the President of the Security Council, S/2015/358, UN, New York, 19 May 2015.
313. Eric Schmitt & Somini Sengupta, "Thousands Enter Syria to Join ISIS Despite Global Efforts", The New York Times, 26 September 2015.
314. John Cantlie, "The Anger Factory", Dabiq, n° 7, Rabi al-Akhir 1436, February 2015, p. 79.

A asks B if he would be willing to commit an act against his principles (such as committing a racist act, theft, etc.) for a million dollars.

B replies « Yes, I think I would ».

A resumes: «And for $5?» and

B, indignant, retorts: « Who do you take me for?

So A explains: « We have already discussed the principle, now I am just negotiating the price![315]

Through this example, Hill attempts to demonstrate that there is a point at which principles tend to fade before the issue at stake, and that the very questioning of the principle calls into question its legitimacy.

This is exactly the same reasoning that leads rule-of-law-minded nations such as the United States and France to violate international law (e.g. by attacking sovereign countries without a UN decision), to practice torture and to officially renounce the application of human rights[316] ! Thus, Western society is unanimous in its condemnation of torture, but is it more acceptable if by torturing a terrorist one can save a million innocent people? And to save a million innocents minus one? ... a million minus two? ... a hundred innocents? ... two innocents? Here we find again, but 'on the other side of the fence', the rationality evoked in General Aussaresses' confession about his activities in Algeria[317].In fact, the radicalisation process of terrorists follows exactly the same pattern.

The media is quick to point out that the terrorists were *«radicalised on the Internet»*, but it is generally very vague as to the nature of the message that leads to radicalisation. Is it the inflammatory rhetoric of Salafist preachers or the images of victims caused by Western action in the Middle East? In fact, it appears - as we shall see - that it is the images of child victims of Western strikes

---

315. Thomas E. Hill, "Making an exception without abandoning the principle: or how Kantian might think about terrorism", in Violence, Terrorism, and Justice, edited by R.G. Frey & Christopher W. Morris, Cambridge University Press, 1991.
316. Blandine Le Cain, «France plans to violate human rights with the state of emergency», lefigaro.fr, 27 November 2015.
317. General Aussaresses, Services Spéciaux - Algérie 1955-1957, Perrin, Paris, 2001.

that fuel the will to act, more than the often abstruse sermons served up by obscure imams.

Arrested and interrogated by the Italian services, one of the four perpetrators of the attempted attack in London on 21 July 2005 was to confess to them:

> *It has nothing to do with religion... we have seen images and videos of the war in Iraq!*[318]

This statement is surprisingly close to that of a member of the «Iraqi network in the 19ᵉ arrondissement of Paris» before the Paris correctional court in March 2008:

> *It was everything I saw on TV, the torture in Abu Ghraib prison, all that, that motivated me.*[319]

In fact, the Internet provides information that is neglected by the media and Western governments, which prefer to «hide the dust under the carpet» rather than face and explain reality. For example, after the Brussels attacks (22 March 2016), the EI published an explanatory video, showing the damage caused by the coalition[320].Instead of tackling the problem head on, the Belgian government preferred not to communicate on the issue, thus leaving the field open to the EI.

In fact, our propensity to explain terrorism by «what is» and not by «what is done» leads us to blame it on fuzzy entities, such as the Internet. This allows us to justify systems of information filtering and mass surveillance, which have no impact on radicalisation, but allow us to 'punish'.

2.6.4.2. The role of religion

During the debates on the law against «separatism» in France, Gérard Darmanin, Minister of the Interior, said:

> *We can no longer discuss with people who refuse to write on paper that the law of the Republic is superior to the law of God.* [321]

This type of statement illustrates the dogmatism and ideological rut in which the fight against terrorism is situated in France, and explains the inability of

---

318. David Leppard & John Follain, "The Third Terror Cell on the Loose?", The Times, 31 July 2008.
319. Élise Vincent, «Quand Chérif Kouachi comparaissait dans l'affaire de la «filière irakienne du 19ᵉ arrondissement», Le Monde.fr, 8 January 2015.
320. Eye for an Eye video, Wilaya al-Furat, 27 March 2016.
321. Marie Lemonnier, «La loi de la République supérieure à la loi de Dieu»: la polémique vue par Olivier Roy», L'Obs, 5 February 2021 (updated 6 February 2021).

successive governments to understand terrorism... We will not elaborate here on the hierarchy that a believer - whether Christian, Muslim or Jew - can establish between religious laws and republican 'laws'. The problem here is to understand the role of religion in relation to radicalisation and - therefore - terrorism.

As a result of more than 50 years of clientelist management of immigration, the French population (known as «de souche») tends to feel - rightly or wrongly - submerged. Unlike previous waves of immigration (Iberian, Italian, Polish, Russian, etc.), the new Muslim population is associated with distinct cultural signs. With the multiplication of jihadist attacks in the West, superimposed on chronic delinquency, an irrational association between violence and Islam has emerged. Thus, an «*Islamophobia*» in the true sense of the word has gradually developed: «*fear of Islam*». Even if the official discourse tries to avoid stigmatising the entire Muslim population by distinguishing between «Islamism» and «Islam», the media and other philosophers continue to maintain the confusion.

Islamist terrorists are often referred to as «*God's madmen*» and are said to be trying to «*impose their religion*» or «*their totalitarianism*» on French society[322]. These polemics are specious and simplistic: recent, less superficial studies based on language analysis tend to show that the Bible is a more warlike work than the Koran.[323]

Our tendency to understand terrorism through its manifestations and effects weakens us and makes people vulnerable. As we have seen, the idea of a *continuum* between the attacks of 1995 and 2015[324] , using religion as a common denominator, is a policeman's approach. It has opened the door to the idea that terrorists fight us *'for who we are, not for what we* do'[325].Terrorism thus becomes an inescapable process and leads us to look for the problem where it is not, and thus to take inadequate measures. In France, the perception of terrorism is clouded by hostility towards immigration, which has turned into Islamophobia through the equation «Islam = Islamism».

The rhetoric about the violence of Islam, repeated by some polemicists, follows the Israeli rhetoric, is meaningless and can even be seen as seeking to generate violence. Multiple studies show that the importance of religion in the radicalisation process is considerably exaggerated. According to a report drawn up by the DGSE and cited by MP Patrick Mennucci during the debates on the disqualification of nationality in November 2014, 70% of individuals who left

---

322. See François Fillon, Vaincre le totalitarisme islamique, Albin Michel, 28 September 2016.
323. Samuel Osborne, «'Violence more common' in Bible than Quran, text analysis reveals», The Independent.uk, 10 February 2016; Christine Talos, «La Bible est bien plus violente que le Coran», Tribune de Genève, 11 February 2016.
324. Jean-Louis Bruguière, Le Grand Référendum, Sud Radio, 19 April 2017.
325. Manuel Valls, 19 November 2015.

to wage jihad in Syria would be of atheist origin and 80% would come from families with no links to immigration[326].

However, in France, at the highest levels of the state[327] , the tension towards Muslim fundamentalist currents is obvious, and extends to intellectuals:

> *We have an enemy, and we must name it: it is radical Islamism. And one of the elements of radical Islamism is Salafism.*[328]

The relationship between terrorism and Salafism is controversial: Salafists have existed for centuries, and it is not clear why this community would suddenly take up arms against France. Symptomatically, in 2009 and 2010, the Dutch intelligence service (AIVD) considered that Salafism was not a vector of jihadism in the Netherlands and even, on the contrary, constituted an alternative to the call to jihad[329].The issue is all the more embarrassing because the behaviour and religious background of terrorists is very irregular. For example, studies show that those who carried out the 2015-2016 attacks in France had only a rather superficial relationship with religion and were far from being familiar with Salafism[330].

The problem is that our Manichean reading of the terrorist phenomenon («you are either with us or against us») ignores nuances and tends to promote language that encourages divisions. For example, *Swiss Radio Television* (RTS), in an effort to communicate after the November 2015 attacks, put a small glossary online for children, *Le terrorisme décrypté pour les enfants*. Under the heading «*jihadist*», the authors give the following definition:

> *A jihadist is a fighter who wages war in the name of Islam, his religion. He wants to spread his religion to as many countries as possible. To do this, he carries out violent actions, such as bombings.*

And under the heading *'Islamist'*:

---

326. François-Bernard Huyghe, «Les Français djihadistes athées à 70% et sans lien avec l'immigration à 80% : pourquoi la DGSE passe à côté d'une partie de la vérité», Atlantico.fr, 5 December 2014.
327. Lionel Bonaventure, «France : Manuel Valls veut engager une bataille identitaire contre les salafistes», RFI/AFP, 5 April 2016.
328. «Manuel Valls: «We have an enemy, it's radical Islamism», AFP/Le Point.fr, 18 November 2015.
329. (Rik Coolsaet, Egmont Paper 97 - Anticipating The Post-DAESH Landscape, Egmont Institute, October 2017, p. 3; The transformation of jihadism in the Netherlands - Swarm dynamics and new strength, General Intelligence and Security Service (AIVD), September 2014)
330. Frédéric Koller, «Olivier Roy: «Le salafisme n'est pas le sas d'entrée du terrorisme», Le Temps, 14 October 2016.

An Islamist is a Muslim who fights to impose a very strict Islamic religion. Some Islamists fight by making speeches. Others do so by committing terrorist acts.[331]

In fact, there is nothing very surprising in this simplification of reality, because the fight against terrorism is in line with the aversion against religion that affects our Marxist-influenced societies. The idea that religion is a divisive factor justifies a secularism that extends not only to the state, but to the whole of society. This issue, crystallised around the Islamic veil or the burkini, has generated an artificial link between Islam and Islamism, which leads to a 'fear of Islam' (Islamophobia).

Moreover, the link between Islam and Islamism is much more strongly expressed in France than in Anglo-Saxon countries, which tend to be more accepting of different cultures. France tends to create its own problem: radicalisation is largely the result of the rhetoric of politicians at all levels and all political tendencies, and the media who like to «throw oil on the fire»...

By overestimating the role of religion, the real causes that drive individuals - even those with little or no religion - to sacrifice themselves in terrorist acts are dismissed. Religion is not central to the terrorist process. On the other hand, there is a religious component, but it must be understood in its proper perspective. It provides a general context and reference points, and is merely the equivalent of an «operating system» that provides terrorism with cultural elements to function, without automatically entering into its purpose. Thus, the attacks in France were not aimed at overthrowing the Republic and replacing it with an Islamic state, but sought to stop the strikes against the one that was being created in Iraq and Syria.

In fact, we refuse to listen and understand what the terrorists tell us. Thus, in June 2018, emerging from his silence, Salah Abdeslam justified the attack of 13 November 2015:

We are not attacking you because you eat pork, drink wine or listen to music, but Muslims defend themselves against those who attack them [...] Put your anger aside and reason for a moment, you are only suffering the mistakes of your leaders.[332]

Our exaggerated vision of the role of religion is only a disguised form of communitarianism, which leads to a lack of coherence and risks increasing the tensions that we would like to combat. Thus, on a strategic level, attempts - in France and Belgium - to 'certify' imams and other preachers risk, on the contrary,

---

331. www.rts.ch/decouverte/monde-et-societe/economie-et-politique/terrorisme/7257733-le-terro-risme-decrypte-pour-les-enfants.html.
332. «13 November: before the judge, Salah Abdeslam justifies the jihadist attacks, according to RTL», France 24, 29 June 2018.

accentuating the feeling that the West is trying to interfere in all aspects of Muslim civil and religious life.

Clausewitz had established that a strategy is the combination of means (or resources), modes of action and objectives. From this perspective, and in the case of jihadist terrorism, religion is a resource, not an objective. It is only a tool to win over the militants and give them a key to the fight, a bit like a «military doctrine» in a conventional army.

Indeed, for an individual to be willing to sacrifice his or her life for a cause, that cause must be worthwhile. In Western culture, the ideas of 'nation' and 'homeland' fulfil this function and have justified sacrifices - but also crimes and injustices - for centuries.

A study carried out for NATO in 2004 had already established that the motivations of jihadists are most often linked to identity claims or a feeling of humiliation, the origins of which lie in societal, historical or political registers[333]. In this context, discussions on the wearing of the veil in schools and public places, driven by a reading of secularism often tinged with Marxism, have largely contributed to fuelling an identity reflex. It is certain that the vast majority of this population is opposed to violence and terrorism; but the permanent stigmatisation of which it feels the object - even if it is sometimes imperceptible - reinforces its sympathy for the *cause of* the Islamists (not necessarily for the methods).

Social, economic or judicial injustices may also enter the equation, but as facilitating factors rather than as central motivators. Indeed, while the Marxist revolutionary takes a hands-on approach to his destiny, the Islamist tends to place it in the hands of God and to accept it more readily. This is why Palestinian terrorists of the 1960s-1980s, who were of Marxist persuasion, would stage cascading attacks to free their arrested and imprisoned colleagues; whereas jihadists sentenced to harsh prison terms accept their punishment and are not pitied by their co-religionists, who make no effort to free them.

As can be seen, the reasons for engaging in violence are multiple and generally secular in essence. To lump them together under the rubric of 'religious violence', as the French government and many experts do, is not only reductive, but makes the terrorist act artificially inevitable. Our emotions and prejudices thus become the main obstacle to identifying solutions.

All these findings were already made in 2008 by the British *Security Service*, or MI5 :

---

333. Report - Suicide Terrorism: The Strategic Threat and Countermeasures, NATO Research & Technology Organisation, August 2004.

Far from being religious fanatics, many of those involved in terrorism do not regularly practice their faith. Many lack religious knowledge and could in fact be considered religious novices. Very few were raised in strongly religious households, and the proportion of converts is higher than average. Some are involved in drug use, alcohol consumption and visits to prostitutes.[334]

In fact, MI5 notes that a well-established religious identity protects against violent radicalisation. This is the opposite of the French reading, which is tinged with Marxism and heavily influenced by the Israeli reading.

The problem is that the French reading leads to the registration of individuals according to their religious beliefs as early as 2020[335] , which could only give an illusion of security. However, as we have seen, the 2020 attacks show that the perpetrators had only a distant link with religion. There is a tendency to restrict freedoms for probably no security gain: this is a response of policemen and not of strategists, as in totalitarian countries.

2.6.4.3. The role of antisemitism

During the Paris attacks of 2015, there was a recurrent - and disproportionate - targeting of Jewish 'targets' (places and people), like a common thread that seemed to link them. It was concluded that antisemitism was a driving force behind jihadist terrorism. A more detailed analysis allows us to qualify this conclusion: antisemitism *is not* at the centre of the Jihadist struggle. It is one of the many factors that can enter into the radicalisation process and is part of a set of criteria that contribute to the choice of targets, but it is not at the heart of the motivation of terrorists. We will come back to this.

The difficulty in identifying the terrorists' approach stems from the confusion between three notions: what is related to the State of Israel («Israeli»), what is associated with Judaism («Jewish») and what is related to Jewish nationalism («Zionist»). This confusion is largely the result of the increasingly widespread adoption of the definition proposed by the *International Holocaust Remembrance Alliance* (IHRA), which makes anti-Zionism a «synonym» of antisemitism, as does Manuel Valls[336] and some French thinkers. It allows criticism of the State of Israel, antisemitism and anti-Zionism to be buried in a single problem to be addressed, but creates two major problems: a) it tends to project the failings of Zionism onto the whole of the Jewish community, and b) it makes it impossible to devise strategies to respond appropriately to each of these problems.

---

334. Alan Travis, 'MI5 report challenges views on terrorism in Britain', The Guardian, 20 August 2008, www.theguardian.com/uk/2008/aug/20/uksecurity.terrorism1 (accessed 13 November 2016).
335. Decree n° 2020-1511 of 2 December 2020.
336. Conference at the Representative Council of Jewish Institutions in France (CRIF), Paris, 7 March 2016.

Yet many Jews even consider Zionism to be anti-Semitic[337] , as can be seen in the impressive gatherings of Orthodox Jews in New York[338] ! This rejection of Zionism by Jews themselves was evident as early as 1897, when 78 out of 80 German rabbis opposed the holding of the first World Zionist Congress in Germany, forcing Theodore Herzl to organise it in Basel (Switzerland) instead of Munich[339].Their questioning of the legitimacy of the State of Israel has a biblical basis, unrelated to the contemporary geostrategic context. In the USA, where there is more freedom of expression on this issue, the number of antisemitic acts is roughly equivalent to that in France, despite a population five times larger[340] .

France, where legal safeguards and some individual or associative actors (such as LICRA) are very sensitive to this issue, sometimes to the point of absurdity, is the country in Europe with the highest number of antisemitic acts between 2005 and 2015[341].

Zionism, which is the ideological foundation of the State of Israel today, is thus an essentially political concept. Moreover, the Zionist movement includes not only Jews, but also Christians, especially evangelicals (mainly in the United States), who see in the Jewish state the fulfilment of a biblical prophecy. They are also partly responsible for President Trump's decision to recognise Jerusalem as the capital of Israel[342].For example, Stephen Bannon, Donald Trump's former chief strategist and far-right activist, declares himself a 'Christian *Zionist*'[343].

On 27 October 2018, in Pittsburgh, the United States suffered the bloodiest antisemitic act in its history[344].Donald Trump was then singled out for not having condemned the extreme right enough after the events in Charlottesville in August 2017[345] , and people then sought to attribute moral responsibility for

---

337. See Rabbi denounces Zionism, YouTube, 4 August 2012; Rebel Rabbis: Anti-Zionist Jews against Israel, YouTube, 7 September 2016; Peter Beinart, "No, anti-Zionism isn't anti-Semitism", Haaretz, 30 March 2016; Matthew Gindin, "The Latest Trend in Zionism? Anti-Semitism", Forward.com, 16 February 2017.

338. See Danielle Ziri, "Tens of Thousands of Ultra-Orthodox Jews in New York Protest IDF Draft Law", The Jerusalem Post, 12 June 2017.

339. See Shlomo Sand, Comment le peuple juif fut inventé, Paris, éditions Fayard, 3 September 2008.

340. "Number of anti-Semitic hate crimes edged up last year, FBI reports", Jewish Telegraphic Agency (JTA), 13 November 2017.

341. Johannes Due Enstad, Antisemitic Violence in Europe, 2005-2015 - Exposure and Perpetrators in France, UK, Germany, Sweden, Norway, Denmark and Russia, Department of Literature, Area Studies and European Languages, University of Oslo, Center for Research on Extremism (C-REX), University of Oslo, Oslo, June 2017

342. Noah Bierman, "Who really wants Trump to recognize Jerusalem? His evangelical supporters at home", Los Angeles Times, 6 December 2017.

343. Ben Sales, "Stephen Bannon: 'I'm proud to be a Christian Zionist'", Jewish Telegraphic Agency, 13 November 2017.

344. Jay Croft & Saeed Ahmed, "The Pittsburgh synagogue shooting is believed to be the deadliest attack on Jews in American history, the ADL says", CNN, 28 October 2018.

345. David Smith, "Donald Trump's rhetoric has stoked antisemitism and hatred, experts warn", The

the attack to him. Thus *France 24* (with AFP), the Belgian *RTBF*, the *Times of Israel* and others reprinted an AFP report:

> *Conspiracy theories, including accusations of Jewish domination of government and finance, are commonplace in the alt-right movement.*

> *A supporter of President Donald Trump, this movement has gained influence in recent years, notably through the president's former strategist Steve Bannon.* [346]

The accusation seems logical, but it is false. Paradoxically, the explanation is exactly the opposite: the perpetrator hated Trump because he was not anti-semitic enough[347] ! If Steve Bannon has been decried by some American Jewish organisations[348] , Zionist organisations acclaim him[349] , which underlines, by the way, the difficulty to associate «Judaism» and «Zionism». We are going in circles!

This type of misinformation complicates the search for the causes of terrorism and delays the adoption of lasting solutions. Strangely enough, victims' associations indulge in a discourse that satisfies their prejudices, but not the search for truth and justice.

It can be observed that the propaganda of the EI, which is very prolix in castigating Western countries, remains very silent on the Israeli-Palestinian question. The wars unleashed by the West against the Iraqi and Syrian governments have rather brought the EI and Israel closer together, and Israel does not see the EI as a main threat[350]. Thus, the Palestinians' fight to recover their land is only timidly

---

Guardian, 29 October 2018.

346. «Pittsburgh shooting: Donald Trump accused of 'emboldening' white supremacists», France 24, 29 October 2018; «Pittsburgh Jews point to Trump's role», 7sur7.be, 29 October 2018; «Pittsburgh shooting: Jewish officials accuse Trump of having a share of responsibility», rtbf.be, 29 October 2018; «Trump, who will arrive in Pittsburgh on Tuesday, would not be welcome», en.timesofisrael.com, 29october 2018.

347. Elizabeth Brockway, "Pittsburgh Synagogue Suspect Robert Bowers Hated Trump-for Not Hating Jews", www.thedailybeast.com, 27 October 2018; James S. Robbins, "Synagogue shooter hated Donald Trump and shows what real hatred, anti-Semitism looks like", USA Today, 29 October 2018.

348. Eric Cortellessa, 'What Jewish leaders say about Stephen Bannon', The Times of Israel, 16 November 2016.

349. Katty Scott, «Zionist Organization of America: 'Stephen Bannon is not anti-Semitic, he is a friend of the Jewish people'», The Jewish World, 15 November 2016; Allison Kaplan Sommer, «Zionist Organization of America Embraces 'Alt-right' Stars - Even Those Too Fringe for Trump», Haaretz, 14 November 2017.

350. Yoav Zitun, Tova Tzimuki & Moran Azulay, 'Ya'alon: In choice between Iran and ISIS, I prefer

supported by the jihadists: in the February 2016 edition of its magazine *Dar al-Islam*, the EI was quite critical of the Palestinian Hamas[351].It can be observed that the 'official' claims and analyses published by the EI after the January and November 2015 attacks do not single out 'Jews', and focus on the response to the French bombings. Even more 'doctrinal' documents, which look back at certain attacks in 'after action analyses' to extract feedback, do not mention Jews in this context.

In Palestine, the resistance is fighting against a territorial occupation, not against a religion. However, the Israeli government considers it as strictly religious and officially labels it as anti-Semitic. Terrorism is then interpreted as an aggression against «what we are and not what we do»; the same speech will be repeated by Manuel Valls in France in 2015[352].In fact, this is a way of dodging the real nature of the problem and maintaining it, because no negotiable solution is then possible and can only be solved by the annihilation of the other.

A poll commissioned by CNN in 2018 shows that for one third of Europeans, the term 'antisemite' is used to neutralise criticism of Israeli policies towards Palestinians[353].The same poll found that for 28% of Europeans, antisemitism is linked to the actions of the State of Israel, while 54% (and 66% in Poland) believe that the existence of the State of Israel is legitimate. In other words, there is no objective link between the legitimacy of the State of Israel and the criticism of its government's policies: it is artificially created!

ISIS', www.ynetnews.com, 19 January 2016; Judah Ari Gross, 'Ya'alon: I would prefer Islamic State to Iran in Syria', The Times of Israel, 19 January 2016.

351. «How to know the truth», Dar al-Islam, n° 8, p. 61, Rabi ath-Thani 1437, January-February 2016.

352. «Speech to the National Assembly - Manuel Valls: 'A risk of chemical or bacteriological weapons'», www.parismatch.com, 19 November 2015.

353. Richard Allen Greene, "CNN poll reveals depth of anti-Semitism in Europe", CNN/ComRes, 2018, http://edition.cnn.com/interactive/2018/11/europe/antisemitism-poll-2018-intl/.

Number of antisemitic acts in France (1998-2018)

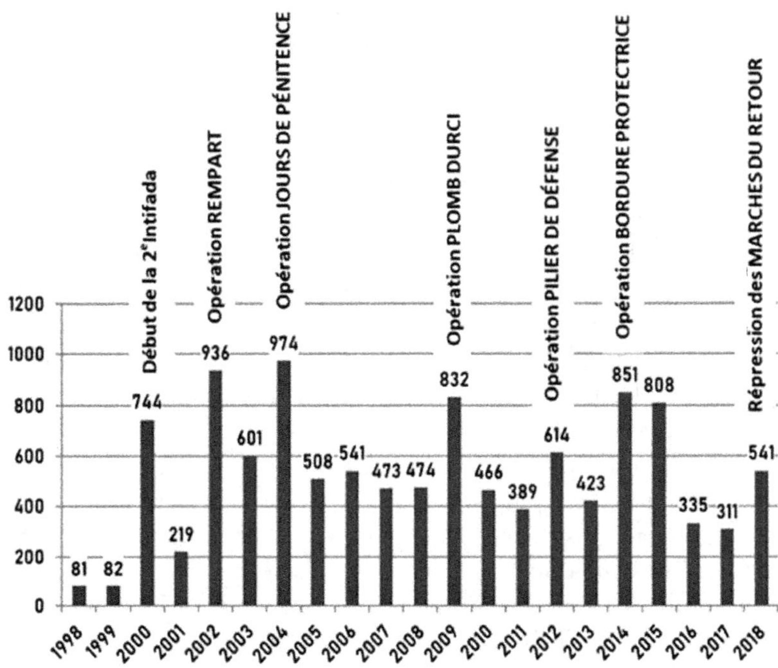

Figure 6. The number of antisemitic acts in France (1998-2018) shows a high correlation with events in the occupied Palestinian territories. The low values (the «troughs») largely reflect latent antisemitism, while the peaks are very clearly linked to the situation in Palestine. If one really wanted to reduce antisemitism, one would try to separate what is religious from what is related to Israeli politics. [Figures: https://www.antisemitisme.fr/]

In France, there is great resistance to the idea of a link between the number of antisemitic acts and the situation in Palestine. However, the annual reports of the *Service de protection de la communauté juive* (SPCJ) show that the outbreaks of antisemitism are very directly correlated with events in the Middle East, in particular with Israeli actions in the occupied territories[354]. Thus, antisemitic acts had been steadily decreasing since the end of the first *Intifada* (1991), but rebounded spectacularly in 2000 with the beginning of the second *Intifada* and its disproportionate repression. Since then, the «peaks» observed correspond exactly to the years in which Israel engaged in brutal operations against the Palestinians: 2002 (Operation REMPARTS), 2004 (Operation PENITENCE DAYS and the assassination of Yasser Arafat with polonium), 2009 (Operation HARD LEAD), 2012 (strikes in March, then Operation PILLAR OF DEFENCE),

---

354. See the reports on www.antisemitisme.fr.

156

2014 (Operation PROTECTIVE BORDER), demonstrating that, rightly or wrongly, the Palestinian conflict has a strong resonance in France:[355].It should also be noted that the operations against Hezbollah in Lebanon (2006) had little impact on antisemitic acts in France, so it is indeed the Palestinian problem that generates this type of action.

In the context of the fight against radicalisation and antisemitic acts, Western governments should seek a more neutral and moderating role in the conflict. More than in other European countries, France tends to forget the sensitivities of a large part of its population: the singling out of the Jewish community, the noisy support of Israeli policy in the occupied territories, the clumsy handling of the Dieudonné affair and the 'BDS' campaign[356] have had the perverse effect of putting the Jewish community at the centre of a whole range of discontent[357]. Had this factor been taken into account by the Sarkozy/Fillon government in 2012[358] , it is very likely that the crimes of Mohammed Merah would not have taken place, as we have seen above.

In a jihadist terrorist environment, political support for religious communities must be exercised with discretion and subtlety so as to prevent deadly confusions. Engaging with the international coalition in the Middle East should have made Western governments more circumspect in this area. The fight against terrorism is not a cockfight based on muscle mass, but above all a fight for legitimacy. In France, no educational effort has been made - especially towards the Muslim population - to explain in a dispassionate way the participation in the international coalition in the Middle East.

2.6.4.4. The role of the social situation

In Europe - and in France in particular - the idea persists that inequality is one of the drivers of terrorism. ᶜOriginating in the French Revolution, then in the social struggles of the 20th century, this idea was probably true in the

---

355. See «Actes antisémites recensés en France de 1998 à 2014», in Christian De Lablatinière, Rapport sur l'antisémitisme: en 2014, le nombre d'actes antisémites recensés sur le territoire français a doubled. Not Islamophobia..., www.europe-israel.org.

356. France is one of the few countries in the world to ban the BDS (Boycott, Desinvestment, Sanctions) campaign, which aims to force Israel to label goods produced in Israel and those produced in the occupied territories differently (as required by international law). Note that the European Union has decided that differential labelling should be used (Peter Foster and Raf Sanchez, «Israel fury after EU orders labels on goods from occupied territories», telegraph.co.uk, 11 November 2015).

357. The ban - in France only - of the organisation for the boycott of products manufactured in the occupied territories but under the label «made in Israel» belongs to the same debate, but is outside the scope of this book. See Jean-Baptiste Jacquin, «L'appel à boycotter Israël déclaré illégal», lemonde.fr, 6 November 2015.

358. Alain Gresh, Gaza, 'Palestine et apartheid', Le Monde diplomatique, 11 March 2012, http://blog.mondediplo.net/2012-03-11-Gaza-Palestine-et-apartheid (NOA: the original text of the Foreign Affairs communiqué has been removed from the web).

1960s and 1970s; but today, with jihadist terrorism, the role of inequality is very small. This phenomenon can be explained simply by the Islamic 'system of exploitation', which tends to make people accept their condition as a way of fulfilling their role on earth.

Indeed, the term 'inequality' hardly ever appears in the writings of the IE. Instead, a considerably more important - but never mentioned - driver is injustice. Expressed in various registers, it is fuelled by the Israeli-Palestinian conflict, but is also strongly associated with Western military interventions, which we have never been able to justify.

The first problem is to link all terrorist attacks to the EI, as used to be the case with «Al-Qaeda». Mysteriously enough, al-Qaeda seems to have stopped committing terrorist attacks altogether... at least if you go by the media! In doing so, the media has implicitly given the EI a driving role in the international jihad, encouraging local groups to give themselves a political base by declaring their rallying *(bayah)* to the EI.

Similarly, in the various descriptions of the EI, particular care is taken to present it as a criminal organisation. This is true of the presentation of its sources of financing, which are often based on trafficking in antiquities, drugs, slavery, etc. That some individuals, members or not of the EI, have compromised themselves in such activities is likely. But it is wrong to present the EI as a bunch of bandits, even if its laws are applied in a brutal manner. What is presented in the West as extortion is often just taxation *(jizyah* and *zakah)*. As for the satisfaction of the people, it should probably be measured by those who regret the regime of Saddam Hussein or the regime of Muammar Gaddafi, which at least guaranteed a certain stability (let us recall here that according to the United Nations, before the Western intervention, Libya had the highest level of human development in Africa[359]).

In this context, it should also be remembered that the civilian victims of Western strikes are undoubtedly much greater than what the media report. The videos disseminated by the EI show images of these victims, particularly children, in a rather generous manner and occupy an informational space that is totally neglected by Western governments, which do not take responsibility for their decisions. Yet it seems that these images have a determining effect on what is called «radicalisation», by generating a feeling of indignation.

Religion is therefore not in itself a reason for violence. The West's tendency to want to control everything and decide for everyone is the driving force behind the revolt that calls for violence. Dr Marc Sageman - a sociologist and psychiatrist, and former CIA officer - has studied nearly 500 cases of jihadist terrorists

---

359. https://en.wikipedia.org/wiki/History_of_Libya_under_Muammar_Gaddafi.

in his book *Leaderless Jihad* and finds that the process of radicalisation of an individual is promoted by four factors[360] :

> *1 - a feeling of anger stemming from his perception of the suffering suffered by his fellow believers in the world;*

> *2 - how the individual places this anger in the context of a more global war against Islam;*

> *3 - whether this 'anger' echoes his or her personal experience within Western society (such as discrimination or difficulties in integrating);*

> *4 - becoming part of a group, whose dynamics may cause them to turn their «anger» into a violent act.*

These observations are confirmed by the doctrinal writings of the modern jihad and are consistent with the claims of the terrorist acts observed in recent years. Once again, we are far from a desire to change Western society or to impose Salafism in Europe.

The problem is that Western governments, convinced by the 'experts' that terrorism is a religious phenomenon with a religious objective, are applying an inappropriate therapy. Caught in the trap of clumsy decisions, governments prefer to adopt a fatalistic attitude based on the idea that terrorism serves a religious purpose and is therefore inevitable.

The perverse effect of this posture is that, for fear of excusing, we do not listen, we do not explain and therefore we do not understand. Thus, the mechanisms of radicalisation are explained according to prejudice. According to the former Minister of Justice, Christiane Taubira, only 15% of extremists are radicalised in prison, while the vast majority are radicalised on the Internet[361] ; according to the Unité de coordination de la lutte antiterroriste (UCLAT), 95% of cases of radicalisation are due to human contact[362] ; according to Pierre Conesa, a professor at Science-Po, *«anti-terrorist judicial services say that 80% of those who*

---

360. Marc Sageman, Leaderless Jihad: Terror Networks in the Twenty First Century, University of Pennsylvania Press, 2008, 208 pages.
361. Interview with Christiane Taubira, Le Temps, 20 December 2015.
362. Christophe Cornevin, 'Islamisme : 8250 individus radicalisés en France', lefigaro.fr, 2 February 2016.

have returned from Syria have not been to a mosque or prison[363] «. Moreover, according to Christine Taubira, then Minister of Justice, none of the perpetrators of the 13 November attacks had been radicalised in prison before these events[364] .

Radicalisation is a complex process in which mosques, prisons or the Internet are only facilitators. Dr Sageman's conclusions are relevant and confirm the observations made in Israel, Iraq and Europe. Terrorist attacks do not come out of nowhere, but are a consequence of events, most often provoked by the West, as one of the most important American *think tanks*, the *CATO Institute*, noted in 2006:

> *Instead of religion, almost all suicide attacks around the world have a specific political objective in common: to force a democratic country to withdraw its military forces from a territory, which the terrorists consider to be their homeland or hold in high esteem.*[365]

To simplify, and based on the concept of 'individual jihad', one could sketch the following scheme:
- *Western action* is the trigger for the process;
- *religion* provides the 'operating system' and will help define the level of commitment and its coherence in the overall action;
- *Personal contacts* or prison contribute to the logistical and support network;
- while the *Internet* provides doctrinal elements, methods and the didactic part.

Our interference in the way of life of Muslims by force or politics is a key element in the radicalisation process and the fundamental reason for armed jihad. But it is probably the bad faith and denials surrounding these interventions, and the casualties they cause, that generate the most outrage and anger. In November 2015, after the attacks Laurent Fabius, Minister of Foreign Affairs, declared:

> *We were among the first to fight against DAECH because they are terrorists who want to destroy us. It is because they want to destroy us that we are in Syria. Moreover, the first attack against Charlie Hebdo, we were not in Syria. So it is really us, our existence that is targeted.*[366]

---

363. Pierre Conesa, «Quelle politique de contre-radicalisation en France?», Report made for the Fondation d'aide aux victimes du terrorisme, December 2014.

364. Christiane Taubira, former Minister of Justice, on the programme On n'est pas couché («Christiane Taubira - On n'est pas couché 6 février 2016 #ONPC», France2/YouTube, 6 February 2016) (36'10").

365. Robert A. Pape, "Suicide Terrorism and Democracy - What We've Learned Since 9/11", Policy Analysis (CATO Institute), 1er November 2006.

366. Interview by Jean-François Achilli, «Laurent Fabius: 'We must unite and defeat these people'», Franceinfo, 19 November 2015, http://www.franceinfo.fr/emission/l-interview-politique/2015-2016/

The statement is all the more cynical as the French government has literally imposed the name «DAECH», which means «Islamic State in Iraq *and* the Levant»! To think that by bombing a group on one side of the border only, it would have no reason to respond to it is foolishness... or disinformation. This denial by the Minister of Foreign Affairs is echoed by some experts who continue to assert that the terrorists struck France first...

> *... when there was no military operation against them [...] The DAECH attacks predated any military action.* [367]

The jihadists are thus able to justify their attacks, in the face of official and expert lies, and thus gain legitimacy among their audience, as we shall see.

Beyond words, if we refuse to state the real causes of radicalisation and attacks, there is no chance of solving the problem, and the measures taken will probably only amplify it. The claims of the January 2015 attacks do not mention the 2005-2006 cartoons or freedom of expression, while the claims issued by the Islamic State on 14 November 2015, then in issue 12 of its official organ, *Dabiq* - published on 18 November - and in its November 2015 *Dar al-Islam* magazine do not mention France's Christian character, democracy or way of life as justification for the attacks, but clearly mention a response to air strikes in Iraq and Syria.

On the other hand, the West tends to interpret the savagery of terrorist attacks as a necessary and sufficient reason to lie and break the rules of law that make democracies strong. The use of torture and the lack of respect for human rights are often presented as a necessary step in the fight against terrorism. This is not true. The US Senate report on the use of torture by the CIA has shown that it is a useless and ineffective tool that creates more terrorism. Above all, this way of dealing with the problem tends to make the state's action lose all legitimacy and thus encourages adherence to the ideas of the terrorists, as a SECRET cable from the US ambassador to Kuwait points out:

> *According to US military intelligence, the primary motivation for most foreign terrorist/combatants (FTCs) is the perceived mistreatment and lack of due process in the treatment of detainees at Abu Ghraib and Guantanamo - making this a key factor in the flow of FTCs and a central element in the lack of confidence in the United States' ability to wage an effective war on terror that remains true to American values.* [368]

laurent-fabius-il-faut-s-unir-et-vaincre-ces-gens-la-19-11-2015-08-04.

367. Jean-Pierre Filiu, programme C dans l'air, France 5, 1ᵉʳ December 2016.

368. Classified Cable (SECRET), Regional CT Strategy for Iraq and its Neighbors: Results and Recommendations from March 7-8 Com Meeting, 18 March 2006, 06KUWAIT913_a, wikileaks.org/

In fact, Western countries have never really been concerned about the impact of their foreign policies on their own immigrant communities. On the contrary, in France there is a form of denial that often borders on misinformation, particularly when it comes to policy towards Israel.

The same causes produce the same effects, yet the countries affected by terrorism in 2015-2016 seem to voluntarily ignore these very clear signs. Curiously enough, the explanations given by the terrorists themselves in their claim texts, and mentioning the strikes in Iraq and Syria, are systematically ignored in the media, as in the 'decoding' of the claim to the attacks of 13 November 2015 by the French-speaking Belgian Radio and Television[369] , which only mentions the most 'offensive' passages, but deliberately ignores the explanations contained in the message. This contributed to the formatting of minds to give the illusion of the inevitability of Muslim terrorism.

2.6.4.5. The role of military intervention

Modern jihadism was born out of American insistence on maintaining a military presence in Saudi Arabia, despite opposition from the government and local populations[370]. Today, the claims of jihadist attacks systematically remind us that their action is aimed at stopping Western military interventions.

Strangely, the role of these interventions is probably the least considered aspect in the study of radicalisation mechanisms. Probably because political and military decision-makers do not want to admit to their public opinion that they caused the attacks that hit their constituents and fellow citizens through carelessness, ignorance, negligence and political ambition. On the other hand, the population and the victims' associations are «good people» and meekly accept the official discourse. So why worry?

---

plusd/cables/06KUWAIT913_a.html.

369. https://www.rtbf.be/info/dossier/attaques-terroristes-a-paris/detail_decryptage-de-la-revendication-officielle-de-l-etat-islamique?id=9136104.

370. Paul Wolfowitz, quoted in William B. Quandt, Peace Process, University of California Press, 2005, p. 503.

Claims of jihadist attacks

Date	Location	Author(s)	Reason given for the attack
22.03.2012	Toulouse	Mohamed Merah	French participation in NATO operations in Afghanistan and «Jews killed our brothers and sisters in Palestine» (telephone claim on France 24). «Injustice and aggression in Palestine, Afghanistan and other Muslim countries» (the «official» claim of Jound al-Katibat al-Khilafah).
07.01.2015	Paris	Chérif KouachiSaïd Kouachi	Bombing of women and children in Iraq and Syria (telephone claim on BFM TV).
08.01.2015	Paris	Amedy Coulibaly	Western] attack on the caliphate, the Islamic State... The regular bombing of civilians by the coalition... (claim via YouTube video).
13.11.2015	Paris	Multiple (Islamic State)	[...] For leading the crusade, insulting the Prophet, boasting about fighting Islam in France, and hitting Muslims in the land of the Caliphate with their planes... (official claim of the EI).
22.03.2016	Brussels	Multiple (Islamic State)	[...] rushed towards the crusader Belgium which has not stopped fighting Islam and Muslims. [...] in response to their [the crusaders'] aggression against our state... (official claim of the EI).
13.06.2016	Magnanville	Larossi Abballa	...Muslim lands are occupied [...] 66 nations are fighting the Islamic State (video message).
14.07.2016	Nice	Mohamed Lahouaiej Bouhlel	... in response to calls to target citizens of nations fighting the Islamic State (claim/Amaq news agency).
26.07.2016	St-Étienne-du-Rouvray	Adel Kermiche Abdel Malik Petitjean	... in response to calls to target citizens of countries that belong to the coalition of crusaders (claim/Amaq news agency)
19.12.2016	Berlin	Anis Amri	... in response to the call to attack members of the coalition fighting the Islamic State (claim/Amaq news agency).
03.02.2017	Paris	Abdallah E-H (?)	No compromise, no return, there is no peace in war (terrorist's Twitter account) [no official claim].
22.03.2017	London	Khalid Masood	[...] in response to the call to target the nationals of the Crusader countries (French text) [...in response to calls to target citizens of coalition countries. (English text).

Date	Location	Perpetrator	Claim
23.05.2017	Manchester	Salman Abedi	[...in an operation to terrorise the polytheists and in response to their attacks on the land of the Muslims (official claim).
17.08.2017	Barcelona	Moussa Oukabir	[...in response to calls to target coalition countries. (claim/Amaq news agency).
25.08.2017	Brussels	?	[...] The operation was carried out in response to calls to target coalition states. (claim/Amaq news agency).
13.05.2018	Paris	Khamzat Azimov	[...] you are the ones who started bombing the Islamic State [...] you are the ones who started killing Muslims (allegiance and claim video/Amaq News Agency).

Table 5 - Content of claims and role of interventions in Iraq and Syria in the logic of the attacks

The few studies conducted on this issue show that Western military interventions have two effects: first, they create the conditions for the emergence of terrorism; second, they generate a phenomenon known as «de-pluralisation» by reducing the number of possible solutions to a problem to the sole use of violence. This is what is happening, for example, in Palestine.

The radicalisation process is therefore driven by a concrete rationality, which means that it is a reversible process, contrary to what the official discourse suggests. But this requires a desire to get rid of terrorism. For as terrible as it may seem, this is not the case. Not only has security become a flourishing economic sector, employing many people who would otherwise have no job opportunities and generating industrial activity, but it also allows for a control of the population that could not otherwise be achieved. Moreover, the measures taken during the state of emergency in France were converted into «normal» law as soon as the state of emergency was lifted!

In France, since 2015, the fight against radicalisation has remained locked in a strictly security framework without a holistic dimension. Instead of trying to win over the population of immigrant origin, the illusion of a national consensus on foreign policy is created. For example, a recurring issue in jihadist propaganda, which fuels moral support for terrorists, is never addressed. While every attack in the West arouses legitimate emotion, with candles and popular demonstrations, attacks outside Europe or the tens of thousands of civilian victims of the international coalition's bombing in the Middle East do not arouse emotion or compassion[371].

---

371. According to the Airwars website, the number of coalition civilian casualties as of 31 January 2018 is between 17,166 and 25,483, airwars.org/civilian-casualty-claims/.

Country	First military engagement in Iraq or Syria	First attack claimed by Islamic State
Germany	Iraq - 4 December 2015 (Decision)	Würzburg - 18 July 2016
Australia	Iraq - October 2014	Sydney - 15-16 December 2014
Belgium	Iraq - September 2014 - (Withdrawal in July 2015) then, resumed in Iraq and Syria in January 2016	Verviers (map) - 15 January 2015Brussels - 22 March 2016
Canada	Iraq - 7 October 2014 (Decision)	Montreal - 22 October 2014
Denmark	Iraq - October 2014 - (Withdrawal in August 2015, then resumed in March 2016)1re strike in Syria, August 2016	Copenhagen - 14-15 February 2015 Copenhagen - 2 September 2016
Spain	Iraq - September 2014	Barcelona - 17 August 2017
Finland	Iraq - September 2014	Turku - 18 August 2017
France	Iraq - 19 September 2014	Paris - 7-9 January 2015
France	Syria - 24 September 2015	Paris - 13 November 2015
United Kingdom	Syria - December 2015	London - 22 March 2017
Sweden	Iraq - August 2014	Stockholm - 7 April 2017

Table 6 - Relationship between countries' involvement in the international coalition and the first
Islamic State attack suffered

2.6.4.6. *Are terrorists psychopaths?*

After the attacks of 9/11 or of 2015-2016 in France, the «experts» competed
with each other to find descriptions such as «*bastards*», «*clueless*» or «*wankers*».
Pseudo-analyses enriched with negative vocabulary such as '*megalomania*',
'*obsessive quest for paradise*', '*unmanageable*', '*paranoid*', etc., are based more
on emotions, prejudices and professions of faith than on a sober and factual
analysis.Thus, terrorists have been portrayed as bloodthirsty or sexually frustrated psychopaths , and their actions the result of mental disorders. So much so
that in 2017, the Minister of the Interior, Gérard Collomb, planned to include
psychiatric hospitals in the fight against terrorism.

This uninformed vocabulary certainly aims to delegitimise terrorism, but
above all it masks a total lack of analysis and knowledge of the phenomenon:
these 'experts' are more part of the problem than part of the solution.

Underestimating one's opponent is a serious strategic error... which we are
fond of repeating and which - paradoxically - only encourages terrorism. In
two ways: first, because relying on simplistic images leads to a false diagnosis
that leads to inadequate solutions, such as the anti-radicalisation measures in

France and Belgium. Secondly, because by refusing to understand the message of terrorists and by systematically belittling them, we push them to persevere, as we saw in Magnanville in 2016. Explaining must allow us to understand, in order to better shape our strategies; an approach that the Hollande/Valls government has deliberately - and openly - rejected in order to satisfy war aims... with murderous effects .

In 2005-2007, the author participated in a NATO-funded study on the behaviour and psychology of terrorism, which highlighted the high level of the majority of individuals involved in jihad. Ironically, while in the West the high demand for security personnel and armed forces has led to a sharp decline in their general level, terrorists bring together high-level individuals. The Islamic State, for example, attracts a large number of academics and individuals with higher education.

However, there are large differences between geographical areas, probably related to the way immigration has been handled. For example, the profile of terrorists in Anglo-Saxon countries (especially Great Britain) and Palestine is different and significantly higher than that of terrorists in France and Belgium. We get the terrorists we deserve...

Studies carried out in Great Britain by Andrew Silke, an expert in terrorist profiling, show a very different profile from the terrorists observed in France. Far from being madmen, terrorists are very lucid individuals:

> *They are remarkably analytical of their own actions and often show surprising insight into how others perceive them. In short, they know how to deal with the violence they commit and are able to justify it in the context of their own perception of the world, and their role in it.*

> *[In analysing the psychology and motivation of terrorists, it is essential, as a starting point, to realise that the vast majority of psychological research on terrorists has shown that they are not abnormal or suffer from a higher incidence of psychopathology. In fact, several studies have shown that terrorists are much healthier psychologically and much more stable than other violent criminals.*

They are therefore able to understand the implications of their commitment:
Involvement in terrorism is a costly activity, involving a mortgage on one's life and limb, the inevitable renunciation - if it were even an option - of a normal life with few benefits to show for it - dreams of victorious triumph seem unlikely to motivate a terrorist, while modes of action have to keep a low profile, precluding compensation in the form of benefits within the community.

In other words, the terrorist sees his commitment as part of a higher purpose for the benefit of the community. It is the injustices committed against the community with which he identifies that motivates him to become personally involved. The British researcher associates this behaviour with a form of altruism, where the terrorist dedicates his or her life to improving the life of the community.

These findings are supported by the work of Diego Gambetta and Steffen Hertog, two sociology researchers at Oxford University in Britain, who studied the psychological profiles of 404 terrorists involved in Islamist attacks, including suicide bombings. They found that between 69% and 48.5% of the terrorists had received a higher academic education. Of these, a majority (56.7%) had studied science, medicine and engineering, not because engineering studies are popular in recruitment areas or because terrorist organisations need bomb designers, but because of the lack of job opportunities after school on the one hand, and the rather conservative and religious nature of engineers on the other. On the other hand, the researchers note that most of the terrorists came from affluent backgrounds and had a stable family life .

These observations are confirmed by other studies of Islamic terrorists, which also show a relatively high intellectual and social level. A 200-page document produced in 2011 by the British *Security Service* (MI5) and classified as «SECRET - UK EYES ONLY» found that more than 60 per cent of the 200 people arrested in Britain for terrorism-related offences were middle-class and mostly highly educated. Furthermore, 90% of them were described as 'sociable' and had normal family lives and many friends, contradicting the widespread image of the lonely, poorly integrated psychopath .

Digging deeper, a number of researchers have long identified an overrepresentation of engineers among jihadist terrorists. Surprisingly, the explanation lies not in bomb design, but in a broader observation from diverse populations around the world: engineers disproportionately combine idealism with conservative ideology.

The situation seems different in France and Belgium, where there is a close link between petty crime and Islamist terrorism. This is due to a combination of clientelistic immigration policies, integration efforts that seem to be limited to a misunderstood secularism, too much vocal support for Israeli policy in the occupied territories, with debates that are more passionate than exciting on subjects such as the Islamic veil or the burkini. Guided by a political mindset, successive governments between 2007 and 2020 have systematically widened the gap between 'native France' and immigration, without considering the domestic impact of their foreign policy, creating a climate conducive to radicalisation.

Since 2007, despite strong rhetoric, governments have done everything possible to create the conditions for radicalisation of a part of their population.

Palestinian terrorism is *sui generis* and does not offer many lessons for the fight against terrorism in other parts of the world. Based on resistance to an occupation, it relies on well-structured organisations with a strong territorial presence. Its recruitment is facilitated by the strategy used by Israel. The main lessons that can be drawn from it come from its asymmetrical character, which has not been integrated into Israeli strategies.

The future «martyrs» are not «brainwashed», as is often claimed. Quite largely recruited in the Al-Najah University of Nablus and the Islamic University of Gaza , their intellectual level and training is high. In 2007, Claude Berrebi, a researcher at the RAND Corporation, noted that in Israel, out of 208 cases where a biography of the terrorists was available, 96% (200) had at least a university education, 65% (135) had a higher education, while in the rest of the population these figures were 51% and 15% .

Interrogations of young Palestinians arrested before an attack show that they do not sacrifice themselves 'for' religion, but that religion provides a cultural framework for their action. Their motivation is not religious, but identity-based and stems from a sense of national humiliation. To claim that Palestinian terrorists are guided by anti-Semitism is inaccurate: it is essentially a question of fighting an occupier, whose prerogatives have only been extended over the years, pushing young people ever more surely into radicalisation, as the path of negotiation appears hopeless.

Paradoxically, the idea that terrorists can be deterred by brutal responses, such as the *Dahiya doctrine* or the *Hannibal directive* (discussed below) in Israel, has instead pushed Palestinian terrorism to become more radical. The terrorists' reasoning becomes: «If you're going to get slaughtered, you might as well do it by causing maximum damage to your opponent! The idea that a terrorist who is willing to die can be deterred by death is simply absurd.

2.7. **The operational dimension of jihad - the «open jihad**

The *Arabian Peninsula Jihad Base* (APJB) (*Qa'idat al-Djihad fi Jazirat al-Arab*) - better known as *al-Qaeda in the Arabian Peninsula* (AQAP) - is one of those so-called 'franchises' that never received Osama bin Laden's approval. However, since 2010 it has become the main doctrinal source of the jihadist movement. In particular, it has developed the concept of *«open jihad»*, which simplifies the preparation of terrorist activities and makes structures, networks and travel unnecessary. Based on the exploitation of new technologies and the Internet, it is a concept of extreme decentralisation of jihad that makes each jihadist an independent cell.

It constitutes a kind of doctrinal *corpus* that is not exclusive to the BDPA, but - as the idea of *open jihad* suggests - can be used by other terrorist structures, which share the same objective, such as the Islamic State. It is based on the idea of 'Resistance' (*Muqāwamah*) which suggests - in the minds of its authors - that it is a fight in response to aggression. Its purpose, as envisaged by theorists of open jihad, is to stop Western interventions:

> *In my opinion, this type of jihadist method can be one of the main reasons for stopping the aggressive war against Muslims [...] Individual jihad against the West, especially when it escalates, will create a climate of terror and anxiety, public resentment and complaints against the governments and policies that brought about the individual jihad [...].*

This is perfectly consistent with the claims of the various attacks that have struck the West since 2003, and France in particular. The terrorism that strikes the West is not a fatality, the fruit of some deranged mind, but follows a perfectly rational logic. This means that it would be possible to put a stop to this violence... if we wanted to.

Jihad theorists have identified four factors of asymmetry between Westerners and jihadists that require an adaptation of their strategy of action :

- the vulnerability of structured clandestine organisations to international security means and international and regional coalitions, and therefore the need for more flexible structures capable of resisting arrest of their members and the use of torture;

- the inability of clandestine structures to reach and integrate the full resource potential of the Ummah's youth who would like to engage in jihad and participate in all kinds of activities without wanting to assume responsibilities in a centralised structure;

- the presence of an adversary (the West) spread over very large areas, with varied objectives and in very distant locations, making it difficult to fight on open fronts and through centralised structures;

- The West's use of air and missile assets to conduct air strikes, piloted by satellites, which can also see hidden objects and facilities, makes open confrontations from permanent positions difficult, and are factors that must be taken into account in combat planning.

To implement this concept, jihad theorists use social networks and the Internet to disseminate technical and doctrinal knowledge, and to provide downloadable learning methods to would-be terrorists...

2.7.1. Objectives of «deterrence operations

In March 2004, jihad theorists realised that the unpopularity of military interventions, and of the governments that initiate them, is a weakness that can be exploited as a factor in deciding to carry out attacks. The Madrid («11M») attack thus became the conceptual basis for *deterrence operations* , which has provided the canvas for jihadist attacks in the West ever since.

Before '11M', 91% of the Spanish population was opposed to the Aznar government's decision to participate in the war in Iraq. The terrorists understood that this opposition could be exploited to push the population to demand a withdrawal of the troops, but they probably did not count on the fall of the government, as the majority of voters had already made their choice before the attack. It was the mismanagement of the crisis (including the attempt to blame it on Basque separatists) that led to the election result.

In fact, after 11M, nobody understood the message and the intentions of the jihadists: the withdrawal of the Spanish contingent was therefore not a response to the terrorists, but the application of an earlier popular will, unrelated to the attack. The problem is that the jihadists interpreted it as the result of their strategy. From this misunderstanding a concept was born, which other terrorists would try to imitate: the concept of «*deterrence operation*».

In Britain, public opinion was also strongly opposed to the decision to intervene in Iraq. On 15 February 2003, the largest-ever peace demonstration in London was reportedly attended by two million people, according to its organisers. This massive opposition led the jihadists to believe that they could achieve the same objective as in Spain and led them to commit the attack of 7 July 2005.

The concept of deterrence operations was only formalised around 2010 by Abu Musab al-Suri, a jihadist terrorist theorist:

> *The mujahideen or resistance must not neglect the importance of deterrence against these enemies. They must strive to create the impression that their arm is ready to reach out and strike anyone who thinks they are participating in an aggression. Generally, the majority of our enemies, from the president to the troops, are in fact cowardly rats. They can be deterred if a strong example is made by hitting and punishing a few of them. This deterrence aims to make those who are engaged withdraw or to act preventively against those who are thinking of engaging.*

In 2015, the combination of the unpopularity of the Hollande/Valls government and the opposition of 68% of the French population to an intervention in Syria were criteria for choosing France as a target. Contrary to the official discourse - relayed by many media and «experts- the January and November operations in Paris had all the characteristics of «*deterrence operations*", as confirmed by the «official» organ of the Islamic State:

> *I don't think it could be any clearer. So it is the indiscriminate French bombings that are the cause of this threat. A threat that was carried out on 13 November 2015 in Paris and Saint-Denis.*

The excuse of «self-defence», put forward by President Hollande on 27 September 2015, to justify the strikes in Syria is specious. It has an asymmetric effect by giving the EI the opportunity to expose a lie:

> *On Friday 19 September 2014 - more than three months before the Hyper Cacher and Charlie Hebdo operations, and more than a year before the Paris and Saint-Denis operations - French Rafales bombed the Islamic State out of hatred for Islam and Sharia law, not in retaliation for attacks allegedly carried out by the Islamic State against France.*

This is compounded by the way France has intervened in Iraq and Syria. As already noted in 1998, air strikes are the surest way to exacerbate the determination of jihadists:

> *Air strikes are perceived as unfair, and this unequal confrontation, without human interaction, is the cause of wider support for terrorism.*

After the attacks of 13 November 2015, the EI produced a video, including footage that no French media has broadcast, in which jihadist Abu Tayssir al-Faransi states:

> *Praise be to God, praise be to God [sic], who allowed us to kill you in your home, in Paris! Praise be to God who sees fear enter your hearts! Praise be to God who has made you taste what we taste in Iraq and in Sham! O you French! O you French! Your president has brought you into a great and long and costly war! [...] Know that this is not the last operation, this is not our last appointment! Unless...* **Unless you put pressure on your government as the Spanish people did several years ago against the war in Iraq**. *Unless you withdraw from this war which is far from your land. Otherwise you will have more Black Saturdays. Otherwise you will be the prey of our lone wolves, and for you, living in peace will be a dream and a luxury! Otherwise, you will pay a high price for your criminal acts on our women and children, because you are fighting a coward's war. You are unable to come to the field!*

In 2016, in a video entitled *Your silence kills you*, the EI repeated the same message, relying on the unpopularity of the Hollande/Valls government:

> *Shredded bodies, women's screams coming from everywhere, children crying, men powerless in front of the catastrophe. It's sad, isn't it? Yes, it is! It's really sad! You have been subjected to a little of what you are doing to Muslims in Syria and other countries! [...] O French people, know that the dramas you are living through today, it is you who caused them (sic) with your own hands. Remember that you were quiet in your homes [when] your government began to attack us. Your real enemy is the one who harms your security. O French people, you know very well now: when you promise, you deliver! And so we promise you that you will see the worst if you stand idly by!* **Because your silence towards the decisions of your government is killing you**.

In May 2018, in his allegiance and claim video before his attack, Khamzat Azimov conveys exactly the same message:

> *[...] You are the ones who started bombing the Islamic State, I am addressing France and its citizens, you are the ones who started killing Muslims, and then when we give you an answer, when we fight back, you cry.* **If you want this to stop, put pressure on your government!** *I am not the first to tell you this. Other brothers before me, who are on the ground there, have already told you, but you refused to listen [...].*

Thus, by hitting people with attacks, the terrorists' aim is to make them demand that their governments stop military interventions, as they thought they understood in Spain in 2004. This is the concept of «*deterrence operations*».

However, there are several problems with this approach. The first is that this logic is the result of a perception that has never really been explained in the West: Westerners systematically reject the idea that terrorism can be motivated by their own action. The second is that the explanations given by the jihadists are not relayed in the media so as not to «give them a platform». The third is that the terrorists themselves (especially with *individual jihad*, which we will see) do not always understand this concept and are more likely to place their action in the context of revenge.

For all these good and bad reasons, our reading of jihadist terrorism is distorted: we tend to see it as revenge with a focus on the past, whereas the concept of *deterrence operations* is future-oriented. As a result, the terrorist risk does not appear in parliamentary, political and other reflections and debates prior to our interventions. It is certain that if Westerners had understood (or wanted to understand) this concept, they would have considered other means of action against the EI *before* engaging in a conflict, and would have - at the very least - taken measures to protect their populations.

By obscuring these concepts and emphasising the vengeful and punitive nature of the attacks (which is only secondary), two things have been suggested: firstly, that terrorists feel like offended victims, and secondly, that Islam is an essentially warlike religion.

This is not true: terrorists do not see themselves as victims, but as fighters in the service of the victims of Western interventions. Moreover, since they put their lives on the line for what they consider a noble cause, they are not afraid of punishment. This explains why, unlike the Marxist terrorists of the 1960s and 1970s, who carried out attacks to free their fellow human beings, Islamic terrorists do not seek to avoid punishment.

As for the warlike character of Islam, we have already discussed this and noted that the Bible is a more warlike text than the Koran: in the end, it is the spirit in which one reads a text that gives it its character. The problem is that the idea has been propagated - not to say created - that France is facing an inevitable fate, linked to the very nature of Islam. This is not true and it is difficult to say what the objectives of this disinformation are, but it has largely contributed to a failure to understand the nature of the problem and has accentuated communitarian tensions in France.

Whether we like it or not, the support for terrorist acts observed on social networks is the result of the perception of three recurrent elements in Islamist discourse: a) the illegitimacy of Western interventions in the Middle East; b) the non-respect of international law for strikes that kill women and children; c) the blind ignorance of Western populations, who accept these interventions without using their democratic rights to stop them.

As we can see, jihadist terrorism is in a paradox. Its cause and its failure have the same origin: the lack of interest of our populations in the wars that we wage abroad (even when they are illegitimate). This lack of interest has two related consequences: the population does not mobilise to stop them, and thus gives the impression that it is complicit and - therefore - not innocent. In fact, we give the terrorists the stick to beat us with...

In fact, the Spanish (in 2003) and the British (15 February 2003) had mobilised against their countries' participation in the war in Iraq, which had incited the jihadists to carry out attacks in 2004 and 2005. In France, there were never any such demonstrations, but it was the unpopularity of the Hollande government that incited the terrorists. For example, the French people had greeted François Hollande's declaration of war in September 2014 at the UN General Assembly with disbelief and only really became aware of being involved in a conflict after the attacks in November 2015.If he had been interested a little earlier, there would probably have been no deaths...

In fact, jihadists have taken strategic analysis further than Westerners have. They have understood that our centre of gravity lies in the popular legitimacy of government decisions. Their strategy is therefore to show that these decisions have negative consequences on the population itself. The problem is that terrorism is a weapon perceived as illegitimate in the West, which is why jihadists insist that their targets are *'carefully chosen'* and aimed at *'those who are most guilty'*.

Despite their brutality, there is therefore a rationality behind terrorist attacks. But because politicians and the media create our belief that this terrorism is divorced from the actions of the West, that it has unstoppable ambitions and is carried out by irrational individuals, we never question our strategies and decisions.

The reasons why President Hollande decided to engage militarily in Iraq (September 2014) remain unclear, and no one has really tried to understand them. In any case, the way France engaged in the conflict shows that neither the armed forces, nor the intelligence services, nor the political institutions anticipated the consequences on the perception of the immigrant population nor sought to understand their implications on the domestic threat. Assuming that the French decision to intervene in Iraq had a valid reason, why were no preventive security measures taken in metropolitan France prior to involvement, as Russia did, for example? The same questioning applies to Belgium.

It can be argued that this strategy of pressuring the population to withdraw from the Iraqi-Syrian conflict was a failure, since no one gave in to this form of blackmail. This is true, but for a jihadist, the logic is different: of course, the ideal would have been to bend the determination of the French government, but on the other hand, the fact of having tried to do so is already a success! We are in asymmetric thinking. We need to understand that our notions of war must be read 'inside out' in a jihadist context: from the moment it was planned, the terrorist act is already a victory, which is accentuated by the efforts of intelligence services to prevent it.

In other words, jihadist terrorism can only be defeated - in the Western sense of the word - when the terrorists' very determination to act is affected. The rest is verbiage.

2.7.2. Military theory of the Call for Global Islamic Resistance (CGIR)

The above findings lead to a reflection on a new articulation of the armed struggle based on two forms of (military) jihad:

- *Jihad by individual terrorism (Jihad al-Irhab al-Fardi)*, which involves clandestine activities carried out by very small independent units, is a first step towards the second form of jihad that it supports.

- *Open-front jihad,* which is a battlefield confrontation from established positions against an aggressor, allowing, when conditions permit, confrontation on

174

the ground and the seizure of territory essential to the emergence of a state - the ultimate goal of the resistance.

This doctrine clearly has its origins in the Iraqi situation, enriched by the experience of Afghanistan. It has two clearly expressed objectives: to consolidate successes against the occupier in 'liberated' areas, through the establishment of an Islamic management structure (in Iraq: *Islamic State in Iraq and the Levant*) and to stop Western interventions that thwart this project. It is very poorly understood in France, where the explanation of terrorism has crystallised around a composite ideology that blindly supports interventions in the Middle East and fights immigration. This can be seen in the debate about the return of foreign fighters to Europe.

The ARIG is a «shield and sword» strategy, which combines *open front jihad* (OFD) against coalition forces to conquer or hold territory (sword) as part of a war of resistance (Afghanistan, Iraq) or seizure of power (Libya, Syria, Mali); and *jihad by individual terrorism* (ITD) with the aim of dissuading Western nations from getting involved in the conflict (shield).

It is important to note that the main fight is at the DFO level: it is the one that will have an impact at the level of the people and their dignity. The DTI is only there to support the main action. This is why the «foreign fighters» went to Syria: if the main fight was France, they would have built up active networks (fighters) there and stayed.

2.7.2.1. Jihad by individual terrorism (Jihad al-Irhab al-Fardi)

2.7.2.1.1. Operating principles

Jihad by Individual Terrorism (JIT) (also referred to in jihadist literature as *'individual jihad'* or *'individual terrorism'*) is a form of combat carried out by individuals or by very small, independent groups.

The attacks of 11 September 2001, Djerba (11 April 2002) and Bali (12 October 2002) can be seen as manifestations before the letter, while the Madrid attack (11 March 2004) provided the model. But ITD was only conceptualised and 'formalised' in the years 2007-2010 by Abu Musab al-Suri of the *Arabian Peninsula Jihad Base* (APJB) after the US intervention in Iraq. Its most spectacular examples were the attacks in Boston (2013), San Bernardino (California, 2015), London (6 December 2015) or Orlando (Florida, 12 June 2016).

DTI is an adaptation of the terrorist concept to the evolution of Western social networks and surveillance means. Its basic principle is to keep the preparation of terrorist action below the detection threshold of (Western) surveillance systems.

- Complex clandestine operational structures (in the target country) are abandoned in favour of independent individuals (or very small groups). Thus, there are no structures, no complex logistical infrastructure and no funding through observable channels. Thus, the number of connections between individuals is very low and the volume of information exchanged is very difficult to detect by security services.

- Terrorist action is structurally disconnected from combat structures in Syria or elsewhere. It is conceived, funded, and executed by the militants themselves. Its objectives are defined in a generic way, sometimes through the conventional media. For example, for the January (Paris) and February (Copenhagen) 2015 attacks, a list of 'targets' was published in 2013 in the BDPA's *Inspire* magazine , aimed at 'individual terrorists'.

- There is no identifiable command structure, and each attack is decided by the militant based on Western action. So, in a way, it is the Westerners who hold the key to triggering the attacks.

This concept has several consequences. The first is that terrorists rarely manage to carry out large-scale actions that meet all these criteria without alerting the security agencies. The second is that the terrorist act tends to be confused with the communal act and can become strategically inconsistent, rendering it unreadable.

As can be seen, the term «*low-cost terrorism*», or «*proximity terrorism*», favoured by some experts and the media, is inappropriate. It should rather be called «*low-visibility terrorism*» or «*stealth terrorism*», because the aim of the operation is not to optimise costs but to escape detection by the security organs.

2.7.2.1.2. Strategic principles
While the operational principles are a consequence of Western technological evolution - as we have seen - the strategic principles were inspired by the Madrid bombing (11 March 2004), which led to the withdrawal of Spanish forces from Iraq.

It is the jihadist version of the American «*AirLand Battle*» concept of the 1990s. It has rapidly acquired a doctrinal dimension for the entire jihadist movement (including the EI), whose central idea is the response to Western actions:

> *[These operations] bring the war to the enemy's territory, just as he does by killing our Muslim brothers and sisters in Islamic countries, destroying their homes and burning their plantations.*

> *They force the enemy to reconsider its aggressive policies against Muslims. When he is hit on his own soil because of his war against Islam and the occupation of Muslim lands, he must change his posture. He who is immune from punishment is behaving badly.*

As we shall see, it implies a redefinition of the war space and the operational objectives of terrorism. For its implementation, the BDPA has articulated the list of possible theatres of operations and ranked them in order of importance. Thus, it can be seen that, contrary to the claims of many experts, the strategic priority is neither Europe nor France:

1- The countries of the Arabian Peninsula (United Arab Emirates, Saudi Arabia, Yemen, etc.), the Levant (Lebanon, Syria, Jordan, Israel), Egypt and Iraq. This area includes the Holy Places, oil, Israel, and the US military and economic presence. It will host the victorious Assembly (Al-Taifah al-Mansurah) that will lead Islam.

2- North African countries from Libya to Mauritania (Maghreb). This area is rich in Western interests, especially for the main European countries, allies of the United States and NATO.

3- Turkey, Pakistan and the countries of Central Asia. They represent the second largest oil reserves in the world, as well as American military, economic and strategic interests. They include important and historically rooted Islamist movements, which constitute the strategic depth of Arab jihadist and resistance movements.

4- The rest of the Islamic world: the Americans and their allies have important interests there. This part of the Islamic world comprises the essence of the resistance, namely hundreds of millions of Muslims, young members of the Islamic Nation, who sympathise with its cause and are ready to engage in jihad and resistance.

5- American and allied interests in Third World countries, especially in countries that participate in crusader campaigns. Because of the weak security measures in these countries, the jihad can rely on the mujahideen who live there and have a normal life. They can move freely, hide and acquire information about the adversary and deal with them easily.

6- European countries that are allies of the United States and participate in its wars. Let us not forget the presence of large and ancient Muslim

7- The heartland of America itself, targeting it with effective strategic actions.

2.7.2.1.3. The notion of the lone wolf

The concept of ITD evokes the notion of the 'lone wolf', of which there is no official definition, only interpretations. Arguments by 'experts' over a definition are akin to the medieval church's debates over the sex of angels, because, whatever our interpretation, what matters is how the jihadists define it. In seeking precision and detail, we lose sight of the essential.In the West, it tends to be seen as a totally solitary individual who decides in the privacy of his room to carry out an attack, without reference to anyone else. For some, the archetype is Anders Behring Breivik, who killed 77 people near Oslo on 22 July 2011 in the name of an extreme right-wing ideology; for others, he is the exception that proves the rule, according to which 'lone wolves' do not exist.

Indeed, reality shows great variation in the application of the concept. Jihadists define the individual terrorist much more broadly than Western experts:

There are differences among theorists within the jihadist movement on the implementation of 'individual jihad'. Some consider this term to be applicable to all individuals and groups who are independent of a larger group or organisation, whether administrative or armed. Among those who adhere to this approach is Abu Musab al-Suri. Others attribute the term to anyone who carries out an operation alone, even if they have been sent by a group or organisation, such as in the operation of Omar al-Farouq [...].

> *In my opinion, an individual mujahid is one who combines the two
> characteristics mentioned above: being independent of any group or organisa-
> tion, whether administrative or armed, and acting alone. This mode of jihad
> is unpredictable for Western intelligence services. It is what they call a «lone
> wolf». It is difficult to discover because it is known only to Allah. He has no
> relationship with any group or individual. That is what we are looking for.*

Western perception tends to confuse the notions of «*mass murderer*» and
«*individual terrorist*». But even if technically or tactically the act is similar, there
is a strategic difference: the objective. For the mass murderer, it is a single act,
which is sufficient in itself: it is simply to kill. In terrorism, the use of violence
serves a strategic process: through his act, he exerts pressure - which will be
repeated if he fails - until the objective is achieved.

Individuals like Breivik are not strictly speaking in a terrorist logic: they do
not use violence to achieve something, but simply to satisfy a fantasy, anger
or revenge. Even if Mohammed Merah's crimes were legally judged as terrorist
acts, technically speaking, they were not part of a terrorist approach situated in
a process to achieve a strategic goal, but were «only» vengeful and murderous.
They are more akin to «mass murders» and/or communal crimes. The problem
is that in the West we use the word 'terrorist' emotionally, not just to describe
a phenomenon, but to attribute a value judgment to it. Its (real) objectives are
never mentioned: it therefore becomes impossible to distinguish between these
two forms of crime, which require separate treatment. Obviously, the word
'terrorist' is more evocative and satisfies our sense of revenge... but it does not
help to conceptualise the answer!

Operationally, what is important here is that the signal to launch an operation no longer depends on a chain of command. It is left to the judgement of
the militants according to objectives, generic watchwords and the situation such
as: «*in response to the call to attack by members of the coalition fighting the Islamic
State...*» Thus, it is Western action (bombing, clandestine action, etc.) that acts
as a trigger for the terrorist act:

> *As for the spontaneous method, [it] began to spread with the intensification
> of the US campaign attacks on Muslim countries, the adoption of the Zionist
> project in Palestine, and the dissemination of news through satellites and
> communication networks.*

For example, the Brussels attacks (22 March 2016) were not initially planned
to hit the capital of Europe, but France: Belgium was only a secondary target. The
problem is that after Salah Abdeslam's arrest, the Belgian authorities, wanting to
show their success, started to spread the rumour that he would denounce his

network. Panic-stricken, his co-religionists then launched an improvised operation in order to act before being caught.In fact, because the Belgian intelligence and security services did not understand how the DTI worked, they needlessly provoked the attacks.

As a corollary to the issue of «lone wolves», the notion of «network» must be understood in a nuanced way. In everyday life, we like to talk about our personal, professional, family and other 'networks'. Traditionally, in clandestine organisations, a network is an organic structure composed of individuals with specific functions. A terrorist group may consist of several cells, usually of 3-4 people, which are compartmentalised to prevent the organisation from being compromised if one of its members is captured. With the DTI, jihadists speak of a «*system of action*» (*nizâm al -`amal*) and not a «*structure of action*» (*tanzîm lil-`amal*).

Thus, with the DTI, there is no network in an organic sense: individuals are connected opportunistically, sometimes without even knowing that they are contributing to a terrorist enterprise. Indeed, in Britain, most individuals arrested in terrorist investigations - 8 out of 10 - are released without charge. This shows that terrorists are not isolated in their world, but communicate with their environment, without belonging to organic networks.

The Western mind is not comfortable with the idea that an individual can operate outside an organic network. When the perpetrator dies, a network is 'needed' in which to find a perpetrator or perpetrators to punish. This explains why, after an attack, those who in one way or another, consciously or unconsciously, helped to carry out the attack (often the immediate family) are sought out... and finally released in most cases. Thus, a mother who sent money to her son just before he died in Syria is prosecuted or we regret that Abdelkader Merah was not sentenced for complicity, because the death of the protagonists no longer gives us any grounds for revenge, but also, and above all, because we have difficulty understanding that the terrorist act can be the result of an individual approach for the benefit of a collective objective.

The idea that there is no such thing as a «lone wolf» is simply because it is no longer possible to «punish» the terrorist, so they try to punish those around them. This is a typically French perspective, more focused on revenge than on solving the problem. In reality, while it is possible that in some cases the perpetrator was consciously helped, the real problem is how to prevent it.

In fact, our tendency to disconnect terrorist acts from rationality leads us to analyse the phenomenon emotionally. We put our pain before the need to solve the problem: that is why we fail to control the problem. But Islamists do not act on the basis of individual impulses and objectives, but for a very real cause and objectives shared with other Muslims, whether or not they are members of a radical movement.

In the concept described by Abu Musab al-Suri, the terrorist is totally disconnected from any organisation and leadership structure, and does not receive any orders or instructions: he organises his action locally with his own means and individual networks. Terrorist trainees are even discouraged from travelling to Islamic countries or areas for training. Thanks to the *open jihad*, they should be able to train alone, discreetly, at home, without contact with external networks, using courses, manuals, and documents accessible on the Net to acquire the necessary technical knowledge. Terrorist actions are analysed, criticised and published on the Net so that the «newcomers» do not repeat the mistakes of their predecessors.

The most important aspect of this concept is that the trigger for terrorist action - or its inspiration - comes from the target country itself. This is the origin of the name of the BDPA magazine: *Inspire*. For example, one year after the Nice attack (14 July 2016), no link to the EI could be established , because the terrorist triggered his operation independently of a hierarchy.

This approach runs counter to Western rationality, as it tends to exclude strategic coordination of terrorist acts. Thus, if the objective of the Islamic State was revolutionary or aimed at conquering the West, such a strategy would not make sense, as it does not allow for the articulation of both the destruction of the existing society and the construction of a new one. This is why Marxist revolutionary organisations were articulated in a military wing and a political wing, the latter taking precedence over the former. There is no equivalent in the DTI.

While the concept of individual terrorism is rather ill-suited to a strategy of conquest, it is on the other hand coherent with the objective that jihadists have set themselves to stop an activity (such as strikes), particularly if it does not meet with the support of a majority of the population of the target country. But the Western reflex is to oppose this with a determination to act: this is a 'pat' situation. This is the problem of the United States in Afghanistan and that of France in the Sahel: if in the short term it works against the terrorists, in the long term it is a problem for our societies. We will come back to this.

Where Westerners seek to see the action of an asocial, withdrawn psychopath, jihadists simply see the legitimate action of a normal individual, but one who is outraged by the attacks on his community. Strategically, this concept helps to show that jihadists retain the initiative.

The subtle analyses of the terrorists' «modus operandi», which are served up by the «experts» on television, are of a police nature and often mask the absence of a strategic reading of the problem. The imperfections in the implementation of the concept are not an expression of a different concept, but simply reflect the fact that terrorists are neither specially trained nor sufficiently experienced to carry out such operations in a totally clandestine and solitary manner. This adds to their unpredictability.

However, experience shows that there is a big gap between doctrine and practice: terrorists find it difficult to remain totally independent and to conceive of their action without sharing the idea with friends or family. This weakness makes the terrorist detectable, even if the signals he gives before the attacks are often difficult to interpret.

In its most 'successful' form, ITD derives its strategic effectiveness from a set of individual and uncoordinated actions against various objectives, which generates a feeling of permanent insecurity:

> *The basic principle of this operational activity is that the mujahid, the member of the resistance, practices individual jihad in his country, where he lives and resides, without the jihad costing him the problem of travelling, migrating and moving to where the jihad is possible. The enemy today is one, and it is everywhere.*

The use of individual terrorism is thus conducted *'in situations where the mujahideen repel their enemies and enemy terror through defensive jihad'*.If not accepted in the West, this reasoning is not inconsistent and could be summarised as follows: «You attack us with means against which we can do nothing. Our only way to respond is to make you stop with acts of terrorism.

2.7.2.2. Open front jihad

Open front jihad (OFJ) is complementary to ITD. It could be likened to guerrilla warfare, which is only likely to succeed in a particular military environment.Jihadist texts do not describe it precisely, but it can be seen as a very fluid fight, conducted by small, highly mobile units attacking specific (often static) targets or by ambush. The conditions described for such a fight correspond to the Middle Eastern theatre, where the authority of the state is very limited and where popular support allows the resistance to move 'like a fish in water', as Mao put it:

> *There is an abundance of weapons and equipment in the region, which also has a great diversity of borders, coasts and passes. Israel provides a motive for the global Islamic cause, and the US occupation adds a revolutionary dimension, which is an excellent key to the jihad.*

The optimal geographical criteria for DFO, identified by jihadist doctrine, are fairly standard for guerrilla warfare and describe the Iraqi-Syrian environment fairly accurately. They do not provide the basis for a conflict that would extend beyond the Near and Middle East:

> *The [enabling] factors include the existence of a cause in which the population can believe strongly enough to embrace the cause of jihad. This cause must be able to mobilise the Islamic nation [in the world] to give moral, financial... and other support to the jihad. The most appropriate cause of all is resistance in response to foreign aggression, to which religious, political, economic and social reasons can be added to make it a revolution and jihad. This is what the literature on guerrilla warfare calls the 'revolutionary climate', and this is what we will call the 'jihad climate' here.*

As can be seen, the EI is applying the ARIG concept to the letter: it was conducting DFO in Iraq and Syria and DTI in Western countries, in support of operational combat.

2.7.3. Operational issues

2.7.3.1. Individual hybrid jihad» operations

The term '*individual hybrid jihad*' has nothing to do with the Western notion of hybrid warfare (which is also extremely vague). In jihadist doctrine, it refers to the joint implementation of terrorist operations by two independent movements or groups. Operational coordination is carried out by the actors themselves, without the intervention of an external authority.

The January 2015 attacks in Paris are a textbook example of a *hybrid individual jihad* operation : the Kouachi brothers' action against *Charlie* Hebdo was under the banner of the *Arabian Peninsula Jihad Base* (APJB), as explained in its magazine *Inspire* and in Chérif Kouachi's telephone statements ; while Amedy Coulibaly's action against the Hyper Cacher was under the banner of the Islamic State (IS), as confirmed by his video and *Dabiq* , the IS magazine. The information found on Coulibaly's computer is only technical advice (not «orders», as the press has interpreted it).

This type of action is quite rare in the context of individual terrorism, which exploits the independence of cells and minimises coordination activities. In contrast, it is relatively common in the Middle East. While the Western media and 'experts' insist on the antagonism between the EI and other Islamist groups, there are many instances of active cooperation between armed groups, regardless of their levels of 'moderation'. Thus, it is not true that the Islamic State and Hayat al-Tahrir al-Sham were (are) enemies.Rather, it should be called competition, as they are all working towards the same goal, sometimes with personal rivalries.

The EI sees no problem in conducting joint operations with other terrorist entities, whose objectives and strategies are different. While the Western mind expects perfect coherence between the two entities, the jihadists are satisfied with a temporary or limited point of convergence.Pragmatically, the groups cooperate on what unites them. This is essential because Western strategy in the Middle East is based on the idea that 'Al Qaeda' is opposed to the EI, thus justifying our support. Our strategies for action are therefore based on false assumptions that contribute to the spread of the problem, as in Syria and Iraq.

2.7.3.2. Suicide actions

The term «suicide action» covers all actions where the tactical objective is achieved only with the death of the terrorist. A particular form of this type of action is the «human bomb».

Contrary to popular opinion, this type of action is not an Islamist 'speciality'. This spirit of heightened sacrifice predates modern Islamism, particularly in Asia, as with Hindu or Sikh extremists. Historically, the West was first confronted with this threat in Beirut on 23 October 1982, when the *Islamic jihad* attacked the headquarters of the US *Marines* with a truck loaded with 2,200 kg of explosives, killing 241 people, followed two minutes later by an attack on the headquarters of the French forces, the «Drakkar», with 820 kg of explosives, killing 58.

Since then, suicide attacks have become one of the most terrible, deadly and effective manifestations of terrorism. The 188 suicide attacks committed between 1980 and 2001 constituted only 3% of the world's terrorist attacks, but accounted for 48% of the victims.*All were* committed in order to regain sovereignty over territory occupied by a foreign force.

Foolish theories, such as that terrorists are not afraid of death because it is 'fixed' in advance by God, are the result of uneducated, simplistic and misleading reading , which has the effect of preventing any preventive action.

In Palestine, the resistance movements of the 1960s-1980s had essentially a secular philosophy, largely tinged with Marxism, and did not develop a «tradition» for human bombs until the early 1990s. Their terrorism then had very operational objectives (obtaining the release of prisoners, eliminating a personality, etc.). It was only after Baruch Goldstein's terrorist attack at the Tomb of the Patriarchs (25 February 1994) that some secular Palestinian groups adopted the human bomb method. But they will abandon it in 2005-2006, after the restitution of the Gaza Strip, in favour of launching rockets.

2.7.3.2.1. The notion of suicide

Since 9/11, in order to delegitimise this mode of action, various exegetes - Christians and Muslims - have tried to repeat that suicide is forbidden in Islam and that, consequently, suicide bombings are also forbidden. In fact, in the

West, the term 'suicide bombing' is often and deliberately reductive to suggest that the perpetrators are not acting as Muslims.

Indeed, in verse 29 of Sura «An-Nisaa», the Qur'an explicitly prohibits suicide (*al-Intihar*):

> *And kill not yourselves: verily Allah is Merciful to you.*

But our interpretation is misleading. For Muslims - as for Christians - the notion of suicide is associated with resignation and flight from adversity. It is a loss of confidence, not to say defiance, in the divine will. Defined as an expression of despair, suicide is exactly the opposite of the notion of jihad.

In fact, jihadists distinguish between two types of fighters: those who engage in combat at the risk of their lives, known as *inghimasyin* (singular: *inghimasi*); and those who engage in combat knowing that they will die, known as *istishadiyiin* ('*those who live the martyrdom*'). The former are ready for anything, the latter are associated with the idea of sacrifice, self-sacrifice, self-victory and courage, the vision of the fighter who goes to the ultimate sacrifice:

> *A martyr is one who dies on the battlefield fighting the infidels.*

Dying is not a desperate act, but a personal act, which transcends life for the sake of a cause: the combatant thus becomes a «martyr» (*shahid*). In 1997, Ekrima Sabri, Grand Mufti of Jerusalem and Imam of the Al-Aqsa Mosque, said

> *In the end, God will judge the person and whether his reason was good or not. We cannot judge. The criterion is whether the person is doing it for himself or for Islam.*

The *istishadiyiin* carry out special actions that could not be carried out by other means. It is the Islamist version of the Japanese 'kamikaze', where we find the same mystical dimension; a comparison contested by some experts, who argue that the Japanese fighters did not attack the civilian population. This is true, but remains a fallacy, because our media 'forget' that the majority of the EI's suicide attacks are carried out in the context of an 'open front jihad' (OFJ), against the troops of the Western coalition in Iraq and Syria in open combat.

For example, in the defence of Mosul alone, the EI carried out some 482 suicide actions between 10 October 2016 and 11 July 2017. This is the case of DFO (on a battlefield), where the suicide action has a primarily pragmatic character: it plays the role of a 'guided missile' against fortified positions or garrisons that are too robust for the mujahedin's weapons. In this context, they are remarkably cost-effective, as evidenced by the losses suffered by the international coalition in the recapture of Mosul in 2017.

Thus, the suicide action is not the result of individual distress, but is a kind of 'last stand', when no other solution seems possible.

2.7.3.2.2. Effectiveness and efficiency of suicide actions

Suicide action is not a gratuitous act: it is a combat technique that aims to achieve a result. In order to analyse it, a distinction must be made here between its effectiveness (comparison of the operational result with the desired goal) and its efficiency (comparison of the operational result with the investment).

The goal has two levels. The first is of a material nature: the ability to destroy an objective. From a strictly operational point of view, the interest of suicide action is that the bomb remains a priori «under control» until it explodes. Its chances of success are therefore high.

The suicide bomb is the poor man's cruise missile: it is a cheap, guided bomb that explodes on target.

The second level is symbolic and strategic. The suicide action shows the determination of the terrorist organisation and its militants. For this reason, the Palestinian movements do not hesitate to record a video tape of each fighter just before his act, which transmits a message that has the value of an «example» for other candidates. Death is no longer associated with the notion of defeat, but with that of victory. Thus, the traditional (symmetrical) notion of combat, which associates victory with the elimination of the opponent, is reversed here.

The situation is therefore asymmetrical: on the one hand, there are terrorists who no longer fear death, or even seek it, and on the other hand, a Western logic that boils down to eliminating individuals who are ready to die. The Western logic therefore loses every time, even - or even especially - in the case of a total crushing of the adversary. This is one of the main reasons why the West and Israel are struggling to fight Islamist terrorism. We understand, among other things, why BARKHANE's successes in the Sahel carry the seeds of defeat...

Western military thinking is still heavily influenced - even implicitly - by the notion of 'balance of power', which makes little sense in an Islamist asymmetry.

Terrorism is often presented as «seeking to maximise the number of deaths». However, while it is obviously deadly, and while some attacks show a determination to kill, such as the attack in Nice (14 July 2016), a slightly more in-depth analysis shows that many attacks were considerably less deadly than they could have been. One could cite the attack in Saint-Étienne-du-Rouvray (26 July 2016), where the terrorists could have killed many more parishioners, or the attack in the Stade de France (13 November 2015), where at least one of the terrorists blew himself up with the clear intention of not causing any victims. Another example is the stabbing of the 18th arrondissement police station in Paris on 7 January 2016, where the terrorist wore a dummy explosive belt , demonstrating that his own death was worth more than the number of deaths he would cause. The same phenomenon was observed on 17 August 2017 in Cambrils (Spain) and in Brussels on 25 August 2017 where the attacker of a Belgian military patrol carried a dummy firearm.

In these examples, the objective is clearly to be killed during the attack: this is the heart of the asymmetric phenomenon where the manifestation of a determination is more important than the number of deaths. The waves of stabbing attacks in Israel and then in Europe illustrate this phenomenon.

In terms of efficiency, suicide attacks are «high yield» because of their low cost. However, suicide attacks are not necessarily less costly than other forms of attack. The preparation, equipping and transportation of the terrorist to the target requires a significant infrastructure and often several (stolen) vehicles. In addition, some organisations, such as Hamas, undertake to support financially the widows and orphans of a martyr. For Hamas, the average cost of a human bomb would be 142.29 dollars, to which would be added financial support to the family of between 2,800 and 5,000 dollars , which further strengthens the popular base of the movement.

Their main 'economic' interest is - paradoxically - to save lives. This is the same principle as with Japanese suicide bombers: with one individual, the same result can be achieved as by risking the lives of several fighters in a more traditional action. This is a characteristic that is particularly observed in the context of 'open front jihad' (in Iraq or Syria, for example). In the context of individual jihad, suicide action allows for strikes with minimal preparation and less detectability.

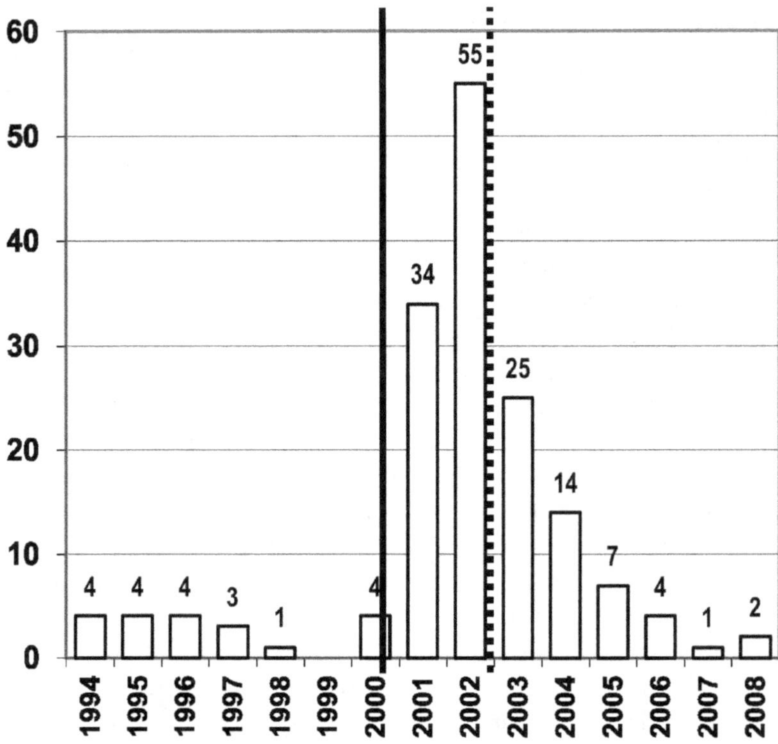

Figure 7. Although it is difficult to establish a formal link between most suicide attacks and Israeli targeted killings, a correlation can be observed. For example, the first suicide bombings in 1994 followed the attack on the Tomb of the Patriarchs. Those of 1996 were provoked by the elimination of Yahya Ayyash. The solid line marks the official resumption of the Israeli policy of targeted eliminations (9 November 2000). The dotted line marks the beginning of the construction of the protective barrier between the West Bank and Israel (see also Figure 5). From 2005, with the return of Gaza, Hamas changed its strategy: it abandoned suicide attacks and adopted the use of rockets to retaliate against Israeli attacks. [Figures: Israeli Ministry of Foreign Affairs]

2.7.3.2.3. A persistent myth: the reward of the 72 virgins

In the aftermath of the 9/11 attacks, attempts were often made to explain the terrorists' actions as the result of mental disorders and they were portrayed as psychopaths with a thirst for blood or unfulfilled sexual needs. Hence the myth of the «72 virgins», to which the martyr would have access in the afterlife, which is more a reflection of the West's inability to explain and respond to this type of attack than of reality. In fact, although the Koran describes paradise in great detail, the legend of the «72 virgins» is not found there. It is found in the *hadiths* (tradition) and even then, it does not apply exclusively to martyrs, but to all Muslims. It is therefore difficult to find a motivation to become a martyr. Nor would it explain the human bombs in Indonesia, where this belief is not widespread among the Muslim population and where studies have shown that the terrorists concerned generally lived in happy households:

> *Far from being lonely individuals, the majority of [terrorists over 30] are in stable relationships, and most have children, [which] challenges the idea that terrorists are young men driven by sexual frustration and lured into 'martyrdom' by the promise of beautiful virgins waiting for them in paradise. It is wrong to think that someone with a wife and children is less likely to commit acts of terrorism.*

Moreover, the legend of the «72 virgins», if it were a major motivation, would not explain the importance of the women martyrs. While it cannot be ruled out that in some isolated cases their actions are the result of external pressure, they are generally voluntary. In Chechnya, young women - often wives, fiancées or sisters of Chechen fighters killed in combat - have joined the ranks of Islamist terrorists in order to carry out attacks, then rather in a spirit of 'vendetta'. Also known as «*black widows*», «*shakhidki*» or «*smertnitsy*», they are involved in most of the most spectacular attacks carried out by Chechen terrorists.

2.7.3.3. Targeting and attacks on civilians

It is convenient to see terrorists as bloodthirsty madmen, but this is a sterile simplification that leads away from solutions. Understanding is not accepting. Even if each attack is unbearable and seems to us to strike unjustly and indiscriminately at innocent people, there is often in the view of the jihadists, a sense of a controlled response; both in the choice of victims, and in the intensity of the action.

The claim of the 13 November 2015 attacks states that the targets were «*carefully chosen*», suggesting that the terrorists did not strike at random in Paris:

> *Eight brothers carrying explosive belts and assault rifles targeted carefully selected locations in the heart of the French capital [...].*

However, the nature of the attacks clearly shows that no specific individuals were targeted. There is therefore a contradiction here, but it is only apparent. The texts published by the EI after the attacks of 2015-2016 show that the selection of targets probably followed a more refined approach than it seems. Indeed, at the tactical level, the attacks hit individuals at random, but at the operative level, there is a relatively precise selection of targets:

In relation to these operations, there are certain factors that need to be taken into consideration to ensure their success. The lives of Muslims must be given the utmost attention. Good targets are places where there should be no Muslims, such as places of perdition, nightclubs like in Bali, Mardi Gras, gambling places, or financial institutions that live on usury like the Twin Towers. Political parties or organisations that persecute Muslims should be targeted.

One must put oneself in the mind of the designers of the attacks and first understand that, contrary to what the «experts» claim, terrorists do not seek to «kill as many people as possible», but to have a maximum impact. These are two different things. They know that striking completely at random is a double-edged sword.

The victims of conflict or attacks are not the result of a 'disregard for life' as is often said, but rather the idea that there is a higher purpose that justifies 'collateral damage'. Indeed, this is exactly the same principle that is being applied by Western forces in Afghanistan, Iraq, Libya, Syria and elsewhere, as we shall see. This is an aspect of violence that is much discussed within the jihadist movements themselves. This is why, in Iraq, some terrorist groups plan their attacks in such a way as to minimise the risks to the civilian population and inform them before committing an attack; but this is explained by the fact that it is essentially a question of fighting an occupier and not forcing a government to make a decision.

As the terrorists have repeatedly made clear, their objective is to mobilise the target population against their government's decision to engage in the Middle East. To this end, instead of hitting them completely 'at random', they *'carefully select'* those who 'are the most guilty' or those who - in their eyes - have contributed or contribute 'more than others' to fuelling hatred against Islam.

After the attack on a gay nightclub in Orlando (12 June 2016), despite the EI's clearly expressed aversion to homosexuality, its claim video does not contain a single word against the gay community and only mentions the US-led war, as with the other attacks. In fact, the terrorists' «*after-action analysis*», published in a special issue of *Inspire* magazine, considers that targeting a «*specific group*» was the main weakness of the operation, as it distracted from the intended message:

The executor specifically chose a gay nightclub, [...] but it is best to avoid targeting minority areas. This is to keep the focus on the operation and to avoid it being portrayed as a small affair, as the US media tries to describe Mateen's case. The Western media focused on the testimony of Mateen's father, who claimed that his son hated homosexuals and had no terrorist intentions. [...]. The media attempted to portray the objectives of the operation as directed against a particular group of people, thereby distracting the American public from the real motives of the operation.

It is interesting to compare this 'first-hand' analysis with the statements of Mohammed Sifaoui on the programme *C dans l'air* of 13 June 2016, who understood nothing at all and stated exactly the opposite.In fact, the 'homophobic' interpretation that some have made of the attack has rendered the terrorists' message illegible and has contributed to the misunderstanding of the motives for the action, thus contributing to the dismissal of possible solutions at the strategic level.

To reach the West, terrorists target those communities (or institutions) to whom they attribute greater moral responsibility or guilt in the war against Islam, the rest being 'collateral' victims. In Paris in November 2015, the Jewish community was more a victim of 'default choices' than of targeting against Israeli or Jewish interests, as confirmed by the testimonies of the Bataclan survivors.

It is important to note that the message conveyed by the terrorist act is not directed at militants, but at the general population. In the Western perception, terrorism strikes civilians, who are innocent by definition. Jihadists have a different logic: they fight Western interventions and consider that the population *knows* that they are illegitimate, but does not use its democratic rights to ask its government to stop these aggressions. Thus, they consider that they bear some responsibility and are therefore not innocent.

Democratic governments are generally considered to be rational and guided by the common interest. But in reality, they engage in conflicts in inexplicable and unexplained ways. The decisions to intervene in Afghanistan, Iraq, Libya and Syria were justified only by lies. Yet these wars are destroying societies. Yet no citizen's movement has called governments and their leaders to account. It is this tacit or explicit complicity of the population that makes it so guilty in the eyes of terrorists.

By understanding the logic of terrorists, we can develop strategies that prevent the emergence of terrorism. In this perspective, we need to (maximum variant) rethink the appropriateness of using more effective and less lethal instruments than armed force or (minimum variant) surround our engagements with a communication campaign to explain their legitimacy.

The problem is that we are engaging in mindless conflict: the West and Israel continue to apply the same strategy that was used against Germany and Japan in the Second World War. This is to strike at civilian populations in order to make them turn against their leaders. This is the concept of the «Five Circles» developed by the American colonel John Warden. This - ironically - is exactly the same logic as terrorist acts:

[...] [The] advantage of targeting civilians is that it stirs up public opinion against administrations, Western governments and their policies.

Thus, in 1990, the United States called for an embargo against Iraq to be adopted by the UN Security Council, whose primary objective is to force Iraq to withdraw from Kuwait and pay reparations. Its secondary objective, however, is to provoke a revolt of the population against Saddam Hussein's regime.

Since the embargo was imposed on Iraq on 6 August [1990] after the invasion of Kuwait, the US has resisted any relaxation in the belief that by making life difficult for the Iraqi people, it will encourage them to remove Saddam Hussein from power.

Not only did the Iraqi population not revolt, but despite its human consequences, the embargo reinforced the legitimacy of the dictator. However, it is said to have caused the death of 500,000 Iraqi children.A figure that did not move Madeleine Albright , then US ambassador to the United Nations in New York:

I think it's a tough choice, but we think the price is worth it.

A line of reasoning that can be compared to Mike Pompeo's statement in November 2018, which introduces the US sanctions to the BBC by ironically saying that the Iranian government will have to do the right thing «*if it wants its people to* eat» .

The fact is that no one in Europe was shocked by this move and the US still enjoys fairly broad support. A comparison with the outcry over the photograph of little Eylan washed up on the Turkish coast in September 2015 shows that the value Westerners place on human life is variable and depends solely on political criteria. Those who advocate the reception of migrants in the Mediterranean are hardly moved by the conflicts created by our military actions and embargoes, which push these unfortunate people to our shores...

Rightly or wrongly, our disregard for the lives of others and our passivity in the face of these injustices make us guilty in the eyes of the Islamists. In fact, they take us to the game of democracy and question our inaction in the face of the decisions of our leaders to engage in conflicts, which we knew from the start were meaningless. In a video published after the Nice attack (14 July 2016), the French jihadist Rachid Kassim explains:

Such is the retribution of the criminal people that is the French people who do not hesitate to go out by the hundred thousands in the streets for their belly, for their work contract, but who knowing that their taxes finance the army of Tsahal and the massacre of Palestinians, that their taxes finance the bombardments in Iraq and in Sham and in the four corners of the planet of the Ummah [...] do not raise a single word!

Just as one crime cannot be justified by another, it is unacceptable that this passivity justifies acts of extreme violence. However, the jihadists' perception of our guilt is not without a certain consistency: it is similar to the notion of collective guilt, which is still applied to the former Nazis, for example. Yet despite the millions of victims, and while the whole world knows that the United States deliberately lied to the UN Security Council to start its war in Iraq, no sanction, no trial, no diplomatic consequences have been applied to the American officials. France opposed the US in 2003, but ended up following its lead in Iraq and Syria ten years later. The result is a sense of 'collusion' between civilian populations and their governments.

The relationship between military intervention and terrorism is surprisingly denied by intellectual and political elites, particularly in France.

In 2013, 68% of the French, 66% of the British, 63% of the Germans, 48-59% of the Americans and 52% of the Italians were opposed to intervention in Syria. Yet we (voluntarily) accept that our leaders engage us in conflicts, without concrete motives. In the minds of Islamists, because we are democracies (the 'power of the people'), this acceptance makes us complicit with the rulers. In their eyes, therefore, we are not innocent:

So what about today, when Western countries like America, Britain and France have opened hostilities against Muslims; killing millions of Muslims and making them suffer the worst. So, I clearly consider that the man who votes for his government and pays taxes to it deserves to be called a fighter. And therefore [shedding] his blood is more lawful than others. I have no doubt about the legality of shedding the blood of mature and sane men, who are capable of fighting, called civilians in the West; until they stop their aggression against Muslims and cease their constant interference in Muslim affairs and countries.

Thus, on a doctrinal level, we can see that, contrary to the official discourse disseminated in the West, the theorists of jihadist terrorism do not seek to «*destroy what we are*" or «*fight our religion*». Moreover, in 2012, Abu Musab al-Suri, who wrote the doctrine of the DTI, applied by «al-Qaeda» and the EI, stated:

[...] A final point about targeting in the heart of enemy countries, America and its Western Allies, is that one must avoid targeting places of prayer of any religion or faith, be it Christian, Jewish or other. Injuries to civilians who are citizens of countries unrelated to the conflict, even if they are not Muslims, must be avoided. This must be done in such a way as to maintain the reputation of the resistance in different circles of public opinion.

However, in July 2015, after the intensification of Western strikes in the Middle East, the EI stepped up a gear and encouraged the targeting of places of worship.

That said, the EI's use of a strategy based on individual initiative, or 'spontaneity' (in its terminology), poses the problem of the consistency of the action. While the literature produced by the EI is quite clear, precise and coherent, the claims expressed by the terrorists in their videos or posthumous letters do not always have the same rigour in the choice of terms. For example, they often speak of «*revenge*» , whereas the real objective goes further, since it seeks to force Western countries to abandon their interventions.

This suggests that not all terrorists always understand the strategic framework in which they operate. In other words, we may have a much greater influence on the choice of targets than we think. Thus, in a way, the emphasis on the religious dimension has unnecessarily exposed places of worship and clerics, whereas jihadist doctrine advised against targeting them, as we have seen above.

2.7.3.4. The antisemitic dimension

Like all discrimination, antisemitism must be fought. But it must be placed in its proper place in the context of terrorism, otherwise it will have the opposite effect. First of all, antisemitism is not the central element or the main motivation of Middle Eastern terrorism, although it is probably underlying. Secondly, a distinction must be made between «global» jihadist terrorism (which is essentially aimed at stopping Western interventions) and the Israeli-Palestinian conflict, which is motivated more by a «hatred of the occupier» than by a «hatred of the Jew».

However, it is clear that the Jewish community certainly suffers more than proportionally from terrorism. This can certainly be seen as antisemitic, but the term 'antisemitic' needs to be examined more carefully. Indeed, using this term tends to mask realities that would allow us to better understand the terrorist phenomenon. For example, the attacks in France in 2015-2016 were certainly aimed more at «French people» than at «Christians» or «Jews».

In 2008, a classified report by the British *Security Service* (MI5) raised the risk that too much support for the Jewish community would create more antisemitism. In this context, the French government accumulated almost all possible mistakes, putting the Jewish community in the terrorist's crosshairs.

Thus, President Hollande's message of support to the Israeli government in July 2014 during Operation PROTECTIVE BORDER and Prime Minister Manuel Valls' overly displayed and assertive link to the Jewish communityhave probably had more tragic consequences than one might imagine. Moreover, the EI took him at his word:

> *Manuel Valls declares that the Jews of France are the vanguard of the Republic, so they must die first in the war between Islam and the Caliphate and France. This was well understood by the brothers Mouhammad Merah and Amedy Coulibaly.*

By ostensibly displaying a personal and privileged link with the Jewish community, Valls undermined the impartiality of the government (secularism) which fuels communitarianism in France. Moreover, he reinforced the existing antisemitism by superimposing the unpopularity of his government, suggesting a collusion between the Jewish community and France's involvement in the Middle East. He thus made the Jewish community appear as a central actor in the fight against Muslims, thus making it «more guilty» than the others: by overexposing it unnecessarily, he placed it in the crosshairs of the terrorists. The best is the enemy of the good.

In January 2015, *Charlie Hebdo*, whose publications had fuelled the violence in 2006, was the main target; the attack on the Hyper Cacher in Vincennes, chosen because of the events in Gaza in July-August 2014 (as Amedy Coulibaly explains in his posthumous video) and probably because no Muslims would be found there, was in reality only a diversion to reduce police pressure on the Kouachi brothers, and not a primary objective.

In November 2015, a similar scenario can be found: the Bataclan, which was usually frequented by the *Jewish Defence League* (LDJ) and *Betar* - two Jewish extremist organisations - was the main target together with the Stade de France; it was on these two targets that the use of bombs was planned and where the terrorists were ready to cause maximum damage. As for the machine-gunning in the streets of Paris, it seems to have had the same function as the attack on the Hyper Cacher in January, namely a diversion to prevent the forces of order from concentrating on the main objectives. This worked well, since the police intervention forces did not arrive at the Bataclan until half an hour after the start of the hostage-taking, after having been engaged in the «machine-gunning» which had already been completed. The Bataclan was targeted because the terrorists believed it was owned by a Jew; in fact, the establishment had been resold in September 2015, but the terrorists probably did not know this.

Thus, antisemitism is not central to the claims of jihadist terrorism. However, it does come into play when terrorists have to choose their targets. Because it appears closer to power, because it strikes Palestinian civilians or because it animates a more virulent discourse against Islam, the Jewish community becomes an operational target, even if the strategic objective has nothing to do with it.

2.7.3.5. *Claiming responsibility for the attacks*

As we have seen above, the terrorist act *always* has a purpose. No one sacrifices his or her life without a reason or purpose. For an attack to be truly 'useful', therefore, its objective must be known, both so that the 'terror' generated can influence behaviour in the desired direction and so that activists can be informed. The terrorist act only exists - and is effective - if it is understood. The claim is therefore essential, as it expresses the meaning of the action. This also explains why attacks are often 'over-claimed', as other groups may then seek to benefit from the momentum they have created.

It is important to remember here that organisations that use terrorism are not afraid to claim it.

This is why the reasons, motives or purpose of the attacks are almost always present in the claims. However, the media almost never report them and replace them with their own interpretation, thus making the claim appear as a simple appropriation. Officially «not to play into the hands of the terrorists», but in reality to mask their real cause: Western interventions, which systematically appear in the text of the claims.

For law enforcement, the claim is also important, as it helps to understand the strategy of the terrorist group and to identify its centre of gravity.

In fact, since 2001 there has been a desire in the West to derationalise the discourse of terrorists. In addition to distracting public opinion from the real causes of terrorism, this concealment tends to fuel an Islamophobic discourse. Indeed, the irrationality attributed to terrorism opens the door to all possible interpretations, including that it is the inevitable consequence of the coexistence between Islam and Christianity, which fuels tensions between communities. Scenarios of intercommunal civil wars are then deduced (in France), whereas the EI has never mentioned them !

It should be noted here that there is a process of claiming responsibility with the EI, whereas there was none with what was called «Al-Qaeda». This is because there has never been an «Al Qaeda» organisation. «Al Qaeda» was only a movement, so called by the United States, but without a leadership structure capable of politically or operationally exploiting the impact of the attacks. This also explains the lack of coherence - visible or expressed - between the various attacks attributed to it. It is with the war in Iraq that we see the appearance of explicit claims and strategic coherence between

196

---

attacks, the most striking examples being Madrid and London. With the EI, not only is there an organisation identified from the outset, but there is also a leadership structure, articulated around the war in Iraq and Syria, with no identifiable offshoots in the West, but with communication channels capable of ensuring strategic exploitation of attacks outside its operational area.

An act that is lost in the fog of crime has no impact whatsoever and is therefore of no interest to terrorists. It must therefore be claimed. But this is complicated by the (theoretical) absence of operational links between the terrorist and the organisation he is acting on behalf of (in this case, the Islamic State), in order to avoid the premature detection of preparations for attacks. Therefore, the problem of individual terrorism is: «How to claim responsibility for a terrorist act, if all the perpetrators are killed?» The problem has been clearly identified by theorists of individual terrorism:

> *This is an important issue. Operations that are claimed to be responsible are certainly more successful. I think there are operations that have been carried out against the United States by Muslims, but because of communication problems have not had maximum resonance. [This is an important issue] especially in recent times, when we decided to stop our direct communications with individual fighters because of the large number of brothers arrested who had not carried out any operations.*

> *To avoid this problem, we came up with a number of ideas for claiming responsibility:*

> *If it is a suicide operation, it is [implicitly] 90% claimed. To complete this claim, you can call in the execution and send your message to someone who will broadcast it, or you can take hostages and negotiate, and then carry out the operation, or [you can] send a scheduled email or any other method that will not affect the success of the operation.*

> *If it is not a suicide operation, you can claim it using Wi-Fi without registering your profile, and then discard the device without leaving a trace. Other methods include leaving a piece of paper near the location of the operation before the operation. The symbol of the individual jihad operation is the burning World Trade Center.*

Technically, terrorists must minimise the risk of being discovered before they carry out their attack. This is why their demands are often recorded at the scene of the attack.

But terrorists often act on the basis of a generic 'call' from the EI. This means that the organisation does not necessarily know the identity of the terrorist or the nature of the act before it is carried out. The organisation must therefore identify the terrorist act and its perpetrator before claiming responsibility. This is why some attacks are not claimed until days later. This does not indicate a malfunction, quite the contrary.

However, this claim process is not without flaws and leads to erroneous announcements: the claim for the Brussels attacks (22 March 2016) mentioned the use of automatic weapons (which were not actually used) and the claim for the Paris attacks (13 November 2015) mentioned 8 terrorists (when there were actually 10). This shows that the EI hierarchy is only partially involved in the planning of operations, in accordance with the principles of «jihad by individual terrorism».

The failure or unwillingness to understand the mechanics of jihadist terrorism has opened the door to conspiracy theories. This is the case with the fairly systematic presence of terrorists' identity cards and Korans at the scene of attacks, as in Madrid in 2004. In fact, it is a way of appropriating the terrorist act, of «signing» it and claiming it «by default». It also means that the Kouachi brothers on 7 January 2015, who had left an identity card in their car, knew that they would die in the operation. The hypotheses formulated by some «experts» who evoke a way to create false leads or a «narcissistic» feeling of the terrorists who seek to acquire notoriety (!) are purely fanciful.

The mechanisms for claiming responsibility allow for a more detailed analysis of the attacks, their objectives or their authorship.

First, there are the 'claims', which are the recognition or acknowledgement of a terrorist act, but which do not necessarily constitute ownership. They arrive fairly quickly and usually before the official claim, most often by the EI's Amaq news agency, and begin with: «*According to a confidential source of the Amaq agency...*", meaning that it is information of external origin. This is the case for the Barcelona attack in August 2017, for example.

Secondly, there are the operations officially claimed by the Islamic State, in the form of an announcement on a blue cartouche with a red header bearing the organisation's logo. These are published simultaneously in several languages, sometimes with small differences due to translation. This is how the attacks of 13 November 2015 in Paris or the attacks of 22 March 2016 in Brussels were claimed. These are operations that the organisation probably knew about before they were carried out, without knowing all the details.

In contrast, the murder in Saint-Quentin-Fallavier (Isère, 26 June 2015) had all the appearances of a jihadist attack. But it was never claimed by a terrorist organisation, and its perpetrator killed himself in prison, which is quite rare for a true Islamist. It is therefore reasonable to think that it was a staged attack.

Finally, there are the reports and analyses in the publications of the EI. These articles glorify the perpetrators and their sacrifice, but not only. Some publications, such as *Inspire Guide,* take the attacks and critically analyse the tactics and techniques used, highlighting the 'positives' and pointing out the mistakes made and how to remedy them. These After Action Analyses (AAA), to use military parlance, and other reports are only about actions for the benefit of the Islamic State, which allows for attribution, even if the formal claim of responsibility is not forthcoming.

As the area covered by the Islamic State has shrunk, its claims have been more rapid and less elaborate, as in the case of the attack of 23 August 2018 in Trappes. This is explained by the fact that, whatever the situation on the ground, it is a matter of the organisation demonstrating that it remains active and does not give up the fight.

2.7.3.6. Terrorist financing

Based on the experience of the fight against Marxist terrorism in the 1970s and 1980s (especially in Italy and Germany), some 'experts' see financing as a major vulnerability of terrorism. This is only partially true, as these «experts» mix up several situations. The funding structure of a terrorist group depends on the nature of the terrorism it practises:

- Terrorism with national ambitions, which aims to overthrow the existing power or to promote a certain policy, is part of a revolutionary process that must maintain a project and political structures. This was the situation of the Red Brigades in Italy in the 1970s and 1980s and that of the Islamist rebel groups in Syria and Libya today, which are very largely supported by foreign countries, especially the West.

- Terrorism in the context of a guerrilla war against a foreign occupation or presence, which must maintain logistics. When it does not have major external support, guerrillas usually live off the population, through donations or support in kind, as in Iraq and Afghanistan.

- Terrorism whose objectives are outside the target country. This is the case of Jihad by Individual Terrorism (JIT), which requires only minimal structures in the target country. A fundamental element of this concept is the self-financing of terrorists, whose actions are usually very simple and inexpensive.

- The organisation of daily life in an area 'liberated' (or occupied) by a terrorist group. This was the case of the Islamic State 'caliphate', which had taken on the tasks of a state, ensuring the reconstruction of infrastructure and the operation of public services in the area it occupied. It was financed mainly by taxes and other levies.

In the early 2000s, the *hawala* system was mentioned as an explanation for terrorist financing. It is a widely used payment transfer mechanism in the Middle East and South Asia. It was designed to allow migrant workers to send their salaries to their families in their home countries, avoiding the often high taxes on earnings, and benefiting from market exchange rates rather than the often unfavourable official exchange rates. It has been in use for many years and has been particularly developed in recent years with mobile telephony. It is very effective in getting money to remote areas quickly and is often mentioned in relation to terrorist financing, although its significance has never been fully appreciated.

Designation of hawala in different parts of the world

Table 7 - Hawala is the most important technique for evading capital flow controls.

The *hawala* operates as a traditional mechanism for shifting debt to a third party: in Dubai (A) goes to the *hawaladar* (A') and gives him a sum of money and asks him to forward it, for a small commission, to (B) in Bombay. The *hawaladar* (A') telephones a *hawaladar* (B') in Bombay, and asks him to hand over a corresponding sum of money to (B), in return for a debt equivalent to the amount of the sum. The *hawaladars* (A') and (B') periodically update their respective credits and debts. One variant uses a receipt code to collect the money, which *hawaladar* A' gives to his client A, and which A' communicates to B so that he can collect the money from B'.

Hawala has also developed in Europe, where it is also used for money laundering[372].Its use in terrorist attacks remains very difficult to detect because of the small amounts of money that circulate. With the doctrine of «open jihad», financing mechanisms are becoming less important in the fight against terrorism.

In fact, the financing of terrorism has become a pretext for the imposition of control measures, which have no impact on terrorism, but serve other purposes. For example, in August 2021, the Israeli authorities confiscated 23 tons of chocolate destined for the Gaza Strip[373] , under the pretext that this chocolate could «*constitute an* alternative *currency*»[374] through which Hamas could acquire weapons. This is a delusion of the Israeli intelligence services, whose effect is

---

372. Hawala money laundering ring dismantled by joint investigation team, Europol, 29 November 2016.

373. «Israel intercepts 23 tons of chocolate it says was intended to finance Hamas", Times of Israel, 16 August 2021.

374. «Israel seizes 23 tons of chocolate intended for Hamas funding", The Jerusalem Post, 16 August 2021.

to reinforce hatred against the Israeli occupier: the Israelis manufacture the terrorism that they then fight...

2.7.3.7. The Jihadosphere

Our understanding of the role of the media and social networks in the jihadist phenomenon is still very sketchy, and explains to a large extent - here too - our inability to deal with the problem.

The jihadosphere is a complex set of diverse communication tools that exploit the capabilities of the Internet and social networks. For the Islamic State, it included Al-Hayat, the Islamic State's media production arm, several magazines distributed on the Net in PDF format, the main ones being: *Dar al-Islam* (in French), *Rumiyah* (in 11 languages), *Dabiq*, *Istok* (in Russian), *Constantinople* (in Turkish), *Al-Naba* and *Islamic State Report*. This is complemented by discussion forums on social networks - in particular Telegram, which offers robust encryption. This set-up was dismantled from 2017 onwards, but it shows the sophistication of the communication and the seriousness that is invested in its implementation.

It is notable that the Islamic State has no website and its communication is decentralised to reduce its vulnerability. Its media structures are extremely flexible. Under constant attack on the Internet by independent hackers or governments, they have developed coping mechanisms by moving very quickly across the web, allowing them to maintain the flow of information to their supporters almost uninterrupted.

These are supplemented by publications produced by the so-called 'al-Qaeda' media outlets, notably the *Global Islamic Media Front* (GIMF), associated with the *Arabian Peninsula Jihad Base* (APJB), such as *Inspire* or *Inspire Guide*. It is noteworthy that while the 'experts' try to persuade us of the antagonism between the Islamic State and 'al-Qaeda' (some of whose Syrian factions are supported and trained by the US and France), the publications of the BDPA complement those of the Islamic State. For example, the fifth issue of *Inspire Guide* provides a detailed analysis of the Nice operation (14 July 2016), noting its positive and negative points, areas for improvement, political exploitation, etc. Clearly, the publications of 'Al Qaeda' provide a doctrinal basis for the actions of the Islamic State.

In addition to these publications, the Amaq (or A'maq) news agency provides commentary covering the entire caliphate area. Considered inoperative since November 2019, it was responsible for disseminating claims for attacks around the world. Its broadcasts are complemented by the Al-Bayan radio station, which transmits news on the Net in several languages, including French and English.

The production of videos and songs («*nashid*») complements this communication device. The videos are usually of high graphic quality, with the clear intention of providing a didactic message. While the Western press only mentions beheadings and other barbaric executions, the video production covers a large number of documentaries on the daily life, structure and objectives of the Islamic State. There are documentaries on the Islamic State's currency, its efforts in agriculture or infrastructure maintenance, the semi-industrial production of weapons and ammunition, etc.

Clearly, these publications are intended to support the efforts of the Islamic State and should therefore be viewed critically. However, the figures and information provided in these publications are mostly accurate, and often more conservative than one would expect from propaganda. They value courage, self-sacrifice and a sense of duty, glorify the great battles of the past, the romanticism of the war adventure and the heroes of yesterday and today. Propaganda plays its role here: presenting the good side of things. It should therefore be the object of healthy suspicion, but should not be extrapolated, as is done in the West, to the point of obtaining a distorted image of the adversary. For example, it can be seen that the efforts of the EI are focused on the struggle in Iraq and Syria. The idea of extending the caliphate to Europe or generating a civil war in France, as some claim, does not appear in these publications.

2.8. Islamic State (IS)

2.8.1. Emergence

The emergence of the Islamic State (IS) is a direct and combined consequence of the mismanagement of the post-First Gulf War (1990-1991), the US intervention in Iraq in 2003 and the US failure to manage the post-Saddam Hussein era. The *Islamic State* (IS) is the most recent iteration of a resistance movement to the US occupation in Iraq, which began in 2004 as the *Group for Unity and Jihad* (*Jama'at al-Tawhid wal-Jihad*) (April-October 2004). Known successively as the *Mesopotamia Jihad Base Organisation* (*Tanzim al-Qaidat Jihad fi-Bilad al-Rafidayn*) (2004-2006), the *Islamic State in Iraq* (*Al-Dawlah al-Islamiyah fi'l Eiraq*) (EII) (2006-2013), then *Islamic State in Iraq and the Levant* (*Al-Dawlah al-Islamiyah fi'l Eiraq wal-Sham*) (EIIL) (2013-2014), it became the *Islamic State* (*Al-Dawlah al-Islamiyah*) (EI) on 29 June 2014.

Before 1990, Sunni Islamist movements were almost non-existent in Iraq, not only because of the strictness of Saddam Hussein's regime - which was fundamentally secular - but also, and above all, because the government was Sunni. After the war, the combination of sanctions (international embargo, no-fly zones, etc.), clandestine support to Shiite rebels by the US and Britain, and their presence in Saudi Arabia generated Sunni radicalism. In 1991, in order to contain this radicalisation, Saddam Hussein gave a more Muslim tone to his regime and added the words «*Allahu Akbar*» to the country's flag.

Completely underestimated and ignored by American and Western intelligence services, this rise of Islamism generates jihadism with the objective of pushing the United States out of Saudi Arabia, a territory considered sacred. At this stage, jihadism is just an idea, a movement that rejects the Western (mainly American) presence in the Middle East. It had no structure and based its action on local initiatives, which culminated on 11 September 2001. But the Americans did not understand anything and their various military interventions only reinforced Islamism. They were thus unable to transform their operational successes into strategic successes and engaged in an intensification of the war, provoking the detestation of the West. Ten years later, it will be the same in Afghanistan, Libya and the Sahel: the absence of a strategy and clear objectives have made our interventions unreadable and have opened the door to all kinds of extremism.

Moreover, the failure of the United States to anticipate the consequences of Iran's new regional role has created an existential fear for the Gulf monarchies. Not because of Iran itself - which has shown no regional aggression since the 18th century[e] - but because their oil-producing areas are all in areas where Shiite minorities are traditionally in the majority.

As early as 2004, obsessed with the Shiite militias resisting their occupation, the Americans distributed arms to Sunni Islamists. However, acting in haste and without organisation, they literally lost about 190,000 small arms, bringing to more than 700,000 the number of weapons delivered by the United States and of which they no longer have any trace[375].Never accounted for and distributed to unknown individuals, they have contributed to the capacity of Iraqi Islamists in the region[376] .

From 2006-2007, General Petraeus' 'strategy' - which the military considers innovative - is merely a 'rehash' of strategies from the late 1940s. Simplistic, decontextualised and disconnected from a holistic approach, it has given the illusion of a buy-in from the Sunni communities of Anbar, whose collaboration has been 'bought' with millions of dollars and arms. This period of apparent stabilisation is strengthening the country's jihadist forces. The main faction to emerge is the EII, which inscribes its action in a form of Sunni nationalism. It fights against the Iraqi government, which is seen as corrupt

---

375. See the quarterly reports of the Office of the Special Inspector General for Afghanistan Reconstruction (SIGAR), which highlights that not only did the US supply weapons based on grossly overstated numbers, but that 43% of the weapons issued were not registered under a valid serial number (SIGAR 14-84 Audit Report).
376. Mark Tran, "190,000 US weapons feared missing in Iraq", The Guardian, 6 August 2007.

because it was established or supported by the West, and whose approach is seen as an extension of the medieval crusades.

While what was known as «Al-Qaeda» only targeted the Western presence, from 2003 onwards, with the communitarian clashes in Iraq, jihadism took on an «anti-Shiite» character. A report by the *Joint Intelligence Committee* (JIC), responsible for intelligence analysis for the British government, confirmed in July 2006:

> *The label 'jihadist' is becoming increasingly difficult to define: in many cases, the distinction between nationalists and jihadists is blurred. They increasingly share a common cause, being united by Shia sectarian violence.*[377]

In March 2007, the JIC confirmed that resistance to the US invasion was indeed behind the establishment of the EII, which later became the EI:

> *There is no shortage of suicide bombers. AQ-I [Al Qaeda in Iraq] seeks high-profile attacks. We believe that AQ-I will try to expand its sectarian campaign wherever possible: suicide bombings in Kirkuk have increased sharply since October, when AQ-I declared the creation of the «Islamic State of Iraq» (including Kirkuk).*[378]

From 2011 onwards, American[379], Turkish and French military support and arms supplies have encouraged a jihadist insurgency in Syria, forcing the government to tighten its grip in the west of the country. The result is a power vacuum in the east and the loss of control over the Iraqi-Syrian border, which provides an opening for the EII, as shown in a dynamic map of the conflict[380].

In 2012, a SECRET report by the *Defense Intelligence Agency* (DIA) already predicted:

> *[Paragraph 8.D.1.] The Islamic State in Iraq could also proclaim an Islamic state by uniting with other terrorist organisations in Iraq and Syria, which will create a great danger to the unification of Iraq and the protection of its territory.*[381]

---

377. Patrick Wintour, "Intelligence files support claims Iraq invasion helped spawn Isis", The Guardian, 6 July 2016.

378. Ibid.

379. David E. Sanger, "Rebel Arms Flow Is Said to Benefit Jihadists in Syria", The New York Times, 14 October 2012.

380. See The Syrian Civil War, every day, Lyria Mapping, YouTube, 19 October 2017.

381. http://www.judicialwatch.org/wp-content/uploads/2015/05/Pg.-291-Pgs.-287-293-JW-v-DOD-and-State-14-812-DOD-Release-2015-04-10-final-version11.pdf.

In 2013, the EII became the EIIL, consecrating its Syrian ambitions. It is however neither Syrian nor composed of Syrians and illustrates the exogenous character of the Syrian insurrection. Led by Abu Bakr al-Baghdadi, its progress in Syria is rapid and it establishes a «caliphate» between Iraq and Syria (al-Sham), straddling the Iraqi-Syrian border, and gives itself the name of *Islamic State* (EI) in June 2014.

For the US, France and Israel, the Sunni insurgency in Syria is a way to weaken Iran's influence in the region and to cut Syria and the Lebanese Hezbollah off from their ally. In early August 2012, in a classified SECRET 'intelligence report' on the situation in Syria, the US DIA explained the advantage of supporting the Syrian Salafists, despite the risks of an Islamic state emerging[382] :

If the situation allows, there is the possibility of establishing a declared or undeclared Salafist principality in eastern Syria (Hasaka and Deir Zor), and this is exactly what the countries supporting the opposition want in order to isolate the Syrian regime, which is seen as the strategic depth of Shiite expansion (Iraq and Iran).[383]

The Americans are not trying to create a terrorist state, as one might think, but to find an outlet for Sunni nationalism, in order to stabilise Iraq for which they feel responsible. Incidentally, this allows the fragmentation of Syria (Israel's declared enemy), to slip a wedge into the Shiite stranglehold around Saudi Arabia, which the 2003 intervention had provoked, and to disrupt the Damascus-Tehran axis. Moreover, the area chosen by the Americans is one of the main oil-producing zones of Syria, so that the Islamists «keep quiet».

In Iraq, the Islamic State in Iraq (ISI) was initially a resistance movement to the US occupation. In 2011, Western efforts to overthrow the Syrian government created an opportunity for the ISI to establish its 'Islamic State' in eastern Syria. Until 2015, its action was limited to these two theatres of operation. It was only after the arrival of the Europeans in 2014, to help the overwhelmed United States, that the EII (now EI) engaged in international terrorist actions. The problem is that France did not get involved in Syria to fight terrorism, but to overthrow the government. Eventually, the Islamic State will physically disappear, but without a clear strategy, the phenomenon remains. Operation BARKHANE in the Sahel suffers from the same strategic deficit.

<hr>

382.   http://www.judicialwatch.org/wp-content/uploads/2015/05/Pg.-291-Pgs.-287-293-JW-v-DOD-and-State-14-812-DOD-Release-2015-04-10-final-version11.pdf.

383   Brad Hoff, "West will facilitate rise of Islamic State 'in order to isolate the Syrian regime': 2012 DIA document", Foreign Policy Journal, 21 May 2015; see also: http://www.judicialwatch.org/wp-content/uploads/2015/05/Pg.-291-Pgs.-287-293-JW-v-DOD-and-State-14-812-DOD-Release-2015-04-10-final-version11.pdf.

2.8.2. Threat to the West?

From 2011, the action of France and the United States aims to overthrow the Syrian regime, and the departure of jihadists to Syria seems to be the subjectof a certain complacency of the French government. In reality, there is, at this time, a convergence of objectives between the government and the jihadists, who become *de facto* the «*occasional collaborators of French diplomacy*», according to the expression of the former anti-terrorist judge Alain Marsaud[384].It was only in April 2014, after about 500 French people had joined Islamist groups, that the government envisaged measures to curb the phenomenon[385].

Indeed, until 2014, all experts agreed that the EI did not pose a direct threat to the West. The declarations of Presidents Obama and Hollande to justify the need for air strikes against the EI in Iraq were met with scepticism, particularly on the other side of the Atlantic. While there was a perceived need to act on the threat to non-Muslim populations in Iraq and Syria, the strikes were of limited use and - on the contrary - stimulated the advance of the EI until Russia arrived in the theatre. Other means of action, such as diplomacy, would have been wiser and certainly less costly in terms of human lives.

On 22 June 2014, when asked about the emergence of the Islamic State at a press conference, President Obama said that it could pose a threat in the «*medium to long term*», but that it was neither an immediate threat nor a necessary and sufficient condition for the United States to engage in external military operations without the approval of Congress[386].A reading confirmed on 29 August 2014 by Jeh Johnson, US Secretary of Homeland Security:

> *At this time, the Department of Homeland Security and the FBI are not aware of any specific and credible threat from the Islamic State against the US territory.*[387]

On 10 September, under pressure from the Republican opposition, President Obama declared:

---

384. Interview with Alain Marsaud, former anti-terrorist judge and chairman of the working group on Syria at the National Assembly, RFI, 24 April 2014.

385. David Thomson, a senior reporter at RFI and author of the book Les Français jihadistes (published by Les Arènes, 6 March 2014), answers questions from Arnaud Rivoire in Paris Direct, France 24, 23 April 2014.

386. Rory Carroll, "Obama: Isis could pose a 'medium and long-term threat' to the US", The Guardian, 22 June 2014.

387. https://www.youtube.com/watch?v=2cmL_PcyoYk, online 31 August 2014 (accessed 13 November 2016).

[...] I have made it clear that we will hunt down the terrorists who threaten our country, wherever they may be. This means that I will not hesitate to act against ISIL in Syria and Iraq.[388]

But since EIIL does not constitute a sufficient threat, one must be created to justify intervention. Then, in a very timely manner, a terrorist group of unknown virulence appears in the media: the Khorasan group. CBS News states:

The sources confirm that the al-Qaeda cell is called «Khorasan» [...].

According to a CIA official, the threat posed by the new Syrian group is more dangerous than ISIL.[389]

On 20 September, it is learned that the *Khorasan* group[390] is led by Muhsin al-Fadhli (an Islamist close to Osama bin Laden), who is said to have participated in the preparation of the «9/11» attacks[391] , and to have financed the operation against the French ship *MV Limburg* in 2002.

He is even credited with using «explosive clothing»[392].US counter-terrorism bodies attribute to him an 'aspiration' to commit a '9/11-like' attack and suggest that he operates in connection with Pakistan, Afghanistan and Iran[393].It was on this basis that on 23 September 2014, President Obama launched air strikes on Syrian territory:

Last night, we also carried out attacks to destroy plots against the United States by experienced al Qaeda operatives known as the Khorasan group. Once again, it must be clear to anyone who would seek to plot against America and harm Americans that we will not tolerate sanctuaries for terrorists who threaten our people.[394]

---

388. "President Obama: 'We Will Degrade and Ultimately Destroy ISIL'", White House Office of the Press Secretary, 10 September 2014 (accessed 1ᵉʳ October 2015).

389. "Al Qaeda's quiet plan to outdo ISIS and hit U.S.", CBS News, 18 September 2014.

390. This group should not be confused with the «Khorasan Province», which emerged on 12 January 2015 in Pakistan from a Taliban splinter group and joined the Islamic State, which was listed as a foreign terrorist movement by the United States on 16 January 2016.

391. Mark Mazzetti, Michael S. Schmidt & Ben Hubbard, "U.S. Suspects More Direct Threats beyond ISIS", 20 September 2014.

392. Josh Levs, Paul Cruickshank & Tim Lister, "Source: Al Qaeda group in Syria plotted attack against U.S. with explosive clothes", CNN, 24 September 2014.

393. Eli Lake, "Al Qaeda Plotters in Syria 'Went Dark' U.S. Spies Say", The Daily Beast, 23 September 2014.

394. "Statement by the President on Airstrikes in Syria", The White House Office of the Press Secre-

It invokes a situation of self-defence, suggesting that Syria was providing sanctuary for terrorists preparing actions against the US. *The Washington Post*, citing Pentagon sources, mentions that the group was about to execute «*imminent*» strikes against Europe or the United States[395].But doubts soon arose:

> *Khorasan intends to strike, but we don't know if their capabilities are what they want.* [396]

Gradually, the plot thickens. It appears that the group (allegedly preparing for imminent attacks) had not defined any targets and the *New York Times* reports the statements of a US official who describes the group as having «aspirations» to carry out attacks and states that it appeared that the group did not even have any concrete plans[397].In late September 2014, the *National Review* confirms:

> *You have never heard of a group called Khorasan because there never was one. It was a name created by the administration, which calculated that Khorasan - a region in the border area of Iran and Afghanistan - had enough links to the jihadist context that no one would question the President's word.*[398]

Clearly, precisely because in September 2014 the EI did not constitute a sufficient threat to justify intervention, the Obama administration created an 'imminent threat' out of thin air in the form of the *Khorasan group*, to claim self-defence and justify strikes. On 1er February 2015, President Obama himself acknowledged on CNN that the EI is not a threat to the West:

> *We will not give these terrorist networks a victory by overstating their importance and suggesting in any way that they are an existential threat to the United States or the world order.*[399]

tary, 23 September 2014.

395. Terrence McCoy, "Targeted by U.S. airstrikes: The secretive al-Qaeda cell was plotting an imminent attack", The Washington Post, 23 September 2014.

396. Ibid.

397. Mark Mazzetti, "A Terror Cell That Avoided the Spotlight", The New York Times, 24 September 2014.

398. Andrew C. McCarthy, "The Khorosan Groups Does Not Exist", National Review, 27 September 2014.

399. Kate Brannen, 'Obama Warns Against Exaggerating the Islamic State Threat', Foreign Policy, 1er February 2015; Ian Schwartz, 'Obama: We Should Stop 'Overinflating' Importance of Terror Groups as If 'They Are an Existential Threat' To U.S.', Realclearpolitics.com, 1er February 2015.

So, in 2014, the EI is not a threat to France, but the French government will make exactly the mistake described by Obama, and will be obliged to lie to the French public in order to clear its responsibility.

The emergence of the Islamic State is the result of a decision by the West to allow this movement, which directly threatened the Syrian government, to grow. Since 2016, this explanation has been confirmed by a first-hand actor of the time: John Kerry, then US Secretary of State. As he explains, the Western coalition deliberately allowed the EI to grow, in the hope that this would force the Syrian government to negotiate:

> *The reason why Russia got involved was because the EI had grown stronger. Daech was threatening to reach Damascus and that's why Russia intervened. Because they didn't want a Daech government and they were supporting Assad.*

> *And we knew it [Daech] was growing. We were watching. We saw that Daech was becoming more and more powerful and we thought that Assad was threatened. But we thought that we could probably manage, that Assad would negotiate afterwards. Instead of negotiating, he asked Putin for help[400] .*

An examination of the maps shows that Western (including French and Belgian) strikes *only* target the EI when it is in contact with Western-backed rebel forces (such as the Kurds), and when it is not in contact with forces allied to the Syrian government[401].Indeed, it was between the end of 2014 (start of Western strikes) and September 2015 (start of Russian strikes), that the territorial expansion of the EI was the fastest[402] .

---

400. John Kerry, recording of a meeting with the Syrian opposition at the UN Mission in the Netherlands, 22 September 2016, published by Wikileaks ("Leaked audio of John Kerry's meeting with Syrian revolutionaries/UN (improved audio)", YouTube, 4 October 2016)
401. Georges Malbrunot, «La France face au conflit syrien : le choix de l'i-realpolitik», Outre-Terre 2015/3 (N°44) (pp. 23-26)
402. See the dynamic maps of the war: https://syria.liveuamap.com/

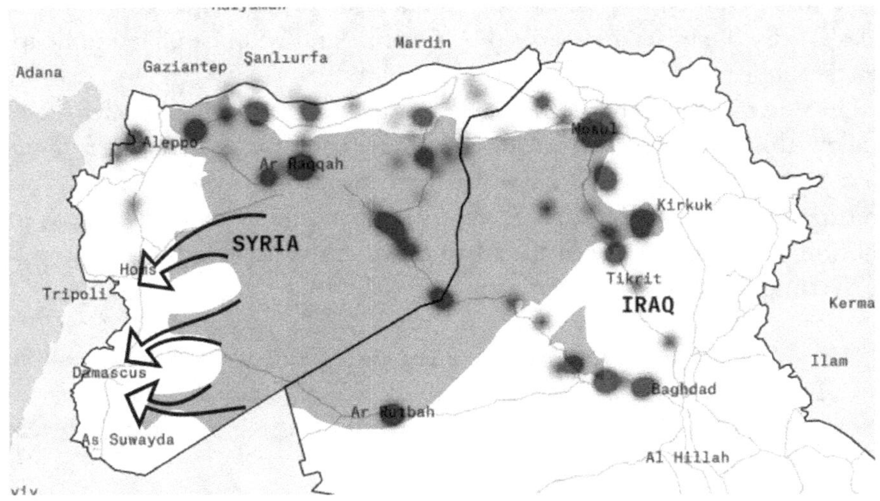

Figure 8 - Map of Western strikes (black spots) against the EI (dark grey area) between 2014 and September 2015 (when the Russians arrived). The arrows show EI offensives towards Damascus. As can be seen, the strikes only hit Islamists who were in contact with the Kurds or Western-backed groups, but never targeted EI forces when they were in contact with Syrian forces. [Source: airwars.org]

It was only at the end of 2015, after the Russian intervention, that the territory of the EI began to shrink[403].At the end of September 2015, Russia proposed to the West the creation of an expanded coalition to fight the EI, but they refused.

For at that time, the West was not interested in destroying the EI, but in dismantling Syria and dividing it into a Kurdish area (in the northwest), a Shiite area (in the west) and a Sunni area (in the east), in which they were prepared to allow a Salafist state to develop. This area is the one described in the *Defense Intelligence Agency* (DIA) SECRET report of 5 August 2012[404].

This area is exactly the one that was spared by the international coalition strikes until the arrival of Russian forces in the region. The idea of a Salafist state in Syria is part of an American plan (drawn up in agreement with Israel) for a partition of Syria, mentioned by John Kerry during his hearing before the *Senate Foreign Affairs Committee* in February 2016[405].This plan will be taken up by the Trump administration and explains the current American presence in Syria[406].

---

403. See "The Syrian Civil War, every day", YouTube (updated daily)

404. Brad Hoff, "West will facilitate rise of Islamic State "in order to isolate the Syrian regime: 2012 DIA document", Foreign Policy Journal, 21 May 2015; see also: http://www.judicialwatch.org/wp-content/uploads/2015/05/Pg.-291-Pgs.-287-293-JW-v-DOD-and-State-14-812-DOD-Release-2015-04-10-final-version11.pdf

405. Patrick Wintour, "John Kerry says partition of Syria could be part of 'plan B' if peace talks fail", The Guardian, 23 February 2016

406. James Dobbins, Jeffrey Martini & Philip Gordon, "A Peace Plan for Syria", Rand Corporation, 2015 (Document PE-182-RC); Jeff Mackler, "The US Plan to Partition Syria", Counterpunch, 9

210

It is not entirely by chance that Abu Bakr al-Baghdadi, and then Abu Ibrahim al-Hashimi al-Qurashi, leaders of the EI, were both shot dead by American special forces *inside* areas that had been sanctuarised by Western forces against Syrian armed forces[407].

In February 2016, Alexander Yakovenko, Russia's ambassador to Britain, revealed that the Russian decision to intervene in Syria was made in the summer of 2015, when the Islamic State (IS) reached the city of Palmyra. The Western coalition then anticipated that the EI would enter Damascus in October, and the US would have been able to establish a no-fly zone over the city. So it was not because of Western weakness, but to prevent the capital from being handed over to the jihadists, that the Russians intervened[408].

It was therefore the Western governments, and in particular the French government at the time, that played with fire, without thinking that their ostensibly and loudly pro-Israel policy would place them at the centre of the terrorists' target. This lack of anticipation is also underlined by the total absence of accompanying security measures in metropolitan France. It is almost as if the terrorists had been challenged to come and commit attacks.

In June 2017, with the battle for Mosul nearly six months old against a coalition of nearly 60 countries, the EI is suffering significant losses, yet its resolve and support do not appear to be waning. It appears to be remarkably resilient[409] , which can be explained by several factors:

- Firstly, their asymmetric doctrine is a key asset: their centre of gravity lies in the determination to resist adversity rather than to crush the opponent. By placing their doctrine under the umbrella of religion, they are defending a community of belief, not territory, which gives them a considerable advantage since victory (or defeat) is not quantifiable. This is a masterful illustration of the notion of 'jihad'.

- By focusing on the EI, Westerners have mythologised it as a symbol of resistance to Western dominance[410].With a strategy based solely on the use of force, they have not succeeded in imposing a value system that appears superior to that of the EI, as illustrated by Ali Arkady's article in *Spiegel*, which shows the brutality of the Iraqi forces supervised and trained by the West, who behave

February 2018; Nafeez Mosaddeq Ahmed, "US military document reveals how the West opposed a democratic Syria", mondiplo.com, 24 September 2018

407. Chantal Da Silva, Ammar Sheikh Omar, Courtney Kube & Phil Helsel, «ISIS leader dies during U.S. special forces raid in Syria, Biden says», NBC News, 3 February 2022

408. Alexander Yakovenko, "Russia and the US are partners in trying to end the war in Syria", The Evening Standard, 15 February 2016

409. Hassan Hassan, «Despite heavy losses, ISIL's structures remain resilient», The National, 10 May 2017.

410. Pieter Nanninga (Assistant Professor at the Department of Middle East Studies, University of Groningen), «Paris through the eyes of IS supporters», religionfactor.net, 24 November 2015.

like lawless torturers, thus feeding the EI's discourse[411]. The EI has now largely become the «reference» in the fight against the West.

In fact, the EI is in essence a Sunni 'nationalist' initiative. It is Westerners - including figures such as Manuel Valls - who have contributed greatly to the mythologising of the group, in order to justify aggressive foreign policies and mask attempts to overthrow a legal government.

The differences proclaimed by the «experts» between «al-Qaeda» and the EI are nothing but sophistry. Moreover, the attack on *Charlie Hebdo* was an action of the *Jihad Base in the Arabian Peninsula*, commonly known as «*Al-Qaeda in Yemen*»[412] , as part of a so-called «hybrid operation»[413]. Their basic «doctrine» converges on the fight against the Western presence in the Middle East. Between 1990 and 2003, it was the American presence in Saudi Arabia that mobilised the jihadists, but they did not have sufficient operational capacity to carry out an 'open' combat. This is the reason for the attacks on the American rear by progressively widening the circle of their actions in Saudi Arabia, Yemen, Tanzania and Kenya, then on American soil. From 2003, the American intervention generated various resistance movements in Iraq. But, in the absence of an Iraqi «Jean Moulin», they clash and eliminate each other. In fact, as with the Taliban in Afghanistan, the *Islamic State in Iraq* (ISI) became the unifying element in the Sunni north of the country.

With great foresight, President Obama warned against the risk of exploiting the overestimation of the threat to abandon our principles and values, which is what France has done with the state of emergency and by renouncing the fundamental rights provided for in the European Convention on Human Rights[414]. This has highlighted the fragility of democracies in the face of the tyranny of counter-terrorism.

2.8.3. Islamic State, ISIS, ISIL, DAECH?

In Anglo-Saxon countries, the use of the abbreviations 'ISIS' (*Islamic State in Iraq and in Syria*) or 'ISIL' (*Islamic State in Iraq and in the Levant*) has caused controversy. Donald Trump and many American commentators[415] criticised President Obama for favouring the abbreviation «ISIL», and thus implicitly denying the existence of the State of Israel (!) Explanation: the «L» in «ISIL»

---

411. Ali Arkady, „Nicht Helden, sondern Monster", Der Spiegel, n° 21/2017, 19 May 2017.

412. Full name: Arabian Peninsula Jihad Base (APJB) (Qa'idat al-Jihad fi Jazirat al-Arab) - also known as Al Qaeda in the Arabian Peninsula (AQAP).

413. The term 'hybrid' here refers to the terminology used by the EI, not that used in the West.

414. Blandine Le Cain, «France plans to violate human rights with the state of emergency», lefigaro.fr, 27 November 2015.

415. Why President Obama Says ISIL And Not ISIS, https://www.youtube.com/watch?v=ea4TK_ISz3M&t=98s.

refers to the «*Levant*» (*Sham*), an area that stretches from the Mediterranean to the Euphrates, ignoring modern national borders, and thus the existence of Israel. The argument is specious because Western countries continue to use the acronym «DAECH» (ISIL), which translates as «*Islamic State in Iraq and the Levant*» (EIIL). Do Western countries deny the existence of Israel?

Our perception of the EI is emotional and the way we call it betrays our weakness. In the French media, the use of the acronym «DAECH», composed from the abbreviation of «*Al-Dawlah al-Islamiyah fi'l Eiraq wal-Sham*», was imposed at the insistence of the French government, and in particular Laurent Fabius, as early as 2014:

> *I would ask you to stop using the term Islamic State, because it causes confusion between Islam, Islamists and Muslims. It is what the Arabs call Daech, and I would call them the cutthroats of Daech.*[416]

This is actually a revengeful play on words inspired by the linguistic proximity to the Arabic word *'daes'*, which means to crush something with one's foot. In fact, Arabs generally make very little use of abbreviations, and the EI has never used the acronym DAECH. Thus, not only is it given a name that limits its field of action to Iraq and Syria - in contradiction with the global ambitions it is said to have - but, paradoxically, it is given the name under which it has never committed attacks in the West! In fact, its first claimed attacks in the West date from the second half of 2014, when it called itself «*Islamic State*» and the West had already launched strikes against it.

In Britain, while 120 MPs urged him to use the word 'Daech', Tony Hall, Director General of the BBC, refused, explaining that the term is *'pejorative'* and *'would not preserve the* BBC*'s impartiality'*[417].

The use of the name «DAECH» is symptomatic of the way the West reacts to terrorism, multiplying inconsistencies and, ultimately, rendering its message totally unreadable. Of course, the initial idea was to remove all legitimacy from a possible «Islamic State». But it is at the same time an admission of weakness, because by not using its official name, one tends to show that one is afraid of it, and thus to make it the main bearer of resistance against Western interventions. Some researchers go even further and show that by using a name that is no longer used, the West denies the evidence and takes refuge behind fictions to justify its actions and exploit terrorism for political purposes[418].

---

416. Armin Arefi, «Daesh-Islamic State: the name war has begun», LePoint.fr, 22 September 2014.
417. «UK questions Daech - BBC refuses to use the term 'Daech' to describe the armed group», lesechos.fr, 3 July 2015. NOA: the BBC favours the term «so-called Islamic State».
418. See Erin Wilson (Faculty of Theology and Religious Studies, University of Groningen), 'Accepting Ambiguity: Being Content with Uncertainties amidst the Urge for Security', religionfactor.net, 17

The same result would be more intelligently achieved with the name «*Islamic State» group*, which shows that the organisation is not recognised as a state, but that its reality is taken into account.

Moreover, this name contains a fundamental contradiction. Indeed, in order to justify its engagement in Syria, France relied on Article 51 of the UN Charter, which authorises the use of force by a state in self-defence. The Charter does not provide for the use of force by a country against a group of individuals, but against countries. France therefore had an extensive interpretation of the notion of self-defence here... unless it considered the *group «Islamic State»* as a state! Thus, contrary to its official statements, it has *de facto* recognised the existence of an Islamic State. Of course, we are playing with words here, but this shows that the fight against terrorism is not a matter of emotions, but of coldly calculated strategy. Otherwise, exactly what happened is happening...

Another element of contradiction is that by denying the EI the possibility of defining itself in relation to a territory, the loss of that same territory was also denied as a defeat! It is therefore logical that the EI does not consider itself defeated.

In the end, the IE is an entity that is very poorly understood and apprehended on the basis of circumstantial elements, i.e. dominated by 'personal impressions' or deductions linked to (Western) 'common sense' according to the circumstances. This is the reason why we do not understand his way of acting, and why the West is systematically 'behind the times'.

As we can see, counter-terrorism is not simply a matter of revenge, police, arrests and over-equipped special forces, but of strategy. This is not the case. Since 2012, there has been a strange doctrinal proximity between the French approach to terrorism and that of Israel: there is no strategy against the EI, but the more or less coherent application of a series of tactical actions. Encouraged by intellectuals and self-appointed «experts», the fight against the EI has been marked by amateurism and has resulted in an aggravation of the problem, including the attacks of 2015-2016.

2.8.4. The emergence of the caliphate

The Islamic State has created a structure to administer the territories it controls. The «black spots» on the maps presented by the media are misleading, because the group's authority is mainly concentrated along the main roads, while the in-between areas are almost deserted. Conversely, when trying to show the coalition's successes, the «blotch» tends to be reduced to the roads, giving the impression of a retreat, when in reality the change is minimal and key areas have remained in the hands of the IO.

November 2015.

Similarly, the Western media tends to give a distorted perception of the acceptance of the local populations of the EI in the areas it administers. Although it is clear that the EI is administering the areas it occupies with an iron fist, it does not seem to be triggering the rejection that one might imagine in the West. This explains why, in June 2014, the EI was able to take Mosul in four days and with only 300-400 fighters, but why the Western coalition will only be able to retake it in nine months with nearly 100,000 men in 2016-2017. As in Afghanistan, Libya, Iraq and Syria, the leaders, even if they are not models of democracy, have far more popular support than the solutions brought from the West.

It is easy enough to take the inflammatory statements of some imam, such as Anjem Choudary in London, to convey the idea of an Islamic state eager to conquer the West. Yet the fear expressed by some of a caliphate that would take over the entire Mediterranean by launching vast military operations is unfounded. In fact, this idea emerged within the American *establishment in the* early 2000s. It was in September 2004, in Lake Elmo, that Vice President Dick Cheney first raised the notion of a caliphate associated with «al-Qaeda» that would directly threaten Western Europe:

> *They talk about wanting to re-establish what you might call the seventh century caliphate. It's the way the world was organised 1200-1300 years ago, when Islam or Muslims controlled everything from Portugal and Spain in the west; across the Mediterranean to North Africa; all of North Africa; the Middle East; all the way to the Balkans; the Central Asian republics; the southern tip of Russia; much of India; and all the way to modern Indonesia. In a sense, from Bali and Jakarta at one end to Madrid at the other.*[419]

The idea was taken up in a report by the US *National Intelligence Council*[420] published in December 2004. Entitled «Modelling the Future of the World», it presents four scenarios for the possible evolution of the world by 2020, including the reconstitution of the caliphate. This report, which is a hypothetical model, will however be presented by the Bush administration - and in the first place by the Secretary of Defense Donald Rumsfeld - as the objective of «Al-Qaeda»[421] :

---

419. «Vice President's Remarks and Q&A at a BC'04 Roundtable in Lake Elmo, Minnesota", Office of the Vice President, 29 September 2004, http://georgewbush-whitehouse.archives.gov/news/releases/2004/09/text/20040929-5.html.

420. The National Intelligence Council (NIC) is an advisory council to the US Director of National Intelligence, which is part of the Intelligence Community and is responsible for providing forward-looking analysis to the country's strategic leadership. It is broadly equivalent to the General Secretariat for Defence and National Security (SGDSN) in France.

421. Elisabeth Bumiller, "21st-Century Warnings of a Threat Rooted in the 7th ", The New York Times, 12 December 2005.

They found that the high resonance of the use of the word 'caliphate' [has] an impact of almost instinctive terror.

This model will provide an explanation for defining the jihadist strategy, which is refused to be understood in the sense of 'resistance', by giving it a more worrying dimension. It will henceforth fuel the West's fear and justify its interventions. The map of the caliphate attributed to the Islamic State[422] , which Western experts believe to be its desired objective, is a mirage[423].Published by the US ABC News on 3 July 2014, it was taken from the Twitter account of the far-right American nationalist organisation *American Third Position (A3P)*[424] , and suggests that it represents the Islamic State's planned progression over the next five years[425].It is used by far-right circles and some services to exaggerate the terrorist threat, such as Markus Seiler, director of the Swiss Federal Intelligence Service, on 4 May 2015, to justify the need for a more intrusive intelligence law[426].

In fact, the EI has never mentioned such a map or such ambitions. Moreover, if the jihadists' objective is to restore the Abbasid caliphate[427] , as some 'experts' suggest[428] , then logically it would first involve fundamental changes in Muslim countries themselves, not in the West. This aspect is perfectly understood by the jihadists, whose priorities are clearly placed in the Middle and Near East[429]. Furthermore, still in this hypothesis, it should be noted that France, Belgium, Great Britain, Germany, Denmark or Sweden have never been part of a historical caliphate. For example, after the Stockholm attack (7 April 2017), some Western journalists falsely claimed that Sweden was not part of the coalition[430] , in order to give credence to the idea of a global jihadist plot to destroy Western society.

---

422. http://www.vox.com/2014/7/10/5884593/9-questions-about-the-caliphate-you-were-too-em-barrassed-to-ask.

423. Mark Strauss, "That ISIS 'Caliphate Map' Is Bogus, So Stop Freaking Out", io9.gizmodo.com, 1ᵉʳ July 2014.

424. See: https://twitter.com/Third_Position/status/478626230418173952/photo/1?ref_src=tws-rc%5Etfw.

425. Colleen Curry, "See the Terrifying ISIS Map Showing Its 5-Year Expansion Plan", ABC News, 3 July 2014.

426. Sylvain Besson, 'La loi sur le renseignement signe le retour en grâce des services secrets suisses', Le Temps, 31 August 2016.

427. A form of Muslim 'empire' between 750 and 1258, without internal borders, which extended from India to the Iberian Peninsula.

428. Daoud Boughezala, 'Daech, c'est le wahhabisme plus le martyre', causeur.fr, 19 August 2016; Hanne Olivier and Thomas Flichy de La Neuville, L'État islamique : Anatomie du nouveau califat, éditions Bernard Giovanangeli, 14 November 2014, p. 178.

429. See Abu Musab al-Suri, "The Jihadi Experiences: The main arenas of operation for individual jihad", Inspire, n° 8, Fall 2011, p. 18.

430. For example, Philippe David, programme Le Grand Référendum, «Terrorisme: Avez-vous peur

While the literature of the EI does encourage its militants to act in the West, there is no mention of a return to the Abbasid caliphate. Moreover, assuming, by hypothesis, that this is a very long-term objective, it can be seen that the Islamists do not see terrorism as a means of establishing it: terrorism plays the role of detonator in an insurrectionary process. However, an examination of the EI texts shows that they do not seek to use this feature to encourage the *Muslim* population to rise up, but to push the *non-Muslim* population to demand an end to military, political, economic or moral interventions in the Muslim world. This is what they call «deterrence operations». This is exactly what the word 'jihad' means in its military context.

In reality, the expansion of the land of Islam (*Dar al-Islam*) will most likely take place without terrorism, but through emigration, in a process that began decades ago. It is not even certain that this is a deliberate process - although opinions differ on this point - but an opportunistic mechanism, based on the negligence of Western governments and the permeability of Western society.

Some experts link immigration from Muslim countries and terrorism in a conquest process, with a scenario similar to that suggested in *Managing Barbary*[431].However, the latter does not describe a continental conquest. The term 'barbarism' refers to occupying forces (considered 'barbarians') and explains how to resist and fight a foreign occupation. The idea that the EI seeks to expand without even consolidating its base is a product of the imagination of Westerners who refuse to see terrorism as a simple response to their destabilising actions.

Moreover, as has been observed so far, if there is an extension of the Islamic State beyond the Levant, it will probably not be the result of a 'colonisation' from Syria, but of rallies (*bayah*) *of* orphaned Islamist groups in search of legitimacy, as in Tunisia, Libya or Egypt. This is exactly the same phenomenon as that observed with 'Al-Qaeda' ten years ago[432].Today, thanks to the «publicity» given to it by Western governments and the importance they have given it, the EI has become the reference, although its territorial objectives are clearly limited to Iraq and Syria.

2.8.5. Terrorism in the West

As we have seen, jihadist terrorism in the West must be understood in the context of our political, military and even humanitarian interventions. It has neither the structures nor the popular support to overthrow governments, but seeks to make Westerners question their interventions.

---

d'aller voter dimanche?», Sud Radio, 19 April 2017, www.sudradio.fr/le-grand-referendum-1468.
431. Abu Bakr Naji, Managing Barbarity - The Stage Islam Will Have to Pass Through to Restore the Caliphate, Paris Publishing, 2007, p. 250 (ISBN 978-2-85162-221-1).
432. Nelly Lahoud et al, Letters from Abbottabad: Bin Ladin Sidelined? The Combating Terrorism Center, West Point, www.ctc.usma.edu, 3 May 2012.

In fact, the terrorists are applying exactly the same strategy as for the Allied bombing of Germany during World War II, the use of atomic bombs against Japan, the strikes against Serbia, the bombing of Baghdad in 2003. The Western strategy for changing regimes is to strike civilian populations to pressure their political or military leaders.

Moreover, the Western media, which broadcast the slightest terrorist attack, never mention that the strikes of the international coalition, of which France is a member, caused between 19,127 and 29,479 «collateral» civilian victims in Iraq and Syria between August 2014 and October 2019, according to the *Airwars* website, a cooperative platform for the analysis of international air strikes[433].Yet after the Brussels attacks in March 2016, the EI explains in a video showing the damage of the strikes:

> *This is a message to the crusader peoples of Europe, America and Russia. This is what your governments are doing to Muslims, and you are responsible!*[434]

In fact, the Americans have probably understood the link between strikes and terrorism. This is why they place their interventions in the framework of coalitions, which associate partners who are not very active and whose military contribution is minimal[435] , in order to «dilute» the terrorist threat that weighs on them. Thus, ironically, members of Western coalitions - such as France - have, in fact, offered their populations as human shields to a terrorism that was initially aimed at the Americans!

In its February 2015 issue, dedicated to the attacks in France, EI's magazine *Dar al-Islam* clearly states the reason that will lead to new attacks:

> *Only a few days after the blessed attacks of brother Aboû Basîr*[436] *[...] the French Parliament voted unanimously to extend the strikes against the caliphate, thus exposing itself to other attacks on national soil.*[437]

---

433. See http://airwars.org/civilian-casualty-claims/ (accessed 7 November 2018). But in November 2015, the Pentagon counted only 6 civilian casualties (!) («US air strike on IS in Iraq 'killed civilians'», BBC News, 20 November 2015) while the British Defence Secretary, Michael Fallon, maintained that there had been no civilian casualties from the Western strikes (!!) (Mikey Smith, "Michael Fallon claims there have been ZERO civilian casualties from air strikes in Iraq", The Mirror, 29 November 2015.
434. Eye for an Eye video, Wilaya al-Furat, 27 March 2016 (02'30").
435. The strikes in Syria are 95.3 per cent carried out by the US, with the remainder shared between Australia, Bahrain, Canada, France, Jordan, Saudi Arabia, the United Arab Emirates, the UK and Turkey (2017 figures, airwars.org).
436. NOA: this is Amedy Coulibaly (nom de guerre: Abou Basir Abdoullah Al-Ifriqi), responsible for the attack on the Hyper Cacher in Vincennes on 7 January 2015.
437. «The History of France's Enmity with Islâm», Dar al-Islam, n° 2, Rabi al-thani 1436, February 2015, p. 10.

218

It is therefore not a question of changing society, freedoms or the expansion of Islam, but, logically enough, a response to decisions taken in the name of a passive French people, and therefore guilty in the eyes of the jihadists...

The problem is that these statements by the EI, which illustrate their approach very clearly, have never been relayed by the mainstream media or by official bodies. Thus, when Manuel Valls asserts that terrorism cannot be stopped by a «*magic wand*», he is right in form, but he is lying in substance: France's inexplicable participation in Western strikes should simply have been stopped. But the government was caught in a trap of its own making: a withdrawal after the attacks would have meant giving in to terrorism. With giddy government leaders, there would be a role for the media in bringing them to their senses... provided they did not behave as spokesmen!

2.8.6. Islamist terrorism in Africa

Terrorism in the Sahel-Saharan strip (BSS) follows the same logic as terrorism in the West. In the BSS, it is above all the subservience of local governments to Western interests that is at the root of the violence[438].Here again, Western short-sightedness and short-sightedness have played a major role in encouraging the destabilisation of the region. Development aid focused on one-off actions, without any overall vision or long-term objectives, led by development workers fresh out of European schools and with no experience of the region, has led to a social and societal disaster.

Interventions that were intended to be humanitarian and humanistic have resulted in disaster. For example, when child mortality in Third World countries was tackled in the 1970s and 1980s - a noble cause in itself - the long-term consequences of a sudden population increase were not taken into account. Nor were the infrastructure construction programmes adapted or the necessary support for this mass of young people provided in order to transform this societal upheaval into economic wealth. This has condemned already poor countries to a deadly demographic asphyxia. It is these young people who are now the migrants flocking to Europe.

What is worse, the immigrants who arrive in Europe come to occupy jobs that Europeans no longer want to do, because they are not sufficiently rewarding or remunerative. These «small jobs» (handymen, maintenance staff, etc.) sometimes constitute a useful contribution to Europe, but can never be valued in the immigrants' country of origin in the - very hypothetical - event that they return home. Moreover, naturalisation by right of citizenship or the allowances they receive tend to prevent any return to their countries of origin. As a result,

---

438. Laurent Bigot, «Le terrorisme au Sahel, conséquence de la prévarication érigée en mode de gouvernance», Le Monde Afrique, lemonde.fr, 16 August 2017.

these countries tend to be dangerously impoverished and live only on the rents received from Europe. No real economy is created, with real local know-how (mechanics, electricians, carpenters, etc.) capable of generating real long-term growth. In the end, the policies pursued by the European left contribute greatly to keeping these countries subservient to the West. In addition to the long-term economic consequences, this form of 'colonialism in the hollow' maintains the anger of Islamists who see it as a real identity challenge[439].

Here again, the short-term visions of politicians, development aid agencies and human rights activists in Europe lead to societal disasters, with security disasters in their wake. There is a widespread view in Africa that Western commitment to development and human rights is primarily intended to address unemployment in Europe. Switzerland, whose foreign policy aims to promote peace and human rights, has thus contributed *volens nolens* to the destabilisation of the countries that were its priorities for engagement: Rwanda, South Sudan, Mali and Niger. So much so that the EI considers it a member of the international coalition in Iraq[440]. This is a strategic intelligence flaw.

---

439. Wakat Séra, «Au Sahel, la 'chimère' de la victoire contre le terrorisme», Courrier International, 16 August 2017.
440. See Islamic State video from September 2017.

3. COMBATING TERRORISM

As we have seen, Islamic terrorism is asymmetric in nature, where tactical success of the security forces can generate strategic success of the terrorist organisation. It can only be combated with strategies developed from a holistic approach, which incorporates all elements of the causal chain generating terrorism.

Whereas the terrorism of the 1960s-1980s was more or less inspired by a Marxist revolutionary idealism seen as part of a 'historical process', Islamist terrorism is not inevitable and could be perfectly avoidable... Yet we are not succeeding. The problem lies in the inability of Western countries to develop holistic strategies for action. Influenced by the American and Israeli approaches - essentially tactical - they have only developed military intervention as a tool for action: the worst and most ineffective solution.

After 9/11, President Bush wanted to be able to intervene quickly abroad against terrorist groups, and thus have a kind of «right of hot pursuit», but he needed the approval of Congress. To get around this problem, Congress passed a *Joint Resolution* on the *Authorisation for Use of Military Force* (AUMF) three days later, which stipulated...

> *That the President is authorized to use all necessary and appropriate force against those nations, organizations, or persons that he determines planned, authorized, committed, or aided the terrorist attacks of September 11, 2001, or harbored such organizations or persons, in order to prevent any future acts of international terrorism against the United States by such nations, organizations, or persons.* [441]

Since 2001, the AUMF has been invoked by different US administrations to strike at terrorism without seeking congressional approval. This is why, in 2003, the United States accused Iraq of being an accomplice of «Al Qaeda»[442].From

---

441. 2001 Authorization for Use of Military Force (AUMF), S.J.Res 23(107th), 14 September 2001.
442. Steven Kull, "The American Public On International Issues - Misperceptions, The Media And The Iraq War", The Program On International Policy Attitudes (PIPA)/Knowledge Networks Poll, 2 October 2003.

2004, the same mechanism was set in motion against Iran: the United States claimed that Iran was harbouring those responsible for 11 September 2001[443], and plans for an attack were studied[444].In total, the AUMF has been used to justify 41 military operations in 19 countries, and the Trump team is again trying to use it against Iran[445].It is the legal basis for the US-led 'perpetual wars', and explains why Iraq, Venezuela or Iran have been accused of supporting international terrorism... Even Obama used it to carry out targeted assassinations.

The AUMF is to the US government what shooting from the hip is to the cowboy: it allows for quick action, without thinking... Its most perverse effect is to preclude political debate on the nature of the problem and how to respond to it. This has led to unnecessary interventions, which have only aggravated the terrorist situation in the world. This is why members of Congress have tried to have it repealed... without success.

The main problem with our interventions is that they are most often launched with a 'good conscience' and without any critical thinking. In the United States, history shows that wars are mostly «*started by Democrats and ended by* Republicans»[446].The combination of a missionary spirit and the feeling of fighting for a just cause tends to generate blindness.

Terrorism is a method, and waging a war against a method has often been used by some to explain the failure of the West. This is a Byzantine argument and the problem is not that the «*War on Terror*» can be read as a mere rhetorical formula. The real issue is that we have never moved beyond the emotional to explain the emergence of terrorism, and we have never been able to define coherent strategies to combat it.

There are three basic reasons why the 'war on **terror**' has failed:

First of all, the Americans, who advocated it, conducted it as a Sicilian vendetta and not as a war. They are fighting terrorists without realising that they are simultaneously encouraging terrorism. Not having grasped the asymmetric nature of the problem, they treat it in a very «symmetric» way. As in Israel, their strategy is to hope for a victory by eliminating all of the opponent's fighters little by little. But this approach, which takes the appearance of a «crusade», generates the emergence of new terrorists and violence. France has not understood this strategic dimension any better, which is why it has become a victim of terrorism on its own territory.

Secondly, this 'war' is only counter-terrorism oriented and has no counter-terrorism component of a preventive nature, and therefore no long-term ambition. It is only a combination of short-term tactical/operational actions, is

---

443. «Bush: U.S. probes possible Iran links to 9/11", CNN, 19 July 2004.
444. James Fallows, "Will Iran Be Next?", The Atlantic, December 2004.
445. "Pompeo says Iran tied to Al-Qaeda, declines to say if war legal", France 24, 10 April 2019.
446. Willie Osterweil, "Democrats Are the Real Party of War", The Baffler, 16 June 2014.

totally reactive in nature and has no effect on the jihadists' willingness to fight the West. The discovery of an explosives laboratory or the arrest of terrorists preparing an attack are actions of a reactive nature, as they occur after the terrorists have decided to strike. But there is no strategy for deterring individuals from engaging in a violent plan. It is like trying to drain a bathtub by leaving the tap running. In fact, in Afghanistan, Iraq, Syria, France and elsewhere, we leave the initiative to the terrorists, and we try to react as quickly as possible when they are planning an action.

Thirdly, as a consequence of the other two factors, it is a war without real objectives, where one «shoots at everything that moves», without focusing one's action. In Afghanistan, Iraq and Syria, the West engaged in wars without knowing how to end them: the absence of an objective that could constitute a criterion for the accomplishment of the mission makes it impossible to define an exit strategy. This is exactly the problem with Operation BARKHANE in the Sahel, which France was «forced» to set up to make up for the absence of a strategy for its engagement in Libya...

In August 2021, the chaotic withdrawal of US forces from Afghanistan gave the illusion that this disaster was the result of decisions taken by Joe Biden, and our media suggested that we should go back. In reality, the West has been losing this war for more than 20 years already due to the lack of a strategy and holistic approach, the inability to curb corruption and the inability to put in place a credible alternative.

3.1. The context

3.1.1. The Cold War years

The West's successes against terrorism in the 1960s and 1980s were deceptive 'strategies'. Hardly any Western country achieved a 'clean' victory against complex terrorism: they were victories by brute force - for example, against *Action Direct* (AD) in France or the *Rote Armee Fraktion* (RAF) in Germany - or benefited from the exhaustion of terrorists (such as the Basque ETA) following the fall of communism in Eastern Europe.

In some countries, the very nature of terrorism has allowed them to solve the problem with the means designed for the fight against organised crime. In Germany, the *Bundeskriminalamt* (BKA) led the fight against the RAF, while in France, the fight against AD relied on the resources of the *Office central pour la répression du banditisme* (OCRB). Like the *Cellules Communistes Combattantes (CCC)* in Belgium, these groups had relatively simple structures, with no popular roots, no political cover and no real doctrine. They could thus be fought with police tools and tactics, without resorting to a strategic approach. Police intelligence, with its networks of 'informants', was sufficient to dismantle organisations that resembled gangs more than clandestine subversive structures, while strategic intelligence played only a marginal role.

This terrorism had a 'symmetrical' form: each success of the security forces - whether the capture or elimination of terrorists - corresponded to a failure of the terrorist organisation. This «symmetrical» character explains, among other things, iterative phenomena, such as the taking of hostages to free previously captured terrorists. With jihadists, despite the large number of them imprisoned for long periods in often very harsh conditions, this phenomenon appears only very sporadically[447] and is not supported by a doctrine.

Few countries can boast of having defeated complex terrorism. One of the few examples is the victory of President Romulo Betancourt in Venezuela against Marxist terrorism in the early 1960s. By combining political measures - which 'took the wind out of the sails' of the revolutionaries - with military measures, which focused primarily on protecting the population and not on destroying the revolutionary forces, the terrorists were forced to abandon violence and engage in a political process, in which they were definitively defeated.

In retrospect, the fight against 'al-Qaeda' has proved ineffective. The failure of Westerners to understand its nature and mechanisms led Western intelligence services down a number of blind alleys. They have treated the threat as if it were a 'simple' criminal organisation. Today, their philosophy has not fundamentally changed and Islamist terrorism is still treated with the same logic.

The decrease in terrorist attacks in Europe and the United States is cited as an example of the success of the fight against terrorism. This is not the case. One only has to follow what is being said and written in Islamist networks to see that the problem has simply shifted. Why would terrorists mount complex and risky operations in the West, while Westerners are sent to meet them in Iraq or Afghanistan? For jihadists, it is not the location that is decisive, but the intention. Thus, it must be noted with some cynicism that the troops sent to Iraq, Afghanistan or Mali have, in a way, protected the Western populations by serving as «lightning rods», without affecting the will of the jihadists. They simply exchanged civilian victims for military ones, without addressing the basic problem.

In short, the West «*is doing the things right, but not the right things*». After each death in Afghanistan or Mali, we repeat tirelessly that «*the guys are doing a good job*», but we never question the nature of this «job» in relation to the objective, because our decisions are not based on facts, but on prejudices:

---

447. This is the case, for example, with the attack in Trèbes (22 March 2018), which was more an individual initiative than a coordinated action of a strategic nature.

Thus, the use of brute force is an unnecessary expenditure of energy. In Syria, France, more than the United States, has claimed a victory over the EI. This is a deception, which is also manifested by the authorities' fear of seeing French fighters return, and which masks the fact that very many fighters - threatened with imprisonment or death on their return - have merged with other jihadist groups (most often supported by Western countries). Since the reason that created jihadism has not disappeared, the problem remains.

3.1.2. The response to Islamist terrorism

3.2. Intelligence

In recent years, the word «intelligence» has taken on a wide variety of meanings in literature and the media. Like the notions of «*counter-terrorism*», «*counter-terrorism*» and «*prevention*», it has been taken out of any conceptual context, and no longer means anything at all. This is true of the distinction

---

448. David Miliband, Foreign Secretary (Britain), «'War on Terror' was wrong», The Guardian, 15 January 2009.

between «*information*» and «*intelligence*», which is the basis of intelligence work. Even in professional circles, the '*information*' that once fuelled police investigations is now indiscriminately referred to as '*intelligence*', and yesterday's '*informants*' have become '*intelligence officers*'.

Beyond the words, it is the understanding of intelligence work that has dramatically declined. After September 11, 2001, the 'experts' blamed the incompetence of the US intelligence services for failing to interpret numerous warnings such as :

- a 1999 British intelligence report stating that al-Qaeda was considering using «*commercial aircraft*» in «*unconventional ways*» «*possibly as flying bombs*»[449] ;

- a note from the French DGSE dated 5 January 2001[450] ;

- messages received by the US authorities on 28 June and 10 July which referred to attacks with «*dramatic consequences on the government or would cause significant losses*» occurring «*with little or no* warning»;

- a note dated 3 September 2001 from Major General Omar Suleiman, head of the Egyptian *Mukhabarat al-Ammah* (General Intelligence) to the CIA station chief in Cairo on the «*advanced state of execution of a major operation against a US target*»[451] ;

- 33 messages intercepted by the *National Security Agency* (NSA) in the summer of 2001[452] , warning of an imminent terrorist attack on the United States; including one from 10 September (processed on 11 September - after the attacks - and released on 12 September) which could possibly have been a concrete indication of an attack on 11 September, although it contained no indication of location, time or targets[453].

But in reality, none of these warnings were able to characterise the threat in time and space. In retrospect, historians see these as very clear indicators, but for an intelligence professional in 2001, with some 11.5 million air movements per year at major US airports, such vague information was virtually useless for taking concrete action. This is the difference between 'information' and 'actionable intelligence'. We will come back to this.

Today, the majority of publications on the subject come from criminologists, jurists or journalists, who know very little about the nature and functioning of

---

449. Sunday Times, 6 September 2002.

450. Its existence was revealed by the newspaper Le Monde in 2007 (Guillaume Dasquié, «11 September 2001: the French knew a lot», Le Monde, 16 April 2007).

451. Gordon Thomas, Globe-Intel, 6 September 2002.

452. Department of Defense agency responsible for electronic intelligence and security in the United States.

453. Testimony of Lieutenant General Michael V. Hayden, Director of the NSA in Report of the US Senate Select Committee on Intelligence and US House Permanent Select Committee on Intelligence, Joint Inquiry into Intelligence Community Activities Before and After the Terrorist Attacks of September 11, 2001, December 2002, p. 375 (TOP SECRET - Declassified).

the intelligence services. It can also be seen that the criticisms levelled at the intelligence services generally concern the detection (or not) of terrorists (tactical intelligence), but never the question of anticipating the emergence of the terrorist phenomenon (strategic intelligence). In fact, even the so-called experts in the field have a limited understanding of what intelligence is.

3.2.1. Defining intelligence

It is important here to define what is meant by the term 'intelligence'. In French, it tends to be related to the verb «renseigner», i.e. to provide information. But in English it is translated into the word «intelligence», which comes from the Latin verb *intellegere*: «to understand». This is its essence.

Technically, a distinction is made between *'intelligence'* and *'information'*: intelligence being the *product of* an intelligence service, after the information has gone through the 'intelligence *cycle*' process[454].

ᶜIn the 19th century, Napoleon had already shown that with the knowledge of the enemy, of his doctrine of engagement, of his available means, of the nature of the terrain, of the weather conditions, of the will to fight of his soldiers and of the quality of their training, it was possible to anticipate his decision for the manoeuvre. It is the same today.

The primary function of intelligence - **and** strategic intelligence in particular - is to *understand* a situation in order to inform *decision-making*. It was during the Second World War that the foundations of modern intelligence were theorised, formalised and systematised to facilitate inter-allied cooperation.

Broadly speaking, a distinction is made between strategic intelligence, which guides the conception of action and the decision, and tactical intelligence, which guides implementation and action. Both have an anticipatory perspective, but with different time horizons: strategic intelligence is more concerned with the medium to long term and tactical intelligence with the short to very short term, without it being possible to define a precise boundary between the two.

Since terrorism is a method of achieving strategic objectives through tactical actions, intelligence must be able to work on both levels. To simplify, counter-terrorism is essentially a strategic intelligence function, while counter-terrorism is a tactical intelligence function. But virtually no Western intelligence service has a doctrinal framework that allows for this distinction, which is why we fight terrorists more than terrorism.

The task of strategic intelligence is to reconstruct the most accurate and reliable picture of the situation, *based on concrete clues* (not professions of faith!),

---

454. The classic Anglo-Saxon literature, which is at the origin of the conceptualisation of modern intelligence, sometimes uses the term 'raw intelligence' instead of 'information', as opposed to 'intelligence' or 'finished intelligence'.

so as to enable political or military decision-makers to take their decisions in full knowledge of the facts. At this level, it is not a question of identifying potentially dangerous networks and individuals, but of understanding the societal, social, political or economic environment, in order to measure and anticipate the possible consequences of our political and military actions on the adversary (or the situation).

A non-trivial problem is to detect *the existence of* a crisis. We generally tend to see the crisis from the terrorist event. This is wrong: we are in crisis from the moment the conditions are created for terrorism to appear. That is why those who deliberately hide these causes are part of the problem.

By treating Islamist terrorism as inevitable, the need to understand its mechanics and causal factors (strategic intelligence) has been eliminated. Virtually all intelligence services have taken refuge in the search for possible clues to the preparation of attacks (tactical intelligence). The result has been the development of ever more sophisticated and intrusive information gathering systems and a gradual shift from strategic to tactical or police intelligence.

In France, a legacy of the Second World War, intelligence is understood and used as a tool for influence and action, with an analysis that is more oriented towards the operational than the strategic decision. The intelligence that the «experts» and other «ex-agents» of an «action service» talk about in their «analyses» is most often tactical intelligence, oriented towards «operational modes», in the immediate proximity of the event.

In the United States, the balance between the action component (the responsibility of the CIA) and the analytical work varies quite a bit depending on the presidents and directors of the Agency. In Israel, intelligence has always favoured action in a security context: this explains its legendary ability to locate and eliminate terrorists. On the other hand, its analytical performance, its anticipation of strategic threats and its understanding of terrorist logics are 'stifled' by politics and ideology, which explains its very mediocre results.

In contrast, in Germany, intelligence has always had a strong analytical component. Since the First World War, it has been guided by the formula *«Nachrichtendienst ist Herrendienst»* (*«The intelligence service is the service of the lords»*). With its methodical, decision-oriented approach to work, the German services are undoubtedly the best equipped to face the complexity of today's challenges.

3.2.2. Forms of intelligence

While 'experts' talk about, comment on and criticise 'intelligence' as a generic activity, it is a plural activity, not only in terms of the tools it uses, but also - and more importantly - in terms of the level at which it operates. The fundamental

228

purpose of intelligence is to inform decision making and it is essential in the study of intelligence to situate it within this process.

Broadly speaking, three forms of intelligence can be defined:

- When it comes to future events, it is called *anticipatory intelligence*. This is the essence of intelligence and its most complex, demanding and (politically) risky form. Its function is to feed into the decision-making process on the probable - not possible - evolution of the situation. It is therefore upstream of the problems and attempts to assess - based on facts - the probability of occurrence and the consequences that would follow. This form of intelligence requires primarily analytical and abstract skills. The personnel needed for this type of intelligence are generally hard to find, and services are reluctant to get involved in this area. This is essentially the role of strategic intelligence, where the word 'strategic' is associated with the 'leader's strategy' and thus his decision. Anticipatory intelligence is based - at least in part - on the results of the other two forms of intelligence.

- *Investigative intelligence* seeks to gather information to explain an event. This is essentially police intelligence. This form of intelligence requires significant collection resources and a high degree of thoroughness. It collects evidence about specific events, objects, organisations or individuals, based on a particular action (arrest, evidence gathering, etc.). It is the intelligence that enables the tracing of leads after an attack.

- The aim of *documentation intelligence is to* build up reference knowledge to support routine decisions. This knowledge must be sufficiently rich to reduce the *need for intelligence in the* event of a crisis and thus save time. This is an activity common to all types of intelligence services, which could be summarised as the constitution of databases for analysis bodies, as mass surveillance systems do. In order to avoid suffocating the services, it must be guided by strategic priorities, which is lacking in almost all countries.

An understanding of these three forms of intelligence is essential in defining the direction of a service, its capabilities and the profile of the intelligence officers it seeks. It must make it possible to manage the interaction between the services and to integrate them, whether private or public, into an overall intelligence concept. The latter must make it possible to manage the overlapping activities of the services in order to avoid «service wars», duplication of effort and waste of resources.

3.2.3. Inadequate intelligence

In the aftermath of 9/11, American intelligence services were immediately pilloried for their inability to predict the event. They were then reproached for their predilection for technical collection systems to the detriment of human intelligence. The same phenomenon was to occur fifteen years later in France with the Islamist attacks. However, a more in-depth analysis of these 'breakdowns' leads to a more nuanced criticism.

First, it is incorrect to claim that human intelligence was abandoned after the Cold War, as is often heard. In fact, with the fall of communism, Western intelligence services shifted their attention to the fight against organised crime and trafficking, requiring the accelerated recruitment of agents from specific ethnic groups, of Asian and Latin American origin. The first Gulf War was the starting point for jihadist terrorism, which required the development of new human intelligence networks, a process that took time. However, from the mid-1990s onwards, the development of mobile telephony and Internet communication gave a new impetus to technical intelligence, whose penetration capacity often exceeds that of human intelligence.

Second, the decision-making power of modern terrorists is concentrated in a very small number of people. Therefore, penetrating the decision-making circle is considerably more complex than with the Soviet General Staff during the Cold War. This difficulty was already noted with Saddam Hussein, whose decision-making circle was limited to a few people in his direct entourage, making it almost impossible to establish informants. Furthermore, simple systems of conduct, with a strong emphasis on oral communication, in regions where the notion of hierarchy is strong, often make access to information very difficult, if not impossible. The adoption of the doctrine of individual terrorism has further exacerbated these difficulties, firstly because an entire population can be virtually terrorist and secondly because decisions are taken by the terrorist himself, and sometimes shared with someone very close to him. Whereas during the Cold War, intelligence services had to uncover secrets, today they are often faced with mysteries. The consequence is that anticipation of tactical action is often impossible, which gives strategic anticipation a decisive role. The fight against terrorism cannot therefore be limited to intercepting terrorists, but must be carried out upstream by identifying the breaking points likely to generate a terrorist will.

Thirdly, since the end of the 1970s, the fight against terrorism has involved all Western intelligence services. There has been a proliferation of bodies for consultation, coordination and harmonisation of services. Thus, the non-detection of a terrorist event such as 9/11 represents more the failure of Western cooperation than the failure of the American services alone, even if they have also had «breakdowns». The *Schengen Information System (SIS)*, the *TREVI group*, the *Club of Bern*, the *Kilowatt Group* are some of the forums for inter-agency information exchange in the field of terrorism. The main problem here is that in the world of services - as in everyday life - a form of single-mindedness has developed, fuelled by a deep analytical deficit. The commissions of enquiry into the intelligence failures in Iraq found that information exchanged between services tends to be taken at face value, particularly when it reinforces preconceived ideas.

Fourth, no one has a «crystal ball», and no prediction can be certain. Most often, and at best, intelligence services have clues that allow them to sketch out a number of possible options, which must then be ranked according to their probability of occurrence. A number of techniques and the experience of analysts can be used to assess the reliability of a prediction in order to turn it into actionable intelligence. The criminal police search for criminals on the basis of objectively related clues. An intelligence service seeks and accumulates information about facts, the links of which are yet to be discovered, about a 'crime' or event that does not yet exist. This is the role of strategic intelligence analysis. Its chronic weakness in all Western countries has led to the collection of huge amounts of information in an attempt to predict terrorist acts.

The USA PATRIOT Act (USAPA)[455] , signed into law by President George W. Bush on 26 October 2001, was enacted in the aftermath of 9/11 to broaden the range of legal instruments needed to combat terrorism in the United States.

USAPA gives new powers to law enforcement and intelligence agencies, and eases restrictions on citizen surveillance activities. It amends laws on wiretapping, electronic communications privacy, computer fraud and abuse, family privacy and education rights, money laundering, immigration and nationality, money laundering controls, bank privacy, financial privacy rights and credit.

Its main innovation is to relax the rules for implementing the *Foreign Intelligence Surveillance Act (FISA)* of 1978, in order to allow foreign intelligence agencies (notably the CIA and the NSA) to operate on national territory, while limiting legislative control over their operations. This is a radical and dangerous change for the rule of law, which has opened the door to the use of mass surveillance systems that developed without the knowledge of Congress and were unveiled in 2013 by Edward Snowden... and that almost all Western countries have implemented on their territories.

In essence, the USAPA opens up the range of cases where a citizen can be monitored on the basis of mere suspicion. Thus, for example, it is possible for the FBI or the CIA to monitor words searched on the Internet using search engines such as Google and emails. It allows surveillance of an individual for offences that are not directly related to terrorism. USAPA also authorises federal agencies to search library and bookstore records for suspicious material (e.g. relating to terrorism or clandestine activities). USAPA also facilitates the imprisonment and forfeiture of assets of individuals to combat terrorist financing sources and mechanisms.

---

455. Its full name is the Uniting and Strengthening America by Providing Appropriate Tools Required to Intercept and Obstruct Terrorism Act of 2001.

The weakness behind the PATRIOT Act is the traditional American inability to understand security as anything other than a power struggle. Its underlying logic is that security is directly related to the amount of information the state has about its citizens. The United States has thus started a security spiral that has been imitated by many countries, which has generated less intelligent, less efficient security that is more often than not inappropriate to the societal context. In 2015, the FBI admitted that the PATRIOT Act had not prevented a single terrorist attack in the US[456].

In September 2003, in a memo, Secretary of Defense Donald Rumsfeld admitted:

> *I have no visibility on who the bad guys are in Afghanistan or Iraq [...] I've read all the intelligence provided by the [intelligence] community, and it looks like we know a lot, but in fact, if you look closely, you'll see that we don't have anything operationalizable. We have a severe lack of human intelligence.[457]*

Clearly: we have ventured into war without knowing the enemy. This is the main weakness of today's intelligence, which fails to understand contemporary wars and the logic behind them. By dint of looking for the trees, we no longer see the forest. This obviously applies to terrorism, but also to other conflicts, such as the one in Eastern Congo or Southern Sudan, which we insist on reading 'in the West' in order to create more manageable peace models. But the inability to understand leads to the inability to anticipate. The result is inappropriate solutions that have, at best, temporary effects and, at worst, none at all.

Intelligence failures are all the more difficult to correct as the opacity of the services has increased. In the United States, the amount of classified information is seen as a factor in the inefficiency of the services. The many studies and commissions that have looked into this issue have observed a general tendency to over-classify information, which leads to significant administrative burdens. In the United States, the CIA alone accumulates about 1,000 terabytes of information (the equivalent of 112 billion pages of text) every 18 months[458] , and - even though much of this information is open - its day-to-day management is very cumbersome and costly.

---

456. M. David & Reagan Ali, "FBI Admits They Haven't Stopped ANY Terrorism With Patriot Act Spying Power", countercurrentnews.info, 22 May 2015.

457. Jennifer Smith, "Donald Rumsfeld 'didn't know who the bad guys were' during Afghanistan war and US had 'woefully deficient human intelligence', reveal documents which exposed fact officials knew conflict was unwinnable", Dailymail.com, 10 December 2019.

458. Transforming the Security Classification System, Report to the President from the Public Interest Declassification Board, Information Security Oversight Office, Washington DC 20408, November 2012.

3.2.4. The intelligence cycle

The intelligence cycle is the essence of the functioning of intelligence services, whatever their size and situation. Virtually all service failures stem from deviations from this cycle. It was theorised during the Second World War, but was only formalised at the beginning of the Cold War and is used by most Western services. There are several variants of this cycle, but the most widely used is probably the American five-phase model: planning and conduct, collection, exploitation, analysis and production and, finally, dissemination. The different variants are simply variations of these phases, with different emphases depending on the capacity of the organisation, but retaining the same functionality.

In recent years, the intelligence cycle has been criticised by some researchers as being ill-suited to the current information processing structure. The main reason for this apparent inadequacy is that the cycle is misunderstood as a static process, which some countries have used to build the organic structure of their services. This is the case with the Belgian *Organe de Coordination pour l'Analyse de la Menace* (OCAM), which was clearly set up according to a «simple» intelligence cycle, which does not reflect intelligence practice, but betrays a conception based on a bookish knowledge of the problem. This design flaw leads to dysfunctions, some symptoms of which were noted in the activity report of *Standing Committee R*, which is responsible for overseeing the Belgian intelligence services[459]. Without going into detail, the dysfunctions of Belgian intelligence are the result, firstly, of poorly thought-out intelligence structures and processes and, secondly, of a deficient leadership that should have noticed these defects long ago. These shortcomings will become apparent during the attacks of 2016, but also during the manhunt conducted in May 2021 against an extreme right-wing extremist. We will come back to this.

In reality, very few intelligence professionals have had the opportunity to work on all the phases and thus understand the subtle mechanism. The compartmentalisation of the services - a fortiori in the «big» services (such as the DGSE, the German BND, the American CIA, etc.) - means that agents only perceive a very small part of this cycle. These criticisms usually come from individuals who are not professionals in the field or whose expertise is limited to one stage of the process. As a result, *think tanks*, private intelligence bodies and other academic institutions generally provide little concrete evidence for improving service performance.

First of all, it is important to understand that the intelligence cycle is not a structural model, but a functional one. It is a process that is not unique and that applies to each issue dealt with by a service, in an iterative way. In other

---

459. Activity Report 2015, Standing Committee on the Oversight of Intelligence and Security Services, , Intersentia, Antwerp, September 2016, p. 100-101.

words, a service is constantly dealing with several overlapping cycles, sometimes sharing the same resources (such as satellite assets), with priorities that must be *constantly* readjusted according to the situation. Furthermore, in addition to the simultaneity of several cycles already mentioned, «mini-cycles» are established, as the information gathered must be refined, specified or cross-checked by other complementary information. Thus, this generic «simple» cycle is constantly completed by short cycles between analysts and information gathering bodies, which can sometimes impact on the resources available. Often represented by a circle for didactic reasons, this cycle is in fact implemented as a sequence of fractal scrolls.

3.2.4.1. Planning and management

The objective of the planning and conduct phase is to identify and prioritise intelligence needs at a given moment, according to the political or military priorities of the decision-maker, the current state of knowledge and the resources available to cover each problem. Technically, it is a question of prioritising the commitment of the technical and human resources available, identifying the possible synergies between the various collection, analysis and dissemination resources, defining the distribution of these resources in time and space, and allocating the appropriate financial means to cover all the missions. Intelligence missions can be very long and overlapping, or even in conflict with each other, and this first phase is crucial for intelligence effectiveness. The calibration of an observation satellite is different depending on the nature of the mission, both in terms of its precession angle, the orientation of its cameras, and the nature of the sensors that can be used under various conditions, to name but a few of the criteria that need to be taken into account in order to cover several missions with a single tool.

This phase is most effective when intelligence agencies are involved earlier in the political or military decision-making process and have a rough idea of the possible intent of the decision-maker. Information gathering and analysis can then be aligned with this rough decision, exploring its possible consequences, particularly in the selection of sources and methods to be employed. It should be understood here that information gathering, like an aircraft carrier, takes time to be redirected. Moreover, while technical intelligence can be redirected fairly quickly, the same cannot be said of human intelligence, which can take years to become fully effective.

3.2.4.2. Collection

The collection phase aims to search for and gather the basic information necessary for the intelligence that will feed the decision. It is a question of coordinating and combining the use of the various sensors available to exploit their full potential and avoid «holes» in the image that we are trying to obtain.

The widespread belief that the scope of intelligence services is limited to classified information is false. Clearly, some services dedicated to clandestine action - such as the UK's MI6 - or working with particular technological means and a limited analytical role - such as the US *National Security Agency* (NSA) and *National Reconnaissance Office* (NRO) or the UK's *Government Communications Headquarters* (GCHQ) - which use technologies whose capabilities must remain discrete, operate in an almost exclusively classified register. This is not the case, however, in the so-called «multi-source» intelligence agencies[460] such as the *Central Intelligence Agency* (CIA) and the *Defense Intelligence Agency* (DIA) in the United States or the Russian *Foreign Intelligence Service* (SVR). In fact, in these services, open sources constitute up to 95% of the information needed for strategic decisions:

> *The Cold War notion that open information is 'second class' information is a dangerous, old-fashioned cliché. Lieutenant General Samuel V. Wilson, former Director of the Defense Intelligence Agency, put it best: «90% of intelligence comes from open sources. The other 10%, the clandestine work, is simply the most theatrical. The real intelligence hero is Sherlock Holmes, not James Bond.* [461]

In the 'big' services, collection by means of classified methods and resources (satellite imagery, electronic eavesdropping, espionage, etc.) and exploitation of open sources (literature and media)[462] are practised by different services. One reason for this is the need to protect the sources and methods used. But this practice hides a trap: that of giving more value to information obtained by classified means. However :

> *Secret information is certainly good, but it does not have to be secret to be good.*[463]

However, this must be qualified. There is often a difference between tactical information (e.g. identification of a terrorist or his contacts) and strategic information. The former is usually classified, as it involves methods and technologies whose capabilities are covered by confidentiality. In contrast, for strategic

---

460. In English: All-source Intelligence Agency.
461. David Reed, "Aspiring to Spying", The Washington Times, 14 November 1997.
462. Also known as «open source intelligence» or OSINT.
463. John G. Heidenrich, "The Intelligence Community's Neglect of Strategic Intelligence", Studies in Intelligence, vol. 51, n° 2, 2007.

decision-making, almost all of the necessary information is available in the open media.

When it comes to the massive collection of data from computer or telephone networks, it is important to understand that unlike the pre-mobile phone era, where 'slings' were placed on telephone lines, 'eavesdropping' on digital networks affects us all. Modern 'lines' are electromagnetic frequencies and channels in optical fibres, shared simultaneously by thousands of users, whose communications are sliced and diced, rather like a zipper, into other communications. This characteristic, which is found in satellite communications, mobile phones and the Internet, requires intelligence services to literally «pick up» everything in electromagnetic space and then «piece together» the bits and pieces of communications to reconstruct messages in order to detect possible terrorist activity. This work is done by computers and therefore concerns all users, not just those under surveillance.

In the wake of the United States, several countries have sought to adopt intelligence laws allowing for the surveillance of individuals. No one has really looked at the number of people involved, which is said to be «*about ten*» in Switzerland[464] and «*a few hundred*» in France[465].This is not true. It is not enough to monitor an individual if we do not know with whom he is communicating; the same goes for the person he is communicating with and so on. Technically, each step is called a «hop», and the NSA monitors three per initial target. Considering that an individual has an average of about 190 friends on Facebook (1er «hop»), the 2^e "hop" concerns 31,000 people (taking into account overlaps) and the 3^e «hop» affects more than 5 million people[466].This is well above the official figures.

In other words, empowering the intelligence services to monitor communications without a specific warrant means that all citizens, companies, senior civil servants, politicians, lawyers, parliamentarians, etc., will have their communications automatically recorded; while the use made of them will be covered by the «defence secret», and therefore beyond the control of those concerned.

As for the actual effectiveness of such a surveillance system, it is somewhat disappointing. Despite an extraordinary system, the United States was unable to detect the Boston attack in 2013 or the San Bernardino attack in 2015. While US capabilities cover the entire globe, including France and Belgium, the attacks of January and November 2015 and March 2016 could not be detected. Electronic intelligence was only able to provide useful elements to the investigation, after

---

464. Julie Conti, «La nouvelle loi sur le renseignement expliquée en trois minutes», Le Temps, 5 September 2016.
465. Christophe Ayad & Jean-Baptiste Jacquin, «Au menu de la nouvelle loi antiterroriste, le suivi des condamnés sortis de prison et la surveillance par algorithmes», Le Monde, 28 April 2021.
466. Ewen Macaskill & Gabriel Dance, "NSA Files: Decoded", The Guardian, 1er November 2013.

the attacks... and even then, very late, allowing the main protagonists still alive to slip away. A very modest result...

In April 2021, Gérald Darmanin claims that 2 out of 35 attacks foiled in France since 2017 were foiled thanks to the digital trace of the perpetrators[467]. According to *Le Monde*, in 2019, only one out of 59 attacks foiled since 2013 was thanks to a surveillance system[468].These figures seem very high.

In addition, there are threats to the rule of law and democracy in our countries. In the United States, the Supreme Court has declared the NSA's mass surveillance activities illegal[469] .

3.2.4.3. The operation

In some countries, the exploitation phase is considered as an analysis activity[470]. This is why some services, such as the American NSA or the British GCHQ, whose function is essentially to collect data and information, have an «Analysis» department. In French terminology, it concerns the «dégrossissage» of the information collected and the extraction of its relevant elements with a view to the analysis and development of intelligence. For information of technical origin, such as electronic intelligence (ROEM) and imagery (ROIM), which collect millions of items of information every month, only a tiny fraction of which will be useful, the purpose of exploitation is to facilitate the reading and use of the data collected.

Depending on the mode of collection, the exploitation may be more or less technical and thus come close to analysis, or even replace it. This is often the case with the collection of data by means of algorithms based on 'typical behaviours' which, in the best of cases, will define a suspect and, in the worst of cases, condemn him to death. This is how drone targets and terror suspects are selected in the US: a combination of criteria (e.g. Muslim, single, made X number of trips to area Y, earns so much per month, frequents A, B and C, telephones B and D, borrowed such and such a book from the local library, etc.) identifies terrorist behaviour that can be placed under surveillance.

Thus, for example, drone strikes use *signature-based* targeting based on metadata collected by electronic intelligence, combined with characteristic profiles established by mathematical algorithms that are supposed to represent typical terrorist behaviour. A phone that frequently connects with phones suspected

---

467. Nicolas Demorand & Léa Salamé, «Gérald Darmanin: face au terrorisme, «il ne faut être ni résigné ni outrancier»», France Inter, 28 April 2021.

468. Jacques Follorou, '58 of the 59 attacks foiled in the last six years have been thanks to human intelligence', Le Monde, 15 October 2019.

469. Dan Roberts & Spencer Ackerman, "NSA mass phone surveillance revealed by Edward Snowden ruled illegal", The Guardian, 7 May 2015.

470. In countries with a Germanic tradition, exploitation is a broader concept («Auswertung») which covers the evaluation of information, its collation, analysis and the production of summary notes.

of belonging to terrorists or located in areas where terrorists are present will be considered to belong to a terrorist. If a strike is decided, it will be carried out on the phone, without knowing who is using it or who is around it (e.g. his wife or a relative).

The problem is that, statistically speaking, the terrorist detection algorithms used in conjunction with mass data collection and eavesdropping systems are not reliable. This is simply because of the very small number of potential «terrorists» and the absence of behaviours that are meaningful for algorithmic analysis. Algorithms that are, for example, effective in combating credit card fraud are thus ineffective against terrorism, largely because terrorists are attributed «Western» and «symmetrical» behaviours. This is why we continue to be «surprised» by terrorists whose profiles are so uncharacteristic that they can hardly be modelled. This is the case of the machete attack of 3 February 2017 in the Louvre by a young Egyptian, newly arrived in France, whose profile had nothing in common with that of the terrorists previously identified in France.

In fact, the inability of intelligence services to deal with terrorism strategically has pushed them into modes of operation that are increasingly akin to the notion of «countermeasures». The response mechanism is triggered without any real decision, a bit like an anti-aircraft missile: very quickly and almost instinctively.

3.2.4.4. Analysis and production

During the analysis phase, information is transformed into a product relevant to a decision on a given problem: intelligence. The analyst will add value to the information he or she receives, making it robust enough to be incorporated into a decision. This is the heart of the intelligence process: reconstructing a relevant picture for decision making.

The fundamental problem with intelligence is the reliability of that picture. Very often, the analysis has to make do with fragmented information from various sources that are often difficult to verify. The temptation is then great to use information as intelligence. The elements that led to the American decision to intervene in Iraq in 2003 were largely fuelled by a confusion (intentional or not) between «information» and «intelligence» by the American and British intelligence services.

In order to enable the 'cross-checking' of information of comparable quality, any analytical process begins with the evaluation of information. For a long time an empirical process, this was codified during the Second World War to enable Allied services to communicate with each other. Several systems exist, but the one selected at the time - and still used today in NATO - is the British Admiralty system: it evaluates the source and the information by combining a letter (A-F) and a number (1-6). This is a very effective system, but services tend to bypass it, because in modern crises, the reliability of sources is generally

238

difficult to establish and information is difficult to «cross-check». Some international organisations, such as the Office for the *Coordination of Humanitarian Affairs* (OCHA), have therefore simplified it by making it less «severe» in order to better justify their decision-making... by increasing the risk of being wrong!

Evaluation of the source		Evaluation of content	
Reliable	A	Confirmed	1
Generally reliable	B	Likely	2
Fairly reliable	C	Very likely	3
Not always reliable	D	Doubtful	4
Unsafe	E	Improbable	5
Reliability not assessable	F	Accuracy not assessable	6

Table 8 - Assessment of information used by intelligence services (different formulations may exist in different countries)

The temptation to place a higher value on classified information can be a major source of error. For example, prior to the 2003 intervention in Iraq, British intelligence did not notice that an Iraqi source was describing Saddam Hussein's chemical weapons to them on the basis of what he had seen in the film *The Rock*[471] !

That said, in the case of Iraqi weapons of mass destruction, it is a little simple to place the blame solely on the United States and Britain, because even in those countries that were opposed to intervention - in particular France, Russia, China and Germany - the intelligence services were unable to provide the evidence that would have countered the American and British allegations. This is particularly true of France, which courageously and decisively opposed the intervention but, in the absence of intelligence, was unable to develop its argument beyond principles. This was clearly the weakness of Dominique de Villepin, who clearly did not have the strategic intelligence to back up his brilliant speech to the UN Security Council on 14 February 2003. Moreover, Germany - which had also opposed intervention in Iraq - appears not to have had a clear picture of the situation in Iraq, since its intelligence service, the BND, had not only provided the Americans with the CURVEBALL source[472]

---

471. Pamela Engel, "A UK intelligence source reportedly based information about Iraq chemical weapons on a Nicolas Cage movie", Business Insider UK, 6 July 2016.
472. CURVEBALL, is the code name of an Iraqi whose real name is Rafed Aljanabi, who has been the main source for German, British and American intelligence analysis of the Iraqi WMD issue. Despite the obvious doubts about the quality of the source, none of the services took the usual precautions in their analyses.

without being able to evaluate its information (which turned out to be lies)[473] , but also supported the American operations thereafter[474] !

When it comes to police intelligence (identification or search for a terrorist), it is generally based on concrete, tangible and indisputable facts: validation is essentially based on observed facts. In strategic intelligence and anticipation, the analysis is based on clues, indicators and models where facts are naturally present, but which rely heavily on judgement. Validation therefore focuses on the robustness of the indicators and the weighting of possible options for the future, in order to avoid it becoming - as is very common - an exercise in divination.

The intelligence services use a number of tools to test the robustness of the assumptions applied to the indicators, of which the best known are

- *Competing hypothesis analysis.* First described by Richard Heuer for the CIA, it is an analytical technique that is based on the fact that the analyst tends to trust more information that supports his or her perception of things, even if it is wrong, and that over time, changing his or her mind requires an ever-increasing amount of information. The tool is therefore to systematically look for evidence that disproves our assumptions.

- *The B Team.* In 1974, President Gerald Ford believed that the CIA was systematically underestimating Soviet capabilities. A procedure was adopted whereby the Agency's analyses were submitted to a «B Team» of outside experts for critical review. The underlying idea is to combat the phenomenon of *group-think, which* can develop within an agency or department.

- *The devil's advocate.* The practice of 'devil's advocate' was introduced in the Israeli military intelligence service (AMAN) after the October 1973 war. It is a relatively aggressive technique, practised by an office reporting directly to the head of intelligence, which systematically contradicts the claims made in the service's analyses. The aim is to critically question all the claims of the analytical bodies in order to push them to develop a solidly fact-based argument.

3.2.4.4.1. Intelligence analysis and 'academic' or 'journalistic' analysis

When talking about strategic intelligence, analysis is too often understood as a variant of academic analysis, when in fact it is very different.

The main difference between intelligence analysis and other forms of analysis is that its purpose is to provide a basis for decision making, not simply to provide insight into a situation. The requirement for rigour associated with it is therefore far greater than that found even at the academic level, as decisions of national importance are derived from this analysis. The intelligence analyst

---

473. D. Banse, U. Müller and L. Wiegelmann, „Wie ein BND-Informant den Irak-Krieg auslöste", www.welt.de, 28 August 2011.
474. Matthias Gebauer, „BND soll USA im Irak-Krieg unterstützt haben", Der Spiegel, 12 January 2006.

has a responsibility to the decision-maker that the academic analyst or journalist does not have. With this responsibility comes the ability to be held accountable, if necessary, for the soundness of their analysis. In Anglo-Saxon countries, 'traceability of analysis' is ensured when intelligence services can be subject to institutional oversight, such as parliamentary scrutiny. It is a question of being able to reconstruct the genesis and the considerations of the decisions taken by the executive. The reports of the commissions of enquiry in the United States on 11 September 2001[475], on weapons of mass destruction[476], on the use of torture[477] and, in Great Britain, the Chilcot report,[478] are very rich documents, which have no real equivalent in other countries, for the study and real improvement of the services.

The complexity and multiplicity of contemporary security problems have led to an increasing complexity and bureaucratisation of intelligence services. This has been accompanied by a growing risk aversion in forecasting and a tendency to produce more descriptive than predictive analyses. In Switzerland, the *Strategic Intelligence Service*[479] has been criticised on several occasions for providing «confidential» analyses from open media without added value[480].

In the United States, this development has encouraged the demand for 'actionable' intelligence[481] that can be integrated into decision making, and thus is anticipatory in nature. Unlike academic analysis, which may rely more on theories and hypotheses, intelligence analysis is essentially fact-based. However, in terrorism, the information available is often unique and therefore difficult to «cross-check» in the short term. When information is lacking, the services use substitutes or complements through the modelling of behaviours according to objective elements (doctrine, established strategy, etc.) The problem is that the modelling of an enemy behaviour must be done according to that enemy and not according to our reading of his way of acting.

---

475. https://www.9-11commission.gov/report/911Report.pdf.
476. http://govinfo.library.unt.edu/wmd/index-2.html.
477. https://assets.documentcloud.org/documents/1376717/cia-report.pdf.
478. http://www.iraqinquiry.org.uk/
479. Today: Federal Intelligence Service (FIS).
480. Martin Stoll, "08/15 statt 007", Facts, n° 25, 2001.
481. In English: actionable intelligence.

Comparison of types of analysis

	Academic analysis	Intelligence analysis
Accent	Study of past (present) events	Impact on the future (basis for decision)
Time constraints	No real time constraints, neither for acquisition nor for analysis	Dilemma between accuracy and completeness of information collected
Nature of the result	The conclusions may have no implications	The conclusions have implications (political, military, other)
Form	Test	Response to a specific problem and evaluation of its impact
Substance	Subject	Problem
Motivation	Personal interest: chosen topic	Decision-maker's need: imposed topic
Customer	Academic experts	Generalist decision-maker
Objective	Good evaluation	The product must be operational, relevant to the question posed and arrive in a timely manner.

Table 9 - A common mistake in Europe is to confuse academic and intelligence analysis. This results in a deficit in the analytical capabilities of the services.

3.2.4.4.2. The weakness of the analysis

After the 2001 attacks in the US and the 2015-2016 attacks in Europe, the tendency has been to increase information gathering capabilities, without significantly improving the situation, on the contrary. Our inability to diagnose the nature of the problem means that we respond poorly.

The nature of the threats, the amount of information available and the rapid evolution of society have created new challenges for intelligence. In general, intelligence services have difficulty in prioritising between very short-term and long-term analysis. The result is a tendency for strategic intelligence services to shift their activities towards police intelligence, which is simpler and brings more visible results... but not necessarily better! Indeed, there is a tendency to move towards a kind of «BARKHANE syndrome», where the number of terrorists killed gives a sense of success, while the strategic situation deteriorates permanently. In Vietnam, the Americans had already noticed that this «*body count*» policy tended to be misleading. In 2005, in an article entitled «*For better intelligence, add courage*», George Friedman noted this tactical drift in intelligence, which led to the dismissal of Jamie Miscik, the CIA's deputy director of intelligence[482] .

In the United States, a commission of enquiry into intelligence capabilities prior to the war in Iraq[483] highlighted the performance of the smallest US

---

482. George Friedman, "For Better Intel, Add Courage", New York Post, 4 January 2005.
483. The Commission on the Intelligence Capabilities of the United States Regarding Weapons of

intelligence service: the State Department's *Bureau of Intelligence and Research* (INR). The syntheses provided by its 305 analysts had been consistently more relevant than those of the CIA and the *Defense Intelligence Agency* (DIA), which at the time had about 1,500 and 3,000 analysts respectively. The commission explained this by the fact that INR analysts had an average of 11 years' experience on the subjects they dealt with (about four times that of their CIA counterparts), while the head of the Near East/South Asia section had 25 years' experience[484].

On the other hand, it can be seen that in a «small» service it is easier for an analyst to have the overall picture of the problems than in a «large» service, where the work of synthesis requires more administrative coordination and is often carried out at a level where the intelligence is already political in nature. Clearly, the performance of an intelligence service is not a linear function of the number of its analysts. On the contrary: while large numbers of staff can be useful in police intelligence work, they can become a handicap in a strategic intelligence service. Thus, paradoxically, increases in the number of security agencies since the early 2000s have certainly contributed to a decline in their efficiency, in accordance with Parkinson's law[485].

This phenomenon affects all Western countries, but particularly the large ones (USA, UK and France). The increase in manpower leads to an increase in complexity that tends to result in inter-service rivalries, a lack of communication or coordination, excessive compartmentalisation, etc. This partly explains why the Russian intelligence services have become better than the Western services, as Vladimir Putin rightly notes when evaluating his services:

> *We are better than the United States because we don't have the same means as them.* [486]

Western weakness in dealing with terrorism is not due to a lack of information, but to a chronic and persistent failure to understand the modern strategic environment. For example, during the state of emergency, most of the «successes» recorded are in relation to «normal» crime, but not really terrorism. Indeed, intelligence is increasingly understood as a discipline associated with security rather than decision-making. In other words, there is a drift away from intelligence as a part of the action and not as the thinking that should shape the action.

Mass Destruction, Report to the President of the United States, 31 March 2005.
484. David Ignatius, "Spy World Success Story", The Washington Post, 2 May 2004, p. B07.
485. See https://fr.wikipedia.org/wiki/Loi_de_Parkinson.
486. «Conversations with Mr Putin 2-4», France 3 (31'15").

The literature on terrorism tends to place little emphasis on intelligence analysis. But they focus on the need for better collection, especially from human sources, and for increased counter-terrorist operations in the form of counter-intelligence and clandestine actions.[487]

However, a fundamental problem is the ability to process the growing volume of information. With more than 200,000 people, 17 agencies and an annual budget of between $50 and $60 billion, the US intelligence community is arguably the largest in the world. In 2013, it was continuously monitoring some 700,000 people around the world, and its electronic component, the *National Security Agency* (NSA), alone was collecting more than 220 billion pieces of information per month[488].According to the British newspaper *The Guardian* (which published the documents leaked by Edward Snowden), its British equivalent, the *Government Communication Headquarters* (GCHQ), harvests the equivalent of the national library every seven and a half minutes, or 21 petabytes (one million billion bytes) per day, just by spying on the flow of fibre optics between the UK, Europe and the US (TEMPORA project)[489] .

The claim that analysis has been neglected in favour of collection is a truism bandied about by journalists and other so-called intelligence 'experts', who point to the huge amount of data collected by surveillance and the inability to absorb it. This is not true. In fact, the problem is not really the amount of data. It is processed by algorithms and artificial intelligence techniques that work in a cascade, reducing the mass of data to a level that is useful and manageable by analysts. The real problem is the temptation for departments to focus on the details and lose the big picture, which is crucial for decision-making.

Experience shows that the very nature of the information provided by mass collection systems rarely allows for real anticipation. By focusing on the «trees», we no longer see the «forest». This mass of information is only really useful at the tactical level, sometimes to prevent the execution of an attack (pre-emptive action), but more often a posteriori to find the perpetrators, but very rarely to prevent attacks (preventive action). In most cases, the data collected is only «deciphered» or «understood» after the event, when a causal link can be established.

After Edward Snowden's revelations, the American establishment tried to justify these wiretaps of American citizens. In June 2013, General Keith

---

487. Erik J. Dahl, "Warning of Terror: Explaining the Failure of Intelligence Against Terrorism", Journal of Strategic Studies, volume 28, issue 1, 2005, pp. 31-55.
488. Glenn Greenwald and Ewen MacAskill, "Boundless Informant: the NSA's secret tool to track global surveillance data", The Guardian, 11 June 2013.
489. Kadhim Shubber, "A simple guide to GCHQ's internet surveillance programme Tempora", wired.com, 24 June 2013.

Alexander, Director of the NSA, claimed that 54 terrorist attacks had been prevented in this way, including 13 in the United States, 9 against American interests abroad, 25 in Europe, 11 in Asia and 5 in Africa[490].However, during the subsequent parliamentary enquiry, General Alexander had to admit that this claim had been exaggerated[491] and that the information gathered had only confirmed existing information, and that only one, perhaps two cases of *'plotting'* could *have* been identified[492].In reality, it turned out to be only one case: the arrest of Basaaly Moalin, a taxi driver from San Diego (California) who had paid $8,500 between 2007 and 2008 to a Somali correspondent suspected of being associated with Al-Shabaab. But in a 2009 report, the FBI even acknowledged that these payments were not related to terrorism, but to tribal ties[493].Thus, in 2015, the 200 billion pieces of information collected monthly by the NSA at that time[494] did not prevent a single terrorist attack ...[495]

While Western parliaments sacrifice the privacy of their citizens, the majority of thwarted attacks are based on information acquired outside mass collection systems. In France, a typical example was the discovery *by chance* in September 2017 of an explosives laboratory in Kremlin-Bicêtre[496] .

One problem that affects intelligence analysis is that in a service, knowledge is at the bottom of the pyramid. The function of a service's managers is not to know, but to manage and aggregate knowledge. The upper echelon is the interface between the intelligence structure and the political power (or military command). Therefore, as intelligence moves 'up' to the decision-makers, it moves from a technical state to a political state: transformed and shortened to be both politically acceptable and readable by a decision-maker in a hurry. In this process, a great deal of substance disappears. Yet in asymmetric warfare, and terrorism in particular, tactical information can be of strategic importance, and the 'smoothing' of analysis sometimes leads to simplification with disastrous consequences.

---

490. Dianne Feinstein, "The NSA's Watchfulness Protects America", The Wall Street Journal, 13 October 2013;Courtney Kube, "NSA chief says surveillance programs helped foil 54 plots", NBC News, 27 June 2013.

491. Travis Gettys, "Patrick Leahy calls out Obama administration on terror plots thwarted by NSA spying", rawstory.com, 2 October 2013.

492. Noel Brinkerhoff, "NSA Director Alexander Admits He Lied about Phone Surveillance Stopping 54 Terror Plots", AllGov.com, 7 October 2013.

493. https://www.emptywheel.net/2013/07/17/what-does-the-government-consider-protected-first-amendment-activities/

494. https://nsa.gov1.info/dni/boundless-informant.html.

495. Maggie Ybarra, "FBI admits no major cases cracked with Patriot Act snooping powers", The Washington Times, 21 May 2015.

496. «Un laboratoire clandestin de fabrication d'explosifs découvert dans le Val-de-Marne», AFP/Liberation.fr, 6 September 2017.

The politicisation of intelligence as it 'flows' up to decision-makers tends to turn it into a product that they will be willing to hear. A frequent behaviour consists in expressing the intelligence in such a way that it is 'right', whatever the situation. This is a way for services to protect themselves from criticism if something goes wrong, but it often renders the intelligence completely useless to the decision-maker. This is why the United States has defined the criterion of *actionable* intelligence. In other words, intelligence that can be acted upon... A non-trivial art...

During the Cold War, Western intelligence services employed a large proportion of military personnel, who could relatively easily assess the military threat by 'putting on the boots' of the adversary and understanding its logic. After the Cold War, strategic intelligence services became more 'civilised' and adapted to a wider range of threats. But they have not acquired the ability to 'bootstrap' the new asymmetric adversaries, who operate with different logics and cultures.

Taxonomy of intelligence problems

	Simple	Deterministic	Random	Undetermined
Basic problem	Information	Quantification	Identify and classify events by probability	Define options for future events
Examples in the context of the fight against terrorism	Technical data Biographical data Tactical doctrine Structures and organisation Arming	Economy Demographics Frequency of travel Ammunition requirements	Short-term forecasts Assessment of the situation (tactical - operational) on the ground Estimated popular support	Long-term forecasts Identification of strategic options Assessment of the risks associated with the decision
Role of facts	Very high	High	Medium-Low	Low
Role of the judgment	Very low	Low	Medium-High	Very high
Analytical task	Selecting information	Select a model	List possibilities	Define the factors affecting the future
Analytical method	Researching sources	Application of the data to the model	Decision matrix	Analysis of possible scenarios
Analytical instruments	Comparison of data	Mathematical models	Calculation of probabilities Influence diagrams Subjective assessment	Holistic approach

Results	Facts	Numerical value	Weighted alternatives	Estimates Range of solutions
Probability of error	Very low	Low	High - depends on data quality	Very high
Type of information	Investigative intelligence Police intelligence	Documentation information Police intelligence	Anticipatory intelligence Military intelligence (operative level)	Anticipatory intelligence Strategic intelligence (strategic level)
Place in the fight against terrorism	Reaction	Pre-emption	Pre-emption or prevention	Prevention

Table 10 - The nature of analytical problems requires certain types of analysts.

Unfortunately, there are few institutional instruments to compel intelligence services to improve the quality of their analytical products. While in Europe parliamentary oversight is perceived as an intrusion into a confidential world and remains embryonic, the American experience shows that it can lead to qualitative improvement. In particular, it gives credibility to the services in the eyes of the political world and administrations.

The taxonomy of problems describes the characteristics of the problems and the generic characteristics of the solutions sought. It should have a direct influence on the selection of analysts, the allocation of resources and the appropriateness of the tasks assigned to them, as experience shows that «deterministic» and «random» problems are most often reduced to «simple» or «indeterminate» problems. Furthermore, too often, «collation» and «analysis» are confused. Analytical tools are often insufficiently developed or staff are not experienced enough to use them. These shortcomings are all the more pronounced for short-term problems.

3.2.4.4.2.1. THE «CRY WOLF» SYNDROME

A danger to the credibility of intelligence services is the repeated and unqualified announcement of all possible events, which trivialises the prediction to the point of ignoring it. The *Central Intelligence Agency*, in its *National Intelligence Daily* of 17 August 1991, announced the imminence of the coup d'état against Mikhail Gorbachev, but no one paid any attention:

The Agency had announced its dismissal so many times that it had ruined its credibility [...]. It was 'the sky is falling' analysis, which no one pays attention to anymore. [497]

This reflex of bureaucratic self-protection that pushes the services to renew cries of alarm, without any real documented basis, with the simple aim of «covering themselves» in the event of an event, is known in intelligence jargon as the «cry-wolf *syndrome*». Combined with the imprecision of available information on possible attacks, it is partly responsible for the relative inertia of US conduct prior to the attacks of 11 September 2001. It was also observed in Belgium after the November 2015 attacks in Paris, and - singularly - in Switzerland, which had no reason to be threatened by jihadists!

3.2.4.4.2.2. THE ROLE OF PREJUDICE AND INTELLECTUAL MIMICRY

In intelligence, experience is often less about knowledge of the facts than about understanding the mechanisms and modes of operation of threats, but also, and above all, about how to perform the analytical task (how to approach a problem, the processes and purposes of intelligence, etc.).

The problem is particularly acute when it comes to asymmetrical threats, because then the thinking has to be done 'behind the scenes', and sometimes against our Western logic. So when prejudice overrides analysis, it can be the source of even greater danger.

A striking example of intellectual mimicry is the reaction of the services after the Madrid attack of 11 March 2004 (M-11). While the Spanish intelligence services were quick to rule out the Basque ETA connection internally, the Aznar government relied on the lack of knowledge of Basque terrorism among the population and the political class to try to influence public opinion:

> *The al-Qaeda lead is confirmed by the discovery of the stolen van with verses of the Koran and detonators on board, and the claim to the British newspaper. Finally, the scale of the massacre, the indiscriminate and massive nature of the attack may make one think of Al Qaeda. However, we must put this lead into perspective, since the claim sent to the London Arabic-language newspaper, Al Quds Al Arabi, comes from the Abu Hafs al-Masri Brigades, a group that is in fact a fake and whose name had already been mentioned during the Sharm el-Sheikh crash, for which it had claimed responsibility. Moreover, Islamist attacks are often carried out by suicide bombers, which*

---

497. «The Agency had been predicting his downfall so many times, they had worn out their credibility [...] It was a 'sky-is-falling' analysis that no one was paying attention to.

does not seem to be the case here. I am more inclined to believe that ETA was responsible, but it is difficult to decide.[498]

In Switzerland, for example, since the end of the Cold War, none of the heads of the various military or civilian intelligence bodies has had any analytical experience of intelligence, while the rule of non-membership of political parties has been abandoned. This has resulted in an impoverishment of the analytical product[499] which affects the quality of strategic decision-making. Thus, after M-11, Jacques Pitteloud, appointed intelligence coordinator in 2000, without having any analytical experience of intelligence or of the specificity of Basque terrorism, blindly followed President Aznar, thus losing precious time[500].

A widely underestimated danger in intelligence is the projection of individual or collective prejudices to compensate for a lack of facts. For example, on 12 September 2001, Major General Peter Regli, former head of Swiss intelligence, declared that the attack on the *World Trade Center* had been accompanied by a computer attack[501] , designed to neutralise the telephone network... In fact, obsessed with cyberwarfare, he had simply failed to consider that, when the towers collapsed, they simply took out the mobile telephone network antennas located on the highest buildings in the city!

As noted before the Iraq war, one of the problems of intelligence in complex logical situations is the tendency of analysts to give in to the phenomenon of *'groupthink*[502].In other words, to align themselves with the prevailing view even if it is not based on fact. Among the many manifestations of this phenomenon is the influence of the 'big' services - notably the American or Israeli services - which are said to perform much better than they actually do, especially because they often provide information that is difficult to verify.

3.2.4.4.2.3. ETHNOCENTRISM

It is not enough to know the names and leaders of terrorist groups by heart to be a terrorist analyst. At the strategic level, it is above all a question of understanding the motivations, objectives and lines of force of the movement. This understanding requires not only knowledge of the strategies of each movement, but also an understanding of its logic of action.

---

498. Interview with Roland Jacquard, Director of the International Observatory of Terrorism, in nouvelobs.com, 12 March 2004.

499. «08/15 statt 007», Facts, 21 June 2001, pp. 38-43.

500. «Jacques Pitteloud, coordinator of the Swiss Confederation's intelligence services, speaks out on terrorism,» Le Matin Online, 20 March 2004.

501. «Der Anschlag basiert auf 'Cyber-War'», Aargauer Zeitung, 12 September 2001.

502. In French: «pensée de groupe» or «pensée unique».

3. COMBATING TERRORISM

Often used to describe the approach of Western intelligence services in general and American intelligence services in particular, ethnocentrism is the practice of understanding, judging and assessing other societies or populations through one's own cultural and societal references. In intelligence terms, ethnocentrism tends to introduce bias into thinking and can radically affect analysis. Although ethnocentrism is often described as a manifestation of superiority, even aggression and violence, and is associated with the notion of racism, experience shows that it expresses a kind of 'default reference point'. It is mostly observed among individuals with little contact or experience with other cultures.

One of the manifestations of this ethnocentrism is the fact of thinking that adversaries, such as terrorist or fundamentalist movements, have the same reasoning and a way of calculating their strategic gains with the same rationality as in the West, in terms of cost/benefit ratio. This phenomenon, which the Anglo-Saxons call «*mirror-imaging*», tends to attribute to the adversary the same reasoning or logic as its own. This is why we fail to understand asymmetrical conflicts, including jihadism. Thus, for Tom Ridge, head of the US Department of Homeland Security, the objective of «Al Qaeda» in the US is to «*disrupt the democratic process*»[503] ; in France, it is against the freedom to sit in bistros[504] and Jews see it as another manifestation of anti-Semitism, etc. But of course, no one is saying that the «Al Qaeda» in the US is a terrorist organisation. But of course, no one suggests the more likely hypothesis that these are individuals who are unhappy about being bombed or occupied by foreign forces!

3.2.4.4.2.4. THE SEARCH FOR «NO MISTAKES

Too often, the decision-maker expects certainty from intelligence. In some types of documentary intelligence or investigative intelligence (police intelligence), certainty is sometimes possible, but it is impossible when it comes to anticipation. Intelligence may come close to a possible future 'truth', but will never achieve real certainty. In this perspective, the decision-maker must always keep in mind that intelligence remains only an estimate - of quality, certainly - of events that no one can predict with certainty. This is a major difficulty in the relationship between the decision-maker and the intelligence analyst.

In simple terms, the analyst can present the result of his or her thinking about a possible future event in two ways: he or she can focus on *precision* - and commit to specific details - or focus on the *accuracy of* the information - and

---

503. International Herald Tribune, 9 July 2004.
504. Alain Finkielkraut, programme C à vous, France 5, 23 November 2015.

250

commit more to the nature of the event without specifying the details. In the former case, the analysis may be useful to the decision-maker, but contains a high potential for error that may render it obsolete, whereas in the latter case, the information will still be accurate, but is so general that it does not provide a basis for supporting a decision. The analysis must therefore offer a fine balance between accuracy and precision.

The most common flaw is to emphasise accuracy to the extent that the information contained is true in all situations and is therefore of no use to the client. During the Gulf War (1991), General Norman Schwarzkopf noted that :

[The [upper echelon intelligence analyses] were so careful, so annotated and so watered down ... that whatever happened would have been correct ... and that's not very helpful to the guy on the ground. [505]

The reality of administrative mechanisms is that an error or misjudgement of an event often leaves more of a mark than a relevant... but useless judgment.

3.2.4.4.2.5. The role of the «experts

Since 2001, the lack of understanding of the terrorist phenomenon and the difficulty of anticipating its action have led to extensive recourse to «experts». After the 2015-2016 attacks in France and Belgium, the phenomenon spread to the French-speaking world.

Often historians or specialists in Islam, sometimes even ex-hostages, their contribution to the reflection on terrorism is often passionate and not very useful to the resolution of the problem. In France and Belgium, some so-called «ex-agents» of the DGSE or other services are in reality only ex-»informants» who have neither the training nor the rigour of intelligence professionals.

Their knowledge of the terrorist phenomenon and intelligence is almost exclusively bookish, not to say novelistic. They tend to confirm American studies which show that 70% of publications on terrorism are simply a recycling of already published knowledge[506] .

This plethora of 'experts' underlines the analytical inadequacy of official intelligence bodies, but contributes to a stagnation of thinking and the growth

---

505. Address by General Schwarzkopf to the Congressional Armed Services Committee, 12 June 1991.
506. Hsinchun Chen, Edna Reid, Joshua Sinai, Andrew Silke, Boaz Ganor, Terrorism Informatics: Knowledge Management and Data Mining for Homeland Security, Chapter 2 - Research on Terrorism: A Review of the Impact of 9/11 and the Global War on Terrorism, Springer Science & Business Media- Business & Economics - 17 June 2008, 558 pages.

of terrorism[507].Too often, rumours become 'intelligence'[508] and hunches become 'analysis'[509].

This explains to a very large extent the chain of bad decisions and hazardous declarations, which add fuel to the fire rather than providing constructive responses. We have seen this in particular with the cacophony surrounding the 'de-radicalisation' campaigns in France and Belgium since 2015.

3.2.4.4.3. Identification of the threat

Only by accurately and impartially identifying the problem (even if it is unpalatable) can an effective response be designed. The lack of honesty in the portrayal of the jihadist threat by our media and 'experts' is largely responsible for our inability to respond to terrorism.

Classically, the threat is defined as the product of two main factors[510] :

$$\text{Threat} = \text{Intent} \times \text{Capabilities}$$

Where intent is defined by the willingness to engage in a campaign of terrorist action, and capabilities[511] are determined by the resources (personal, material and training) needed to carry it out. As can be seen, the threat is not a function of probability, but of factual elements.

A common mistake is to confuse capacity and intention, limiting thinking to the idea that if there is one, there is the other[512].Thus, there is a tendency to see radicalisation as a capacity and as an indicator of intention. Indeed, while the violent act is clearly an expression of a radical posture, some jihadists involved in recent attacks do not show a discernible radicalisation phase. In fact, at the tactical level, the «effective» intention of individuals to commit the act does not depend on a process of «brainwashing» or on attending a Salafist mosque. Conversely, many «radicalised» individuals (or even, in France, those

---

507. Clément Parrot, «Qui sont les 'experts en terrorisme' qui squattent les médias après un attentat?», Franceinfo, 8 July 2016; Olivier Toscer, «Télévision : La face cachée des consultants en terrorisme», TéléObs, 7 May 2016; see also Pascal Boniface, Les pompiers pyromanes - Ces experts qui alimentent l'antisémitisme et l'islamophobie, Max Milo, May 2016.

508. The term «RUMINT» (Rumor Intelligence), which is widely used by the Anglo-Saxons, was even derived from this.

509. See Émilie Gavoille and Erwan Desplanques, «Les experts à la télé, ils parlent à tort et à travers», Télérama.fr, 29 March 2016.

510. See Assessing and Managing the Terrorism Threat (NCJ 210680), Bureau of Justice Assistance, U.S. Department of Justice, Office of Justice Programs, Washington DC, September 2005.

511. NOA: sometimes opportunity or training is added to cover the English term 'capability', which cannot always be translated correctly into French.

512. See Bart Schuurman & Quirine Eijkman, 'Indicators of terrorist intent and capability: Tools for threat assessment', Dynamics of Asymmetric Conflict, volume 8, n° 3, 2015, pp. 215-231.

on an «S» file) are not terrorists. Our indicators are not adapted to the reality of modern jihadist terrorism and make us look in the wrong direction.

Furthermore, when capabilities (material and training) are atomised within an entire population, as is the case with Jihad by Individual Terrorism (JIT), they are difficult to detect and therefore cannot become an indicator of intent.

3.2.4.4.3.1. Detecting and assessing intent

The assessment of the opponent's intentions is the most problematic part of threat identification. Especially in France, it is often more ideological than factual.

Two major errors impact on our perception of terrorist intent. The first is that terrorism is an inevitable fate that affects us «for what we are, not for what we do», the result of a Machiavellian plot to «impose a global caliphate». Initially propagated by Israel to justify its abandonment of negotiations with the Palestinians, this convenient rhetoric was gradually adopted by the American, British, French, Belgian and German governments. In this model, terrorist intent is an invariant over which we have no control: terrorism can only be solved by exterminating the adversary.

This leads to the second mistake: because terrorism is seen as inevitable, strategies to influence the intentions and decisions of terrorists are useless. There is a tendency to deal with terrorism only *after* the terrorist has made his or her decision (and thus the intention is already expressed). This explains why what we call «prevention» is really «pre-emption», i.e. trying to intercept the terrorist when he is already in the execution phase. While the art of war suggests influencing the opponent's decision in order to be in a favourable position to act (like a chess player), we tend to leave the initiative to the terrorists and deal with the problem in a tactical or «police» manner. This is why Israel has never been able to control its terrorist threat, and why Westerners are not doing much better.

Yet the sacrificial dimension of Islamist terrorism suggests that jihadists perceive an existential threat that justifies their own death. It is hard to imagine that individuals would sacrifice themselves simply for the sake of 'dividing' France! The historical caliphate - whose reconstruction is the objective of the EI - has never contained France. Moreover, in their demands, the jihadists do not mention changes in French, Belgian or German society. Yet the inevitability of terrorism has slowly become part of the official discourse[513] and prevents us from implementing strategies to influence the terrorists' intentions. In fact, the opposite is true: we have done everything to stimulate them.

---

513. See Prévention de la radicalisation. Training kit, 2ᵉ edition, Secrétariat général du comité interministériel de prévention de la délinquance, September 2015.

Since 2001, when jihadist terrorism was associated with nihilism, «nuclear terrorism» was seen as the logical extension of «9/11» and some people spoke of «super-terrorism» or even «hyper-terrorism». Now, fifteen years later, attacks are carried out with knives. Clearly, we have not understood anything. We tend to imagine the capabilities of terrorists based on how *we* would act if we were practising terrorism.

The aim here is to evaluate the real capacity of a terrorist movement to carry out attacks. The term «capacity» covers two realities: a qualitative dimension that must qualify the group's ability to carry out its project (in English: *capability*) and a quantitative dimension, its human and material potential (in English: *capacity*).

The *ability to* carry out violent actions has taken a turn for the worse with the concept of «*open* jihad» and the DTI, which advocate that terrorists train themselves through online manuals. This method generates terrorists who are sometimes imperfectly trained, but potentially very numerous and difficult to detect. On the other hand, the success of ARIG is not based on the sophistication of the attacks, but on their number and wide distribution. Even basic «training» of terrorists is perfectly sufficient to realise the concept.

From a quantitative (*capacity*) point of view, the potential of a terrorist force is expressed in strategic and tactical terms. Strategically, it is the capacity of the group or movement to mobilise sympathisers, militants and fighters, who will constitute three circles that frame its action. It is important to make a distinction between the capacity to mobilise and the phenomenon of radicalisation. Mobilisation takes place on the basis of a legitimacy - real or perceived - generated by (Western) action and which will be extended by 'radicalisation'.

If we want to combat the growing capabilities of a terrorist movement, we must first combat its ability to mobilise militants. It is therefore at the level of the perception of legitimacy that we must operate.

3.2.4.4.3.3. INDICATORS AND ECONOMETRIC MODELS

During the Cold War, the Warsaw Pact had leadership structures and a regular rhythm of activity that allowed for the identification of a measurable «normal flow» that allowed for the establishment of indicators. Deviations from these indicators (also known as the «signal-to-noise ratio») constituted warning elements, the intensity and nature of which determined the intelligence services' level of surveillance or triggered operational measures. Most of these indicators were calibrated to possible preparations for a conflict in Europe. These included changes in the coal trade, military assets allocated to wheat harvests, increased signal traffic, activation of reserve transmission channels, raw material flows, the number of observation satellites in orbit, the number of reconnaissance flights, and many others.

This intelligence discipline, which aims to study «*indices and warning criteria*» or «*indices and warning indicators*», is better known by professionals under the generic abbreviation of I&W[514].It involves two concepts: a) the *indication* and b) the *indicator*. Often confused, they have very specific meanings in terms of intelligence:

- the *index* is a generic signal in a particular domain (e.g. the fuel gauge of a car). By nature, it is simply observed information;

- The *indicator* is a specific value or *threshold value* in the genesis of a problem, which indicates that a stage has been reached and triggers an alert for a reaction (by analogy: the red light on the gauge indicating that one is on reserve). It is determined empirically or calculated statistically from clusters of indicators. Its identification is crucial in determining the imminence of an event.

While it is relatively easy to identify concrete crisis indicators, it is often much less trivial to identify the indicators that should trigger a response. All too often, the problem is circumvented by simply renaming lists of indicators as «lists of indicators». For example, in 2010, in order to better address violence against women, the UN Department of Peacekeeping Operations created a list of violence indicators. However, contrary to the author's advice, this was only a list of indices, with no defined threshold for operational action, and therefore did not lead to any significant improvement in this area.

During the Cold War, Western services monitored the number of Soviet Kosmos observation satellites in orbit (usually 3-4 units): 5-6 satellites in orbit was considered an indicator, as this was the minimum number needed to monitor a long-term crisis continuously. They also monitored the number of Soviet submarines in the various seas of the world according to similar principles. The simultaneous conjunction of several indicators was then a warning of a possible major crisis and triggered a move to a higher alert level.

With a complex set of concrete, quantifiable and observable indices and indicators, it was possible to develop econometric models to quantify and evaluate a degree of threat in terms of probability, and thus risk, in advance. The intelligence services thus had at their disposal, alongside the continuous analysis of the politico-military situation and the available potential, effective tools for dynamically measuring the evolution of a situation in order to put political actions into perspective. It was such tools that enabled the author, then working for the Swiss strategic intelligence service, to predict in 1986, to within

---

514. NATO Glossary of abbreviations used in NATO documents and publications, AAP-15, 2013.

a few thousand troops, the Warsaw Pact's troop reductions that were announced more than two years later by Mr. Gorbachev, on 7 December 1988[515].

There are two types of I&W[516] :

- *Tactical I&W*, which are action-oriented and are used to combat or prevent the execution of an attack, assault or other damage. They contain information on perpetrators, locations, weather conditions, etc. ;

- *Strategic I&W*, which should allow for a better perception of changes in the security environment and threats by anticipating, for example, the change in attitude of a state or non-state actor.

In fact, in a strict sense, tactical warning indicators are not considered an intelligence discipline, but an operational activity, because at this level - and this is particularly true in the case of terrorism - the indicators do not shape policy, but are translated into direct action. Strategic indicators, on the other hand, are more oriented towards building a picture of the situation that should detect potential risks, but whose significance is not necessarily linked to their imminent realisation.

During the Cold War, in order to make it more difficult to read the war indicators, the adversaries on both sides of the Iron Curtain routinely carried out a higher level of activity than necessary (reconnaissance flights, satellite launches, naval presence, etc.). The indicators were thus 'drowned' in artificially high ambient 'noise', making the signal-to-noise ratio almost insignificant. This is what the Soviets understood by the term 'active measures', a discipline of '*maskirovka*'[517] , itself part of 'counterintelligence' activities[518] .

With the concept of *Jihad by Individual Terrorism* (JIT), the idea is exactly the opposite, but with the same objective: to lower the 'signal' to the level of 'background noise' so that their ratio is rendered insignificant in determining a threat level. The inability of the intelligence services to distinguish between these two elements is at the origin of the almost irrational application of the precautionary principle and literally at the origin of the *lockdown* in Brussels from 21 to 25 November 2015, just after the Paris attacks.

The search for indicators of attack requires sensors of such granularity that the very foundations of our democratic society would be called into question. Moreover, the nature of these indicators is difficult to determine. For example,

---

515. See : Status of Soviet Unilateral Withdrawals, National Intelligence Council, NIC M89-10003, Washington DC, October 1989.

516. Jack Davis, "Strategic Warning: If Surprise is Inevitable, What Role for Analysis?", The Sherman Kent Center for Intelligence Analysis, Occasional Papers, volume 2, n° 1, January 2003.

517. A term that could be loosely translated as 'concealment'.

518. The Russian term is «kontrrazvedka», frequently and incorrectly translated as «counter-espionage».

the «*warning signals*» mentioned by the Egmont Institute[519] , which could have prevented the attacks of 22 March 2016 in Brussels, are in fact independent events that could at most have constituted clues, useful for historians, but not indicators for intelligence analysts.

In fact, the race for details is becoming a «race to the bottom»: tactical intelligence is no longer sufficient to fight this type of terrorism. The report drawn up after the attacks on the American embassies in Nairobi and Dar-es-Salam on 7 August 1998 already clearly indicated that it was insufficient to anticipate attacks:

> *The commission found that the intelligence and policy communities have relied excessively on tactical intelligence to determine the level of potential terrorist threat to overseas posts. The Inman Report[520] noted, and previous experience tells us, that terrorist attacks are often not preceded by advance intelligence. The establishment of the Counter-Terrorism Centre with inter-agency units has produced tactical intelligence that has thwarted a number of terrorist attacks. But this type of intelligence cannot be relied upon to prevent this type of attack.[521]*

Yet, 17 years later, the lessons have not been learned and we are back to thinking in terms of tactical intelligence, the only kind that the media and non-professionals understand, because their results are more visible (arrests, strikes, etc.). With threats more diffuse, difficult to discern or define, intelligence services must learn to move away from tactical questions and focus on how terrorists think.

Indeed, when the nature of the threat does not allow us to obtain intelligence that can prevent the problem, we must deal with it upstream, by going back to the causes[522].This is the conclusion drawn by the Americans following the Beirut bombing in 1983:

---

519. Thomas Renard (editor) (with contributions from: Sophie André, Elke Devroe, Nils Duquet, France Lemeunier, Paul Ponsaers, Vincent Seron), Counterterrorism in Belgium: Key Challenges and Policy Options, Egmont Paper 89, October 2016.

520. The Inman Report, named after Admiral Bobby Ray Inman, who chaired its preparation, and officially known as the «Report of the Secretary of State's Advisory Panel on Overseas Security», was published in 1985, following the attack on the US Marine barracks in Beirut in November 1983.

521. Admiral William J. Crowe, Chairman, Report of the Accountability Review Boards - Bombings of the US Embassies in Nairobi, Kenya and Dar es Salaam, Tanzania on August 7, 1998, Washington DC, January 1999 (also known as the Crowe Commission Report)

522. Jack Davis, "Strategic Warning: If Surprise is Inevitable, What Role for Analysis?", The Sherman Kent Center for Intelligence Analysis, Occasional Papers, volume 2, n° 1, January 2003.

While specific intelligence on terrorist intentions was almost impossible to find, the intelligence community could and should have made an extra effort to better analyse the socio-political situation in Lebanon, even if the decision-makers had not asked for it.[523]

But here again, 35 years later, we have learned nothing...

3.2.4.4.4. Determining the risk

The purpose of intelligence is to anticipate risks in order to inform decision-making (that is why the Dutch word for intelligence is *'inlichtingen'*, 'lighting'). Since the decision will, by definition, have its effects in the future, the risks must be identified at least in the period of time when the decision will have its effects.

But since no one has a crystal ball to read the future, forecasting or anticipation is a difficult art. Like weather forecasting, intelligence anticipation is not - or, more accurately, should not be - the product of chance or impressions, but is a projection based, on the one hand, on concrete and identifiable clues and, on the other, on clearly observed doctrines or patterns of action.

The concepts of «risk» and «threat» are often confused: while the threat is essentially a function of relatively easily definable factual elements, as we have seen, the risk is a function of a probability that is often difficult to quantify. All too often, the precautionary principle tends to overestimate risk and associate it with a 100% probability, which, in short, reduces the risk of the threat to an unavoidable level.

At the intelligence level, risk assessment should not be the result of impressions, but of fact-based analysis. We will use here as a reference the UN risk assessment mechanism for the adoption of necessary security measures in crisis areas[524] :

Risk = Threat x Vulnerability x Probability

Derived from a formula developed by the British intelligence services, this risk calculation takes into account the nature of the problem (threat), the existing or potential vulnerabilities to that threat and the probability of the event occurring, based on indices.

---

523. Shaun P. McCarthy, The Function of Intelligence in Crisis Management: Towards an Understanding of the Intelligence Producer-Consumer Dichotomy, Ashgate, Aldershot, 1998.
524. «Security Risk Management, Security Policy Manual, Department of Safety and Security, United Nations, 2011.

3.2.4.4.4.1. Quantifying the threat

Once a threat has been identified, its intensity needs to be assessed in order to include it in the definition of risk. To this end, some countries have developed rating scales to guide the implementation of preventive measures. Overall, however, experience shows that these systems do not work well, mainly because they do not define what is expected of them.

In March 2002, the United States adopted a warning system - the *Homeland Security Advisory System (HSAS)* - designed to alert government agencies, private companies and the public to terrorist threats and to harmonise threat perceptions and corresponding security levels. It was divided into five «Threat *Conditions*»[525] , which confused the concepts of «risk» and «threat». It was expected to be able to accurately warn of an impending attack, but no intelligence system in the world is currently capable of doing this. Activated on a precautionary basis, rather than on the basis of intelligence capabilities, it has generated a large number of false alarms, resulting in a loss of credibility: preventive measures and evacuation drills planned for different levels of alert in companies or administrations were quickly abandoned. For many Americans, the fluctuations in alert levels were more the result of administrative reflexes than of relevant information and analysis.

In fact, in the United States, between 2002 and 2011, the alert level changed 17 times without ever dropping to the lower levels (blue and green) and only once reaching the highest level (red). Its stagnation in the upper intermediate levels (yellow and orange) eroded citizens' ability to differentiate between no threat and a diffuse threat, leading to fatigue and disinterest in the system. It was therefore abandoned in 2011[526].

In Belgium, the confusion between *threat* and *risk* has probably had operational consequences, which have not really been analysed. The Kingdom has a body whose specific mission is the determination of the threat level - the *Office for the Coordination of Threat Analysis* (OCAM) - the inconsistencies of the system briefly caught the attention of a few media, but without generating in-depth reflection. Apparently, the intelligence oversight body (*Committee R*) had suspected the inadequacy of OCAM's assessment tools already in 2015, but no significant changes were made[527] .

In Belgium, OCAM defines four levels of threat:

- Level 1 (Low): the person, group or event under analysis is not at risk;

---

525. «Low Condition» (green): normal situation and low terrorist risk; «Guarded Condition» (blue): general risk (of an unspecified nature); «Elevated Condition» (yellow): significant risk; «High Condition» (orange): high risk; «Severe Condition» (red): imminent attack.
526. Jessica Zuckerman, National Terrorism Threat Level: Color-Coded System Not Missed, The Heritage Foundation, 26 September 2012.
527. Standing Committee on the Oversight of Intelligence and Security Services, Activity Report 2016, Intersentia, Antwerp - Cambridge, 2017, p. 72-73.

- Level 2 (Medium): the threat to the person, group or event under analysis is unlikely;
- Level 3 (Serious): the threat to the person, group or event under analysis is possible or likely;
- Level 4 (Very serious): the threat to the person, group or event under analysis is serious and imminent.

These levels are obtained by cross-referencing two scales that measure coefficients of «*likelihood*» (from 2 to 6) and «*severity*» (from 1 to 5) of the event. These coefficients are added together for each event and the result (between 3 and 11) determines the threat level.

This scale calls for several remarks. Firstly, it does not distinguish between the scope of the threat. In other words, the threat against a person is placed at the same level as a threat of national scope. This is what justified the assessment of a possible performance by Mr Dieudonné in Brussels on 17 May 2015 as 'serious' (level 3), an assessment that was widely questioned by the Belgian media[528].This particularity can create inconsistencies in the way the state responds to the threat[529]. This is what happened with Jürgen Conings, a far-right military man for whom a manhunt was conducted throughout Belgium in May 2021: he was defined as a level 3 threat (i.e. the same level as the Islamist threat in 2016). The problem is that this scale of measurement is completely meaningless and depends - in the final analysis - on discretionary judgement to be (possibly) useful.

Secondly, the notions of threat and risk are mixed, without reference to the notion of probability. In other words, these threat levels do not really allow for effective crisis management and tend to take away the responsibility of the intelligence services for the quality of the analysis they provide. In fact, we arrive at assessments that are always 'right'. Indeed, although the terms *'possible'* and *'likely'* are used in common parlance as synonyms for *'probable'*, in reality they are not. The notion of «*possibility*» is associated with material conditions, not with probability[530] : «In a race with two horses, one of which has three legs, both have the possibility of winning, but the probability that the one with only three legs will win is very low»...

As for 'likelihood', this can only really be measured experimentally, as it can only be determined in relation to a reference event. Threat levels defined in this way are not really binding on the body making the judgement and can hardly form the basis of an effective preventive strategy. In fact, this type of

---

528. «Dieudonné: was the level 3 threat justified?», https://www.youtube.com/watch?v=O9DSVXabonE.
529. «OCAM threat analysis after the police killings in Magnanville (Paris)», Syndicat Libre de la Fonction Publique - Secrétariat National, trade union statement, 15 June 2016.
530. Sherman Kent, "Words of Estimative Probability" (CONFIDENTIAL), Studies in Intelligence, Central Intelligence Agency (CIA), Fall 1964.

criterion is a bureaucratic means of protection against the incompetence of «civil servants-analysts».

Thus, when the Belgian government decided to raise the alert level to 4 in Brussels, from 21 to 26 November 2015, one week after the Paris attacks, there was no objective threat to the city at that stage. Indeed, according to the logic of the jihadists, Belgium is no longer part of the coalition in Iraq, and it is difficult to see what the terrorists' motives could have been at that time: level 4 was decreed in the period that probably presented the least risk for the city. Two months later, when Belgium resumed its participation in the strikes in Iraq, the threat level was reduced to 3. It is precisely at this moment that it should have been raised to 4 and could have helped to prevent the attacks of March 2016. Moreover, we note that in 2015-2016 level 4 was *only* invoked *after* the crises, whereas it is intended to prevent them.

The instrument is therefore ill-suited to its purpose and badly used. It is reasonable to conclude that the Belgian services did not understand the asymmetric dynamics of jihadist terrorism, and the political power committed itself to Iraq and Syria later on without measuring the likely consequences. Belgians will pay the blood price on 22 March 2016. That said, Belgium is far from being an exception: France and Switzerland have the same deficits.

3.2.4.4.4.2. IDENTIFICATION OF VULNERABILITIES

The responses to the 2015 and 2016 terrorist attacks in France and Belgium show that not only was the intrinsic nature of terrorism poorly understood, but that the vulnerability of the population was virtually ignored in the assessment of risk and the proposed responses. Clearly, governments failed in their «*Responsibility to Protect*» (R2P). They have even taken measures that have increased the vulnerability of the population.

In assessing risk, a distinction must be made between strategic and tactical vulnerabilities.

At the strategic level, civilian populations have become the transmission belt of the message that jihadists send to governments intervening in the Middle East, according to the Madrid model (2004). In this context, the greater the vulnerability of a country, the more its population opposes the government's policy. This is why Spain and Britain were targeted in 2004-2005, but not Poland, Italy or the Netherlands, which had a strong presence in Iraq. In Britain, opponents of the war had formed the largest popular rallies in British history[531] , while in Spain 91% of the population were opposed to the engagement[532].

---

531. "'Million' march against Iraq war", BBC, 16 February 2003.
532. Giles Tremlett and Sophie Arie, «Aznar faces 91% opposition to war», The Guardian, 29 March 2003.

It was probably because it was unpopular that the Hollande/Valls government sought military success in Iraq in September 2014. But it was also this same unpopularity that, as in Spain in 2004, provided a wake-up call for terrorist actions to bend the government's will. This explains why France, despite a relatively low participation (4.7%) in the strikes in Iraq and Syria, seems to attract the wrath of the jihadists.

At the tactical level, actions were taken by police officers, not strategists, based on preconceived ideas and without even attempting to understand what the enemy was after. After the incident in Verviers (Belgium), where the police apprehended a terrorist cell that wanted to specifically target the police in Brussels and Molenbeek, the response was to put more police on the streets. Thus, in a way, the designated 'targets' were placed in the heart of the population, instead of being made less visible. The same was true of the attack on 3 February 2017 against four soldiers at the Louvre[533] : their deployment was a response guided by police and not intelligence thinking, disconnected from an asymmetric context.

France and Belgium have engaged in Iraq and Syria without addressing their strategic vulnerability - thereby encouraging terrorists to strike - or their tactical vulnerability.

3.2.4.4.4.3. THE EXPRESSION OF THE PROBABILITY

While measuring the probability of an event occurring is a non-trivial exercise in itself, the way in which it is expressed in an analytical intelligence product is essential because it influences the decision. This topic is not generally addressed by the so-called European intelligence «experts». However, since the beginning of the Cold War, it has been the subject of research within the CIA, with the aim not only of better communicating risk at the level of analysis, but also of having a common and transversal language for reading intelligence analyses. These studies were largely inspired by the work of Sherman Kent, the modern American intelligence theorist, and his empirical table[534] :

Probability	Variation	Vocabulary
100 %		Some
93 %	±6 %	Almost certain
75 %	±12 %	Likely
50 %	±10 %	50/50
30 %	±10 %	Unlikely
7 %	±5 %	Very unlikely
0 %		Improbable

Table 11 - Expression of probability in CIA analyses (1964)

---

533. Eugénie Bastié, 'Avec Sentinelle, les militaires sont devenus des magnants à terroristes', lefigaro.fr, 3 February 2017.
534. «Words of Estimative Probability (CONFIDENTIAL), op. cit.

Several variations of this table exist. In Canada, detailed studies were carried out within the *Intelligence Assessment Secretariat* (IAS) of the *Prime Minister's Privy Council Office* to establish a method of quantifying the subjective probabilities expressed in intelligence briefs. The aim was also to encourage analysts to systematise their thinking and identify the consequences of their assessments. As a first step, a scale was established to express probability and then coupled with a 'mapping' of probabilistic vocabulary. The result is a correspondence table with commonly used vocabulary and a scale from 0/10 to 10/10, which was adopted in 2010[535] :

Vocabulary	Quantification	Remarks
Will happen Is certain	10/10	There is no plausible scenario - however remote - in which this event would not occur
Almost certain Extremely likely Highly likely	9/10	There are conceivable - but remote - scenarios in which this event would not occur
Likely	7-8/10	
A little more than a 50/50 chance	6/10	Used rarely, only when the probability is greater than one in two, but cannot be described as probable.
One in two chances	5/10	
A little less than one in two chance	4/10	Used rarely, only when the probability is lower than one in two, but cannot be described as improbable.
Improbable Unlikely	2-3/10	
Very unlikely	1/10	There are conceivable - but remote - scenarios in which this event could occur
Will not happen Will not be	0/10	There is no plausible scenario - even remote - in which this event would occur

Table 12 - Expression of probability in the Intelligence Assessment Secretariat (IAS) analyses (2010)

It is interesting to note that in this process - in which departmental staff were involved - analysts showed concern that the quantification of the probability of their information could be used to evaluate their own work. A recurring phenomenon is the feeling among analysts that, to be successful, the intelligence they produce must always have a high degree of probability. This is obviously

---

535. Alan Barnes, "Making Intelligence Analysis More Intelligent: Using Numeric Probabilities", Intelligence and National Security, volume 3, n° 3, 2016, pp. 327-344.

not true! It is not the analyst who makes the event, but he or she must determine to what extent it can occur, and with what likely consequences.

Experiments with this table show that decision-makers have a more precise idea of the assessments proposed to them. Furthermore, this quantification has forced analysts to be more cautious about the time horizon associated with their forecast, preferring to limit their scope to one or two years, for example.

The formulation of the probability of occurrence of an event has a direct impact on the perception of decision-makers. It is therefore essential that the analyst estimate this probability with the greatest intellectual rigour. The problem is that the latter does not coexist well with bureaucratic reflexes, such as pleasing one's superiors, not provoking conflict with the decision-maker, conforming to prevailing opinions, preferring 'too much' to 'too little', fear of being 'favourable to the enemy', etc.

In the report, published on 6 January 2017 by the US intelligence community on Russia's alleged attempts to influence the US elections, a grid for interpreting the probability formulation is given, which can be translated as follows:

Probability	Variation	Official terminology	French translation
100 %	-10 %	Almost certainly, nearly certain	Almost certain
80 %	±10 %	Very likely, highly probable	Very likely
70 %	±10 %	Likely Likely	Likely
50 %	±10 %	Roughly even chances, roughly even odds	Approximately equal chances
35 %	±10 %	Unlikely, improbable	Unlikely
18 %	±10 %	Very unlikely, highly improbable	Very unlikely
5 %	±5 %	Almost no chance, remote	Almost no chance

Table 13 - Expressions of probability in analyses by the US Office of the Director of National Intelligence (2017)

In Britain, similarly, the intelligence services use a unified 'probability *yardstick*' to simplify communication between services:

Probability	Gap	Official terminology	French translation
95-100 %	5 %	Almost certain	Almost certain
80-90 %	10 %	Highly likely	Very likely
55-75 %	20 %	Likely Likely	Likely
40-50 %	10 %	Realistic possibility	Realistic possibility
25-35 %	10 %	Unlikely	Unlikely
10-20 %	10 %	Highly unlikely	Very unlikely
0-5 %	5 %	Remote chance	Almost no chance

Table 14 - Expression of probability in UK analyses (Probability Yardstick) [536]

---

536. Professional Development Framework for all-source intelligence assessment, Professional Head of

Perhaps the most famous case of risk distortion was the *National Intelligence Estimate* (NIE) of 1ᵉʳ October 2002 on Iraqi weapons of mass destruction, which was prepared by the CIA[537].In the version sent to members of Congress, in order to make the message clearer and reduce ambiguities, the vocabulary used and the tense of verbs had been changed and the conditional tense replaced by indicatives. In this way, the agency's doubts were smoothed out and superimposed on a prevailing opinion, which was not based on facts and corresponded to the executive branch's expressed intentions in favour of an operation in Iraq.

3.2.4.5. Dissemination

While analysis is at the heart of intelligence activity, it is not the end of it. The decision-maker still needs to receive and accept the intelligence. The dissemination phase is therefore a critical aspect of the intelligence process, as it determines the manner and degree to which intelligence is integrated into the decision. It is the indicator of the existence - or not - of an 'intelligence culture', as it materialises its purpose. In the final analysis, the effectiveness of the intelligence system therefore depends on the quality of the relationship between the decision-maker and his services.

This leads to the need for caution when judging a policy decision: it may be the result of poor quality intelligence itself, a distortion in the way intelligence is transmitted, or the non-adherence of the decision maker.

In the framework of the rule of law, the main function of intelligence is to provide factual and non-partisan elements in the decision-making process. Insofar as the 'services' are central actors in the decision, to which they contribute with high-quality and reliable analyses, they constitute - in theory - a sort of 'standard meter' of information. In theory, they set the *pace* for understanding the strategic environment. This is why intelligence should be detached from any political affiliation. Sherman Kent (1903-1986), the American intelligence theorist, declared a political bias in intelligence «inexcusable»[538].This is the major weakness of many Western services.

This can be seen in the decisions taken in France, Belgium or by the European Union. Clearly, leaders are making decisions based on their own prejudices, not on robust intelligence. This can be seen in situations such as the hijacking of Ryanair Flight 4978, where decisions by Charles Michel or Ursula von der

---

Intelligence Assessment (gov.uk), January 2019.

537. Iraq's Continuing Programs for Weapons of Mass Destruction, NIE 2002-16HC, National Intelligence Estimate, (S//NF), October 2002 (TOP SECRET), p. 6 (Approved for release 12 September 2014).

538. Jack Davis, 'Sherman Kent and the Profession of Intelligence Analysis', The Sherman Kent Center for Intelligence Analysis, Central Intelligence Agency, Occasional Papers, vol.1, n° 5, November 2002.

Leyen are taken long before any analysis can be carried out: they therefore decide autocratically on the sole basis of their 'infallibility'.

The various forms of intelligence are integrated into policy-making in different ways. In most Western countries, for example, police intelligence tends to lose its tactical role and become part of strategic decision-making, leading governments into a form of 'micro-management'. The result is a confusion between the tactical and strategic levels, which works to the disadvantage of the latter and largely explains decisions that lack rationality.

3.2.4.5.1. The integration of intelligence into the decision

The relationship between the intelligence services and decision-makers is complex. They are the result of both the inexperience of political leaders in using this instrument and the reluctance of the services to «sell» their product. The complexity of security problems requires ever greater interaction between intelligence and decision-makers. However, several obstacles to this interaction are recurrent, but poorly combated:

- The purpose of intelligence is poorly understood. There is a tendency to attribute to it a documentary role and to ignore its role in the decision-making process. This tendency is shared both by the services, which prefer to explain rather than anticipate, and by the decision-makers, who are reluctant to integrate intelligence into the preparation of the decision.

- Services are often associated more with 'action' than with reflection. This phenomenon affects services such as the CIA or the DGSE, which generate an image of both respect and distrust, but which obscures their role in decision-making processes. Within the CIA, this phenomenon has led to a deep rivalry between the *Directorate of Operations*[539] and the *Directorate of Intelligence*, stimulating an improvement in its analytical products.

- The analytical result is all the more acceptable to the decision-maker as it confirms his ideas.

- The bureaucratic reflex encourages 'flat' analyses, expressed in vague and accurate terms, but without risk for its authors. Since the mid-1980s, virtually every crisis has been preceded by clues that were picked up, but almost never translated into clear warnings for the political authority. The information was available, but the crisis was not - or was badly - announced by the services. In Switzerland, several crises, which had been anticipated in good time by analysts, were not reported to the political level... for fear of being wrong.

The integration of intelligence into the decision is the responsibility of the decision-maker and requires a certain humility on the part of the services: whether they take it into account or prefer to decide according to their intuition remains their

---

539. Now called the National Clandestine Service (NCS).

266

prerogative. But in any case, the decision-maker must be aware of the intelligence, and must be ready to assume his choices.

3.2.4.5.2. The expression of the reliability of the information

During the Cold War, the issues were essentially strategic in nature and satellite imagery, wiretaps, human intelligence and even economic intelligence could be combined to produce quality intelligence. The analyses provided to decision-makers were generally of a measurable and known quality. However, the further down the line one goes, the less assurance one can have of the quality of intelligence provided.

In the case of terrorism - as in the initial phase of acute crises - intelligence is often forced to work with unique, uncross-referenced and unverifiable information. On the one hand, because sources are very scarce or even unique and, on the other hand, because the urgency does not always allow for a collation process and a thorough analysis. This is why, in order to use this information in a decision-making process, it is essential to specify its degree of reliability, which is very often low.

This was done in the report published on 6 January 2017 by the US intelligence community on Russia's alleged attempts to influence the US elections. Attached to the report is an interpretive grid that defines the degrees of reliability used in the document in relation to the claims it makes, most likely because the information available did not allow for a 'normal' analysis[540] :

English expression	French translation	Interpretation
High confidence	High confidence	High confidence generally indicates that judgements are based on high quality information and multiple sources. High confidence in a judgment does not imply that the product is a fact or a certainty; such judgments may be wrong.
Moderate confidence	Moderate confidence	Moderate confidence means that the information is based on credible sources and is plausible, but is not of sufficient quality or sufficiently corroborated to ensure a high level of confidence.
Low confidence	Low confidence	Low confidence means that the credibility of the information and/or its plausibility is uncertain and that the information is too fragmentary and insufficiently corroborated to provide a basis for sound analysis, or that the reliability of sources is questionable.

Table 15 - Expressions used by the US Office of the Director of National Intelligence to indicate confidence in a judgment (2017)

---

540. Background to «Assessing Russian Activities and Intentions in Recent US Elections: The Analytic Process and Cyber Incident Attribution, Intelligence Community Assessment (ICA), Office of the Director of National Intelligence, ICA 2017-01D, Appendix B, 6 January 2017, p. 13.

This grid makes it possible to decode the text of the report and thus to put the accusations against Russia into perspective. It should be noted that with regard to the notion of «high confidence- which appears seven times in the report - the *Director of National Intelligence* specifies that it can refer to false judgements[541] ! However, hardly *any European media* picked up on this warning, preferring to emphasise the role of Russia and condemn it unreservedly. An illustration of the «post-truth» phenomenon... It is exactly the same phenomenon that led the international community to blindly accept the American claims about Iraqi weapons of mass destruction.

3.3. Defining a strategy

Winning a hundred times in a hundred battles is not the height of excellence. Defeating an opponent without fighting is the pinnacle of excellence.

(Sun Tsu)

The first essential condition for combating terrorism is to understand that it is not a fatality: it has serious consequences, but objective causes that must be dealt with in a transparent and neutral manner. The fatalistic discourse - particularly strong in France - must be definitively abandoned.

The second condition is to understand that the fight against terrorism does not start *after* it has struck, but *before*. This sounds simple, but *no* Western country does it: you create the conditions for terrorism to occur and then limit yourself to trying to limit its effects.

The terms «strategy» and «prevention» are the most overused terms in counter-terrorism. When not confused with a «doctrine» or «idea», «strategy» usually takes the form of a list of activities, rarely coherent with each other, directed at symptoms and not at causes. In fact, *no* Western country has a real strategy against terrorism.

The weakness of the West is its overly conventional thinking and its inability to understand insurgent conflicts beyond the tactical issues. The «unconventional» dimension often mentioned in the media is reduced to coups de main or raids, following the World War II model. We repeat the same mistakes and we are always behind the terrorists. In February 2015, Lieutenant General Douglas Lute admitted about the start of the war in Afghanistan:

---

541. Op. cit.

Clearly, the Americans had no clear strategy or objectives for their war in Afghanistan[543] .

The same applies to Operation BARKHANE in the Sahel. Its strategy is based on three axes: a) maintaining pressure on the armed terrorist groups; b) accompanying the armies of partner countries; c) acting on behalf of the populations[544].Without going into detail, it can be seen that it is not geared towards measurable objectives that would make it possible to define success: instead of explaining how to transform tactical successes into strategic successes, the operation is reduced to a sum of tactical actions.

In February 2021, at the G5 Sahel summit, President Emmanuel Macron stated that he wanted to continue the effort of Operation BARKHANE in order to 'decapitate' Islamist organisations and thus reduce the level of the terrorist threat[545].In fact, he is thinking as he did in 1914, when the effectiveness of an adversary was based on pyramidal command structures. The problem is very different with floating, very flat structures: eliminating 'leaders' tends to stimulate terrorist activity rather than paralyse it.

Conversely, the Islamists' strategy is the result of the multiplier effect of their tactical actions: it turns the local populations against the French forces.

The only countries that have effectively fought complex terrorism of an asymmetric nature have been Italy (with the Red Brigades) and Spain (with ETA). Through a combination of political, strategic and tactical measures, Spain managed to defeat its domestic terrorism by gradually eroding its popular base: through democratisation and dialogue measures, the state succeeded in reducing the radical left-wing base of ETA and - through legislative measures - in cutting off the pro-independenceists from their nationalist base.

On the contrary, no country in the world has been so ineffective as Israel in its fight against terrorism. Locked into fixed doctrines, an intellectual inability to break out of a tactical framework and a culture that tends to underestimate its opponents, it is the only country in the world to have fostered a quantitative and qualitative increase in hostility in the territories it controls. Moreover, the

---

542. "Interview with Ambassador Douglas Lute", NATO Permanent Rep, former Director Iraq/ Afghanistan, NSC 2007-2014, Office of the Special Inspector General for Afghanistan Reconstruction, 20 February 2015.

543. "How Government Officials Misled The Public About The Conflict In Afghanistan", npr.org, 18 December, 2019.

544   «Operation Barkhane», press kit, Media Relations Office of the Armed Forces Staff, November 2019.

545. «Sahel: Macron wants to 'decapitate' the groups affiliated to Al-Qaeda», AFP/Le Point, 16 February 2021.

unpopularity and ineffectiveness of its internal security policy has encouraged antisemitism in the rest of the world.

To be effective, the fight against jihadist terrorism must move beyond tactical thinking. The establishment of a strategy must take into account the specificities of jihad:

- Deterrent action has no conceptual impact, because jihad inherently implies that one refuses to be impressed by the strength of one's opponent. By attempting to deter individuals who are ready to die by death, our logic of action is doomed to failure.

- It is the determination to resist that counts, and this is where the 'obligation of result' of the mujahid lies. In other words, he must show that he does not bend the knee and must - in a way - 'have the last word'. It is important to emphasise that this determination does not necessarily have to be expressed in an act of violence, but can be expressed in other ways (verbally or in writing, for example).

- Victory in jihad is not measured by the number of victims it causes or the intensity of its action, but by its determination.

One strategy for combating Islamist terrorism is to offer it 'escape routes' so that its determination can be expressed in ways other than violence. But such a strategy requires tact. It is necessary to avoid showing that one is giving in to the blackmail of violence, while at the same time offering the terrorist an opening so that he can show his determination, without necessarily resorting to violence.

In contrast to conventional or symmetrical conflicts, the state's firmness in the fight against Islamist terrorism cannot be expressed solely in terms of capabilities. The weakness of the American and Israeli approaches to terrorism is precisely that they are 'implacable' and deny the adversary any way out. Sometimes effective against serious crime or certain types of 'symmetrical' terrorism (notably right-wing or fringe terrorism), they do not work against asymmetrical terrorism that feeds on the 'strength' of its adversary. The more intractable the situation appears to be, the stronger the determination to engage in extreme actions (suicide attacks). This is the phenomenon that has been observed in the use of drones for air strikes, as we shall see.

The problem is that in the West, there is a tendency to apply a kind of standardised intellectual schema based on intransigence, which should be applied to any form of terrorism without trying to understand its different drivers. More energy is spent on avoiding losing face than on finding solutions that would prevent militants from engaging in terrorism.

Terrorism must be fought firmly, but not blindly!

The formulation of a counter-terrorism strategy must therefore take into account a very broad spectrum of societal, social, cultural and security factors. This is reflected in the notion of a «*holistic approach*», which is poorly understood in security circles and often confused with the «*comprehensive approach*» used by NATO. The latter assumes that a problem is dealt with by combining the efforts of several actors, whereas the holistic approach implies dealing with the problem along the entire chain of causality that caused it. A holistic strategy must address all the military, societal, cultural or social factors that generate and reinforce terrorist resolve.

This confusion largely explains NATO's failure in Afghanistan, which France is repeating in the Sahel. To put it simply, NATO sees itself as an organisation whose scope is limited to collective defence issues. In an asymmetric context, its narrow scope tends to complicate the situation. The author has seen this first-hand in Afghanistan and with his Mediterranean Dialogue partners (mainly Algeria, Egypt and Tunisia), where NATO tends to have a destabilising role. Not because it seeks to destabilise these countries, but because it is unable to understand the logic of its partners. On the one hand, it has neither the culture nor the skills to deal with the whole 'counter and anti-terrorist' spectrum, and on the other, its mere presence feeds the Islamist opposition. This is why, in February 2018, Tunisia refused the establishment of a NATO operational command centre on its territory[546].

3.3.1. The centre of gravity

In the 19th century, Clausewitz and Jomini had identified the existence of a chain of causality linking the various politico-military actions towards an objective that would lead to victory. However, it was necessary to find criteria for setting this objective. Both strategists had identified a 'point' or determining element on which the strength or effectiveness of an opponent depended. Jomini describes it as a «strategic decisive point», while Clausewitz uses the expression «centre of gravity»[547] defined as :

> [...the centre of all power and movement, on which everything depends; the characteristic, capacity or location from which enemy and friendly forces derive their freedom of action, physical strength or will to fight.[548]

---

546. Yacine Babouche, 'Tunisia rejects NATO's proposal to install a command centre on its territory', TSA-Algérie, 13 February 2018.

547. «...] ein gewisser Schwerpunkt, ein Zentrum der Kraft und Bewegung bilden, von welchem das Ganze abhängt, und auf diesen Schwerpunkt des Gegners muß der gesammelte Stoß aller Kräfte gerichtet sein", Karl von Clausewitz, Vom Kriege, Achtes Buch, Dümmlers Verlag, Berlin, 1832.

548. «The hub of all power and movement upon which everything depends; that characteristic, capability, or location from which enemy and friendly forces derive their freedom of action, physical strength, or the will to fight», Glossary, FM 100-5 (German: Schwerpunkt). Also found: «...characteristic(s), capability(ies), or locality(ies) from which a nation, an alliance, a military force or other grouping derives its freedom of action, physical strength, or will to fight.», Office of the Joint Staff, DOD Dictionary of Military and Associated Terms, Joint Publication 1-02 (Washington DC, 1984)

In the fight against a terrorist movement, identifying its centre of gravity is a central task of strategic intelligence services. It requires an intimate and dispassionate knowledge of the terrorist movement, its objectives and its doctrine. It is a non-trivial task, particularly in an asymmetric context where the thinking must be done «behind the scenes». In the absence of a real understanding of Islamist terrorism, the Western mind tends to project its own patterns and identify the centre of gravity according to its own cultural biases. This is why the elimination of Osama bin Laden or Abu Bakr al-Baghdadi seemed so important to us, when in fact their disappearance in 2011 and 2019 had no impact on global terrorist activity[549].

For each protagonist, the centre of gravity is therefore the 'keystone' of its strategic edifice: its removal causes the collapse or destruction of the whole. It can be a charismatic leader, a geographical position, a particular weapon system (e.g. nuclear weapons) or it can be intangible, such as the legitimacy of a fight or popular support.

The centre of gravity of terrorist movements is generally located in the intangible fields and in the *legitimacy of* their action vis-à-vis an audience. This legitimacy is of varying importance depending on the nature of the strategic objective: it must be won by terrorists seeking to establish a new regime, it is generally fairly well acquired in resistance terrorism, but plays only a minor role in common law terrorism, for example.

For other types of terrorism - such as ordinary terrorism - the centre of gravity is in the material domain. This is the case with narco-terrorism, whose motivation (and objective) is profit, and whose centre of gravity is often the (monopolistic) position of the traffickers in the market. This is why some strategists advocate opening up the narcotics market in order to impose a market on the traffickers, thereby attacking their centre of gravity and thus their main motivation: profit[550].

Once the centre of gravity has been identified, one can begin to develop a strategy. In some cases - for reasons of political expediency or legitimacy, for example - action may not be directed at the adversary's centre of gravity, because it cannot or should not be reached. In Northern Ireland, the British did not systematically target the known leaders of the terrorist networks in order to avoid radical changes in network structures and thus keep the networks under permanent 'control'. When the centre of gravity is poorly identified, its neutralisation can lead to a worsening of the situation, as was the case with the targeted

---

p. 188

549. Nicole Gaouette, "5 years ago the U.S. killed Osama bin Laden. Did it matter?", CNN, 2 May 2016; Ryan Pickrell, "Killing ISIS leader Abu Bakr al-Baghdadi hasn't hurt the terror group's operations, Pentagon warns", Business Insider, 4 February 2020.

550. See Dirk Chase Eldredge, Ending the War on Drugs - A Solution for America, Bridge Works, New York, 1998.

eliminations carried out by the Israelis, who systematically overestimated the importance of the movement's leaders (such as Sheikh Yassin, leader of Hamas) and underestimated the virulence of their successors.

With the concept of 'open *jihad*', the centre of gravity is entirely based on an immaterial factor: the legitimacy of the action. It derives from the legitimacy of resistance to international military interventions in the Middle East, interpreted as a crusade against Islam. Religion is a critical factor here, enabling the federating of resistance efforts (jihad), the ironing out of possible differences between rival groups, and even joint operations («hybrid operations"). In France, this centre of gravity has not been «captured» at all by the intelligence services and the government. Instead of tackling it, it has been reinforced with highly publicised and often childish debates:

- Campaigns against the Islamic veil ('hijab'), the burkini, the 'burqa' (which is, in fact, a 'niqab'), women's swimming pool times, or actions against individuals such as Dieudonné have - rightly or wrongly - given rise to a sense of 'persecution'. In the argument of the jihadists, they add to the interventions against Muslim communities around the world[551] and give credence to the idea of a crusade against Islam.

- Prime Minister Manuel Valls' ostensibly expressed link to the Jewish community (and Zionism[552]) has had the effect of reinforcing the centre of gravity of the jihadists, superimposed on antipathies that may be deplored, but which exist[553].

Without discussing the relevance of the substance here, the form was totally inappropriate and it was totally unnecessary to put them in the spotlight at this stage: these discussions could have been postponed to a quieter period. There is no point in the state fighting content on the Internet if, on the other hand, it openly positions itself as an enemy, thus fuelling the jihadists' desire to fight. It is like emptying the bathtub and leaving the tap running.

In such a context, the task of intelligence is obviously not to decide on the banning of this or that clothing, but to know whether the timing of the debate is judicious, and above all whether the decisions taken should be surrounded by accompanying measures (particularly in terms of communication).

If in the years 2015-2017, France was more targeted than other countries in the international coalition, it is largely because there was no management of the conflict at the level of communication in metropolitan France.

---

551. «Rohingyas, Uyghurs... : the map of persecuted Muslims in the world», France Culture, 6 September 2017.

552. See YouTube, «When Manuel Valls compares anti-Zionism and antisemitism», speech of 7 March 2016 at the CRIF.

553. «The history of France's enmity towards islâm», Dar al-Islam, n° 2, February 2015, p. 10 (NOA: the author of the article refers to Manuel Valls' speech of 19 March 2014, in Paris).

3.3.1.1. *Critical factors*

To enable the centre of gravity to exist and be effective, Clausewitz and Jomini had identified 'points', a sort of gateway to the centre of gravity, the destruction or control of which made it possible to reach the latter. Clausewitz called them «*neuralgic points*» and Jomini, «*decisive points*». They can be military positions, weapon systems, means of transmission, means of intelligence, etc.

In order to take better account of the complexity of the modern battlefield and the interweaving of a wide range of factors, these principles had to be refined. Thus, the neuralgic or decisive points have been redefined as a set of material or immaterial «critical factors», indispensable for carrying out actions or maintaining freedom of manoeuvre, the combination of which allows the centre of gravity to exist.

These critical factors can be broken down into a combination of critical functions, critical resources and critical vulnerabilities. In the context of the fight against terrorism, their general characteristics can be outlined as follows:

- *Critical functions* are those functions that are essential for action. They include, for example, communications, command and control capabilities, joint capabilities, etc. For a terrorist movement, this includes the leadership and coordination of various factions, the coherence between the objective of the movement and popular demands, which often boils down to the legitimacy of the terrorist movement.

- *Critical resources* can be popular support, national cohesion, industrial capacity, etc. In the case of terrorism, it may be financial support, logistical support (caches, shelter, etc.) or human resources - including the availability of 'fighters' willing to sacrifice their lives.

- *Critical vulnerabilities* are the potential weaknesses of the system, its 'Achilles heel', such as an over-sized logistical network, dependence on popular support in a difficult social context, poorly protected or unprotectable critical infrastructure, etc. In a terrorist context, these may be insufficiently compartmentalised leadership structures, insufficiently trained militants, or driven more by the romance of revolutionary action than by deep-seated convictions. In a terrorist context, it may be a question of insufficiently compartmentalised leadership structures, insufficiently trained militants or militants driven more by the romance of revolutionary action than by deep convictions. Thus, the Italian Red Brigades, after an initial phase led by a highly politicised core, rapidly expanded into student circles, where the romance of action exceeded political convictions, which introduced a critical vulnerability. This allowed the Italian security forces to infiltrate the organisation and exploit the 'repentant' system. A critical vulnerability can exist when the movement or its legitimacy depends on a charismatic personality, as in terrorist groups.

At the end of the 1990s, the American colonel John A. Warden developed a model[554] which generically articulates the critical factors in five concentric circles, with leadership and conduct at the centre, followed by critical infrastructure, communication infrastructure, the population and, finally, the forces deployed on the ground. It derives an air strategy based on a catalogue of targets chosen from among the critical factors to reach an adversary's centre of gravity.

In reality, Warden was simply formalising and adapting the theories of Clausewitz and Jomini to the technologies of the 21st century[e].By deliberately bombing German civilians between 1940 and 1945, and the Bulgarian population in 1941, the British had tried to shift their support to the Nazi regime and thus weaken it[555].This is the same strategy that was applied against Saddam Hussein in 1991 and 2003, against Serbia in the Balkan conflict during the 1990s and against the EI since 2014: the civilian population was deliberately targeted in order to isolate the 'leaders' (centres of gravity) from their base and provoke insurgencies. Today, sanctions against Iran or Venezuela have the same objective[556].Yet in neither of these examples has this strategy worked.

In fact, the opposite is true: the strikes have become a central element of Islamist propaganda. They play a mobilising role, reinforce the spirit of resistance and legitimise terrorism in the minds of jihadists. A bomb brought by a terrorist into a crowd of innocent civilians is undoubtedly a terrorist act, but what about a bomb brought by air over the same crowd? By applying this analogy, the EI has implemented exactly the same strategy as Western countries in using terrorism to push public opinion against the decisions of their governments[557].But this approach has been no more successful than its Western model.

Ironically, Western countries and the Islamic State have made the same error of judgement: whatever the final objective, attacking the civilian population tends to weaken the legitimacy of the action, which is their centre of gravity. In fact, the only ones who have understood this asymmetry are the Palestinians of Hamas: the Israelis attack the civilian population excessively, while the retaliation (rockets and mortar shells) is spectacular, but kills very few people and mainly during Israeli operations. As a result, their cause continues to attract sympathy, to the detriment of Israel. As a result, the very legitimacy of its existence is

---

554. Col. John Warden (USAF), "Air Theory for the Twenty-First Century", Air Power Journal, 1995.
555. Contrary to what history books suggest, it was only after British strikes on German cities and civilians in 1940 that Germany unleashed its Blitz on London (Richard Overy, The Bombing War: Europe 1939-1945, Allen Lane, 26 September 2013).
556. "Secretary of State Mike Pompeo's Interview with Hadi Nili of BBC Persian", Washington DC, 7 November 2018; Brendan Cole, "Mike Pompeo Says Iran Must Listen To U.S. 'If They Want Their People To Eat'", Newsweek, 9 November 2018.
557. See the video, Your Silence Kills You, by the Islamic State, released in December 2016 and «The History of France's Enmity with Islâm», Dar al-Islam, n° 2, Rabi al-thani 1436, February 2015, p. 10.

increasingly being questioned, forcing Western states to legislate to make such questioning criminally punishable.

The classical principles of warfare apply universally, but they must be carefully adapted to the context. Particularly in asymmetric conflicts, the understanding of the underlying nature of the centres of gravity and critical factors must be analysed uncompromisingly and objectively, otherwise the results will be exactly the opposite of what was intended.

3.3.1.2. Respect for our values

In November 2015, Manuel Valls stated:

We must therefore fight this terrorism in the name of universal values. [558]

For once, he was right... just before announcing that France would give up applying human rights in its fight against terrorism[559] , thus abandoning its centre of gravity to the terrorists! This firm speech was - in fact - a failure: at no time did Manuel Valls understand that he was in an asymmetric context!

The centre of gravity of countries fighting terrorism is mostly intangible in nature and is an essential factor in their legitimacy to act. It can be simplified by saying that it is composed of our «values», such as the rule of law and respect for individuals and their rights and freedoms. For democracies, these values are *critical resources* of the centre of gravity. They underpin the legitimacy of our struggle against violence, especially abroad. This means that we must preserve them. Thus, in strategic terms, abandoning respect for human rights - as France did[560] and the United States did in Guantanamo and Abu Ghraib in 2004 - means abandoning one's centre of gravity to the enemy and losing the legitimacy of the struggle. It is a resignation or, in military terms, a betrayal.

The problem is that we tend to think that fighting terrorists allows us to get away from the law. There is a real problem here, which is never addressed by our politicians and which contributes to the development of terrorism. Since the early 2000s, under the influence of the United States, Western countries have tended to move away from international law to apply another system called *«rule-based international order»* (RBIO). Whereas international law is a norm that applies equally to all (in theory), RBIO is based on principles defined by

---

558. Answers of Mr. Manuel Valls, Prime Minister to questions in the National Assembly, Paris, 18 November 2015, https://il.ambafrance.org/Lutte-contre-le-terrorisme-Politique-internationale-Mesures-de-securite-Lutte.
559. Blandine Le Cain, «France plans to violate human rights with the state of emergency», lefigaro.fr, 27 November 2015.
560. Ibid.

276

one actor, in this case the United States. This is a way of subordinating our 'values' to other interests.

This is the case in the United States, where Donald Trump pardons a soldier who stabbed a child for no reason and poses for a photo with his 'trophy'[561] , which puts pressure on the International Criminal Court (ICC) by imposing sanctions on its prosecutors[562] , so that it does not investigate US and Israeli crimes in Afghanistan and Palestine[563].The same phenomenon can be observed in Israel, which has been repeatedly criticised by the UN for its failure to comply with international law and norms: soldiers simply kill for fun[564] or break the bones of captured Palestinian youth[565].These heavy-handed approaches flatter 'primitive' minds, but are a strategic weakness. They run counter to the 'hearts *and* minds' strategies that have made the British counter-terrorism effort in Malaysia so successful. As a result, neither the Americans nor the Israelis are respected adversaries: this is a *critical weakness in* their centre of gravity. This partly explains why they never manage to move beyond tactical success to strategic victory.

During the events in Gaza in May 2018, some journalists blamed the Palestinians (and Hamas in particular) for the massacres, accusing them of placing children in front of Israeli guns. Videos released by the UN show that this was not the case[566].However, even admitting this, there is no justification for shooting at unarmed children... or at medical personnel who came to treat them! The law of war is very clear on this subject: the means must be adapted and proportionate to the threat and - ultimately - it is up to the shooter to refrain from shooting (even if his orders are different!) It is, moreover, exactly according to the same principle that former SS non-commissioned officers and soldiers have been condemned: hiding behind the order given cannot be invoked when it comes to applying the law of war.

In the Israeli army, the only soldiers who deserve respect are those who have the courage to come together in the *Breaking the Silence* association in order to

---

561. Richard Luscombe, "Navy seal pardoned of war crimes by Trump 'freaking evil', colleagues say", The Irish Times, 28 December 2019.

562. «US Sanctions International Criminal Court Prosecutor, Human Rights Watch, 2 September 2020.

563. «Statement by the Prosecutor, Karim A. A. Khan QC, after requesting the judges, under Article 18(2), to rule on his application for authorisation to resume investigative work in the situation in Afghanistan', International Criminal Court, 27 September 2021.

564. Israeli occupation soldiers kill Palestinian kids for fun, "Israeli soldiers cheer after shooting a Palestinian protester in the village of Madama", B'Tselem/YouTube, 24 April 2018.

565. Amira Hass, "Broken Bones and Broken Hopes", Haaretz, 4 November 2005.

566. "Video screened at UN Human Rights Council meeting, February 28, 2019", Haaretz/YouTube, 28 February 2019.

bear witness to the abuses regularly carried out in Palestine[567] : they contribute not only to saving the Israeli army's lost honour, but also to removing the legitimacy of terrorist acts.

The policy of people like Donald Trump is to see the application of *international humanitarian law* (IHL) as a weakness. In fact, it is a strength in all cases, but especially in asymmetric conflicts, it is a way to show oneself stronger than the terrorists.

In fact, those countries that claim to fight terrorism through the use of torture, violation of privacy, indiscriminate bombing, and even extra-judicial killings, use exactly the same intellectual scheme as the terrorists: the end justifies the means and justifies forgetting our values to achieve it. While IHL - or *the law of war* - imposes restraint on belligerents when civilians are threatened, Westerners hide behind the imprecision of their weapons to justify 'collateral damage', which then becomes a justification for the terrorists:

> *Artillery, like terrorism, leads to the loss of non-combatant lives. A missile hitting a city, which is obviously not a precise weapon, is no different from a bomb in a city in a country that is at war with Muslims.*

> *...] it is clear that Muslims are allowed to target populations in countries that are at war with Muslims, with bombs, guns or other forms of attack that inevitably lead to the death of non-combatants.*[568]

The jihadists' very cold and technical reading of terrorism allows them great strategic coherence. It avoids moral questions, often insoluble, such as the differentiation between «*resistance fighter*», «*freedom fighter*» and «*terrorist*». When France supplies arms to a group affiliated with «Al-Qaeda» in Libya or Syria, is it participating in jihadist terrorism or not? Is bombing a civilian population in order to make them rebel against their leaders (as in Iraq and Syria) terrorism? Is torturing a terrorist compatible with the values we defend against terrorism or not? When the international coalition kills more civilians than the Islamic State in Afghanistan[569] does it respect the values it claims to defend?

We are often our own enemies.

---

567. Israeli Soldiers Breaking The Silence on the Occupation of Palestine, YouTube, 24 October 2012.
568. Inspire, n° 8, Autumn 2011, p. 42.
569. Midyear Update on the Protection of Civilians in Armed Conflict: 1 January to 30 June 2019, United Nations Assistance Mission in Afghanistan (UNAMA), 30 July 2019, p. 12; Amy Woodyatt & Arnaud Siad, "More civilians are being killed by Afghan and international forces than by the Taliban and other militants", CNN, 31 July 2019.

Westerners continue to understand warfare as it was in the Middle Ages and to see the centre of gravity of terrorist movements in their leaders, which is why they spend considerable energy tracking them down and eliminating them. But this is the result of a misunderstanding of jihadism itself and the concept of ARIG. This is why the elimination - ingloriously[570] - of Osama bin Laden has had no impact on jihadist terrorism[571].Similarly, the repeated eliminations of Palestinian leaders have not changed the influence of their movements, on the contrary...

In fact, the centre of gravity of Islamist movements is not individuals, but the very legitimacy of their struggle. To fight them, the solution does not lie in targeted eliminations, but in the suppression of the very cause of the fight. In the Palestinian case, Israel and the Palestinians have very different centres of gravity:

- For Israel, the objective is to establish its sovereignty over the entire territory between the Mediterranean and the Jordan River. Its centre of gravity lies in the legitimacy to occupy the whole of the land of Palestine. But this legitimacy is not given to it by international law (which only grants it a *part of* Palestine, according to UN Resolution 181). This is why politicians prefer to invoke the Bible. However, scientific research in the fields of history[572] , archaeology[573] and genetics[574] tends to weaken this approach little by little. The critical factors that Israel has to take into consideration are: a *critical resource, the* political and financial support of the United States; a *critical vulnerability*, the non-compliance with international law, which tends to discredit it within the Jewish community, especially in the United States[575] ; and a *critical function*, the communication in order to maintain the American and Diaspora's support

- The centre of gravity for the Palestinians is the will of the younger generation to resist, without which their rights under Resolution 181 will be slowly «phagocytised» by Israel and the US. Their *critical resource* is respect for international law, which gives legitimacy to their resistance. Their *critical function* is to maintain the memory of the mass deportations and massacres of civilians (*Al-Nakba*) carried out by Jewish militias from 1947 onwards, and then the

---

570. Sandip Roy, "Osama Bin Laden was a Prisoner in Pakistan: 5 Shocking Facts Revealed from Hersh's Expose," May 12, 2015, http://newamericamedia.org/2015/05/osama-bin-laden-was-a-prisoner-in-pakistan-5-shocking-facts-revealed-from-hershs-expose.php.

571. Nicole Gaouette, "5 years ago the U.S. killed Osama bin Laden. Did it matter?», CNN, 2 May 2016.

572. See, Shlomo Sand, Comment la terre d'Israël fut inventée, Flammarion, coll. Champs histoire, 2012.

573. See Israel Finkelstein and Neil Asher Silberman, La Bible dévoilée - Les nouvelles révélations de l'archéologie, Gallimard, coll. Folio, Paris, 2002.

574. See Kate Yandell, "Genetic Roots of the Ashkenazi Jews", The Scientist, 8 October 2013.

575. Jonathan Cook, "Can young Jews in US turn tide against Israel?", The National, 26 June 2017.

occupation of the land from 1967 onwards, which are the primary source of legitimacy for their resistance. Their *critical vulnerability* is the risk of falling into aggressive terrorism, which would alienate them from the growing sympathy that the Palestinian cause has in the world.

The multiplication of settlements in the occupied territories, contrary to international law[576] , fuels the Palestinians' will to resist. Thus, contrary to appearances, the centre of gravity of the Israelis tends to weaken, while that of the Palestinians tends to strengthen over time. A report published in 2017 by the *Brand Israel Group*, which monitors Israel's image in the world, shows that between 2010 and 2016, support for Israel among young American Jews dropped by 27%[577] , with a sense of growing divergence between the values of the two countries[578] , and ever greater sympathy for the Palestinian cause.

Number of Israeli settlers in the West Bank (1976-2017)

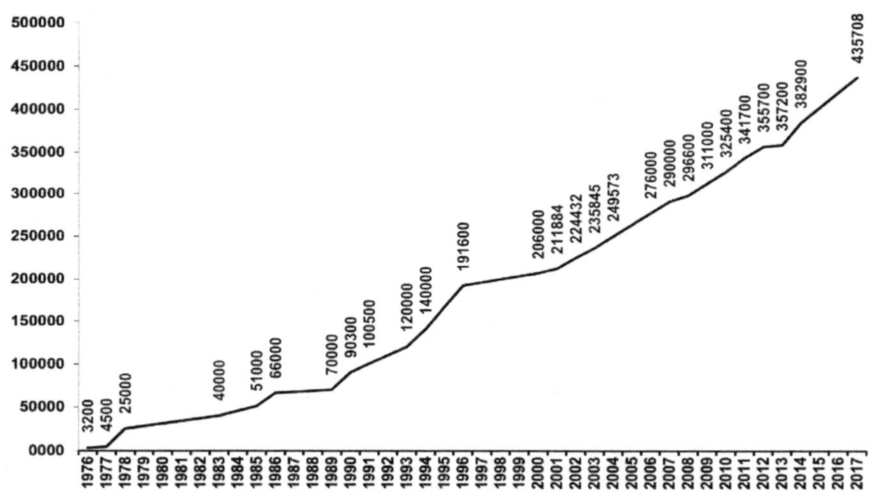

Figure 9. The number of settlers in the occupied territories is constantly increasing, despite the repeated commitments of the Israeli governments to freeze these settlements since the Camp David agreements (1976). The resistance of the Palestinians is thus more about identity than religion, even

---

576. These are essentially the Hague Convention on the Laws and Customs of War on Land of 1907 and the IVe Geneva Convention relative to Civilian Persons in Time of War of 1949, which regulate the behaviour of occupying powers in «occupied territories». The problem is that Israel - in opposition to the interpretations of the international community - does not recognise the status of «occupied territories» to the Gaza Strip and the West Bank, as these lands have never been claimed by Jordan and Egypt, and therefore Israel would not have taken these lands from «contracting parties». The cause of this situation is the very notion of a border in traditional Arab culture, which recognises entities of populations, but not delimited territory.

577. Jonathan Cook, "Can young Jews in US turn tide against Israel?", The National, 26 June 2017.

578. Amanda Borschel-Dan, "'Devastating' survey shows huge loss of Israel support among Jewish college students", The Time of Israel, 21 June 2017.

if the latter supports the former. A reduction of these settlements - which are contrary to international law - could be an important factor in a real counter-terrorist strategy. (Figures not including Jerusalem) [Sources: B'Tselem, Israeli Ministry of Internal Affairs and Israeli Central Bureau of Statistics].

Thus, Israeli actions feed the Palestinian centre of gravity: in addition to the legal aspects of the occupation, its policy of fait accompli and its brutality maintain the Palestinians' will to fight. As we saw during the Palestinian «return marches» in Gaza, and during the events of May 2021, Israeli violence generates a growing disaffection for Israel among the Western population. In France and the United States, it has been necessary to adopt an increasingly stringent legal framework to prevent criticism of the State of Israel and to protect a critical resource in its centre of gravity.

The paradox is that the Israelis - who are mainly from Europe - have neither the mentality nor the culture of the Middle East, where they claim to come from: their reactions are tactical or - at best - operative, while the Palestinians, on the other hand, have a more strategic thinking and culture.

In this asymmetric context, the Israeli government's policy feeds the Palestinian strategy. This is the main flaw in the Western approach: we try to deprive terrorism of its legitimacy by criticising its brutality, but we also feed it by maintaining its raison d'être, a foreign occupation.

3.3.2. The strategic concept

It is a question of defining what you want to do. This seems trivial, but it is the main weakness of Westerners. In France, after the 2015-2016 attacks, the lack of reflection on the real causes of the attacks and their objectives led to measures being taken to prevent the execution, but not the conception of the attacks.

The failure of NATO's *International Security Assistance Force* (ISAF) and the US Operation ENDURING FREEDOM in Afghanistan is a clear illustration of the West's inability to deal with terrorism strategically. It stems from a lack of clear concepts and confusion of terms. At the beginning of the ISAF engagement, each country intervened within the framework of a «strategic vision» of the Alliance, but also according to national doctrines that were not coherent. Thus, not only was NATO materially and intellectually unprepared for this type of conflict, but each member state had a different reading of how to carry out the mission.

In fact, from the beginning, the NATO high command did not really understand the nature of the conflict it was fighting. For example, ISAF was given a 'peacekeeping' mission[579] , when there was no peace to keep. In the absence of a prior peace agreement, ISAF could at best impose peace, which it failed to do...

---

579. «NATO is ready for its mission in Afghanistan», NATO Update, 6 August 2003 (updated 8 August 2003), www.nato.int/docu/update/2003/08-august/f0806a.htm.

Secondly, from the outset there was confusion between *counter-insurgency* (COIN) and counter-terrorism. COIN is a dynamic issue, which seeks to combat a process that is not only military, but also social, societal and political. The fight against terrorism requires a different range of measures, which may or may not fit into a COIN framework. For example, at the beginning of the engagement in Afghanistan, countries such as Germany, the Czech Republic or Norway sent counter-terrorism units. But these units were designed for intense, short-term engagements against specific objectives (hostage rescue, neutralisation of terrorists, etc.), and were totally unsuited to a conflict that would last... 20 years! The staffs had understood nothing of the nature of this new battlefield and the units had to be repatriated after only a few weeks.

Comparing insurgency and terrorism

	Insurgency/Resistance	Terrorism
Nature	Process	Method
Centre of gravity	Population-centred	Focused on activists
Strategy element	Aims at policy objectives	Facilitates the achievement of objectives
Guiding principle	Guided by a perceived need	Part of a strategy
Time horizon	Medium to long term	Short to medium term
Objective	Taking powerResistance	Imposing a change Reinforcing a status quo Reinforcing political gains

Table 16 - Differences between insurgency and terrorism relevant to the development of action strategies. The main reason for Western failure in Afghanistan, the Middle East and North Africa is their inability to conceptualise their actions.

3.3.2.1. Possible strategies

Starting from Mao Zedong's famous expression that the guerrilla must «*be in the civilian population like a fish in water*", several simple lines of strategy can be outlined. These are most applicable in counter-insurgency situations, but some of them can be used in counter-terrorism situations:

- *Catch the fish*. This is the most obvious strategy, which forms the backbone of current Western action against terrorism. However, it requires a remarkable knowledge of the 'fish' and its behaviour. It is only really effective with «simple» forms of terrorism, when the terrorist group does not have a strong popular base. This is the case with common law or marginal terrorism: everything happens at the police and tactical level, and the strategic dimension of the action is weak or non-existent. This is the case of the *Symbionese Liberation Army (SLA)* in California, *Action directe* in France, the *Cellules communistes combattantes* in Belgium and the *Rote Armee Fraktion* in Germany.

- Remove the water. This involves isolating the terrorists from the population in which they are embedded. This is a particularly effective strategy in a COIN situation, where the terrorist movement depends on popular support which it obtains by force. There are two basic ways to achieve this result. The first is to try to physically separate the terrorists from the population. This is what the French tried in Algeria by isolating villages or grouping rural populations in more controllable areas; it is also the British strategy of «New Villages» in Malaysia and the American concept of *Provincial Reconstruction Teams* (PRTs) in Afghanistan. We will come back to this later. The second is to 'charm' the civilian population so that they no longer see any point in supporting the guerrillas/terrorists. These are the *'hearts & minds'* operations, which aim to win the hearts of the population. In a situation of terrorism in the West, the problem is more complex: with *Jihad by Individual Terrorism* (JIT), the terrorists are embedded in society and difficult to identify. The risk here is that security action accentuates a communitarianism that facilitates the recruitment of new activists. The exaltation of Western values, secularism or the assertion of proximity to another religious community will only stimulate the desire for «jihad» (resistance) and encourage the development of violence.

- Remove the water and the fish. This is essentially the strategy pursued by Israel to recover Palestinian land and eliminate Palestinian resistance, seeking to push the entire Palestinian population out of the occupied territories. This strategy has been applied since 1948 with the mass deportations of populations, and has been prolonged by a slow nibbling of the occupied territories by settlements and the security fence, the construction of which was initiated in 2002.

- Add another fish. The aim is to create competition between rival groups by creating a kind of «counter-fire». This was the strategy adopted by Israel to fight Fatah in the late 1980s[580]. Very early on, the Israeli government tried to divide the Palestinian movement with the help of Islamists[581]. As early as 1979, Brigadier General Yitzhak Segev, military governor of Gaza, had regular contacts with Sheikh Ahmed Yassin, then leader of the *Mujama al-Islamiya*, precursor of Hamas, and financed the construction of mosques in Gaza in order to favour the emergence of what would become Hamas[582]. This policy continues today, as Benjamin Netanyahu himself confirmed at a Likud faction meeting in March 2019, prompting former Defence Minister Avigdor Liberman to say that Israel is *'funding terrorism against* itself'[583]. This is also what the US, Britain, France

580. Andrew Higgins, "How Israel Helped to Spawn Hamas", The Wall Street Journal, 24 January 2009.
581. Richard Sale, "Hamas history tied to Israel", UPI, 18 June 2002.
582. Robert Dreyfuss, Devil's Game - How the United States Helped Unleash Fundamentalist Islam, New York, 2005, ISBN: 0-8050-8137-2, p. 169.
583. Lahav Harkov, "Netanyahu: Money to Hamas part of strategy to keep Palestinians divided",

(FUKUS) and Israel have done in Syria, deliberately allowing the EI to grow, in the hope that it would become such a threat to the Syrian government that it would be forced to negotiate, as confirmed by John Kerry, the US Secretary of State:

> *The reason why Russia got involved was because the EI was getting stronger. DAECH was threatening to reach Damascus, and that's why Russia intervened. Because they didn't want a DAECH government and they were supporting Assad.*

> *And we knew it [DAECH] was growing. We were watching. We saw that Daech was becoming more and more powerful and we thought that Assad was threatened. But we thought that we could probably manage, that Assad would negotiate afterwards. Instead of negotiating, he asked Putin for help.[584]*

As we can see, this is an extremely delicate strategy to engage and requires a perfect political and cultural knowledge of the opposition, which neither the FUKUS nor Israel have.

- *Add a predator.* This is basically the strategy that the United States employed in Southeast Asia (Laos and Cambodia), Latin America and Afghanistan, by encouraging lucrative agricultural production (in this case the cultivation of poppies and coca). The aim was to encourage peasants to resist the advance of communism, which was then based in the countryside, in accordance with the ideas of Mao and Che Guevara. This strategy, innovated by the French in Indochina («Operation X»), worked remarkably well... But, uncontrolled, this drug market quickly became a problem for the West itself. For this strategy to work and have lasting effects, the two 'fish' must have distinctly opposing interests. This is why General Petraeus' 'Awakening' strategy in Iraq, and later in Afghanistan, yielded no tangible results other than the arming of militias that - in the absence of political follow-up - gradually coalesced into... the Islamic State[585] ! A variant of this strategy is the creation of 'anti-guerrilla guerrillas', such as the *Vandenberghe Commando* (or *Commando No. 24*) in Indochina, or the engagement of 'anti-terrorist terrorist' groups, such as the Anti-Terrorist Liberation Group (GAL) in Spain during the 1980s. Implemented in Central America by the CIA in the 1970s and 1980s, this strategy produced «death squads» that did not provide a long-term solution to the

---

Jerusalem Post, 12 March 2019.

584. John Kerry, recording of a 22 September 2016 meeting published by Wikileaks, "Leaked audio of John Kerry's meeting with Syrian revolutionaries"/UN (improved audio), YouTube, 4 October 2016.

585. Ehab Zahriyeh, "How ISIL became a major force with only a few thousand fighters", Al Jazeerah, 19 June 2014.

conflict. To be effective, such a strategy needs very strong political backing, which intelligence services are generally unable to provide.

- *Feed the fish enough so that they lose their aggression.* This strategy is based on treating the causes of terrorism. In other words, it is about making its demands meaningless, so that it loses the desire - and the legitimacy - to fight. It is a delicate tool to use, requiring an excellent knowledge of the adversary and its motives, because it must not be thought that the use of violence has been successful. It must necessarily be integrated into a negotiation process - the mere existence of which is sometimes enough to stop the violence - in order to determine the area of convergence between demands and requirements, to make the terrorist movement responsible for political choices. The aim is to avoid an uncontrolled spiral of political demands and claims. This is how the Colombian M-19 ended its involvement in violence. For jihadist terrorism, this strategy consists of removing anything that might justify its action. This is primarily, but not exclusively, a question of foreign intervention. In France, before committing itself to the Middle East in September 2014, the government took absolutely no account of public opinion of Muslim origin. Thus, the cases of the Islamic veil, the burkini, and Dieudonné were conducted too noisily and inopportunely, contributing very largely to accentuating the polarisation of the population, pushing moderates to have sympathy for the cause of the Islamists (even if they are opposed to terrorist violence).

The choice of strategy depends on what you are trying to achieve, which derives from two things: the opponent's centre of gravity and the political and military (or security) end state you are seeking.

3.3.2.2. Defining the objective and success criteria

Westerners are often satisfied with tactical successes and lose sight of the strategic objective. This was the case in Algeria and Vietnam, where tactical - even operational - successes were unanimously recognised, but, disconnected from a real strategy, they were not enough to bring victory. Today, the same causes produce the same effects. This is even more dramatic in an asymmetric context, where what seems to be a success generates a failure.

In Afghanistan, at the beginning of the US intervention, consensual objectives such as 'nation-building' or 'women's rights' were mentioned. But no one asked whether war was the best way to achieve this... Moreover, it was not even clear what kind of war to fight: was it counter-terrorism or counter-insurgency? The British wanted to fight opium cultivation, but Afghanistan never produced more drugs than under the Western presence... In short, not knowing which direction to go, we went nowhere.

The Western military establishment seems unable to describe what should constitute a strategic 'victory' or 'success'. For *'fighting the Islamic State'* is not an objective, it is a modality. Success is measured by the clear willingness of the 'loser' to accept defeat and build peace. Thus, even the destruction of the EI does not mean the end of the problem, because since 2014, fighters have been migrating to other less exposed Islamist movements, even supported by the West itself, thus contributing to the 'radicalisation' of more moderate groups[586].

Without understanding what motivates the adversary and what would constitute a strategic victory, Western military planners are reduced to interpreting strategic victory as a sum of tactical successes. NATO countries were unable to defeat the Taliban or 'Al Qaeda' in Afghanistan and Iraq: after short-lived tactical successes, these organisations thought to be subjugated have reappeared with very similar objectives under different names, such as the Islamic State. Without a strategy, the West is simply (re)generating its own enemies.

The fight against terrorism is marked by a constant confusion between tactics and strategy, which could be summed up in the idea that eliminating terrorists leads to the eradication of terrorism. This reading dominates Operation BARKHANE in the Sahel: its success is measured by the number of jihadists killed, with no long-term perspective and no vision of the «end state» sought. The logical consequence is that the death toll is rising and the situation is deteriorating[587].If we don't know where we want to go and if we don't look at where we are going, we get nowhere!

3.3.2.3. *Preventive and pre-emptive action*

In English, the strategic vocabulary distinguishes between the terms «*prevention*» and «*preemption*»: the former expresses the measures taken so that an event is not decided, while the latter designates those that disrupt its execution. In French, this distinction does not exist and the word «*preemption*» is not really used in security matters. The term «*prevention*» is preferred to designate obstacles to both the conception and execution of the action, which is too broad to develop a strategy. However, even in English, the term prevention tends to be preferred as it is more rewarding. For the practitioner, however, while «preventing» an attack is generally understood as an act of prevention, it involves very different means if it results from an action on the determination of terrorists or simply on the execution of a terrorist act.

We will therefore adopt the Anglo-Saxon terminology for the purposes of this book, for which linguists will excuse us.

---

586. Jason Burke, "Al-Qaida moves in to recruit from Islamic State and its affiliates", The Guardian, 19 January 2018.

587. Laurent Larcher & Corinne Laurent, 'Barkhane, le temps de la remise en cause', La Croix, 13 January 2021; Nicolas Normand, 'Le Sahel en 2021: pour empêcher la détérioration de se poursuivre', Le Point, 29 January 2021.

In the fight against terrorism, these linguistic subtleties have very concrete implications. This distinction should allow for a better division of roles between the services acting at the strategic level (prevention) and the security and police services acting at the operational level (pre-emption). The former act on the determination of radical groups and contribute to strategies aimed at preventing them from taking violent action, while the latter will try to interfere in the application of violence after the terrorist decision.

3.3.2.4. Focusing on the objective

The development of a strategy must be based on a holistic view of the problem that seeks, through a combination of offensive and defensive, civilian and military means, to «fight» the entire process that transforms an individual from a citizen to a terrorist. The understanding of this process must be developed without prejudice. In France, there is an emotional tendency among politicians to overestimate the role of religion in the terrorist phenomenon, which leads to poor prioritisation of actions, explains the failure of measures against radicalisation and increases the vulnerability of the nation[588].

It is also important to mention that a comprehensive strategy aims to hit the opponent's centre of gravity, but must not forget to preserve its own centre of gravity. Thus, for example, it will be necessary to ensure that popular support for the terrorist movement (a critical resource) does not become a critical weakness in our own countries[589].A mistake that was made by the Valls/Hollande government, which coldly entrenched itself behind republican principles, but made no effort to win the hearts of the immigrant population: the lack of a clear explanation for intervening in the Middle East, a loud assertion of support for Israel, the over-mediatisation of foreign policy actors of questionable legitimacy[590] , an out-of-proportion campaign against the comedian Dieudonné with a very personal involvement of Prime Minister Valls, all in a very degraded domestic political climate, combined to create a rift in the centre of gravity in France. The opinion of a significant part of the immigrant population became a critical vulnerability that the EI was able to exploit perfectly.

As we will see in more detail below, the scope of the strategy must be articulated along two complementary lines:

- *Counter-terrorism*, which is the set of measures designed to combat terrorism *before the* terrorist decision is taken. It is the preventive component of the action and involves a thorough knowledge of how terrorists think. It is essentially the

---

588. See «Sébastien Pietrasanta: «Fighting against radicalisation without talking about religion is half the battle», Europe 1, 24 February 2018.
589. Shiv Malik, "Support for Isis stronger in Arabic social media in Europe than in Syria", The Guardian, 28 November 2014.
590. NOA: like Bernard-Henri Lévy.

result of strategic intelligence and is mainly implemented through a combination of political and communication measures. It requires a small but highly specialised staff and close international cooperation.

- *Counter-terrorism*, which consists of all the means of fighting *after the* terrorist decision (in other words: after the terrorists have decided to act). It combines the pre-emptive and reactive components of action, and is often the result of a failed or lacking counter-terrorism strategy. It usually involves heavier structures, a large surveillance system requiring expensive technical means and a large personnel presence. It also requires a specialised response capability, usually found in police or paramilitary forces.

One of the few countries that managed to control an asymmetric situation without a spillover of violence was Venezuela in the early 1960s. President Romulo Betancourt was the first democratically elected president of Venezuela to complete his term and effectively combat terrorism in his country. In 1961-1964, the *Armed Forces of National Liberation (FALN)* manifested itself through a brutal insurgency campaign, which culminated in 1962-1963 in a series of bloody attacks in Caracas. Inspired by Carlos Marighella's strategy, the FALN's action, initially directed at the police forces (notably through a «kill a policeman a day» campaign), mutated in September 1963 into a campaign of indiscriminate actions against the population. President Betancourt's strategy centred on a combination of the minimal use of force and the exploitation of the December 1963 elections to propose a political alternative. By 1964, the influence and support of the FALN had diminished considerably and the movement dissolved.

In Europe, Italy was probably the most effective in combating the terrorism of the 1970s and 1980s, given the complexity of the problem. But this was not without its legal, moral and even ethical shortcomings. The *Red Brigades* and all the small groups that emerged from or gravitated around them enjoyed a high level of prestige in intellectual, student and certain working-class circles animated by a widespread revolutionary romanticism. This important anchoring limited the possibilities of 'frontal' action by the state. Collaboration with mafia networks and extreme right-wing terrorism was the price of an effective eradication of left-wing terrorism.

Germany, which is often cited as an example of its effectiveness in the fight against the *Rote Armee Fraktion (RAF)*, in fact had an adversary of a fundamentally symmetrical nature, with a weak popular base and behaving like a criminal group with a marginal political audience. It was therefore possible to apply classic methods, similar to those used against organised crime. The same problem can be found in the fight against *Action directe (AD)* in France at the same time: simple terrorism, with a very weak popular base and symmetrical in essence.

In an asymmetric context, an effective counter-terrorism strategy must provide the adversary with exit routes: he must have the opportunity to place his action in a symmetrical perspective or to refocus his struggle within a legal framework.

The objective is neither to satisfy the terrorist movement nor to endorse its action, but to prevent it from consolidating its popular roots and increasing its legitimacy, while at the same time having an exit strategy for both parties.

3.3.2.5. *Define your opponent*

It is also important to have a functional approach to the designation of armed groups, so that specific strategies can be applied to them. In Afghanistan, the Americans were careful not to define the Taliban as terrorists, in order to keep the door open for possible negotiation.

3.3.2.6 *Identification of the mechanisms of asymmetry*

In order to design an effective strategy, it is necessary to understand the mechanics that fuel its asymmetry. For example, for some Marxist movements, demands are merely a front for a process that can only succeed through violence. In such a situation, democratic concessions and responses become an obstacle to revolution and indirectly fuel the cycle of violence. This is the case of the Basque *ETA* or the Peruvian *Shining Path* (in its first period).

Islamist terrorism of the 'Al Qaeda' type, based on open networks, is very difficult to combat tactically, as new actors are constantly and randomly entering the scene. On the other hand, it would be relatively easy to combat on a strategic level. The 11 March 2004 attack in Madrid would never have happened without the US intervention in Iraq, and the 11 September 2001 attacks would not have happened without the clumsy US strikes of August 1998.

After the 2015 attacks in France, as after '9/11', the authorities tried to decontextualise terrorism in order to present it as irrational. Not only is this untrue, but the government has trapped itself by making it impossible to devise a coherent strategy. This is why the fight against terrorism in France is not played out at the strategic level, but exclusively in a reactive and tactical manner. This being said, France is far from being the only one and, almost everywhere in the West, there is a cruel absence of strategy and a concentration on tactical solutions. We have thus settled into a «race to the bottom» in which we leave the initiative to the terrorists.

3.3.2.7. *Maintaining a holistic dimension*

The defeat of the West in Afghanistan and their surprise at the return of the Taliban to Kabul is a perfect illustration of their complete lack of a comprehensive strategy. A holistic counter-terrorism strategy must include a *nation-building* component *from the outset*.

The problem with Westerners, whether in NATO or in a national context, is that they treat terrorism as a military problem and see peace as the next phase. At the end of the war - as in 1918 - you sign a treaty and you have **peace**!

This is a simplistic view, but one that explains successive Western failures in counter-insurgency. In fact, peace-building is a process that must begin with and accompany counter-terrorism actions. The refusal to imagine that one can have peace with one's adversary (whatever methods he uses) comes from the Israeli doctrine that is applied in the West after having permeated American military thought.

Counter-terrorism according to the terrorist process

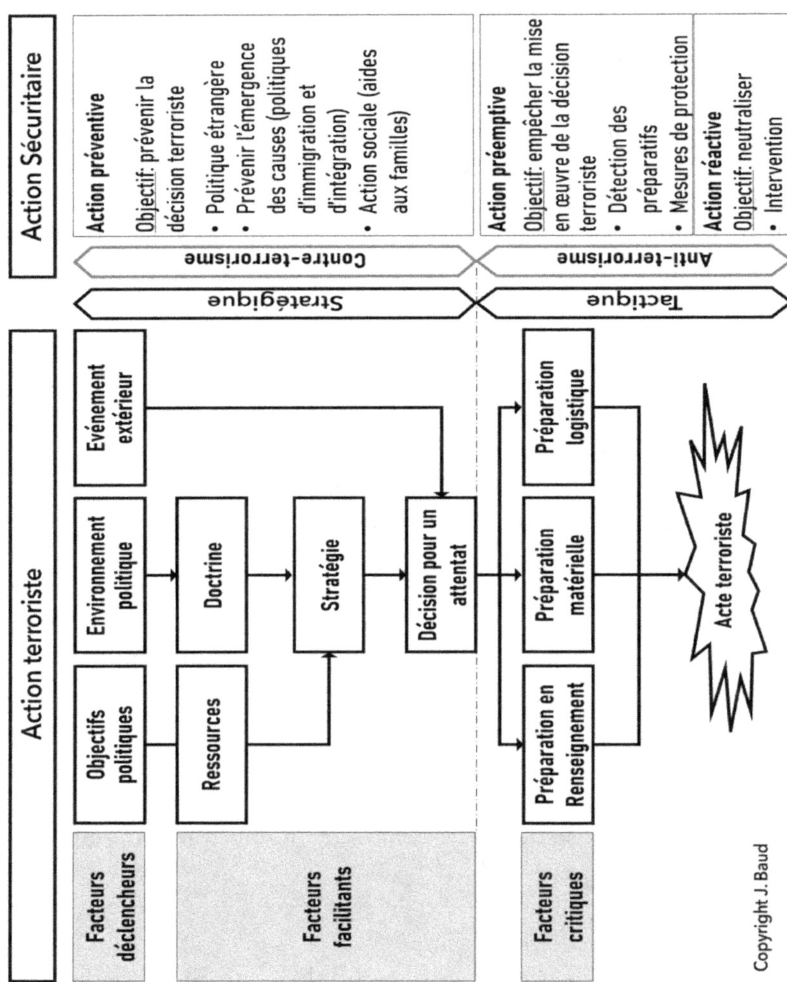

Figure 10. The fight against terrorism needs to be more clearly articulated between the notions of counter-terrorism and anti-terrorism, which are too often confused today. As an example, if we place the «National Plan» produced in February 2018 by the government of Édouard Philippe against this graph, we see that none of the proposed measures affect terrorist decision-making processes (prevention).

Terrorism is a phenomenon that must be fought on a broad front in terms of prevention (counter-terrorism) and in a very specific way in terms of tactical response (anti-terrorism).

3.3.3. Operations

3.3.3.1. Extra-judicial executions

Extra-judicial killings are the elimination of terrorists, outside of a judicial process, using killers or «ad hoc» strikes such as air strikes. Legally questionable, they are often not very effective strategically. Three countries use them regularly: the United States, Israel and France. Presented as a preventive measure, they are generally carried out in a punitive manner like Sicilian vendettas, without any real assessment of their strategic consequences and, in practice, they fuel a growing process of violence and are a source of legitimacy for terrorism. In fact, they reflect the lack of a real counter-terrorism strategy in these countries.

The archetype of this mode of action is Operation ANGER OF GOD (*Mivtza Zaʿam Haʿel*), also known as Operation BAYONET, carried out by the Mossad to punish the perpetrators of the attack against the Israeli Olympic team in Munich in 1972 (Operation BERIM & IKRIT). In one year, almost the entire Palestinian commando was eliminated: Wae Zwaiter (Rome, 16 October 1972), Mahmoud Hamchari (Paris, 9 January 1973), Abd El-Hir (Nicosia, 24 January 1973), Basil Al-Kubaissi (Paris, 6 April 1973), Ziad Muchassi (Athens, 12 April 1973), Mohammed Boudia (Paris, 28 June 1973), Kamal Nasser, Mahmoud Najjer and Kamal Adouan (Beirut, 9 April 1973). Its leader, Ali Hassan Salameh, was killed in Beirut on 22 January 1979 and was followed by his second in command, Khalil al-Wazir (alias Abou Djihad), on 16 April 1988 in Tunis. In the end, only one member of the terrorist group, Jamal al-Gashei, seems to have escaped the «Wrath of God»[591] , and an innocent man was killed by mistake in Lillehammer (Norway).

Other similar eliminations have been carried out, the most publicised of which was that of Mahmoud Al-Mabhouh, one of the co-founders of the *Izz ad-Din al-Qassam Brigades* - the armed wing of Palestinian Hamas - in a hotel in Dubai on 19 January 2010[592].

The Americans are not to be outdone, but tend to limit themselves to drone actions in war zones. Some spectacular actions, such as the elimination of Osama bin Laden (2 May 2011) and Abu Bakr al-Baghdadi (26 October 2019), are half-hearted successes. On the one hand, they were carried out without glory: OBL was then under house arrest[593] and Baghdadi was in the Idlib pocket, where the

---

591. Simon Reeve, One Day in September, Arcade Publishing, London, 1998.

592. See details of the operation on Wikipedia: https://en.wikipedia.org/wiki/Assassination_of_Mahmoud_Al-Mabhouh.

593. Sandip Roy, "Osama Bin Laden was a Prisoner in Pakistan: 5 Shocking Facts Revealed from

West is training and supporting Islamist groups against the Syrian government[594] and, on the other hand, they had no impact on terrorism[595].In fact, carried out without strategic thinking, they mainly allowed the Americans to strut their stuff at home.

However, a distinction must be made between assassinations carried out in foreign countries by clandestine units and eliminations carried out in an area where an occupation force is operating.

The eliminations in the occupied Palestinian territories are similar to those carried out in areas of resistance to foreign intervention (Iraq, Afghanistan, Syria, Yemen, Mali, etc.). In addition to drones and other aerial means, the Israeli army has special units - called *Mista'aravim* - which operate clandestinely (in Arab clothes - hence their name), whose main missions are reconnaissance and intelligence gathering, but which can occasionally carry out «direct actions», although the latter are obviously not favoured for security reasons. It is indeed «safer» to «mark» the target with lasers or positioning satellites, and then to use more sophisticated means, such as drones or guided missiles.

ᵉWith some 2,300 known operations, Israel rivals the United States as the country that regularly assassinates opponents and terrorists[596] , with the perverse effect of making the Jewish community - until now well integrated - an object of distrust and perceived as a «column» in many countries of the Near and Middle East. The implementation of an «elimination» in a foreign country is a complex operation, which relies on a network of information gathering using local operators («*sayanim*»), most often recruited within the Jewish diaspora.

Practised as clandestine operations, extra-judicial killings pose a significant political risk if they fail. In 1997, the Mossad's attempt to poison Khalef Mashal, the political leader of Hamas in Jordan, was unsuccessful: the two Israeli agents carrying Canadian passports were arrested; then Israel had to provide an antidote and release Sheikh Ahmed Yassin in exchange for the release of his agents. The result was a loss of Israeli credibility with the international community and distrust from Jordan - with whom Israel has a peace treaty.

Hersh's Expose," May 12, 2015, http://newamericamedia.org/2015/05/osama-bin-laden-was-a-prisoner-in-pakistan-5-shocking-facts-revealed-from-hershs-expose.php.

594. David L. Phillips, "Turkey protected Abu Bakr al-Baghdadi", The Jerusalem Post, 5 November 2019.

595. Nicole Gaouette, "5 years ago the U.S. killed Osama bin Laden. Did it matter?", CNN, 2 May 2016; Ryan Pickrell, "Killing ISIS leader Abu Bakr al-Baghdadi hasn't hurt the terror group's operations, Pentagon warns", Business Insider, 4 February 2020.

596. Ronen Bergman, Rise and Kill First: The Secret History of Israel's Targeted Assassinations, Random House, 30 January 2018; Charles Glass, "'Rise and Kill First' Explores the Corrupting Effects of Israel's Assassination Program", The Intercept, 11 March 2018.

The main problem with extra-judicial killings is that they tend to legitimise illegal violence and terrorism, as evidenced by the *Arabian Peninsula Jihad Base (APJB) Inspire* magazine:

> *[The assassination of leaders of the unbelievers, both civilian and military, is one of the most important arts of terrorism and one of the most advantageous and deterrent types of operations. These are methods also used by the enemies of Allah. The CIA has the authorisation of the US government to assassinate presidents, if it is in the national interest of the US, and they have used it more than once. In the CIA, there is a special department for that! Therefore, I don't know why we are prevented from doing it?* [597]

It has been observed that the announcement of US and then French airstrikes against the EI from August 2014 led to a surge in foreign volunteers in Syria. According to a UN Security Council report published in May 2015, the number of foreign volunteer fighters in these countries increased by 71% between summer 2014 and March 2015[598].Once again, the West is the architect of its own problems.

Human bombs versus extrajudicial killings (1996-2003)		
Targeted elimination (Date) (Target) (Affiliation)	Response (Date) (Victims)	Comment
06.01.1996 Yahya AyyashHamas	25.02.1996 1 death 25.02.1996 27 deaths 03.03.1996 20 deaths 04.03.1996 13 deaths	The elimination of the 'engineer' was the source of the largest wave of human bombs.
14.01.2002 Raed al-Karmi Fatah	27.01.2002 1 death 16.02.2002 2 deaths 02.03.20021 1 death	The Israeli action led the Al-Aqsa Brigades to engage human bombs.

597. Abu Musab al-Suri, "The Jihadi Experiences: Individual Terrorism Jihad and the Global Islamic Resistance Units", Inspire, n° 5, Spring 2011, p. 32.
598. Letter dated 19 May 2015 from the Chair of the Security Council Committee pursuant to re-solutions 1267 (1999) and 1989 (2011) concerning Al-Qaida and associated individuals and entities addressed to the President of the Security Council, S/2015/358, UN, New York, 19 May 2015.

08.08.2003 Fayez al-Sadr Izz al-Din al Qassam	12.08.2003 2 deaths	
15.08.2003 Mohammed Sidr Al-Quds Brigades	19.08.20032 1 death	Riposte claimed by the Al-Quds Brigades and by Hamas.
21.06.2003 Abdallah 'Awashmeh Hamas		

Table 17 - The «human bomb» technique is not a «tradition» of Palestinian movements. It was used between 1994 and 2005-2006, in response to Israeli extra-judicial executions.

In an asymmetric Islamist context, the effectiveness of extra-judicial killings is highly questionable, and often the 'cure' is worse than the 'harm'. Without even considering the legal and moral issues here, the killing of leaders does not deter and almost never leads to the end of terrorist action, but tends to stimulate it. Elimination does not necessarily weaken the terrorist group, but it does cause its hierarchy to renew itself more quickly and to apply new methods and policies of action. This is what happened with the Islamic State, which might never have emerged in its current form if Abu Musab al-Zarqawi had not been eliminated by the Americans.

While the perpetrator was in training with the British services, and the *Irish Republican Army* (IRA) hierarchy was known in great detail (including addresses, family, friends and acquaintances, movements, etc.), eliminating a leader was out of the question, as the organisation was then totally predictable. Eliminating a leader or hierarchy creates uncertainty that works in the terrorist group's favour.

To measure the impact of a targeted elimination, one must know the targeted terrorist groups extremely well, which is rarely the case. Paradoxically, while Israeli operations have all been models of tactical mastery, they have generally been strategic failures due to a chronic analytical deficiency:

- On 16 April 1988, the assassination of Khalil al-Wazir (alias Abu Jihad) - Yasser Arafat's right-hand man and considered to be the operational leader of the first Intifada - was intended to put an end to the Palestinian uprising. Not only did this not happen, but it deprived Arafat of a wise advisor.

- On 16 February 1992, the elimination of Sheikh Abbas Moussaoui allowed the accession of Hassan Nasrallah, more radical, to the head of Hezbollah.

- The elimination of Fathi Shikaki, the leader of Islamic Jihad, on 26 October 1995, was based on the assumption that his likely successor, Abdallah Ramadan Sallah, would not have the qualities required to lead the organisation, and would therefore have been a less ferocious opponent. In fact, history has shown that this assessment was wrong: the number and effectiveness of Islamic Jihad attacks increased after his death.

- On 6 January 1996, the elimination of Yahya Ayyash (alias «the engineer»), an explosive device specialist, while he was observing a truce with Israel, discredited Yasser Arafat and discouraged Hamas moderates who expected results in a negotiation process.

- On 27 August 2001, in response to an attack[599] that killed three Israeli soldiers, Israel eliminated Abu Ali Mustafa, Secretary General of the Popular Front for the Liberation of Palestine (PFLP). This action provoked the assassination of the Minister of Tourism, Rehavam Ze'evi, on 10 October 2001, and the launch of a campaign of suicide attacks, which the PFLP had never carried out before. In the end, the Israeli action indirectly caused two Israeli deaths and 48 injuries[600].

- On 22 March 2004, the assassination of Sheikh Ahmed Yassin[601] , spiritual and historical leader of Hamas, did not weaken the movement. On the contrary. It pushed Abd el-Rantissi, more virulent than his predecessor, to its head, who will have to be eliminated in his turn on 17 April. On 31 August 2004, a double suicide attack in Beersheva, killing 16 people, was claimed in the name of Hamas, to avenge the death of Sheikh Yassin and Abd el-Rantissi[602] .

- On 23 July 2002, the elimination of Salah Shehada with a 1,000 kg bomb dropped by an F-16 aircraft killed 14 people (including several children) and wounded 150 others, while the elimination of Sheikh Ahmed Yassin in March 2004, by a salvo of Hellfire missiles, caused the death of a dozen innocent civilians.

- On 9 March 2012, Israel's elimination of Zohair al-Qaisi, secretary general of the Popular Resistance Committees (PRC), killing some fifteen innocent civilians[603] , and French support for the operation will motivate Mohammed Merah's attacks on 22 March.

These eliminations illustrate the characteristic of the Israeli services: a great capacity to locate their targets, but a profound inability to understand their enemies, which is the fundamental criterion for judging the capabilities of a service. The result is that far from weakening their adversary, the Israelis have strengthened its combativeness by discouraging the efforts of moderates within Hamas and Fatah. In short: tactical success, strategic failure.

The counter-productive nature of extra-judicial killings is even more important and systematic when they are carried out during a negotiation process or during a

---

599. NOA: In fact, the attack was carried out by a commando of the Democratic Front for the Liberation of Palestine (DFLP)!

600. The subsequent PFLP attacks on 24 April 2003 (which was also claimed by the Al-Aqsa Martyrs Brigades) and 22 May 2004 can probably no longer be associated with this process.

601. He was eliminated a week after a double suicide attack on an ammonia depot in the port of Ashdod. This attack - which killed ten Israelis - was seen as an attempted chemical attack and was interpreted as a new level of terrorist action.

602. Jerusalem Post, 1er September 2004.

603. The Guardian and The Washington Post, 10 March 2012.

truce: a recurrent practice of the Israelis. In fact, Israel does not consider targeted eliminations or drone attacks as ceasefire violations[604] !... Thus, Palestinian rocket attacks, always presented by the Western press as moody demonstrations, almost *always* take place *after* raids or cease-fire breaches by Israel[605] .

Targeted killings and human bombs in the middle of a negotiation process

Israeli targeted elimination	Palestinian response	Comments
(Date) (Target) (Membership)	(Date) (Victims)	
06.01.1996 Yahya Ayyash Hamas	25.02.1996 1 death 25.02.1996 27 deaths 03.03.1996 20 dead 04.03.1996 13 deaths	The elimination of the 'engineer' was the motive for the largest wave of suicide bombings.
31.07.2001 Jamal Mansour Hamas	09.08.2001 15 dead	The Israeli action broke a nearly two-month ceasefire by Hamas.
23.11.2001 Mahmoud Abou Hanoud Hamas	01.12.2001 11 deaths 02.12.2001 15 dead	The Israeli action rendered null and void the agreement between Hamas and Fatah not to attack targets in Israel after «9/11».
23.07.2002 Salah Shahada Hamas	04.08.2002 9 deaths	The Israeli action left 15 people dead, hours before a widely publicised Tanzim and Hamas ceasefire was to take effect.
26.12.2002 3 fighters Fatah, Palestinian Islamic Jihad and Al-Aqsa Brigades	05.01.2003 22 dead	The Israeli action comes as representatives of Fatah, Hamas and other factions negotiate a ceasefire on attacks against Israeli civilians in Cairo.

Table 18 - Impact of extrajudicial executions on negotiations between 2001 and 2003. More recent comparisons are difficult given the abandonment of negotiation processes on the one hand, and the different nature of the Palestinian resistance's means of action on the other.

These eliminations do not contribute to improved security. Intuitively, it could be seen as an arithmetic reduction of the threat, and some studies have attempted to show that these eliminations have reduced the number of suicide attacks[606].But in reality, the opposite is true. The gradual disappearance of this

---

604. "Senior official: 'Israel didn't agree to halt targeted killings for ceasefire'", The Times of Israel, 15 November 2019.
605. http://blog.thejerusalemfund.org/2012/12/israeli-ceasefire-violations-in-gaza.html.
606. Ophir Falk, "Measuring the Effectiveness of Israel's 'Targeted Killing' Campaign", Perspectives on

type of attack from 2005 onwards is the result of a change of strategy initiated in 2002 by Mohammed al-Deif, leader of the *Kataeb Izz al-Din al-Qassam*. Linked to the construction of the Israeli «barrier», it was a question of abandoning a «disorganised» terrorism for a more structured resistance fight, including the use of rockets and mortars as a means of action.

In the United States, extrajudicial killings were banned by *Executive Order 12333*, issued by President Ronald Reagan in 1981[607].EO 12333 defines the roles and missions of the US intelligence community and states that *«No person employed or acting on behalf of the United States Government shall be engaged in, or conspire to be engaged in, assassinations»*, thus formalising a policy already established by President Gerald Ford in 1976. But many American jurists justify the use of assassination by arguing that an executive order is not law (it can be modified or overturned by another executive order) and that the principle of 'just war' authorises the elimination of opposing leaders in order to spare the lives of innocent people. This is a very «Democratic» intellectual construction, which led President Bill Clinton to sign, in 1998, a classified *«intelligence finding»* authorising the CIA to eliminate Osama bin Laden (OBL). True to a Democratic tradition, President Barack Obama will continue the policy of extra-judicial eliminations, including OBL, without any effect on terrorist activity.

3.3.3.2. Death squads

In an environment of political, fringe or urban guerrilla terrorism, the idea of *'terrorising the terrorists'* has often led to the formation of *'death squads'*. In Spain, the government has attempted to combat terrorism through 'anti-terro-rist' groups, such as the *Commandos DELTA*, the *Antiterrorist Liberation Group (GAL)*, the *Batallón Vasco Español (BVE)*, which operated in Spain and France. The GAL was responsible for 24 assassinations in 1983-1987 and its main leaders were tried in early 1995.

This method conceals several weaknesses: in addition to the state's inability to respond holistically to terrorism, it is in fundamental contradiction with the values it defends, and thus legitimises the use of terrorism. Thus, on a strategic level, the trap of this 'tool' is that it enters into the logic of terrorists, allowing them to move to a higher level of violence, as Carlos Marighella advocated:

> *The government will only be able to intensify repression, which will make the lives of citizens more unbearable. Homes will be violated, police beatings organised, innocent people arrested, roads closed. Police terror will set in,*

Terrorism, vol 9, n° 1, 2015.
607. Executive Order 12333 - United States Intelligence Activities (As Amended by Executive Orders 13284 (2003), 13355 (2004) and 13470 (2008)), 4 December 1981, para 2.11, www.cia.gov/about-cia/eo12333.html.

In other words, the government is playing into the hands of the terrorists and contributing to the development of the insurgency: its leaders thus become doubly criminal!

But the use of «death squads» is not exclusive to dictatorships. Countries that call themselves «democracies» also use them. The United States[609] , Great Britain[610] and France[611] have used clandestine paramilitary (unofficial) units to eliminate terrorists or civilians in order to deprive the terrorists of support.

Main US paramilitary formations in Afghanistan

Common name	Operational area
Force 01	Wardak - Logar
Force 02	Jalalabad
Force 03 (Kandahar Strike Force)	Kandahar
Force 04	Kunar
Sangorian	Helmand
Khost Protection Force	Khost
Shahine Force	Paktika

Table 19 - Paramilitary forces in Afghanistan. They were organised and funded by the US CIA and led by the Afghan National Directorate of Security (NDS). Their aim was to cut off the Taliban from popular support.

The use of these «death squads» is only really effective when the guerrillas or terrorists lack popular support and legitimacy. The problem is that Westerners fight their wars tactically. In Afghanistan, the widespread corruption of the authorities by those who had the money to do it - the West - doomed efforts to transform society. As a result, violent counter-terrorism or counter-guerrilla actions were highly unpopular. This is why, in March 2013, President Karzai demanded the

---

608. Carlos Marighella, Urban Guerrilla Manual, chapter «Supporting the Population», June 1969, www.terrorisme.net.

609. Rod Nordland, "After Airstrike, Afghan Points to C.I.A. and Secret Militias", The New York Times, 18 April 2013.

610. Niall Stanage, "Britain's tame death squads", The Guardian, 26 June 2002.

611. Vincent Nouzille, Les tueurs de la République, Fayard, 21 January 2015.

withdrawal of US special forces and their auxiliaries from certain provinces; the Americans did not do so after accepting the decision[612].

3.3.3.3. Air strikes and drones

While air strikes seem to be an elegant solution, with maximum effect for minimum risk, they are seen to reinforce a sense of solidarity with the populations concerned and a sympathy for the jihadists. This is exactly what happened in France and - to a lesser extent - in Belgium in 2015-2016. The government, the media and the 'intellectuals' totally ignored the cultural realities of their own population and only saw *their* reality from *their* ivory tower, leaving the population to pay the price of their fantasies...

The increased operational role of intelligence services has led to an ever greater use of their technical means to eliminate individuals. To this end, the use of drones is regularly practised by countries such as Israel, the US, France and Britain. Since 2012, the CIA and the US *Joint Special Operations Command* (JSOC) have been authorised to conduct strikes on individuals they have not identified, who are simply targeted according to the nature of their move-ments[613]. Thus, in January 2015, a CIA drone killed two «al-Qaeda» hostages in Pakistan - who had not even been detected despite several «*hundreds of hours of surveillance*»- without touching the targeted terrorists[614] !

Official rhetoric presents these methods as 'surgical', but this is not exactly the case, and their use needs to be carefully measured as they have been identified as a source of radicalisation.

First of all, these strikes are not 'surgical'. Moreover, whereas during the Second World War the US Air Force defined precision bombing as a strike within a 25-foot (7.6 m) circle, it defines it today as a 39-foot (12 m) circle[615] !...

Furthermore, technically, it must be understood that these executions are rarely carried out on the basis of positive identification of individuals (as films and TV series tend to suggest), but on the basis of behaviour measured from data provided by mobile phones or other devices. In other words, it is the mobile phone that is the target, not the individual, based on a certain number of calls in given areas, of a given duration, with given individuals: this is so-called «*signature-based*» targeting.

---

612. Azam Ahmed, "Afghans Compromise Over Ban on Elite U.S. Troops", The New York Times, 20 March 2013.

613. Greg Miller, "White House approves broader Yemen drone campaign", The Washington Post, 25 April 2012.

614. Peter Baker, "Obama Apologizes After Drone Kills American and Italian Held by Al Qaeda", The New York Times, 23 April 2015.

615. Nicolas J. S. Davies, "The Persistent Myth of US Precision Bombing", Consortium News, 20 June 2018.

As General Michael Hayden, former Director of the National Security Agency (NSA) and the Central Intelligence Agency (CIA), was to admit:

We kill on the basis of metadata! [616]

The drones use metadata collected by service providers and passed on to intelligence services. This data is associated with characteristic «profiles», which are derived from mathematical algorithms that are supposed to represent the typical behaviour of terrorists. Thus, in simple terms, a phone that frequently connects with phones suspected of belonging to terrorists or located in areas where terrorists are located will be considered to belong to a terrorist. It will be targeted without knowing who the actual user is at the time or the identity of the people around him (e.g. his family), who are automatically considered terrorists.

Thus, we kill without really knowing, with a method that is inherently imprecise and creates collateral damage. According to classified documents released in 2015[617] , 90% of drone victims are innocent. According to the *Bureau of Investigative Journalism* (BIJ), between June 2004 and October 2014, US drones killed some 2,379 people in Pakistan (which is not at war with the US), of whom only 84 (4%) were identified as terrorists[618].

The problem is that American (and Western) intelligence is not up to the technological capabilities of these weapons. As the Iraq campaign showed, electronic intelligence, traditionally a key source of information, becomes extremely unhelpful with an adversary that has figured out how to evade it and must be supplemented by human intelligence, or else there will be many collateral casualties.

This is true of the various attempts to eliminate the leaders of the Islamic State. Already, Abu Musab al-Zarqawi, founder of the *Islamic State in Iraq* (ISIL), had been considered killed three times (2003, 2005 and 2006). The same thing is happening with his successor, Abu Bakr al-Baghdadi, leader of the EI:
- 18 March 2015, he is considered seriously injured, in an air strike[619] ;
- 11 October 2015, he is briefly thought to have died in an air strike in Iraq[620] ;
- 9 June 2016, he is announced as dead by Iraqi television[621] ;

---

616. "Former NSA & CIA director: 'We kill people based on metadata'", YouTube, 11 June 2014.
617. "The Drone Papers", The Intercept; Andrew Blake, "Obama-led drone strikes kill innocents 90% of the time: report", The Washington Times, 15 October 2015.
618.   http://www.thebureauinvestigates.com/2014/10/16/only-4-of-drone-victims-in-pakistan-named-as-al-qaeda-members/ (accessed 25 January 2015).
619. "Islamic State chief Abu Bakr al-Baghdadi seriously injured after US-led air strike in Iran", Firstpost, 22 April 2015.
620. "ISIS figures killed in air strike; Baghdadi not believed among them", Reuters/The Daily Star, 11 October 2015.
621. "U.S, Iraqi officials can't confirm report Islamic State leader wounded", Reuters, 10 June 2016.

- 12 June 2016, he is reported dead in a coalition strike in Raqqa (Yenis Safak, 13 June 2016);

- 3 October 2016, he was allegedly poisoned by an EI member[622] ;

- 28 May 2017, he is probably killed in Raqqa[623] ;

- 10 June 2017, he is considered dead, according to Syrian television[624] ;

- 23 June 2017, he was killed, according to the Iranian news agency IRNA[625] ;

- 11 July 2017, he dies in Deir ez-Zor, according to the Syrian Observatory for Human Rights[626] .

... But, he reappears in a video at the end of April 2019[627] ... Finally, he is shot dead by American commandos, on October 27, 2019[628] in Barisha, Idlib province, inside the sanctuary created by the Westerners for the «moderate rebels», whose limits are monitored by NATO military!...

Similarly, on 14 June 2015, the elimination of Mokhtar Belmokhtar[629] , by an American air raid[630] on the Libyan town of Ajdabyia, is celebrated as a victory in the media[631].Five days later, it turns out that the information is false[632] ; but the victims are real, and there will be no apology or compensation for them... It is easy to understand why this 'collateral damage' becomes a major motivation for recruiting militants.

---

622. Sam Webb, 'Report: Abu Bakr al-Baghdadi and three other IS commanders poisoned by assassin', The Sun, 4October 2016.

623. Jared Malsin, "Russia Claims Airstrike May Have Killed ISIS Leader Abu Bakr al-Baghdadi", Time Magazine, 16 June 2017.

624. Charlie Parker, "ISIS leader Abu Bakr al-Baghdadi 'killed in a massive airstrike in Syria', the country's state TV channel claims", The Sun, 11 June 2017; "Syrian media claim ISIS leader killed in artillery strike", World Tribune, 11 June 2017.

625. "Khamenei's representative says Islamic state's Baghdadi 'definitely dead': IRNA", Reuters, 29 June 2017.

626. Lisa Barrington & Ellen Francis, "Syrian Observatory says it has 'confirmed information' that Islamic State chief is dead", Reuters, 11 July 2017.

627. Martin Chulov & Dan Sabbagh, "Isis leader Baghdadi appears in video for first time in five years", The Guardian, 30 April 2019.

628. News, France 24, 27 October 2019.

629. NOA: Mokhtar Belmokhtar is reputed to be a terrorist from the Jihad Base in the Islamic Maghreb. In reality, he is a little-known character whose speciality was smuggling goods (including cigarettes and weapons) in southern Algeria. His exact role in terrorist ventures has never been formally established and he is credited with many actions, such as the attack on the Amenas oil base in Libya. In fact, the operations attributed to him are not consistent with other Islamist actions and are more akin to 'simple' banditry.

630. NOA: This action was carried out by F-15 aircraft and not by drones, but it illustrates the US policy towards victims.

631. "Mokhtar Belmokhtar: Top Islamist 'killed' in US strike", BBC News (US & Canada), 15 June 2015.

632. Richard Spencer, "Mokhtar Belmokhtar has survived several previous claims to have killed him," The Telegraph, 19 June 2015, http://www.telegraph.co.uk/news/worldnews/africaandindianocean/libya/11686244/One-eyed-sheikh-Mokhtar-Belmokhtar-alive-says-al-Qaeda.html.

In the first five years of Barack Obama's presidency, the US conducted eight times as many drone strikes as during the entire George Bush presidency. Officially, the number of civilians killed in each strike has been halved[633] , but Obama was a lawyer, and this reduction is just a legal sleight of hand: neither the procedures nor the modes of action have been changed, only the criteria for counting victims. Thus, the US considers that all

> *[...males of combatant age in a strike zone are combatants, unless it can be explicitly demonstrated posthumously that they were not.[634]*

In other words: we shoot and ask questions afterwards.

Another problem is that in the US, strikes are managed by two separate entities: the US Air Force and the Central Intelligence Agency (CIA). When carried out by the military, the selection of targets (*'targeting'*) follows strict and traceable criteria and procedures (even if they are classified). This is not the case with CIA strikes, where targeting criteria and procedures are completely opaque, and are sometimes carried out by civilian contractors without any supervision. In a combat zone where national forces are engaged, target selection is relatively easy to justify. In theatres of operation that are not open combat zones, however, it is more difficult to qualify a target as an «imminent threat» or a case of «self-defence».

Eliminations can therefore become a backdoor way of applying the death penalty without trial. In the United States, the issue arose after the elimination of Anwar al-Awlaki[635] , a US citizen radicalised after the invasion of Iraq, who was shot down by a US drone on 30 September 2011.

France also practices targeted eliminations. According to journalist Vincent Nouzille[636] , President Hollande is the president of the Fifth Republic who has made the most use of clandestine operations to physically eliminate individuals with the *Action Service* of the *General Directorate for External Security* (DGSE) (HOMO operations).

---

633. Jack Serle, "More than 2400 dead as Obama's drone campaign marks five years comments", The Bureau of Investigative Journalism, 23 January 2014.

634. Jo Becker & Scott Shane, "Secret 'Kill List' Proves a Test of Obama's Principles and Will", The New York Times, 29 May 2012.

635. Sheikh Anwar al-Awlaki is an imam born in the United States, considered as a specialist in Islamism, he was invited to the Pentagon shortly after «9/11» in order to present the situation of radical Islam in the world to senior officials. Very critical of '9/11', he strongly criticises 'Al-Qaeda' and approves the American decision to intervene in Afghanistan. But the invasion of Iraq, the Abu Ghraib scandal and the use of torture by the United States radicalised him and he moved to Yemen where he became one of the theoreticians of jihadism. He escaped several drone attacks until 30 September 2011.

636. Vincent Nouzille, Les tueurs de la République, Fayard, 21 January 2015.

The clandestine operation makes it possible to «personalise» the elimination and minimise collateral effects. But France also carries out eliminations by means of air strikes. In fact, these operations have the appearance of success, but they are not really.

The US targeted killing programme in Yemen illustrates the inadequacy of the Western war on terror. First, legally, it is difficult to justify it as self-defence because Yemen is not at war with the US and does not threaten it. Secondly, according to a study by the *Center for Strategic Studies at the University of Jordan*, in cooperation with the American universities of Princeton and Michigan[637] , for 73.5% of the Yemenis questioned, these strikes justify hitting Americans all over the world.

This is why air strikes - and drone strikes in particular - have been identified across the Atlantic as a motive for radicalisation. In 2015, Tom Pettinger, in the *Journal for Deradicalization*, observed:

> *In areas where the US drone programme has been engaged, there is a perception of a dishonourable, cowardly and unequal war, as air strikes are not associated with a risk to US personnel. For this reason, «there is an al-Qaeda acceptance» against such «remote warfare» everywhere. Such a way of waging war generates a sense of invulnerability for those who intervene, and the sense of powerlessness of living under the threat of drones or air strikes can lead - especially when there are civilian casualties - to individualisation, and thus to the radicalisation of individuals quickly, even for those who would previously have supported counter-terrorism measures.*[638]

In 2012, the *New York Times* wrote:

> *Drones have replaced Guantánamo as the tool of choice for recruiting militants.*[639]

A lesson that France and Belgium would ignore two years later, sacrificing their citizens:

---

637. Arab Barometer Survey Project - Yemen Report, http://www.arabbarometer.org/sites/default/files/Yemenreport1.pdf.

638. Tom Pettinger, "What is the Impact of Foreign Military Intervention on Radicalization?", Journal for Deradicalization, Winter 15/16, n° 5, pp. 92-114 (ISSN: 2363-9849).

639. Jo Becker & Scott Shane, "Secret 'Kill List' Proves a Test of Obama's Principles and Will", The New York Times, 29 May 2012.

It is wrong to say that the attacks are taking place in France in response to and to put pressure on governments that are intervening militarily in the Middle East.[640]

French exceptionalism or head in the sand? In any case, it is exactly this type of (lack of) thinking that is behind the attacks that hit France in 2015-2016. The Islamic State videos clearly explain the relationship between the strikes and the attacks[641].

Thus, in an asymmetric context, strikes may bring a tactical gain, but hardly ever a strategic gain. On the one hand, they legitimise the action of terrorists, on the other hand, they become a consecration for the terrorists who are shot and become a source of radicalisation for the survivors and families of those who were collateral victims.

This is where strategic intelligence comes into its own in terms of informing decision-makers about the fundamental mechanisms of terrorism, in order to anticipate - given the facts, the individuals, their background, their character, their political environment, etc. - the possible consequences of decisions taken and to assess the strategic gain or cost of eliminating an individual or individuals. - It can also be used to assess the strategic gain or cost of eliminating an individual or individuals.

3.3.3.4. The body count policy

In Vietnam, in order to convince Washington to maintain its financial support for the war, General Westmoreland instituted the *'body count'* policy, which consisted of counting the number of enemy dead, wounded and prisoners in order to quantify his operational success. This practice proved to be a failure and had to be quickly abandoned: on the one hand, it encouraged American units to overestimate Viet Cong casualties and, on the other, because the Vietnamese practised a multitude of small ambushes with very few losses. From then on, the body count was no longer an indicator of success[642].

Today, in the fight against terrorism, the «*body count*» policy is practiced in varying ways[643].In Afghanistan, the NATO command measured the effectiveness of Operation RESOLUTE SUPPORT by the number of insurgents killed[644].In France, each time Operation BARKHANE is killed, the 'success' of the operation

---

640. Philippe Cohen-Grillet, journalist, in Le Grand Référendum, Sud Radio, 23 March 2017.
641. Eye for an Eye video, Wilaya al-Furat, 27 March 2016.
642. Kate Brannen, "When Is a Body Count Not a Body Count?", Foreign Policy, 22 January 2015.
643. Micah Zenko, "Checking the Math on the Pentagon's ISIS Body Counts", Foreign Policy, 16 August 2016.
644. Bill Roggio, "NATO command touts body count of 'Taliban irreconcilables'", The Long War Journal, 23 July 2018.

in terms of the number of militants killed is recalled[645]. These figures are increasing without reflecting success: the situation does not seem to be improving and hostility to the foreign presence is growing. With no measurable objectives defined, only the number of adversaries killed remains to illustrate success. This brings us back to the military thinking of the 1914-1918 war. The application of a 'comprehensive approach', as NATO has done in Afghanistan, by adding a socio-humanitarian component to military action (rebuilding schools or rehabilitating hospitals), has no multiplier effect, as would a holistic approach[646].

This lack of strategic thinking around BARKHANE leads to a paradoxical situation. For as we have seen, dying is not considered a defeat for a jihadist, but a sign of determination. Therefore, highlighting the number of jihadists killed is counterproductive: it only helps to demonstrate the determination of the mujahideen and tends more to stimulate new vocations than to discourage potential fighters. The official French discourse is simply superimposed on the propaganda of the EI, which values the example of martyrs who sacrifice their lives.

The '*body count*' policy tends to reduce success to a body count, and to mask our lack of strategic thinking: in an asymmetric conflict, high casualties weaken the position of the 'victor' in the minds of local populations and are therefore not a measure of success.

A variant of this ineffectiveness 'strategy' is to eliminate the leaders of jihadist groups one by one. This is related to a discussion the author had during his counter-terrorism training in Britain, when the Provisional IRA was wreaking havoc: British intelligence had detailed organisational charts of each unit, with their commanders, addresses, telephone numbers, eating habits, family details, etc. Yet they did not eliminate these 'leaders', so as not to have to deal with the terror. Yet they did not eliminate these 'leaders', so as not to be left with new leaders they knew nothing about, which would have weakened the British themselves. In other words, tactical success led to strategic weakening. This is exactly the problem with the French strategy in the Sahel...

The logic of France's war must change. In April 2021, the *Citizens' Coalition for the Sahel* noted that the current measure of success was insufficient[647] :

> *For the Citizens' Coalition for the Sahel, a security approach that does not include concrete measures to ensure the protection of civilians is doomed to failure. The Citizens' Coalition therefore calls for a drastic reordering of*

---

645. «G5 Sahel: some of Barkhane's military successes amidst terrorist chaos', France 24, 15 February 2021.
646. «Operation Barkhane», press kit, Media Relations Office of the Armed Forces Staff, July 2019.
647. «Sahel: What needs to change for a new people-centred approach, recommendations of the Citizens' Coalition for the Sahel, April 2021.

priorities, so that the measure of success of interventions is not only military (the list of «neutralised terrorists»), but also takes into account the number of displaced people voluntarily returned to their homes, schools reopened, fields cultivated again.

3.3.3.5. The fight against the financing of terrorism

The emphasis on terrorist financing by some experts stems from the fight against organised crime and fringe terrorism in the 1980s. After 2001, the idea was extended with the image of an exalted multi-millionaire - Osama bin Laden - using his fortune to overthrow the world order in the manner of Dr Strangelove. But after twenty years and countless investigations, very little is still known about the financing of '9/11'[648].

In fact, by seeing «Al Qaeda» as a «criminal organisation», the problem has been approached as the fight against organised crime, by tackling money laundering mechanisms. However, while organised crime tries to use illegal money for legal activities, the opposite is true in the case of terrorism: it tries to use legal money for an activity that is not legal. Thus, there is a tendency to apply inappropriate logics to this type of problem, as in Belgium[649].In the emotion that followed 9/11, it was necessary above all to demonstrate that the terrorists were «bad guys», and funding from illegal activities (prostitution, arms trafficking, drug trafficking, etc.) was attributed to the Islamist networks. Thus, the international community lost precious time looking for networks that did not exist.

The way the West seeks to deal with this issue is outdated and reflects our misunderstanding of contemporary jihadist terrorism. First, it is necessary to define the terrorism we seek to combat. In the case of the Islamic State, a distinction must be made between *open-front jihad* (OFJ), carried out on the ground by fighters with relatively sophisticated weapons, and individual terrorism (ITD) carried out by isolated individuals and with the «means at hand».

With the adoption of the «open jihad» strategy, where the resources (doctrinal and technical) of terrorism are openly available and the initiative is left to the individual or a very small group of individuals, the issue of financing takes on a whole new dimension. The underlying idea is to make terrorism invisible to surveillance systems. The means used (knife, car, etc.) do not necessarily require large investments and can be financed literally out of the current expenses of the

---

648. John Roth, Douglas Greenburg, Serena Wille, Monograph on Terrorist Financing - Staff Report to the Commission, National Commission on Terrorist Attacks Upon the United States, Washington DC.

649. See Thomas Renard (editor) (with contributions from : Sophie André, Elke Devroe, Nils Duquet, France Lemeunier, Paul Ponsaers, Vincent Seron), Counterterrorism in Belgium: Key Challenges and Policy Options, Egmont Paper 89, October 2016, pp. 11-12.

terrorist or his family. The granularity of this type of financing is such that it passes through most means of surveillance. Moreover, from a legal point of view, the distinction between terrorist financing and everyday life becomes almost impossible. This is the case of Mme Nathalie Haddidi, who sent money to her son Abbes Bounaga (who left for Syria to wage jihad) to enable him to return to France and who found herself before the correctional chamber for financing terrorism[650].

If the same logic were to be applied, the American, British and French leaders should be brought to justice, for not only did they do everything in their power to generate hatred against the West, but they also provided them with the weapons to carry out their project. Indeed, by exploiting Islamist groups to destabilise secular regimes, these countries have grossly misjudged the intentions and doctrines of their allies and their ability to keep them in check.

3.3.4. The information war

Information warfare is a complex set of measures designed to frame military policy or operations. In an asymmetric situation, the central and strategic issue in information warfare is the legitimacy of the action, which can only be achieved within the framework of an overall holistic strategy.

All too often, Western countries focus on cyber warfare, imagining threat scenarios that are more real than fictional. Without denying its importance, it is a very secondary area in the fight against terrorism.

Western countries feel legitimised by the very nature of the values they think they are defending and seek to propagate by force. The problem is that the countries we operate in do not want to have these values imposed on them: they should be their choice, not ours. The objectives of information warfare are therefore often at odds with military operations.

In this information war, jihadists have a considerable advantage over Western countries because they fully accept their use of terrorism. By openly displaying their crimes and fully acknowledging their terrorist nature, they reduce their vulnerability to Western communication.

On the other hand, engaged in operations that are often contrary to international law, Westerners are forced to be discreet - even to lie - in order to maintain their legitimacy. Thus, it is not enough to declare that we are fighting terrorism in the name of our values; we must also respect them ourselves. We practice

---

650. Jean Chichizola, «Jugée pour avoir financé son djihadiste», lefigaro.fr, 5 September 2017.

torture (directly or indirectly[651]) and do not respect human rights[652] , we cause more civilian casualties than the EI in Afghanistan[653] , we carry out strikes and wars in defiance of international law[654] , we support Islamic terrorist groups[655] , etc.

The civilian casualties of Western strikes, modestly called «collateral damage», fuel radicalisation among Muslim minorities. The policy of most Western countries in this regard is to keep them quiet, as disclosing them could encourage acts of violence. This is the argument that was raised after the Wikileaks and Bradley/Chelsea Manning revelations about US practices in Iraq. For example, Belgium hardly communicates about its strikes in Iraq and Syria[656] , and never about civilian casualties[657].The Americans stopped communicating about their strikes in Syria in 2017. As for France, it systematically denies its numerous 'blunders' in the Sahel, such as the one in Bounti (Mali) on 3 January 2021[658].

This strategy of «not seen, not taken», typical of bureaucracies, may appear judicious at first glance. But it is counterproductive, because the phenomenon becomes asymmetrical: by not communicating, we are absent from the information field and leave it to the terrorists. Without an appropriate strategy in 2014, France has failed to win the hearts of its immigrant population and has created a potential enemy within itself.

In fact, the Western countries see information warfare as operations were conceived in 1914: by constantly seeking superiority. This is their main weakness. Without a strategy, with actions on the ground that contradict the official discourse, they are incapable of transmitting a message that is capable of creating a solid legitimacy around their action.

---

651. In addition to the practice of torture to obtain information, some countries (such as France, Germany, Great Britain or Switzerland) authorise the acquisition of information obtained through torture in other countries. («No questions asked» - Intelligence cooperation with countries that torture», Human Rights Watch, 29 June 2010).

652. «État d'urgence: la France prévient qu'elle ne respectera pas les droits de l'homme», AFP/Le Point. fr, 27 November 2015; Blandine Le Cain, «La France prévoit d'enfreindre les droits de l'homme avec l'état d'urgence», lefigaro.fr, 27 November 2015.

653. «Midyear Update On The Protection Of Civilians In Armed Conflict: 1 January To 30 June 2019', UNAMA, 30 July 2019, p. 12.

654. Marko Milanovic, 'The Syria Strikes: Still Clearly Illegal', European Journal of International Law, 15 April 2018; Doug Bandow, 'End America's Illegal Occupation of Syria Now', CATO Institute, 13 June 2019.

655. "U.S., Britain, France block Russia bid to blacklist Syria rebels", Reuters, 11 May 2016.

656. "Improving Belgian transparency and public accountability in the war against Daesh", Airwars. org.

657. Laurie Treffers, 'De mythe van nul burgerslachtoffers', De Standaard, 24 September 2020; Laurie Treffers, 'Belgian airstrikes and the myth of zero civilian casualties', Airwars.org, 2 October 2020.

658. Pierre Alonso, 'Frappe française au Mali : les appels à la transparence se multiplient', Libération, 21 January 2021 (updated 22 January 2021).

3.3.4.1. Generic objectives

It is a truism that information is a key issue in a conflict. However, it is important to understand the complexity of this issue. Beyond its strategic objectives, information warfare targets several types of operational objectives, which are articulated in a matrix fashion. These are functional objectives:

- The mastery of information *upstream of decision-making*, which aims to give the decision-maker the overall vision necessary for his decision. It implies a capacity to manage the knowledge of the battlefield (physical or virtual) and to integrate all the information necessary for the conduct (intelligence, logistics, own troops, etc.). It includes in particular the capacity of intelligence to anticipate the actions of the adversary.

- Information control *downstream of the decision*, which essentially aims to acquire and maintain the technical means and processes of command and control to provide the necessary information to the executors to accomplish their missions. It also includes the ability to feed back the information gathered by the executors, so as to ensure the steering of operations, or even the adjustment of decisions in response to the evolution of the situation. This is an essentially technical issue, which we will not address here.

- Controlling *communication* between the state and public opinion, which aims to manage the perception of conflict. It is not only about controlling the content of the information disseminated, but also the way in which information is shared. It also has the function of preventing the adversary from dominating the information fields.

These objectives are combined with structural or facilitating cross-cutting objectives:

- The *control of information vectors*, which implies the availability of communication means and the technologies associated with them. It implies their physical availability, but also the human and technical capacities to implement them.

- *Control of the content of the* information and its integrity, which means that the elements that circulate are not corrupted in technical terms. In other words, it is not a question of whether the information is «right» or «wrong», but that it is able to circulate as intended.

3.3.4.2. Controlling information upstream of the decision - knowledge

While intelligence is essentially the relevant information about the «adversary», it is not all the information needed to make a decision. It must be complemented by information about our own capabilities and limitations (e.g. operational availability of equipment). Combined with intelligence, this information constitutes the knowledge needed for specific decisions. Knowledge management implies the management and continuous updating of this knowledge, while allowing continuous access to it within an institution.

In most government (and intelligence) agencies, expertise and factual knowledge are concentrated at the «bottom» of the pyramid, while the higher echelons must have an integrative and synthetic function of this knowledge. Since terrorism is the use of tactical actions to achieve a strategic objective, tactical information - usually located at the 'bottom' of the pyramid - can have strategic importance. The result is often a tendency for the higher echelons to 'descend' to the tactical level to substitute for the experts and focus on the details (*micromanagement*). This often means a loss of the big picture and a tactical handling of the problem. Functionally, overlapping competences are created which encourage the retention of information at all levels. In complex conflicts, this is a major weakness of security agencies and probably the main reason for failures in the fight against terrorism.

The aim of knowledge warfare is not only to know more and faster than the adversary, but also to make this knowledge more quickly available to operational elements, so that they can act more quickly, more precisely and more effectively. It also includes all means designed to prevent the adversary from building up his knowledge. It therefore includes all measures that serve to remove information from the adversary's acquisition systems (camouflage, protection of information, etc.) (passive measures), as well as all measures that provide the adversary with false information in order to deceive him about our operational intentions (active measures)[659] .

Knowledge management is essential for strategic coherence of action. In overly bureaucratised intelligence services, institutional compartmentalisation favours the vertical circulation of information (*'stovepiping'*) and tends to isolate analysts. This situation is a weakness if the «chiefs» do not assume their function as integrators of information. This is the case in most 'large' departments. It is probably for this reason that the 'smaller' services are better predisposed to take a global view of the threat, such as the *Bureau of Intelligence and Research (INR)* of the US State Department or the *Office of National Assessments (ONA)* in Australia.

3.3.4.3. *Control of information downstream of the decision - the means of control*

In management, knowledge management is essentially about providing each operational level with information relevant to its task. In pyramidal hierarchical structures, this is fairly straightforward, as each level supplies the next level with «tailor-made» information in both the top-down and bottom-up directions. The problem is more complex in an open, networked and information-rich environment, which offers each

---

659. What the Russians call «maskirovka».

level the same wealth of information. The risk is that the same information enters the same process several times and that higher quality information is ignored.

This is particularly the case in strategic analyses of the jihad that use *mainstream* information because it is more easily accepted. This is the case with Osama bin Laden's responsibility for the 9/11 attacks, which is still considered an established fact, even though there is no evidence to prove it to this day.

3.3.4.4. *Mastering communication - mastering perceptions*

Perception management is a weapon of war. Virtually no major conflict since the Second World War has started without a disinformation or communication operation.

Terrorism is a tool of influence: it exploits uncertainty, insecurity and fear in order to influence decision-making mechanisms. In fact, terrorism - like air disasters - is an extreme phenomenon that constitutes only a tiny fraction of the causes of death. Yet it disproportionately affects the lives of individuals and the state.

As we have seen, asymmetric warfare - particularly jihadist asymmetry - is based on a cognitive differential. Rightly or wrongly, jihadists perceive Western interventions as aggression against their societies, and link them to the Crusades. The point here is not to know whether they are right or wrong, but to note this state of affairs. In France (and to some extent in Belgium), no effort is made to correct this perception. One sometimes gets the feeling that terrorism is being exploited for domestic political purposes.

As we have seen, the key issue in the fight against terrorism is to avoid the slide of sympathisers towards activism, by targeting the national population as a priority. One could envisage, for example, to :
- minimise the gap between governments and their (mainly immigrant) population, which could be a vulnerability to terrorism;
- communicate on the legitimacy of interventions abroad, explaining their motives and their imperative necessity... if any... ;
- To show that interventions abroad do not stem from defiance towards a religion (in this case Islam) or different cultures, but from the higher imperatives of winning the hearts and minds of the population which could express a form of solidarity with the populations affected by our interventions, giving pledges of trust to the immigrant population and avoiding misplaced polemics on peripheral issues (Islamic veil, burkini, etc.) which have no bearing on terrorism.

To achieve this, government policy must be clear and understandable. In France, participation in the American operation in Iraq and Syria has been justified in a jumble of reasons: self-defence, protection of the Yezidi minorities, overthrow of the Syrian government and the fight against the EI. Yet for each of these actions, more effective, more sustainable and less lethal means for the civilian population could have been implemented.

It is also essential that acts of terrorism be analysed in a non-partisan way in order to curb the fears of the population and find appropriate ways to deal with them. The option chosen in France - as in American religious circles - has been to situate them within a conquering will of Islam, presented as inescapable («France is attacked for what it is, not for what it does»). The idea that terrorism is only the prelude to a quasi-civilisational conflict between Islam and Christianity within our own countries has thus been allowed to develop. By dubiously associating 'Islam' and 'Islamism', notably through sterile polemics on the Islamic veil (hijab) or the burkini[660] , the state has promoted tensions within its own population.

Moreover, the lack of critical analysis of the causes of terrorism has led to further internal divisions. This was particularly the case after the *Charlie Hebdo* attacks, where those who were not 'Charlie' were accused of condoning terrorism[661].Here we enter the realm of 'post-truth', which reflects the official position of the countries involved in the international coalition and conceals the fact that the real objective of the attacks was to push France to withdraw from the Middle East conflict. Western countries have adopted a discourse that masks their bad decisions and seeks to «smooth out» the thinking on terrorism.

Unlike autocratic governments, democracies are responsive to public opinion and accountable to it at every election.

As we have seen, the importance we give to terrorist events helps to express vulnerability. Giving each victim national importance implicitly tells terrorists that each individual becomes a «juicy» target. So much so that today terrorists no longer need to target personalities: the assassination of a «simple» policeman or soldier automatically acquires strategic importance.

The looping of images of the attacks, the return to the scene of the event, the «micro-trotters» of citizens with only limited knowledge of the issue provide little substance, but a lot to the terrorists who see that their attack «worked». By their insistence, and the disproportionate echo they give to the event, the media thus become the objective accomplices of the terrorist act.

What is new is not the phenomenon, but the fact that it is not remedied or even cultivated.

This has been particularly the case in France, where the Hollande-Valls government has presented it as an inescapable phenomenon (because it is linked to religion or a transformation of society), given it a resonance out of all

---

660. Mohammed Sifaoui in the programme On a tellement de choses à se dire, «'Le voile n'est pas islamique' mais 'islamiste' selon Mohamed Sifaoui», RTL/YouTube, 25 September 2019 (06'30").
661. «Aged 8, he is heard for apologie du terrorisme», Europe 1, 29 January 2015.

proportion to the risk it poses to the state, and thus produced a multiplier effect that has only served the Islamic State and encouraged violent action. As this comment by Abu Bakr al-Baghdadi, leader of the EI, attests:

The sheer size of the forces amassed to fight the Islamic State is a testament to its strength and that it is on the right path. [662]

Government communication is a complex activity, which must be part of a strategy that balances political objectives, security objectives and the cultural specificities of the target audience.

This starts by communicating about the action of the state. In France, it is often attributed the *'monopoly of violence'*, according to the theories of the German philosopher Max Weber. Yet violence is defined according to criteria that invariably involve emotion and brutality, which perhaps explains why the term 'legitimate' is sometimes added to it[663].State interventions are - in theory, at least - the result of a process that owes nothing to emotion or brutality, but involves the use of force, armed or unarmed. In short, the state has a monopoly on the use of *force*, not *violence*. The confusion stems from a mistranslation of the German, in which the word (*'Gewalt'*) does not distinguish between *'violence'* and *'force'*. In English and French, however, a distinction can be made. This is why, in Anglo-Saxon terminology, force is the responsibility of the state (*«Use of force»*), while violence belongs to criminals. Paradoxically, in French-speaking European countries (France, Belgium and Switzerland), this distinction is hardly ever made. This vagueness allows 'opponents' to denounce the state as an instrument of oppression (police *violence*) and 'loyalists' to authorise practices contrary to international law.

Thus, in terms of communication, a distinction must be made between the use of *force*, to solve a problem in a considered manner and according to carefully weighed criteria, and the use of *violence, which is* a brutal, emotionally driven and often poorly controlled outburst:

The state uses force; the enemy uses violence.

However, this approach should not just be an exercise in vocabulary, but should be accompanied by concrete measures. Police officers who disregard traffic rules by (ab)using flashing lights and sirens, arrest individuals without reason and lie about the circumstances[664] or use their weapons inappropriately[665]

---

662. Quote from a chat captured in April 2017.
663. Max Weber, The Scholar and the Politician (1919), Union Générale d'Éditions, 1963.
664. «Brussels: a young man dies after being stopped by the police», belga/lesoir.be, 11 January 2021.
665. «'Yellow waistcoats': police prefect Michel Delpuech sacked, Didier Lallement replaces him», europe1.fr, 18 March 2019.

, contribute to the delegitimisation of state action. Technically (but not legally!), this is treason.

In Europe, although communication is well recognised as a strategic factor, the means to manage it are generally lacking. Yet, as the main instrument of influence, it has become an indispensable condition for the implementation of policies, strategies and, more generally, decisions.

At the end of August 2004, after two journalists were taken hostage in Baghdad[666], the French government put in place a remarkable and skilful communication, in which the French Muslim community was spontaneously involved. Efforts were made to explain the reasons and purpose of the law on the «Islamic veil» in order to convince the hostage takers that Islam was not under threat in France.

Strategically, however, it is questionable whether there was sufficient advance notice of the problem when the law was passed (10 February 2004). The debates around the law were widely commented on by Arab television channels - notably Al-Jazeerah - and were the subject of an intervention by Dr Aïman Al-Zawahiri, Osama bin Laden's right-hand man, on 24 February 2004, as well as demons-trations in Gaza, Lebanon, Bahrain, Jordan and Indonesia. But in France, the problem was perceived, in a very Cartesian way, as a «Franco-French» issue, and was not understood as a possible breaking point, requiring a communication campaign. In the general context of hypersensitivity towards Islamist movements that prevailed at the time, the 'simple' non-participation in the war in Iraq was no longer enough to forge a positive image.

Later, the French government's political support for the Israeli government in its operations in Gaza, which contributed considerably to polarising the perception of the Muslim population in France, was never communicated to this population. The same is true for the reasons that led the French govern-ment to become involved in the Middle East in 2014, which were never the subject of a message addressed to the Muslim part of its population or a warning to the population as a whole about the risks that could arise from this involvement. Whatever the relevance of these decisions, the fact that they were not communicated to the French population - and to the Jewish population in particular - left them open to the vindictiveness of Islamists. These conse-quences were not only foreseeable, but foreseen.

Perception management does not necessarily mean «misinforming», but should also help to bridge perception gaps between adversaries. For example, Switzerland, although not part of the international coalition fighting it, was threatened by the Islamic State in a 4-minute video entitled *No Respite*[667] : its

---

666. They are Christian Chesnot and Georges Malbrunot and their Syrian driver Mohammed Al-Joundi, on 24 August 2004.

667. Propaganda video released on 24 November 2015, http://heavy.com/news/2015/11/new-isis-islamic-state-news-pictures-videos-no-respite-english-language-propaganda-full-uncensored-youtube-

flag was among the 60 banners of the coalition countries. To make the video, the Islamists took their information from Wikipedia, where Switzerland was mistakenly associated with the international coalition[668].Switzerland has provided humanitarian aid to Iraq, but has never been part of the international coalition. In this case, not only did the intelligence services fail to detect this problem, but no information campaign was conducted by Switzerland - and particularly by the *Department of Foreign Affairs* - to correct this misperception among potential jihadists. Surprisingly - and irresponsibly - this «mistake» was seen as an opportunity to get closer to the Western community at a lower political cost. In other words, Switzerland could have been the victim of a terrorist attack because of an editorial error by the EI that the intelligence services did not detect! This may be the explanation for a radicalised French couple's plan to carry out an attack in Geneva in 2017[669] .

The services are thus torn between the duty of reserve that binds them to the decision-maker and the imperative need to create and maintain public confidence. This largely explains their silence. But this is not the only reason: very often, the intelligence services are also in a state of uncertainty because the nature of the problem is such that no answer can be given. Silence allows one to hide what is known and what is not known, and thus to give the illusion of knowledge. In some cases, however, this policy can be counterproductive. In Switzerland, in the aftermath of 9/11, the information embargo imposed by the Department of Defense led some commentators to suggest that the intelligence services did not have the necessary expertise... which was unfortunately true.

Communication control is exercised at two levels: at the level of information content (i.e. protecting the messages sent out by the government or individuals from being altered, diverted or replaced by other messages) and at the level of information vectors (i.e. the infrastructure and structures put in place to process and disseminate information).

3.3.4.4.1. Influencing actions

Influencing actions should :

- to meet strategic objectives shared by civilian and military law enforcement agencies;

- be based on close collaboration between civilian and military intelligence agencies;

---

daesh/.

668. Military intervention against ISIL, https://en.wikipedia.org/wiki/Military_intervention_against_ISIL. (NOA: After the author detected this Wikipedia error, the mention of Switzerland was removed from the page in question on 11 December 2015, at the request of the Swiss Foreign Ministry).

669. V.B-G., 'Annemasse: un couple radicalisé prévait de «se sauter à Genève»', Le Dauphiné, 23 September 2017.

- be designed jointly by civilian and military bodies;
- be designed to achieve specific psychological objectives for a specific target audience.

Influencing actions have three basic purposes:
- gaining legitimacy for action;
- to restore and/or maintain the confidence of the civilian population in the authorities;
- weaken the combative will of the opposing force.

3.3.4.4.2. The war of influence

As we have seen, legitimacy is an essential component of the centre of gravity of both terrorists and governments engaged in conflicts contrary to international law. The war of influence is therefore an issue for both sides, but it cannot be treated symmetrically by both.

In a democratic country, whose illegal actions are often at the root of terrorism, information warfare has to take circuitous routes and sometimes requires accommodation with the media.

The centre of gravity of modern warfare in general, and asymmetric warfare in particular, is the legitimacy of the fight or struggle. Overly clear-cut campaigns, the categorical rejection of certain ideas, the marginalisation of certain schools of thought, or even their banning, can have unpredictable and counterproductive effects. This is the case with the extreme right, which is constantly on the rise in Europe and especially in the United States, stimulated by the mythification that results from poor communication. Transparency and credible - and unbiased - communication are essential ingredients for effective influencing.

In an asymmetrical context, our thinking often has to develop 'in the hollow'. The war of influence is no exception to this rule.

Today, while the EI has defined its main battleground in the Near and Middle East region, its external operations in the West are very much dependent on the knowledge that its supporters have of the situation in Iraq and Syria. Much more than the religious message, the videos showing the casualties and destruction caused by the international coalition are, in fact, the main motivation for European jihadists. It is therefore tempting to try to cut off this source of information through cyber warfare. This is done by Western intelligence and cyberwarfare agencies as a matter of routine, with two major consequences.

The first is that, since terrorism is a means of communicating a cause and the Internet is also a means of communication, cutting off the Internet encourages jihadists to use only terrorism as a means of communication.

The second is that, since most of the information obtained on terrorists comes from the surveillance of computer networks, locking them down will push terrorists towards alternative means of communication that will be beyond the reach of our «cyber-police». This is what happened in Afghanistan, where Afghan resistance fighters reactivated old methods of communication, using carrier pigeons or messengers that are totally beyond the reach of Western technology. In the West, this has resulted in networks being tightened around siblings or families. It was in fact the anticipation of this phenomenon by Islamists that formed the basis of the concept of 'individual terrorism' between 2007 and 2010 by jihad theorists.

In other words, there is a strategic choice to be made here and a balance to be found between the ability to detect and the ability to circumscribe propaganda capabilities. Information dominance does not necessarily mean the annihilation of the enemy's communication, but rather a better developed active communication, capable of competing with the terrorists towards the target populations. This is an area that has not been mastered at all by the West since the beginning of its war in the Middle East, and which France in particular has tried to deal with by denial.

3.3.4.5. *Controlling information vectors*

The control of information vectors includes all active and passive measures aimed at preserving the civil, economic and military information environment. This environment includes first and foremost the means of leadership, but also the means of management, as well as the means that allow the maintenance of links between the population and the political leadership of the country.

The control of information vectors is a combination of static means (physical protection measures for installations and hardening of systems) and dynamic means (defensive and offensive action capabilities in cyberspace). The objectives are: a) the possibility to use them permanently with a minimum of restrictions and b) the ability to prevent their neutralisation.

Cyber warfare is the most frequently mentioned aspect of information warfare (and sometimes even considered alone as information warfare). It is easy to imagine disaster scenarios - mentioned before Y2K - where ill-intentioned individuals could disrupt air traffic, or even cause considerable damage by taking control of particular facilities (nuclear power plants, aircraft, etc.). Computer action by an individual or group of individuals against a particular target is a real threat. However, a war aimed at the collapse of a country or an economy through a succession of actions in cyberspace seems unrealistic. There are several reasons for this. An attack on networked computer systems can have unpredictable effects, including an unexpected backlash against the attacker himself. Another reason is related to the structure of the networks: it was noted during the Y2K prevention work that in most countries sensitive computer systems (air safety, banking or financial networks) are generally managed independently of the large computer networks[670] .

This is not to minimise the risk of cyber warfare, but to put it in perspective. During the Y2K rollover, the American imaging satellites were inoperative for three days: the computers designed to decipher the signals from the radar and optical satellites at Fort Belvoir (Virginia) were no longer working, and the signals had to be relayed to the White Sands Missile Range (Minnesota) to be deciphered manually. The reason for this incident was not the «bug», but the «patch» applied to the software which was not adapted[671] ! Terrorist threats in cyberspace cannot be ignored. However, as with superterrorism, it must be remembered that terrorism is doomed to «success», which is why terrorists limit themselves to applying simple methods that work. Action in cyberspace, while tempting, is very random and its effects are not nearly as emotionally charged as more «traditional» attacks.

3.3.4.6. *Controlling the content of information*

Information content management is the ability to manage the adequacy of information in relation to the objectives of the forces involved. It has an essentially qualitative role. It presupposes as a prerequisite the control of information vectors and the guarantee of a communication offering a minimum of distortions due to technology. It implies the permanent maintenance of two-way information flows between the censor and the user.

3.3.4.6.1. Censorship

From this imperative of trust, it follows that a relationship of partnership must be established with the media, in order to manage the dissemination of 'critical' information, while avoiding falling into a system of censorship - or propaganda - contrary to the principles of a democratic society. This can only be done on the basis of a «*gentlemen's agreement*» which is the result of a common will and transparency acceptable to all partners.

In Anglo-Saxon countries, cooperation between the state and the media in cases of crisis, terrorism or security is institutionalised and generally accepted. In Great Britain, the D-Notice system is a system of self-censorship of the press, in force since 1912. The D-Notice is only advisory and informative. It informs the recipient that a given subject may be covered by the *Official Secrets Act* - which has the force of law - but there is no formal link between them. It takes the form of a letter of request, addressed confidentially to the print, broadcast and audio-visual media, asking them

---

670. The «Y2K bug» gave a distorted picture of the risks. It was indeed a risk that could affect the entire computer population, but independently of the networks.
671. Stone Martin, "Satellites Blinded By Y2K Bug", Daily News, Newsbytes, 14 January 2000.

318

to consider a given subject as being of particular importance to the security of the state and not to publish anything about it. In 1982, *D-Notices* covered eight areas deemed sensitive. In August 1993, their number was reduced to five and they were renamed «DA-Notices». In 2015, they were redefined and renamed DSMA-Notices:

Evolution of D-Notices in Great Britain

	D-Notice (1982)	DA-Notice (1993)	DSMA-Notice (2017)
1	Defence planning, operational capabilities, military training	Military operations, planning and capabilities	Military operations, plans and capabilities
2	Defence equipment	Nuclear and non-nuclear equipment and weaponry	Nuclear and non-nuclear weapons systems and equipment
3	Nuclear weapons and equipment	Protected numbers and communications	Military counter-terrorism forces, special forces and intelligence agency operations, activities, methods and communication techniques
4	Transmissions and radars	Sensitive facilities and personal addresses	Property and physical assets
5	Cryptography and data transmission	UK Intelligence and Special Forces	Staff in sensitive positions and their families
6	British intelligence and security services		
7	Defence preparations and infrastructure		
8	Photos and images of military installations		

Table 20 - D-Notice is a way of involving the media in the fight against terrorism. In Britain, it has evolved in response to the nature of the threats.

Since 1988, the Home Office[672] has also had a comprehensive legal arsenal - including the *Official Secrets Act* and the *Prevention of Terrorism Act* and others - to prevent the publication of the activities of Irish activists or even legal political parties such as Sinn Féin, without reference to Parliament.

In Israel, the military censor *(Ha'tzenzura Ha'tzva'it)*, which is subordinate to the military intelligence services, has extensive powers to ban the publication of information that could affect national security, although its zeal has been relaxed in recent years.

All these systems of media cooperation or control are primarily aimed at cases where state security is involved, not at manipulation of minds in the sense

---

672. UK Home Office.

of propaganda or disinformation, although the distinction is often blurred. In Israel, for example, press access to troubled areas is restricted both for security reasons (for journalists) and because the presence of journalists tends to encourage violence. It is a fact that the presence of visual media often stimulates bold, demonstrative and violent behaviour, and gives combatants the opportunity to valorise themselves or dramatise a situation. On the other hand, keeping the press at bay also keeps certain methods of the security forces hidden, such as the systematic elimination of protest leaders by snipers[673] .

With the development of social networks, other mechanisms of influence have developed. The networks themselves have been forced by Western governments to impose censorship. This censorship basically concerns hate speech and incitement to violence, but by extension it also concerns divergent political opinions (then considered potentially violent). The most caricatural example was the closure of Donald Trump's Twitter account on 8 January 2021, after the Capitol Hill incident, which was considered to be 'domestic terrorism' and used for political purposes. One could also mention the suspension of Instagram accounts favourable to General Soleimani, after his elimination, in January 2020[674] .

In an increasingly superficial society, the deletion of messages that support Iran, Hezbollah, the Palestinians, the Muslim Brotherhood, Russia, China, etc., and that criticise Israel[675] may seem legitimate. In fact, it ignores the fact that social networks also play a role as an outlet. Therefore, censorship closes this option and pushes for 'physical' action, as we saw in the chapter on cyberwarfare.

That said, it is clear that the inability of the security and counter-terrorism services to counter terrorism is largely due to the perception conveyed by the media and 'experts'. An effective tool would be to make the media and other agencies that theorise about terrorism accountable for the poor quality of the information they transmit, which becomes the basis for thinking about the fight against radicalisation.

3.3.4.7. Protection of information

With the spread of networked computer communication and control systems, knowledge protection has become an issue for governments and armed forces, but also for companies and individuals. It includes a whole arsenal of means ranging from individual discipline (which is largely underestimated) to network

---

673. Maj Eugene Sockut, "License To Kill", Defence Update, n° 89, p. 50-53.
674. Jeffery Martin, "Instagram Censoring the Accounts of Farsi Media Outlets and Iranian Influencers, International Federation of Journalists Says", Newsweek, 10 January 2020; Chris Mills Rodrigo, "Instagram takes heat for removing pro-Soleimani content", The Hill, 16 January 2020.
675. Sam Biddle, "Facebook's Secret Rules About the Word 'Zionist' Impede Criticism of Israel", The Intercept, 14 May 2021.

hardening, which we will not deal with here. One of the central elements of this protection is cryptology, the science of encrypting information. Access to and control of this technology is therefore also an issue. Cryptology is one of those technologies that were once reserved for the strategic level but are now accessible to all. It can certainly be used by terrorists or criminal organisations, but by protecting the information of honest citizens or companies, it contributes to the consolidation of a liberal and free society.

Since the mid-1970s, cryptographic technology, which had changed little since the Second World War, has exploded. Paradoxically, it was not the main stakeholders, the intelligence agencies, who were the promoters of this explosion. Military systems based on maintaining secrets did not include mechanisms for exploiting feedback and remained static. The new cryptological systems of civilian and academic origin are developed in a dynamic context. For example, the RSA algorithm, invented in the United States in 1977, had already been invented a few years earlier by the British GCHQ, but the latter had preferred not to file a patent in order to maintain the secrecy surrounding its invention. In fact, GCHQ was looking for a method to disseminate encryption keys for a new tactical military communication system, while the three inventors of the RSA algorithm had already foreseen the civilian possibilities of their encryption system in an open communication world.

The evolution of cryptology involves a series of challenges for the intelligence services. First of all, it is a question of mastering the technology of cryptology itself, which does not tolerate second best. It is constantly evolving and requires a permanent adaptation of the research and development apparatus, both for the development of new encryption techniques and for new decryption capabilities. Added to this is the capacity to absorb the information gathered. The development of an information acquisition capacity must be accompanied by a calculation capacity (cryptanalysis), but also - and this is essential - by an analysis capacity. Finally, it is a question of ensuring knowledge management that enables threats to be dealt with transnationally and universally, while preserving the integrity, personality, privacy and dignity of honest people.

Intelligence services have an ambiguous relationship with modern cryptology. In the United States, it is often noted that cryptology is used by the «*Four Horsemen of the Infocalypse*», which are traffickers of all kinds, terrorists, organised crime and paedophile networks. The intelligence services therefore often express unease about a technology that is constantly evolving. Whether it is the setting up of a third-party guarantor system for encryption keys or the export of encryption software, the various mechanisms often provoke strong reactions from the public and the political world.

In 1993, in order to be able to monitor the communications of criminal, terrorist and other organisations, the US attempted to introduce an encryption processor that would have been used as standard (initially mandatory) in all mobile phones, with the encryption key held by the National Security Agency (NSA). The system was eventually abandoned under pressure from civil liberties groups. The following year, the United States introduced the *Communications Assistance for Law Enforcement Act* (CALEA), which obliges ISPs and telecommunications companies to provide law enforcement agencies with a technical capability to intercept communications. At the same time, the NSA initiated a «third-party guarantor» programme to collect encryption keys for surveillance purposes.

Of course, cryptology also protects terrorist movements, as well as the privacy, intimacy and property of individuals and companies. This is, for example, the case of the cryptographic technology integrated in the GSM system of mobile phones or in computer data protection software. Many legends have overstated the importance of this technology, such as the report that the 9/11 terrorists communicated by hiding their information in pornographic images using steganography and then sending them by email or through the Usenet network[676].In fact, this information, which was given by the *New York Times* in October 2001, has never been proven...

3.3.5. Special operations

Special operations have become one of the pillars of the fight against terrorism, developed during the Cold War to fight wars of liberation.

The US special operations system is perhaps the most comprehensive. They can be 'overt' or 'acknowledged', for example in the context of military operations (e.g., conducting air strikes, damage assessment, etc.). They can also be 'covert' in order to 'influence political, economic, or military conditions abroad, where it is desired that the role of the US government not be apparent or publicly acknowledged'[677] or 'clandestine', where the very existence of the operation is not acknowledged. Covert or clandestine operations can be undertaken under two conditions: the existence of a written «presidential *finding*» establishing the national security significance of the operation, and notification to the Congressional intelligence committees «at the *earliest* possible *time*»[678].It should be noted, however, that these steps are not required when the United States is at war or when a deployment of US forces is planned in a given region. The notion of a 'war on terror' is not simply seen here as a figurative expression, but as a real strategic condition, which justifies a commitment[679] .

---

676. Steganography is the technique of hiding information, in particular by «embedding» it in a digital image.
677. Intelligence Authorization Act 1991.
678. Ibid.
679. Jennifer D. Kibbe, "The Rise of the Shadow Warriors", Foreign Affairs, March/April 2004.

Summary typology of special operations (US)

		Action	
		Recognised	Not recognised
Author or beneficiary Not declared	Declared	Open operation (overt operation) (Example: engagement in a multinational operation, etc.).	Clandestine operation (clandestine operation) (Example: espionage, strategic reconnaissance, etc.)
	Discreet operation (covert operation) (Example: influence operations)	Covert operation (Black operation) (Example: murders, terrorist attacks, drug trafficking, etc.)	

Table 21 - Categorisation of special operations in the US nomenclature, which is probably the most comprehensive.

One difficulty with clandestine action is mainly its clandestine nature, which tends to take it away from strategic coherence. This is particularly a problem when the intelligence bodies are also the ones carrying out the action. In a situation where the same actor is responsible for analysing the situation and responding to it, the producer tends to be the consumer, and there is a great risk that the action becomes an end in itself.

This is the result of a situation inherited from the Second World War, when the clandestine action of the Resistance was very largely associated with intelligence work and thus had a meaning. Today, this type of mechanism tends to be counter-productive. This can be seen in post-Gaddafi Libya, where clandestine action collides with political coherence[680] or in the Sahel. The example of the CIA's torture programme shows that the intelligence system tends to operate in a closed circuit to the detriment of a holistic approach to solutions.

Special forces are forces that are specially trained and equipped to perform a broad spectrum of missions outside the capabilities of «conventional» military forces. The very concept of special forces and their engagement varies considerably from country to country. Moreover, the term 'special forces' itself is used for all kinds of military or police forces, but does not always cover identical capabilities. It (too) often refers to intervention troops capable of eliminating terrorists quickly and with minimal collateral damage.

For example, in 2002, in the hysteria following 9/11, several European countries sent their anti-terrorist units to Afghanistan in support of Operation ENDURING FREEDOM. It was an «anti-terrorist» operation, so these countries

---

680. Jean Guisnel, «Trois militaires français tués en Libye», lepoint.fr, 27 July 2016.

sent «anti-terrorist» units. However, the German KSK or Polish GROM units, for example, are intervention units designed to respond to a specific, one-off situation (hostage rescue, neutralisation of a terrorist, etc.) and not formations intended for prolonged operations; they quickly found themselves totally out of step with the needs of Operation[681] , and had to be repatriated.

The lack of a robust anchoring of special forces in a holistic counter-terrorism doctrine often contributes to the problem. In fact, most European countries have units to intervene against terrorists, but no clear concept of how to combat terrorism.

In many countries, for example, special forces are used to protect public figures. As the commander of the British Royal Family's bodyguards pointed out, a special forces fighter is trained to survive and kill, whereas a bodyguard is trained to protect, even at the cost of his or her own life: the psychic preparation is diametrically opposed.

After the Second World War, with the increase in insurgent conflicts related to decolonization, 'special forces', initially created to organize and support resistance movements in Europe in the event of a Soviet invasion, were used to operate in enemy zones. They were transformed from 'resistance' to 'antiresistance'.

In Vietnam, contrary to what the *Rambo* films of the 1980s suggest, US Special Forces (SF) (also known as 'Green Berets') were responsible for supporting local populations in Viet Cong-controlled areas: training fighters, coordinating propaganda campaigns in rural areas, advising peasants on irrigation and cultivation, and organising educational facilities for children, all with the aim of empowering villagers. This ability to create loyalty and support for the government in enemy territory was remarkably effective.

Today, some of these tasks, such as the *Provincial Reconstruction Teams (PRT)* concept in Afghanistan, have been handed over to NGOs with very limited success. As for the SFs, they are used as commandos to eliminate individuals with precision rifles or laser-guided weapons. Spectacular, but totally ineffective in the fight against jihadist terrorism.

In fact, Western special forces have gradually adopted an Israeli model. Israeli special forces have acquired a solid and well-deserved reputation for daring, creativity and efficiency. They are essentially composed of reconnaissance units (*sayeret*), which have gradually become specialized for specific tasks. Generally speaking, Israel's strategy is anti-terrorist in nature: it is more «pre-emptive» than «preventive» and favours violent action. This is largely the reason why Israel has never succeeded in eradicating terrorism.

Its special units have distinguished themselves in spectacular operations, but exclusively focused on the fight against terrorism:

---

681. «Wunderwaffe ohne Ziel", Spiegel Special, 2/2004, p. 112.

324

- The most famous - and prestigious - special forces unit is the *Sayeret Mat'kal* (*Unit 269*) subordinated to the Israeli General Staff[682].Its most spectacular operation was undoubtedly the liberation of the hostages held in Entebbe, Uganda, in July 1976 (Operation THUNDERBOLT).

- The *Sayeret Egoz* (*Unit 621*) was created in 1956 and disbanded after the Sinai War. It was reconstituted in 1963 to monitor the border with Syria. In 1985, after the partial withdrawal of Tsahal from Lebanon, the *Sayeret Egoz* was engaged against Hezbollah in a *Terrorist Killing Zone*[683] several kilometres wide. Disbanded once again, it was reactivated in 1995 and reinforced by personnel from *Sayeret Shimshon* to conduct raids against Hezbollah.

- In the occupied territories, Israel uses the «*mista'aravim*». These are *ad hoc* units that operate clandestinely, to carry out reconnaissance, intelligence gathering or «direct action» missions. Their personnel comes from other reconnaissance units, such as the *Sayeret Duvdevan* (*Unit 217*) (for the West Bank), the *Sayeret Shimshon* (*Unit 367*) (for the Gaza Strip, but deactivated in 1994, following the Oslo agreements)[684] , the Yamas (*Yehidat HaMista'arvim*) border guard unit (under the command of the SHABAK Security Service and operating in the West Bank, Gaza and Jerusalem) and the *Gideonim* police unit (operating in Jerusalem). In early December 2002, the Palestinian security services uncovered and arrested members of a cell set up by the Israeli intelligence services and acting as an «Al Qaeda» cell[685].

This clandestine system is completed by airborne means dedicated to the elimination of terrorist leaders («extrajudicial executions»): precision air-to-ground missiles, guided by laser or GPS. The designation of the targets is ensured by the *Sayeret Shaldag (Unit 5101)* of the air force, which had already operated during the first Intifada (1986-1987). On 16 February 1992, it was a commando of the Sayeret Shaldag that designated the car of Abbas Moussaoui, Hezbollah's secretary general, to the missiles of the AH-64A Apache attack helicopters.

The Special Forces frequently work in cooperation with the Mossad's *special operations division, Metsada*, which has a special unit dedicated to elimination operations, *Kidon*. In 1997, it was Metsada agents who tried to eliminate Khalef Mashal, the political leader of Hamas, in Jordan. It was also the Metsada that carried out the car bombing of Izzedine Sheikh Khalil, considered to be the head of Hamas' external military wing, in Damascus on 26 September 2004.

---

682. Hence its name, derived from «Mate Klali» (General Staff).
683. «Terrorist Elimination Zone».
684. It seems that a new clandestine unit was set up in 2001, subordinated to the Southern Command of the Israeli armed forces and composed of reservists from the Sayarot Duvdevan and Shimshon.
685. Middle East Online, 7 December 2002.

Israeli SF is a tool for eliminating terrorists, but not terrorism. Thus, despite spectacular immediate successes, they have been unable to solve the problem due to ill-conceived, doctrinaire and inadequate strategies.

3.3.6. Negotiation and concessions

On 17 December 2017, in the debate on the possible return of jihadist fighters to Belgium after the defeat of the EI, the Belgian Prime Minister, Charles Michel, declared: 'There is *no negotiation possible with such* people'[686].In fact, attributing to Islamists the will to destroy «*what we* are»[687] excludes from the outset any negotiation with terrorists. This intransigence is deeply rooted in the mentality of Europe and Israel, but it masks a lack of strategy to respond to the problem.

Indeed, it is easy to understand that, with the exception of resistance to an occupation, terrorism is an expression of «dictatorship from below», through which a minority tries to impose a decision on the majority. On the other hand, refusing to negotiate under pressure is a perfectly legitimate principle in any situation. On the other hand, collaborating with terrorist groups is not a problem of values or morality for Western countries, since they do not hesitate to do so (discreetly): in Libya with the *Islamic Group fighting in Libya*, in Syria with phalanxes associated with *Jabhat al-Nosra* and the Islamic State, in Iran with Modjahedin e-Khalq or in Palestine where Israel finances *Hamas*, which it is also fighting[688] ...

In fact, the problem often comes from a poorly posed problem, because we generally start talking about negotiation when we are already in a situation of failure. Thus, we start fighting terrorism *after we* have let it hatch and *after* we have let it take the initiative, when we are already in a process of violence. It is too late. We have this situation in the Sahel, with operation BARKHANE.

3.3.6.1. *The terrorist group and its centre of gravity*

The first problem is to understand the nature of the terrorist group, its centre of gravity and its objectives. For example, jihadist groups do not generally commit terrorist acts to free co-religionists or to demand money: this would be contrary to their operational doctrine. In the few cases where such demands

---

686. «Charles Michel: «There is no negotiation possible with Belgian EI fighters»», rtbf.be, 17 December 2017.

687. Frédéric Encel, programme C dans l'air, France 5, 23 August 2018.

688. Robert Dreyfuss, Devil's Game - How the United States Helped Unleash Fundamentalist Islam, New York, 2005, ISBN: 0-8050-8137-2, p. 169; Richard Sale, 'Hamas history tied to Israel', UPI, 18 June 2002; Lahav Harkov, 'Netanyahu: Money to Hamas part of strategy to keep Palestinians divided', Jerusalem Post, 12 March 2019.

326

have been made, armed gangs have been draped in jihadism in order to be more credible.

In most cases, jihadist terrorist groups do not seek negotiations. This is true of the Islamic State, whose attacks are not intended to push a government to negotiate, but to push the population to demand the withdrawal of its armed forces from the theatre of operations (following the model of Spain in 2004).

3.3.6.2 Identification of the nature of the terrorist targets

It is essential to distinguish between terrorist actions that directly serve a strategic purpose (the final objective of the terrorist movement) and peripheral actions, whose objective is purely instrumental. For example, hostage-taking to free imprisoned fighters or to obtain a ransom often does not have a final, but a strictly capability-based role.

These objectives have a different value in terms of negotiations. Final or strategic objectives are the object of the struggle. They therefore have a known dimension, are 'unique', and vary very little (land reform, repeat votes, withdrawal of a law, withdrawal of troops, political autonomy, etc.). Experience shows that these objectives are often negotiable before the violent action. Indeed, if the objective is generally expressed very clearly, the modalities to reach it are often much less so. This vagueness can sometimes indirectly offer a great deal of room for negotiation on the very nature of the objective, on its modalities or the timetable for its implementation.

This type of negotiation can be part of a *counter-terrorism* strategy, aimed at preventing the outbreak or development of violence. It must be based on an identification of breaking points, which allows the state to define its room for manoeuvre before a violent process is triggered. It is the role of the intelligence services to detect situations that require 'letting go' (if necessary) before the pressure of conflict is applied.

On the other hand, for tactical objectives of a capability nature, which are the result of opportunities and can be repeated (hostage-taking for the release of comrades, means of financing, etc.), the concessions made are risky, as they can constitute a «call for air» for other terrorist actions.

The Spanish withdrawal from Iraq just after the Madrid bombing («11-M») in March 2004 is an interesting case study that has different impacts at the strategic and tactical levels. At the strategic level, the withdrawal kept Spain out of terrorism thereafter. In fact, Spaniards had always been opposed to involvement in Iraq, and it was the government's response to the attack that led to its overthrow, and to the resetting of a failed and corrupt foreign policy. So the attack was only a minor factor in the decision making. But the jihadists interpreted it as a success and it became a model for the London bombings the following year. The problem in this case was the failure of British intelligence to understand that they were in exactly the same strategic situation, and thus to take action that could have 'short-circuited' the terrorists' decision. France and its services will make exactly the same mistake ten years later, by taking the decision to intervene in Syria and Iraq in a totally illegal context - when nothing forced them to do so - despite the warnings of the Islamists.

We will not go so far as to claim, as some American authors do, that the EI is not terrorist[689] : an organisation - or a state - that uses the method of terrorism is terrorist. But, as with 'Al Qaeda' previously, the EI is in the situation of a resistance organisation. It is therefore up to the intervening powers to reflect on the justification for their presence: all Westerners were involved in the Middle East before the emergence of the EI, with the sole aim of calming a situation that they themselves had triggered in the early 2000s (in the early 1990s for «Al-Qaeda»).

As can be seen in Afghanistan, where the war is now clearly understood to have been totally unnecessary, our motives are not existential, but opportunistic and political. Therefore, unlike the situations in the 1960s and 1980s, there is a potential for accommodation.

But this aspect is rarely identified by intelligence services, which devote too much energy to «making history» rather than identifying the future. In all cases where there is a need to respond to terrorists, intelligence services have failed to do so... or have knowingly facilitated destabilisation.

3.3.7. The problem of returnees

A strict application of the principle of non-negotiation leads to inconsistencies and tends to prevent individuals from leaving a terrorist environment if they wanted to. Thus, the very idea of using repentant individuals becomes a legal problem, stemming from the fact that the legitimacy of a fight is denied from the start. So-called «*hearts and minds*» operations aim to «turn around» the confidence of a terrorist group's sympathisers on the one hand, but also the militants themselves. Intransigence thus runs counter to operational strategies and pushes militants to extreme behaviour. The phenomenon is very clear with the end of the EI, instead of finding a way to get the fighters back and show them the futility of their fight, they are pushed to continue the jihad under other banners[690].

Firstly, we need to have a clear idea of what a terrorist is. It is certainly convenient to define as such all those who are in contact with violent individuals, but often such a designation is purely emotional and satisfies the imperatives of revenge for a

---

689. Audrey Kurth Cronin, "ISIS Is Not a Terrorist Group", Foreign Affairs, March/April 2015.
690. Andrew Illingworth, "Breaking: Defunct ISIS affiliate militia in northwest Syria re-brands itself to become more 'moderate'", AMN, 13 March 2018.

situation that one has not been able to control earlier. Is a young girl who went to Syria to follow her friend *ipso facto* a terrorist? If she has contributed materially to violent actions, the answer is clear, but if it is only love for a man or even sympathy for a cause, it is less so.

3.4. Counter-terrorism - Preventive action

The victorious warrior wins the battle, then goes to war. The defeated warrior goes to war, then seeks to win the battle.

(Sun Tsu)

Counter-terrorism consists of all measures aimed at combating terrorism *before the* terrorist decision is taken. In other words, it includes all measures and actions that should influence and prevent individuals (or groups of individuals) from *wanting to* engage in violence. In counter-terrorism, the initiative lies with the state.

It is not a question of granting the opponent everything he or she claims, but of 'cutting the ground from under his or her feet' so that any calls for violence do not have a 'hold'. For example, in France, for electoral and clientelistic reasons, the cultural links between the immigrant population and the Muslim world have been underestimated. In 2014, for example, no accompanying measures were taken before intervening in the Middle East to explain and prevent the 'radicalisation' of sympathisers on national soil. In Russia, the government took preventive measures *before* intervening in Syria.

It is therefore not only a question of preventing the terrorist from *carrying out* an action that he has *already* decided to take (pre-emptive action), but of influencing his will so that he does *not decide to* engage in violence.

When viewed as part of a comprehensive strategy, counter-terrorism is the true offensive dimension of the fight against terrorism, even if, paradoxically, it requires less force. It includes: a) all political measures (including influencing actions) aimed at preventing the outbreak of terrorist violence; b) operational measures aimed at fighting terrorism at its core (infiltration of movements, preventive eliminations, etc.).

Counter-terrorism requires a thorough understanding of the terrorist movement, its strategy and doctrine of action, its legitimisation mechanisms, its popular roots and its local and international political support. This understanding must be the result of an unprejudiced analysis, which allows policy options to be identified, based on the opponent's centre of gravity. This is the most effective part of the fight against terrorism, if used judiciously.

For example, the *Charlie Hebdo* attack was explicitly committed in the name of 'Al Qaeda'. But, for political reasons, it was attributed to the EI. As we saw with the mobilisation of 11 January 2015, through poorly thought-out communication, France thus established the legitimacy of the EI as the true bearer of Islamist demands. This phenomenon was concretised by the influx of foreign fighters in Syria, who massively went to the EI, whereas it affected all Syrian jihadist movements until then.

3.4.1. The role of intelligence

In 2002, George Tenet, Director General of the U.S. Central Intelligence Agency, said:

> *[The role of intelligence] is not to observe and comment, but to warn and protect.*[691]

In counter-terrorism, the problem of strategic intelligence is not to identify terrorists, but to understand their doctrine and strategy in order to anticipate the likely consequences of policy decisions before they are taken.

Today, virtually no Western intelligence service is capable of this work. As we have seen, while the timing and location of the attacks in France and Belgium in 2015-2016 could not be anticipated, the wave of terrorism generated by the interventions of both countries was perfectly predictable. Since 1995, we have known that our military interventions are a primary cause of jihadist action. At the very least, we could have expected that measures to protect the population would have been taken to accompany the decision to participate in the Western coalition in Iraq and Syria. But this was not done. Worse, the absence of measures to protect the population before the attacks was superimposed on campaigns that only served to warm up the community spirit at the same time. The Dieudonné affair, the burkini and the endless Islamic veil have demonstrated the inability of the services - and the political authorities - to anticipate and manage the threat from a strategic angle.

Russia has taken into account the mistakes of the French and Belgian governments: before engaging in Syria, the security services conducted actions in jihadist circles and strengthened domestic protection measures in order to minimise the effects of its future intervention. It should be noted, however, that

---

691. Cynthia M. Grabo, Anticipating Surprise: Analysis for Strategic Warning, Defense Intelligence Agency, Washington DC, December 2002.

public support for the government in Russia is considerably higher than in many Western countries.

Terrorism is not the result of chance and does not appear «by spontaneous generation». Whether the problem is societal, social, economic, political or even religious in origin, terrorism is part of a process. Even before violence erupts, there are usually warning signs of discontent. The task of strategic intelligence is to answer the question: how can the process of violence be controlled and what are the elements that can influence its development in one direction or another?

In France, the process of radicalisation, which marks the turning point of an individual into a radical, has been combated in a police manner by emphasising the way in which the turning point occurs and not the reasons that provoke it. This has left us with simplistic schemes based on religion[692] , whereas Islamic terrorists do not have any particular 'religiosity'. In the case of terrorism that has affected the West for a quarter of a century, our military interventions constitute this external phenomenon and form the basis of the radicalisation phenomenon by exacerbating the feeling that they are guided by a desire to subjugate the Muslim world.

While in Anglo-Saxon countries the confusion between 'Islam' and 'Islamism' remains confined to certain extremist circles, in France this debate spills over into the public and political debate. It is fuelled by certain agencies, experts and other journalists who have set themselves the objective of fuelling communitarianism.

In the United States, the idea of using artificial intelligence (AI) to anticipate terrorist decisions is an old dream. Advances in intelligent systems, particularly in the field of crime prevention, offer hope for results. Indeed, it is now possible to anticipate the behaviour of burglars and their likely area of action at a given moment. The results are relatively good and make it possible to act as a deterrent, but they must be qualified: a burglar behaves symmetrically and his risk is a linear function of the expected gain.

Such technology will only be effective against terrorists if their logic is correctly reflected in the system's algorithms. However, in the case of jihadist terrorism, on the one hand, the relationship between risk and reward is not linear and, on the other hand, the notion of reward is very different from Western logic, as we have seen. Clearly, until we understand the true asymmetric nature of terrorism, AI systems, no matter how sophisticated, will be of no help in preventing terrorism.

3.4.2. Political integrity

The first and probably most difficult condition for tackling the issue of jihadist terrorism is the intellectual and moral integrity of our political *establishments*, on which the legitimacy of action depends. Analysis of the decision-making

---

692. Antoine Hasday, «La pensée djihadiste décryptée», slate.fr, 6 November 2017.

processes that led to Western interventions in Afghanistan and the Middle East shows deep weaknesses in Western executives.

The question here is whether interventions abroad or participation in international coalitions are consistent with real national interests. The controversial election of George W. Bush and his inability to lead the state in 2001-2002, Nicolas Sarkozy's drop in the polls in 2011, before the 2012 presidential election, the fall in popularity of the Hollande government in 2012, the fall in political support for Theresa May at the end of 2017 are some of the examples where leaders, in difficulty at home, have sought to 'restore' their image through a more aggressive foreign policy.

The problem is not new, but it is attributed to dictatorships, whereas it is democracies that are most vulnerable to it. Much more than dictators, politicians in democracies are 'slaves' to the image they project. This leads to the temptation to exaggerate external threats, or even to cover up wrongdoing. It is the role of parliaments to monitor these deviations... but parliamentarians generally do not assume their role, and the population accepts *de facto* the lies of their leaders.

As the jihadists note, the French population willingly takes to the streets to refuse a change in labour law[693] , but does not react when it comes to starting a war or violating international law. For example, President Hollande's admission that he violated the EU embargo to supply arms to Syrian rebels, and thus militarised the situation, was not publicly debated in France. This is why the jihadists do not see the civilian population as 'innocent'.

It is noticeable that Italy, a democratic and deeply Christian country, home to the seat of Christendom, where significant criminality thrives, where the influx of refugees has stimulated racist behaviour and which is active in the Middle East with international coalitions, has been considerably less affected by terrorism than France, whose values it shares. The difference is that in France, interventions in Libya and the Middle East have been celebrated in a noisy and demonstrative manner. At the same time, pseudo-intellectuals such as Bernard-Henri Lévy, Alain Finkielkraut[694] and others served up absurd theories about Islamism and its objectives, suggesting that French policy was dictated by Jews[695]. The conditions were thus created for the unpopularity of the government to add up to «anti-French» feelings, and then to antisemitism, even though it was not - a priori - an issue in these conflicts.

---

693. See note 470.
694. Alain Finkielkraut, in the program C à vous («Finkielkraut face aux terroristes - C à vous - 23/11/2015», France 5/YouTube, 23 November 2015) (03'20"), http://www.lepoint.fr/societe/finkielkraut-le-djihad-est-une-obligation-leguee-par-mahomet-a-tous-les-musulmans-11-12-2015-1989225_23.php.
695. «Libya: BHL is committed «as a Jew»», lefigaro.fr, 20 November 2011.

The main objective of jihadist terrorism is to show that it does not give up the fight. It is therefore important to avoid giving it an opportunity to «have the last word». To this end, political action must be as discreet as possible: both successes and failures must remain modest. We have done exactly the opposite...

3.4.3. Foreign policy as a strategic weapon

3.4.3.1. Coping with the effects of globalisation

The *EU Counter-Terrorism Strategy*[696] refers to the issue of globalisation in the context of terrorism prevention, but limits itself to its tactical aspects (ease of transport, communications and travel, etc.) without drawing any conclusions of a preventive nature. It illustrates the Western failure to identify the mechanisms that guide the emergence and persistence of terrorism.

In the West, industrial and economic development has taken place in harmony with the evolution of society and its culture. Since the 16th century[e] , urbanisation, scientific discoveries and the integration of technology into the life of society have been processes that have been «synchronised» with the evolution of minds. Thus, the decline in the role of religion, the size of families, social progress, the place of women in society, etc., have been interrelated processes that have caused society to evolve in a certain coherence specific to each country.

Globalisation is a continuation of this development and of Western economic dynamism. Its ambition is undoubtedly economic, but it is also intended to bring prosperity - and the well-being that goes with it - to the rest of the world. Under this label, with the help of new technologies, Western society is now more than ever infiltrating societies with different histories, shaking up their foundations and local cultures. Good or bad, the phenomenon seems unavoidable and the question is how to manage it in a coherent way.

Just as in the past our missionaries went to bring the 'good word' of civilisation to the Third World, globalisation today wants to bring free markets, good governance and human rights. The motivation is noble, but it must be expressed with tact and respect. It is the temptation to want to change traditional societies that has led to identity-based outbursts, the rise of fundamentalisms and terrorism.

The «clash of civilisations», predicted by Samuel Huntington[697] , is not a doctrine - as it is often presented - but an observation: societies that lived relatively far from the West found themselves, as a result of globalisation, in sudden contact with societal, economic, social or legal norms for which they were not

---

696. European Union Counter-Terrorism Strategy, Council of the European Union, 30 November 2005.
697. Samuel Huntington, The Clash of Civilizations and the Remaking of World Order, Simon & Schuster, 1996 (in France: Le Choc des civilisations, éditions Odile Jacob, 1997).

prepared. Huntington foresaw that the rapid expansion of Western influence in culture, economic exchange, law, etc. (mainly through the Internet, but not only) would 'saturate' traditional institutions and provoke violent reactions. Blinded by the wisdom of its approach, the West embarked on the globalisation process without taking any precautions. The Middle East is the loudest example of this.

In most disadvantaged countries, development continues to be imposed from outside and is not the result of a 'harmonious' development of society. Decolonisation began with a revolutionary dynamic serving the foreign policy interests of the USSR, and then continued with a kind of humanitarian utopia focused on material well-being and not on the evolution of minds. The acceleration of democratic or economic processes in the Third World often gives the illusion of an outcome, but progress remains very superficial and poorly anchored in hearts and cultures. This is the case of South Sudan, whose independence from the Islamic government of Sudan had aroused a great deal of enthusiasm in the West. Countries with no expansionist agenda, such as Switzerland, were deeply involved in this process, but guided by an ideology that was resistant to security issues, they skewed the peace process and helped shape institutions that were totally unsuited to the nature of the country, thus contributing to its destabilisation. Simply put, the Sudanese government (anti-Christian, corrupt and brutal) was seen as the main, if not the only, source of destabilisation in the South. This was completely wrong. A potentially rich country, financially supported by the entire international community, South Sudan had already 'lost' $4 billion less than a year after its independence[698].The South Sudanese army, although trained in the laws of war by Swiss army officers, was guilty of countless war crimes[699] , simply because the nature of the power relations in the country was not understood, the training programmes did not take into account the structural specificities of the armed forces, and the instructors had no knowledge of local conditions.

The road to hell is paved with good intentions. It is the lack of understanding of cultures and the inadequacy of command structures and processes based on the Western model that have a multiplier effect on violence.

---

698. Hereward Holland, "South Sudan officials have stolen $4 billion: president", Reuters, 4 June 2012.

699. Annual report of the United Nations High Commissioner for Human Rights and reports of the Office of the High Commissioner and the Secretary-General, Assessment mission by the Office of the United Nations High Commissioner for Human Rights to improve human rights, accountability, reconciliation and capacity in South Sudan: detailed findings, Human Rights Council, 10 March 2016, http://www.ohchr.org/EN/HRBodies/HRC/RegularSessions/Session31/Documents/A-HRC-31-49_en.doc.

The weakness of the West is that the rule of law, democracy and human rights are strong enough values that we allow ourselves to deny them and impose them on others by force.

This way of thinking is particularly exacerbated in the United States. As a country of immigration, it has attracted (and continues to attract) those who voluntarily or under duress have abandoned other 'systems', and have thus been condemned to succeed in order to survive. Strongly influenced by Protestantism, American society has been built around the notions of 'success' and 'determinism'. From the individual level to the strategic level, control of events is encouraged and little room is left for fate, an image widely celebrated by American cinema. The slogan of a well-known American sports shoe brand perfectly symbolises the American mentality: «*Just do it!* In the United States, social welfare is more about opportunity than about achievement. Americans like to refer to their country as the «land *of* opportunities». Social equality is understood as equality of opportunity, not equality of status. The result is a society which, although not very egalitarian by European standards, is surprisingly stable, constantly striving for efficiency, and whose latent individualism is counterbalanced by a deep attachment to religion and country. This society, which seems so individualistic, so «heartless» and so harsh, is in fact the most generous society on the planet. The American people are the biggest contributors to mutual aid, charity and humanitarian work, but this aid - relayed on the ground by religiously based charitable organisations - frequently takes the form of proselytising.

The Western, mainly American, vision guiding globalisation has had - at least in its early stages - a quasi-messianic dimension, aiming to open up access to prosperity for all regions of the world through economic development and democracy. This 'market democracy' should reduce the growing gap between rich and poor countries, and ultimately reduce the potential for 'North-South' tensions. Paradoxically, left-wing ideologies and the most liberal capitalism tend to come together in this vision. Thus, prosperity and democracy would open the door to universal peace.

But the reality is more complex. With sometimes laudable intentions, and often guided by ignorance, Westerners attempt - with varying degrees of success - to eradicate ancestral practices and beliefs that they perceive as obstacles to the achievement of democracy and the universalisation of human rights. In doing so, however, they often create new imbalances and tensions within these societies.

In the absence of demands, attempts have been made to explain '9/11' by the unequal distribution of wealth in the world. We fit the causes of terrorism to our explanations, instead of fitting our explanations to the causes:

> *Poverty is the breeding ground for terrorism. Although the attacks of 11 September were carried out by wealthy intellectuals, one of the foundations*

This is totally false. There is no jealousy or need for prosperity in the emergence
of jihadism. Firstly, because Islamists have a rather fatalistic attitude towards the
human and social condition. ᶜAs in the Catholic religion, as it was practised until
the beginning of the 20th century, there is the idea that life is a trial that must
bring the individual closer to God. In the West, it was Marxism that 'liberated'
the individual from God and changed our relationship to religion in the second
half of the 20th centuryᶜ.Such an evolution has no real equivalent in Muslim
thought: believers do not really feel frustrated by their social situation. Religion
provides them with a form of resilience that can be found in all aspects of society.

Paradoxically, while the West saw in '9/11' the need to fight poverty and to
become more involved in the Third World, the Islamists want to tell us exactly
the opposite. They want to remain masters of their own development.

Our foreign policies are driven by a desire to do the right thing, but they
are guided more by a form of ideology than by listening to the real needs of the
people we want to help. Where we hear 'rule of law' and 'human rights', others
understand 'cultural imperialism' and loss of identity. The duty of «humanitarian interference» advocated by Bernard Kouchner[701] , which often motivates
our interventions, is unfortunately double-edged and must be put into practice
without missionary blindness, but with sensitivity and circumspection. However
noble our ideas may be, they cannot be imposed by force without generating
legitimate violence.

3.4.3.2. The importance of culture

Technological or social progress as envisaged in the West is often destabilising
in the Third World. Thus, while in the West the media are seen as vectors of
democracy through information, in many 'developing' countries television is
seen as an instrument of cultural and identity disintegration. Paraphrasing the
notion of *Weapons of* Mass *Destruction* (WMD), E. Anders Eriksson defines the

---

700. «How to fight terrorism effectively and sustainably», Groupe de recherche et d'information sur la
paix et la sécurité (GRIP), analysis note, Brussels, 27 September 2001.
701. The notion of the «right» or «duty of humanitarian interference» is attributed to Bernard Kouchner, a French politician and co-founder of Médecins Sans Frontières, and to Mario Bettati, a professor
of international public law at the University of Paris II in the late 1980s.

336

perception of television in some Central Asian countries as a *Weapons of Cultural Disruption* (WCD)[702].

Globalisation implies major cultural leaps that some societies are unable or unwilling to make. The evolution of societies is the result of a constantly renewed compromise between tradition and innovation. It is even this mixture, specific to each community, that creates diversity. However, the weight of tradition (in its historical, cultural and religious dimensions, etc.) differs from one society to another, and its 'speed of accession' to prosperity in the Western sense varies considerably. Thus, globalisation is often perceived as interference, if not aggression. Wanting others to reach our standard of living does not imply that they have to be 'like us'. This is the mistake the West made in Afghanistan.

By refusing - voluntarily or not - to listen to these messages, the West places itself in an asymmetrical situation. It is true that the situation of women under the Taliban regime, excision in certain African countries, child labour in South-East Asia and coca cultivation in Latin America rightly shock the Western mind. But we tend to forget that these phenomena are each part of a social, cultural or economic coherence that has been established over the centuries, just like an ecosystem. Occasional intervention upsets these balances, awakens consciousness and stimulates the identity reflex.

Thus, in an asymmetric Islamist context, humanitarian or human rights actions do not 'compensate' for our military actions, but are additional to them! This does not mean that our humanitarian actions should be abandoned, but that they should be designed in a more subtle way. On the one hand, it is a question of avoiding militant action that could be interpreted as provocative and, on the other hand, of avoiding - or better delimiting - the work done with religiously inspired charitable organisations. For example, the Swiss missionary Beatrice Stoeckli, kidnapped by *Ansar al-Dine* in Mali on 14 April 2012, was released on condition that she would not return to the country; but she returned, breaking the agreement, and was kidnapped again on 7 January 2016 and killed in 2020.

Too often, humanitarian action is aimed at satisfying ourselves and not the target populations. Our relationship with these cultures and civilisations needs to be rethought. We need to prioritise our aid efforts and limit ourselves to creating conditions that are favourable to their development rather than imposing them. The problem is that the management of interactions between Third World countries and the West is dispersed among many actors: governments, international organisations, private companies, non-governmental organisations (NGOs) and individuals. NGOs have become powerful, flexible and effective

---

702. E. Anders Eriksson, "Information Warfare: Hype or Reality?", The Nonproliferation Review, Spring/Summer 1999.

actors. On the other hand, driven by different and uncoordinated objectives, they often play a counterproductive role, especially in an asymmetric context:

> *Unintentionally, NGOs reinforce racist stereotypes and emphasise the successes, benefits and (loving and harsh) compassion of Western civilisation. They are the secular missionaries of the modern world.* [703]

... and this is further exacerbated by the considerable importance of American NGOs, often funded by churches and other religious communities, which are often a stimulus to jihad. NGOs such as *Worldvision*, which are ostensibly Christian and proselytising, are regularly targeted more than other international organisations.

The necessary dialogue with civil society - of which NGOs are a part - must be aimed at better coordinating international presence and action so that they can be integrated into a global policy, which also takes into account a counter-terrorism strategy. The former UN Secretary General Kofi Annan promoted the maxim:

> *There is no development without security, there is no security without development, and there can be neither security nor development if human rights are not respected.* [704]

The problem is far from trivial, as these three components can only be considered in different time frames. The mistake lies in our tendency to try to deal with them simultaneously.

3.4.3.3. Parallel diplomacy

Foreign policy plays an essential role in counter-terrorism, but diplomacy is not the only possible instrument. Intelligence services can make a valuable contribution here through *'second track diplomacy'*. The advantage of intelligence services is that they combine the credibility of a close relationship with the authorities, access to the actors of violence and the possibility of exploiting 'discreet' communication channels. They thus constitute a sort of 'back door' for communicating with an adversary. Moreover, this discretion allows them to hide possible failures or the granting of concessions that might be controversial.

A good example of parallel diplomacy is the links between the US CIA and the Palestinians. In late 1969, concerned about the security of the US embassy in

---

703. Arundhati Roy, «Les périls du tout-humanitaire», Le Monde diplomatique, October 2004, p. 24.
704. In larger freedom: towards development, security and human rights for all, Report of the Secretary-General, UN document A/59/2005, p. 6.

Beirut, President Richard Nixon asked the CIA to make contact with the PLO in order to recruit informants. The CIA quickly identified Ali Hassan Salameh (Abu Hassan), Yasser Arafat's right-hand man and later head of the PLO's *Jihaz al-Razd*[705] , as a potential informant, but only succeeded in «recruiting» him in 1974. At the beginning of the 1970s, the United States officially refused any contact with the Palestinian organisation, which was then qualified as terrorist. But the PLO was looking for respectability and Arafat exploited his clandestine contacts with the CIA. Thus, an agreement was made with the PLO not to attack American citizens in exchange for the lifting of the American ban on Arafat's access to American territory, which allowed him to attend the United Nations General Assembly and deliver his speech on 11 November 1974, which led the PLO on the road to legitimacy[706].Contact with Salameh was maintained without the knowledge of the Israelis, with the idea, on both sides, of starting a dialogue that could lead to a negotiation process. The elimination of Salameh on 22 January 1979 in Beirut by the Mossad, because of his participation in the attack against Israeli athletes at the Munich Olympic Games - a guilt that was known to the Americans - stopped the process.

It was not until the late 1980s that contact between the CIA and the PLO was renewed. In 1988, negotiations in Tunis led to the appointment of Amin Al-Hindi as liaison officer with the CIA. At this stage, however, the dialogue remained limited to the prevention of attacks against American nationals[707] .

After the signing of the Oslo Accords in 1993, the CIA was called upon by the Palestinian Authority to provide training for its security services. President Bill Clinton signed an «*intelligence finding*»[708] authorising the CIA to train and equip the Palestinian security services. The underlying idea was to strengthen the Palestinian Authority's counter-terrorism capabilities, and thus to reinforce it against extremist movements such as Hamas. The CIA assistance was led by Brigadier General Amin Al-Hindi. The cadres of the Palestinian security services (mainly the *'Amn al-Wiqa'i*[709] and the *Moukhabarat al-Ammah*[710]) were trained in information gathering techniques (electronic listening systems, night vision devices, photography, etc.).

This link between Americans and Palestinians will be particularly useful during the second Intifada. In 2002, when relations with Israel were at their

---

705. Fatah's Internal Security Service, which he headed between April and December 1973. Ali Hassan Salameh was also one of the instigators of the Black September operation at the 1972 Munich Olympic Games.
706. David Makovsky, "The Covert Channel Between CIA and PLO", Haaretz, 10 November 1998.
707. Rony Shaked, "Mr. Stanley's CIA sweets", Yediot Aharonot, 27 August 1999.
708. Presidential Directive for Intelligence.
709. Preventive Security Service.
710. General information.

lowest, Egyptian President Mubarak sent Major General Omar Suleiman[711] , director of the Egyptian *Mukhabarat al-Ammah, to* mediate between the Israeli and Palestinian authorities. From the beginning of the uprising, an important solidarity movement had developed in Egypt, which provided logistical and political support to the Palestinians. Working in close cooperation with the American CIA, the Egyptian services were a pivotal point in convincing the various Palestinian factions to engage in a negotiation process.

Two years later, after Ariel Sharon's decision to evacuate the Gaza Strip, the Egyptian services quickly imposed themselves as a key interlocutor to prevent Gaza from becoming a terrorist state. In June 2004, General Suleiman started negotiations with *Hamas* and *Islamic Jihad in* order to stop the *Qassam* rocket attacks against Israel and to set up a mechanism to prevent the development of violence in the Gaza Strip: the training of Palestinian Authority officers in Egypt, the confiscation of illegal weapons, the dismantling of Palestinian militias and an information campaign aimed at promoting the rule of law[712].Ariel Sharon's policy directed personally against Yasser Arafat will undermine these efforts.

3.4.3.4. Discontinue external interventions

As we have seen, jihadism is an expression of resistance against Western interference - military or otherwise - in the affairs of the Muslim world. Logic leads one to question the relevance of our participation in these interventions.

In doing so, it should be remembered that these conflicts were initiated by the United States and that the US continues to bear the vast majority of military operations. The reason they seek to form coalitions is clearly not to have additional capabilities: the contribution of the coalitionists to the overall war effort is very small. In Afghanistan, when Germany set up its own *Provincial Reconstruction Team* (PRT), it sought to have a Swiss 'contingent' of two officers to give credibility and a 'non-NATO' connotation to its presence in a previously unmilitarised area.

In fact, in this type of operation, multilateralism does not bring any obvious benefit, except that of diluting the terrorist response by offering a multiplicity of targets, and the Americans know this. As of early March 2016, French strikes accounted for 4.7 per cent and Belgian strikes for 1 per cent of the total number of strikes conducted by the international coalition in Iraq and Syria, while the

---

711. Major General Omar Suleiman had been leading the Mukhabarat al-Ammah since 1993. He gained unparalleled prestige with the Egyptian president in 1995, after advising him to take his armoured limousine during his trip to Ethiopia. President Mubarak was the target of an attempted Islamist attack in Addis Ababa and was saved by his limousine. General Suleiman is a privileged point of contact with the American administration.

712. Jerusalem Post, 23 June 2004.

United States had conducted 68.1 per cent[713].Yet France has 'attracted' the bulk of the Islamic State's attacks. The reason for this is twofold: a) France was 'loudly' engaged and b) the popularity of the Hollande government was very low, and the jihadists thought they could force public opinion to make him stop the strikes. Certainly, the terrorists underestimated the French people's lack of interest in their foreign policy, but the French government did just about everything it could to have attacks on the mainland.

This is why some countries (such as Sweden, Finland or Denmark) remain discreet about their participation in counter-terrorism operations in Iraq, Syria or the Sahel. Even if their impact on the ground is minimal, the risk of the country becoming a terrorist target is disproportionate. The cost/benefit of such participation (in an operation contrary to international law) is of little interest.

Conversely, when a country refuses to participate in an external operation, it must communicate this! In May 2021, in Belgium, Theo Francken, parliamentarian of the right-wing N-VA party, was sanctioned for having disclosed that Belgium would not participate in the BARKHANE mission in the Sahel[714]. Beyond the procedural problem (as he would have violated the rules of confidentiality), the fact of disseminating such information is likely to reduce the terrorist threat.

3.4.4. Domestic policy

3.4.4.1. Controlling immigration

Clearly, the large Muslim minorities in our countries have expectations of the authorities with regard to their policies in the Near and Middle East. The perception of biased, prejudiced actions motivated by fear of Islam reflects on the credibility of governments and their actual «secularism».

Broadly speaking, the issue of immigration covers three realities:

- The presence of a long-standing legal immigrant population from the 1950s-1970s, when our countries had a great need for low-skilled labour. In France, it comes mainly from the Maghreb, in Belgium from Morocco, in Germany from Turkey, in Great Britain from the Indian subcontinent, etc. This population is generally well integrated socially, economically and culturally. This population is generally well integrated socially, economically and culturally.

- A population that has entered illegally since the 1990s, and which - not surprisingly - tends to live on the margins of society. No one knows exactly how large it is. Not having the same access to work and services as other categories,

---

713. http://airwars.org/data/ (accessed on 6 March 2016).
714. «Theo Francken heavily sanctioned for a tweet published after a closed-door commission», 7sur7. be, 6 May 2021.

this population tends to group together and help each other in a form of parallel economy. This is the development model of the «mafias».

- Refugees in distress as a result of conflicts or natural disasters, hosted in our countries under international humanitarian law. Since 2014, they have mostly come from conflict zones, almost systematically created by Western interventions. The problem is not so much their reception as their management, because, in theory, they are only temporary guests and should return to their country of origin as soon as the situation is normalised. With one difficulty, however: those who flee the countries in which we are fighting wars are often... Islamists.

In discussions of immigration policy, the focus is usually on issues related to delinquency and crime and, more recently, terrorism. However, very little thought is given to the long-term impact of changing perceptions on international relations by a population that does not always share the same cultural references.

Paradoxically, the reluctance observed in most Western countries to manage migratory flows - often for political rather than humanitarian reasons - benefits mafia networks, whose action generates illegal structures, which in turn generate tensions and intolerance. Countries with a high proportion of immigrants (Germany, France, Great Britain, the Netherlands, Switzerland, etc.) are also those where significant racial crime is developing.

In fact, the policies of European countries have done everything possible to create a feeling of 'fed up' that feeds populism and a form of communitarianism. It is in this area that strategic intelligence has failed most obviously, by being unable to identify the breaking points caused by the lack of control over immigration. Indeed, European progressives, by treating immigrants as numbers, assumed that their culture of origin would slowly fade away in favour of a European culture.

It is not immigration as such that is the problem, but the way it is managed, with the added difficulty that over time the situation requires drastic measures that no one has the courage to take.

As of summer 2014, Europe is facing an unprecedented wave of immigration from Syria, Kosovo, Afghanistan, Albania, Iraq, Pakistan, Eritrea, Serbia, Ukraine and Nigeria[715]. We will not dwell on the fact that Kosovo, Albania, Serbia and Ukraine are countries that already rely heavily on Western aid. In Afghanistan and Iraq, two countries where human rights, democracy and the Western way of life were supposed to bring development, corruption reigns, fuelled by the very people who wanted to eliminate it[716].

---

715. "Migrant crisis: Migration to Europe explained in graphics", BBC News, 27 October 2015, http://www.bbc.com/news/world-europe-34131911.

716. Dan Wright, "Special Investigator's Report Details US Corruption In Afghanistan", Shadowproof, 6 August 2015, http://www.mintpressnews.com/special-investigators-report-details-us-corrup-

Fifteen years of war and billions of dollars of investment have only brought insecurity and despair. In fact, the West is caught in its own trap. In order to bring about regime change in a number of target countries, they have created unbearable living conditions there, including through sanctions. Described by Richard Nephew, who was in charge of sanctions at the State Department under Obama and then delegated to Iran under Joe Biden, in a book entitled *The Art of Sanctions*[717] , this mechanism was intended to stimulate insurrectionary movements. But it has also encouraged an emigration that drains these countries of their cultural, intellectual and labour substance.

In the case of Syria, this emigration has left the field open to Islamists, allowing Israel, France and the United States to attempt to overthrow the regime of Bashar al-Assad. But at what cost? Whatever their motives, the commitment of France and the United States to overthrow the Syrian government by force could only generate a humanitarian catastrophe in the short, medium and long term.

The West has thus been overtaken by its own policies. The migratory flow resulting from the Western intervention in Syria was (temporarily) curbed thanks to an agreement with Turkey. But Turkey realised that the refugee camps were a time bomb, like the Palestinian camps in Lebanon in the 1960s and 1970s. Indeed, a large part of these refugees are opponents of the secular Syrian state, which is why the countries in the region do not want them...

In 2020, immigrants to Europe come mainly from two countries where the West is seeking to impose regime change (Syria and Afghanistan[718]) and from a country that was in sixteenth place in 2018[719] , and has moved up to third place in 2020, after the application of sanctions that are suffocating it: Venezuela. So our strategies are not working.

Western humanitarian organisations are not contributing well to the solution. Their actions are dogmatic and motivated more by a feeling of guilt than by a real desire to help. They contribute to the impoverishment of countries of emigration by «sucking out» the most dynamic and industrious part of their populations.

At the same time, a profound societal change is affecting Western countries, and European countries in particular: the Judeo-Christian «operating system» on which the West was based is migrating towards a more Muslim software.

---

tion-in-afghanistan/208365/

717. Richard Nephew, The Art of Sanctions - A View from the Field, Columbia University Press, New York, 2018.

718. «File: Figure 2 Top 30 citizenships of first-time asylum applicants (non-EU citizens), EU, 2019 and 2020 (thousands) v2.png", Eurostat (ec.europe.eu), 23 March 2021.

719. "File: Countries of origin of (non-EU) asylum seekers in the EU-28 Member States, 2016 and 2017 (thousands of first time applicants) YB18", ec.europa.eu, 20 March 2018.

In France, this change has already begun; it is developing behind the screen of secularism and the disinterest of the authorities who refuse to listen to what is called the «extreme right». Yet this slow change makes political decisions resonate differently and enters the radicalisation equation, especially when combined with what is perceived as injustice. This is the case with the Western silence on the plight of the Palestinians and the noisy campaigns against the burkini or the comedian Dieudonné, which would probably have gone unnoticed a few decades ago. But today, this adds to interventions perceived - rightly or wrongly - as crusades, and contributes to the radicalisation of young people and the rise of anti-Semitism.

The logical answer would be to increase the resources allocated to development aid, so as to encourage a *real* economic base, effectively fighting corruption. The problem is that hundreds of billions have been given to the Third World for over 60 years without any real development strategy. But such policies cannot be implemented at the point of a bayonet, as is currently the case: the idea of crushing peoples in order to develop them is an idea that does not sit well with the populations concerned. Thus, our strategies do not allow us to get involved in certain regions, even for noble reasons, without awakening nationalist feelings.

As after '9/11' in the United States, the European media (especially French and Belgian) relayed the official discourse sharing *de facto* the responsibility of the government in the radicalisation of a part of society.

Western interventions have been fatalistically explained away by the *establishment* and have provoked violence by a minority. But we are slowly approaching the limit of the resilience of the people of the Middle East. «Al Qaeda» was just an idea, but today the Syrian and Iraqi rebels (including the EI) are tangible entities, which crystallise the indignation of young Islamists and push them towards radicalism. This mechanism in turn triggers a rise of extremes in the West.

3.4.4.2. Secularism

It is common to think that Muslims - and Islamists in particular - are opposed in principle to Christianity and other religions. This is not true. First of all, Muslims themselves recognise that they have a common religious heritage in the concept of the *'peoples of the book'* (*Ahl al-Kitab*).

Muslim - and therefore Islamist - distrust of Westerners is fuelled by two main perceptions. The first is that Christians systematically seek to impose their culture, notably through their military interventions (which they have never really justified other than by lies). The second stems from the first: Westerners are generally opposed to religious practice and seek to impose this view, which explains the recurrent use of the term *'miscreant'*[720] or *'apostate'* in Islamist literature.

In France, several factors affect the perception of Islam today. Firstly, the idea that there is a linear relationship between Islam and terrorism ('ancestral jihad'); secondly, the increasing number of people dressed in North African fashion in the French streets, which gives the 'native' population a feeling of submersion and slow phagocytion of their own culture; and thirdly, a reminiscence of the Marxist reading of conflicts, which advocates the disappearance of religion as a factor of social peace.

After the attacks of 2015-2016, the idea that secularism is the key to «living together» has imposed itself in an almost irrational way in French political discourse and is brandished as the solution to terrorist violence. It results both from the importance attributed by Western 'experts' to religion in Islamist terrorism and from the idea that terrorism is a 'religious variant' of the class struggle.

In France, what is called «laïcité» has no recognised official definition. It is derived from the *1905 law*[721] , which essentially aimed to separate the Catholic Church from the State, so that the latter would no longer be an extension of the former's power. This law seeks to impose denominational *impartiality on the state* in order to avoid conflicts of interest in its governance and to ensure that it serves the interests of all citizens equally. It implies that the state and its representatives must refrain from openly advocating or supporting a religion. But it does not impose anything on citizens who remain free to exercise their faith, within the limits of public order and respect for others. The law is clear and coherent, but its doctrinaire and inadequate application has only encouraged the phenomenon of radicalisation, as the terrorists themselves have noted[722].

The real problem is political and institutional bias. In 2011, the intervention in Libya - which was based on lies and clearly led to regional chaos - was loudly claimed by Bernard-Henri Lévy, who himself declared that he had done it *«as a Jew»*[723].An admission that goes exactly against the republican principles he claims to defend: the fundamental reason for republican secularism[724] is precisely to avoid politics being guided by religious considerations. BHL thus directly - and unnecessarily - associates his religion with an operation that has been a humanitarian and regional disaster, and that President Obama himself has considered the *«worst* mistake»[725] of his presidency.

---

720. Which literally means «unbeliever».

721. See: www.legifrance.gouv.fr/loda/id/LEGITEXT000006070169/

722. See: «The History of France's Enmity with Islam», Dar al-Islam, n° 2, February 2015, p. 10.

723. «Libya: BHL is committed «as a Jew»», Le Figaro/AFP, 20 November 2011.

724. The famous "Law of 1905".

725. "Barack Obama says Libya was 'worst mistake' of his presidency", AFP/AP/The Guardian, 11 April 2016.

Similarly, in 2012, Manuel Valls, then Minister of the Interior, in hailing the «*symbiosis between the Republic and* French *Judaism*»[726] , and then on 18 September 2014, then Prime Minister, in addressing «*his brothers and sisters*» at the Paris Synagogue goes exactly against the spirit of the 1905 law. His affinity for the Jewish community is perfectly legitimate, but it must be accompanied by the necessary restraint in the context of official activities, in order to inspire confidence and not to suggest partiality. This is the meaning of the separation between state and religion, which guarantees the impartiality of the rule of law.

Manuel Valls, for whom opportunism and ideology take the place of intelligence, has thus undoubtedly been the greatest promoter of the radicalisation of Islam in France.

But it is part of a political tradition that cuts across the French political spectrum. Some politicians, such as Jean-François Copé, have railed against the demand of Muslim communities for separate hours for men and women in swimming pools in order to preserve secularism. However, the same demands made by the Jewish community in the late 1970s do not seem to have affected it[727] ... In October 2020, Gérald Darmanin, then Minister of the Interior, declared himself «*shocked*» by the presence of «halal» shelves in supermarkets, but not by the «kosher» products which are the Judaic equivalent ...[728]

However, the 1905 law has a perverse effect: in order to guarantee its separation from the State, it imposed autonomous financing on the Catholic Church. Today, Muslim places of worship are subject to the same constraints[729]. This opens the door to foreign funding (such as from Saudi Arabia or Qatar) and to the propagation of a reading of Islam that is not necessarily violent, but which does not correspond to the Islamic tradition of the Maghreb countries and adds to other sources of division.

To think that the problem of terrorism can be addressed through the imposition of secularism on the population is a simplistic fallacy. Firstly, because it concerns institutions and not individuals. Secondly, because it stems from an overestimation of the religious character of terrorism. Contrary to what is claimed, the immigrant population does not seek to live in a society without Christianity, but simply refuses to have a way of thinking imposed on them.

---

726. «Manuel Valls salutes the «symbiosis between the Republic and French Judaism»», Representative Council of Jewish Institutions in France, 23 May 2012, http://www.crif.org/lecrifenaction/manuel-vallssalue-la-symbiose-entre-la-république-et-le-judaïsme-français/31266#.
727. Muriel Bernard, «Des créneaux réservés aux élèves des écoles juives», ledauphine.com, 20 October 2011.
728. A. Peyrout, J. Assouly, A. Brogat, P. Caron, X. Roman & V. Gustin, « Gérald Darmanin : déclaration polémique sur les rayons halal et casher des supermarchés «, francetvinfo.fr, 21 October 2020.
729. NOA: with the notable exception of the Alsace-Moselle region, which has a concordat authorising state funding of religious institutions.

As part of a strategy to combat jihadist terrorism, the desire to eliminate religious differences by abandoning their symbols only confirms the discourse of the Islamists. For example, in Belgium, the idea of 'secularising' Christian holidays, such as renaming 'Christmas markets' as 'winter markets', or the removal of the cross from the mitre of St. Nicholas by the association Solidaris in Belgium[730] , was even considered harmful to the Muslim community[731].These measures only make us look down on the Islamists.

The Islamists do not blame us for being Christians, but for wanting them to renounce Islam. In 2006, during the cartoon crisis, the author - then serving as the UN's chief of intelligence in Sudan - met with Islamist extremists linked to the Muslim Brotherhood. Received with an ironic comment about Christians on his arrival, he addressed the «leader» of the group: «Be careful, because you and I have the same God!» The Islamist then smiled at him and said, «You're right, let's talk!» and the discussion went on in a very cordial manner... The same phenomenon concerns Judaism. In February 2018, the Tunisian Islamist party *Ennahdha* - close to the Palestinian Hamas - carried a Jew on its electoral list in Monastir[732] ! Of course, the French media barely noticed[733] ...

As so often, the problem lies in our own contradictions. The same people who claim a 'multicultural society' tend to use secularism to homogenise the cultural landscape: exactly what feeds jihadism. Our ethnocentrism thus tends to encourage Islamist discourse. Living together does not require a smoothing of the religious landscape, but a mutual understanding of each other's religious practices.

In France, nothing symbolises the irrationality of the fight against terrorism better than the endless debates on the wearing of the Islamic veil («hijab»), the «burqa» or the burkini, which has been stirring up passions since 2004:

> *The Islamic veil is also a symbol of Islam, as the Muslim woman is clai-*
> *ming her adherence to the Koran and all its murderous verses which call for*
> *the killing of Christians, Jews, unbelievers, apostates and many other innocent*
> *people. The Islamic veil is finally a political symbol that is at war with the*
> *West and our European civilisation.[734]*

---

730. «Polemic: Solidaris removes the cross on the mitre of Saint Nicholas», lalibre.be, 23 November 2017.

731. «St Nicholas' cross: 'Muslims didn't ask for anything'», 7sur7.be/RTL-TVi, 27 November 2017.

732. «Simon Slama: I am proud to represent Ennahdha in the elections», www.mosaiquefm.net, 20 February 2018.

733. «Tunisia: polemic around a Jewish candidate on an Islamist list», Le Point.fr, 29 April 2018.

734. Louise Langlois, «Ces étudiantes musulmanes qui imposent le voile dans les écoles d'infirmières», Résistance Républicaine, 15 November 2018.

In fact, the diversity of so-called «Islamic» clothing shows that it is more a question of local or regional traditions than of a strict religious prescription. For example, the «burqa», which is often mentioned, is hardly ever worn in the West and is specific to Afghanistan. It is generally confused with the «niqab», which originated in the Arabian Peninsula. In some Islamic countries, such as Sudan, women wear clothes reminiscent of Indian «saris» with a coloured veil, sometimes slightly transparent. As for the «scarf», it is found in practically all Mediterranean traditions: The Virgin Mary is always represented with a headscarf, Catholic nuns continue to wear headdresses, the headscarf is still worn (less and less) in the Italian, Spanish or Greek countryside, while practising Jews wear the headscarf in public, as do Muslim women... A sign of submission to man for Westerners on the left, a symbol of war for those on the right, the headscarf is more often than not the expression of a cultural identity for Muslim women It has become the all-too-visible symbol of a foreign presence that politicians have never dealt with and sends back to their voters the image of a failure they have deliberately ignored for more than half a century.

In December 2003 - shortly after the Istanbul bombings - Syria extradited 22 suspects to Turkey. Among them were two girls of Turkish origin who had gone abroad to study in an Islamic school, because Turkish laws prohibit the wearing of the «veil» in class[735].In other words, instead of letting them wear the veil and get an education in a secular Turkish school, these girls were pushed towards an Islamic school and radicalisation.

The burkini controversy is symptomatic of the ignorance surrounding the nature of Islamism. Designed by an Australian designer in 2006, it was intended as beachwear in a country where skin cancer is rampant and beachwear is commonplace[736].But in France, a subtle combination of silliness and politics has turned it into an Islamic garment, strongly opposed by the mayors of some cities, who have even enacted a ban on its use on beaches. Paradoxically, as the Israeli newspaper *Haaretz* notes, these ill-considered actions have relayed the discourse of the Islamic State and facilitated its recruitment efforts[737].This is for three reasons: firstly, they gave the opportunity to the Islamic State to show its opposition to women going to «expose themselves» on the beaches; secondly, in the eyes of Muslims - even «moderate» ones - this controversy served as an eye-opener for the Islamic State.- Secondly, in the eyes of even 'moderate' Muslims, the controversy has served to reveal a form of institutional 'Islamophobia' at the political and judicial levels, well beyond the realm of republican secularism; and thirdly, it has helped to reinforce extreme views.

---

735. «Veiled threats 0148", The Economist, 6 December 2003.
736. «Australia is the country with the most skin cancers», AFP/20 minutes. fr, 16 December 2010.
737. Allison Kaplan Sommer, "The Burkini Ban Is a Gift to ISIS", Haaretz, 22 August 2016.

In fact, these polemics are only a way of «fighting the problem», without providing any solution to living together, and go exactly against a strategy of fighting terrorism: more than the «veil», it is the debate that becomes an additional factor of radicalisation.

3.4.4.3. The fight against antisemitism

As we have seen, antisemitism is not a driving force in jihadist terrorism, as evidenced by the links between Israel and jihadist movements[738].However, it is present in many acts of hatred and is a «facilitating factor» in jihadist terrorism. Combating antisemitism helps to reduce the number of factors that push towards violence, but is not enough to solve the problem. Attacks such as those on Mohammed Merah in March 2012 and the Jewish Museum in Belgium in May 2014 may have more to do with our handling of the Israeli-Palestinian conflict than with global jihadism.

In France, Islamophobia and antisemitism are intertwined, feed into each other, and will probably never be completely eradicated[739].The only way to reduce their influence on violent extremism is to deal with them in a dispassionate way, which is far from being the case today: current strategies to combat antisemitism only generate it.

The fight against antisemitism tends to ignore its real causes and to attribute them to the very existence of the Jewish people. It is therefore more focused on sanctioning its symptoms, than on addressing its causes and their perception. This is a counterproductive approach, which leads to an ever more extensive interpretation of the notion of «antisemitism». Thus, the adoption of specific laws (such as the laws against «BDS»[740] in favour of Palestine) tends to generate a much deeper resentment than the one they are meant to combat: they allow for short-term responses, but their long-term effects work against both the Jewish community as a whole and the State of Israel.

For behind a «surface» antisemitism (which is most often manifested in stupid and sterile acts) there is a growing distrust of Israel. This is not antisemitism per se, but rather «anti-Zionism», which is more about Israeli politics than the State of Israel itself.

This is not a matter of «cutting ties» with Israel, but of helping it more actively to resolve the Palestinian problem in a just manner. Israel's repeated violations of international law and immigration from North Africa and Asia Minor have resulted in a slow change in sensitivities towards the Israeli-Palestinian conflict.

---

738. Elizabeth Tsurkov, "Inside Israel's Secret Program to Back Syrian Rebels", Foreign Policy, 6 September 2018.
739. Pamela Duncan, "Europeans greatly overestimate Muslim population, poll shows", The Guardian, 13 December 2016.
740. BDS: Boycott, Divestment, Sanctions.

Today, the fight against antisemitism inevitably requires a more critical stance towards Israeli policy and a greater determination to impose international law in this context. The policy of fait accompli, camouflaged by a rewriting of history, has allowed Israel to escape its international obligations by creating a legitimate sense of injustice.

3.4.5. Operational measures

The first requirement for sustained success is to know what you are trying to do. This is what is lacking in virtually all Western operations against terrorism.

In Afghanistan, there are, very quickly, two distinct forces: a legitimate force (ISAF) under a UN mandate and an 'illegal' force in the eyes of international law (OEF-A) under US command. The former has a peace-building mandate, while the latter is waging a war with unclear objectives[741].

The coexistence of two operations, with different objectives, under different commands, in the same theatre of operations quickly drifted towards the pooling of logistical elements and led, in August 2009, to the merger of the two operations. Thus, the initial peacebuilding mandate was considerably diluted, as confirmed by the American General David McKiernan, Commander of ISAF:

> *The fact is that we are at war in Afghanistan. This is not peacekeeping. This is not stability operations. This is not humanitarian assistance. This is war.*[742]

This collision of mandates within ISAF gave rise to numerous legal and political discussions within the coalition: two missions, with sometimes contradictory objectives, were being conducted by the same countries. As had been the case in Beirut in 1983 and in Somalia in 1993, the simultaneous presence of combatants and peacekeepers - sometimes wearing the same uniform and therefore indistinguishable - could not bring coherence to the situation. The result was a confusion that made the international community's message unreadable for the local population and for the forces involved, and could only lead to disaster.

Not only did the West commit itself with questionable legitimacy to a conflict with vague objectives, but it was unable to present a strategic coherence that could have facilitated the operations, or even generated the support of the local populations. This phenomenon will be repeated in Iraq, Libya and Syria.

---

741. Steve Coll, 'We Can't Win in Afghanistan Because We Don't Know Why We're There', The New York Times, 26 January 2018.
742. General David McKiernan, Atlantic Council, Washington DC, 18 November 2008.

3.4.5.1. Social action and building loyalty among the population

Gaining the trust of the populations in which the discontent that will fuel the terrorist drive is developing is essential. This is obvious. It is also necessary to understand what the population wants and why they take up arms.

In order to address this issue effectively, a distinction must be made between internal security in the West, where terrorism is an expression of a very minority struggle or indirect resistance (Western Europe), and counter-insurgency situations, where terrorism is an expression of direct resistance to a regime or occupation (Afghanistan, Iraq, Libya, Syria, etc.)

Even if the basic idea is similar, the tools for its implementation will differ.

In the West, where jihadist terrorism is linked to illegitimate interventions in the Middle East, and where large Muslim minorities reside who condemn violence in general but have an understanding of its motives, societal action must proceed with subtlety. It must aim to smooth out any factors that might facilitate a shift to violent action. The integration of minorities must be carried out with respect for their specificity.

In a counter-insurgency environment, in order to change the mindset of a society in depth, even to adapt it to universal values, it is first necessary to win its 'hearts and minds'. *Hearts and minds»* operations were developed by the British in the 1950s, and successfully implemented in Malaya, then - with more relative success - in Northern Ireland. The problem is that the West was never really prepared to win this battle. Unlike 'physical' operations, psychological warfare must be sustained to be effective. Western armies are not equipped for this. They can carry out 'psychological operations' of limited scope, to support combat, but not to change a society.

In Afghanistan and Iraq, the West has treated - and continues to treat - the «rebels» as insurgents. But they are resistance fighters. Beyond the vocabulary, this corresponds to different characteristics of the conflict. The 'revolutionaries' seek to change society and aspire to a better future, economically, socially or socially; to fight against them, it is relatively easy to rely on the part of the population that does not want change. Resistance fighters, on the other hand, seek primarily to restore the *status quo ante*, without necessarily wanting societal change; they generally enjoy much broader popular support.

Thus, in Afghanistan, the goal of improving the status of women was undoubtedly a noble one, but it could only be achieved with the help of society, not by fighting *against* it. Malalai Kakar was the first woman to reach the rank of lieutenant colonel in the Afghan police. Her appointment was celebrated in the national and international media as an example of how Afghan society has changed after Western intervention. She was shot dead in front of her home on 28 September 2008, demonstrating the naivety of the West in wanting to change a society that has not been pacified in a few years.

This is especially true since 'universal' values (such as human rights) are understood in much of the world as values imposed by the West. For example, the *International Criminal Court* (ICC) is perceived by Third World countries as a Western court, which does not even seek to punish those who, through lies and bad faith, such as President George W. Bush and British Prime Minister Tony Blair, have done everything in their power to generate unnecessary and murderous wars.

Under these conditions, to want to transform societies with which one is at war is both naive and foolish. The trust and loyalty of populations, a necessary condition for initiating a process of change, have never been established in Afghanistan, Iraq or the Sahel. Yet this loyalty is essential to create trust and remove the legitimacy of terrorists.

The aim is to limit the recruitment base of violent movements, to cut off popular support for terrorism and to create a favourable climate among the population for law enforcement operations. To this end, there are many approaches:

- Strengthen and energise the presence of the state - but not necessarily the security presence - in troubled areas (strengthening education programmes, spending and capital works in rural areas, social measures, etc.);

- to valorise the actions of the state in order to discredit and criminalise the activities of the guerrilla or terrorist movement;

- Empowering local people in matters of public order and enhancing their sense of security by being responsive to their security concerns.

When carried out against the adversary, it should help to point out other courses of action than violent action. Thus, even if the social situation of Islamist terrorists is not in itself a factor in radicalisation, the fact that they feel closer to their co-religionists in the *Ummah* than to the French citizens they come into contact with on a daily basis is the result of a failure of integration and facilitates a change of tack.

In France and Belgium, very little effort has been made since the 1960s to build loyalty among immigrant populations: initially, work and then the appeal of a democratic society were supposed to be enough to generate support for Western values. Today, these two countries have completely lost control of this «loyalty». Even if the proportion of the immigrant population in favour of violence is very small, the cause defended by the Islamists has significant support.

Thus, amnesty laws, the reconversion of combatants, and the prospect of 'reconciliation' are all instruments that offer combatants another perspective than that of dying with their arms in their hands or under the knife of justice.

Conversely, there is no doubt that the water and electricity cuts in Iraq helped to sustain popular discontent that served - and probably also legitimised - resistance to the occupier (which quickly translated into terrorism), even if these phenomena were not central to the terrorists' demands.

In Vietnam, psychological operations to gain the trust of the local population have been remarkably effective, largely because terrorists or guerrillas are very often recruited by force or by some form of social pressure. In Vietnam, it was found that only about 8 per cent of Viet Cong fighters were committed to communist principles and that the harshness of underground life made the rest vulnerable to government propaganda.

3.4.5.2. *Population control*

In a COIN situation, some security can be achieved by physically separating civilian populations from terrorist groups that seek to intimidate and exploit them. This method was used in the 1950s-1970s with some success.

In South-East Asia or Algeria (during the Algerian war, but more recently also during the Islamist insurgency), insurgent movements had recruited personnel by force, launched punitive raids on villages (often for personal vendettas), extorted a 'revolutionary tax' or committed other crimes.

Counter-measures may be, after a state of emergency has been declared, to regroup populations in areas where they are both protected and controllable. It is important to note that these are not measures to punish local people, but to help them:

- The creation of well-organised and structured 'new villages' (e.g. Malaysia in the 1950s). This system, set up by the British, was successful because it combined material and security advantages for the local populations.

- Systematically mining areas that are difficult to control so as to push populations towards populated areas. Less costly than the previous solution, this solution has been widely applied in Africa and South-East Asia, notably in Vietnam, southern Laos and Afghanistan. Its humanitarian and economic consequences are counterproductive and have long-term consequences that are difficult to calculate. Furthermore, it undermines the restoration of economic activity necessary to stabilise a region in a post-conflict phase.

In 2002, the US forces in Afghanistan realised that the military actions of Operation ENDURING FREEDOM would not, in the long run, solve the Afghan problem. This led to the creation of the *Provincial Reconstruction Team* (PRT) concept, which consists of setting up economic and social reconstruction centres in the areas recently liberated from the Taliban.

This concept is derived from the experiences in Vietnam. It is about re-establishing normality just after the fighting. In concrete terms, this means bringing aid organisations to a newly 'liberated' area, guaranteeing them a security perimeter and letting them work with the local population. In this way, a military success is exploited to move the liberated population as quickly as possible from a combat logic to a reconstruction logic. The objective is to cut the insurgent movement off from its popular base, which quickly finds an economic advantage in the pacified areas. A tactical success is thus transformed into an operational success[743] .

In Vietnam, this type of activity was largely CIA-led, employing military personnel from Special Forces and *Civil Affairs* (part of the Special Operations Command) to set up schools, irrigation projects, local public information facilities and to defend villages from falling back under Viet Cong influence. In Afghanistan, forty years later, the same principle was applied, but with a plethora of non-governmental organisations. Civilian non-governmental organisations were 'injected' into the military area of operation to create 'islands' of development, coordinated by the *Civil Affairs* units of the *US Special Operations Command* (USSOCOM).

In Afghanistan, the implementation of the concept was officially launched on 21 November 2002 and included the establishment of 16 PRTs. The first PRT was established in Gardez on 31 December 2002. The project was supported by the Afghan government, which deployed a battalion of the new Afghan army to Bamiyan and another to Gardez. The PRTs are staffed mainly by US forces and reinforced by officers from New Zealand, the UK, Italy, France and Romania.

Placed under NATO command on 11 August 2003, the *International Security Assistance Force (ISAF),* initially deployed in the Kabul area, gradually expanded to cover the whole of Afghanistan until 2006. Straddling the line between the temptation to fight and the promotion of peace, NATO embraced the concept of PRT, but never really defined a real strategy. Taking over a peacekeeping mandate, ISAF initially wanted to stay out of the fighting and set up its PRTs in areas where international aid organisations had already been operating freely for many years. Thus, the PRTs in the combat zones (south and east of the country) are operated by British and US forces, while those in areas with little or no combat (north and west of the country) are operated by NATO forces that are not part of Operation ENDURING FREEDOM. This is the case of the German PRT in Qunduz, which had the effect of militarising an environment that did not need it. Whereas the American PRTs were an attempt to 'civilise' a military area, the German PRT tended to 'militarise' a peaceful area.

The gradual expansion of NATO's presence is almost «mathematically» followed by an increase in terrorist activity and suicide bombings. From 2003 onwards, NATO - which until then had only had a presence in Kabul - was allowed to cover the whole country. This expansion was carried out in phases. Phase I: the north (2004), phase II: the west (2005), phase III: the south (summer 2006) and phase IV: the east (autumn 2006). At the same time, the number of suicide attacks in the country, which had been 2 between 2003 and

---

743. The term 'operative' is taken here in its Clausewitzian sense of 'relating to operations', a level between the strategic and tactical (operational) levels.

2005, rose to 93 in 2006, 137 in 2007 and 136 in 2008[744].The UN security maps - which show the levels of danger in various areas of the country by colour - show that the maximum level of danger steadily follows the expansion of the NATO presence. While insecurity was initially highest along the Pakistani border, the deployment of troops in traditionally calmer areas in the north of the country by Alliance members who, for political reasons, wanted to participate in the operation without getting involved in the fighting, such as Germany, thus generated a sense of foreign occupation, which led to a rise in violence in these areas. The map that was almost «green» in 2003 became red in 2014.

Moreover, it quickly became apparent that ISAF lacked logistical means, such as helicopters capable of flying in mountainous areas, and protection means. Thus, ISAF uses resources from the American operation. This collaboration required close coordination, which led to a gradual integration of the leadership structures of ISAF, the PRTs and US Operation ENDURING FREEDOM under a single command, headed by an American.

The West thus creates an objective confusion between a war operation and a 'peacekeeping' operation, and their message becomes totally illegible for the Afghan population. As a result, the military presence generates the idea of an occupation of the country and all military actions are then perceived as hostile, stimulating terrorist activity and increasing insecurity throughout Afghanistan - not just in the south-east where the Taliban predominate.

This confusion, extended to all aid activities, is at the origin of several terrorist attacks against international humanitarian agencies, notably in Mazar-e-Sharif (causing the humanitarian demining organisation *HALO Trust* to cease its activities), in Qunduz, as well as in the Herat region (causing *Médecins Sans Frontières* to leave in March 2004). It was also in 2003 that terrorism emerged in Afghanistan[745].

That said, reports on the operation of PRTs in Afghanistan are generally complimentary. Indeed, they have 'worked' well. The problem is that they did not generate the expected regional dynamics. Unlike in Vietnam, where the work of building population loyalty has been the subject of outreach work in the countryside, the Afghan PRTs have concentrated on certain urban centres and have had only a limited effect on the surrounding populations, which are still largely subservient to local lords[746].In conclusion, the 'blind' application,

---

744. Robert A. Pape & James K. Feldman, Cutting the Fuse, University of Chicago Press, 2010, pp. 34-37.
745. Anthony H. Cordesman, Global Trends in Terrorism Through 2016 and the Relative Role of ISIS and the Taliban, Center for Strategic and International Studies (CSIS), Washington, D.C., 14 June 2017.
746. The United Kingdom Parliament, Examination of Witnesses, 16 March 2003.

without a clear strategy, of the concept that had proved successful in Vietnam led to a negative development in an asymmetric situation.

3.4.5.3. *Taking the initiative*

The success of terrorist movements is essentially their ability to retain the initiative and seek to put the state and the forces of order in a defensive position. It is therefore a question of ensuring that the initiative is regained, both politically and operationally.

A distinction must be made here between counter-insurgency situations (e.g. Afghanistan, Iraq, Sahel, etc.) and counter-terrorism situations in Europe, which are not insurgent in nature. Nevertheless, some similarities (which we will not detail here) can be exploited in both situations.

One option is to take the fight to the areas occupied by the subversive movement. In Indochina, Vietnam, and then Afghanistan, this strategy resulted in the creation of «hunting commandos», tracking down the guerrillas on their home ground. In this way, «anti-guerrilla guerrillas» are created, living and operating in the same conditions as their opponents, sometimes with the same uniforms and weapons. The troops used for this type of engagement must be of above-average quality. In Rhodesia, South Africa, Indochina, and Vietnam, guerrilla defectors were frequently used under the supervision of special forces officers. The author had the opportunity to follow the operations of ex-SWAPO guerrillas in Namibia: trained in special warfare schools in the USSR, they worked for the South African army with spectacular results. In Vietnam, from the end of 1962, the *Civilian Irregular Defense Groups (CIDGs)* programme was set up, which were local villagers trained, armed and supervised by American special forces officers. By 1963, their numbers had grown to about 15,000 fighters.

The formation of irregular groups carries certain dangers. In Latin America or the Philippines, this strategy has often led to the creation of local militias and the use of «snipers» who quickly became «death squads». It must therefore be managed in a very precise manner, with combat plans based on extensive intelligence, and only be directed against combatant adversaries. Beyond the obvious humanitarian aspect, it is also a question of avoiding conflict with a *«hearts and minds»* strategy that would be applied in the same region.

In India, for example, the fight against the Sikh insurgency involved a combined strategy:

- The government favoured the use of ethnic Sikh police to restore order. Besides being familiar with the terrain, the local population and their customs, it helped to preserve the central government in New Delhi by giving the image of a 'home-grown' solution;

- the response to the insurgents' tactic of abducting family members of law enforcement officers through 'counter-abductions' and subsequent exchanges;

356

- substantial remuneration and protection for informants;

- the construction of a sophisticated fence on the Pakistani border to disrupt and reduce the flow of arms and insurgent movements to sanctuaries in Pakistan.

This strategy was reinforced by the gradual criminalisation of the insurgency by the insurgents themselves, who routinely engaged in kidnapping, murder and extortion, thus cutting themselves off from popular support.

In Iraq in 2006, these concepts translated into the creation by the Americans of the '*Iraqi Awakening*' and '*Sons of Iraq*' movements organised around local tribes and communities to fight global jihadist groups. The problem is that the strategy was implemented in a partial way, developing their 'military' capabilities and neglecting accompanying measures to create a deep democratic base. These movements developed in a totally uncontrolled manner and will be the source of the Islamist groups that will eventually lead to the EI.

3.4.5.4. Amnesty

Amnesty can be useful in defusing the spiral of violence necessary for the revolutionary process, and thus 'pull the rug out from under' terrorism. It is a strategy that can be used in counter-insurgency and counter-terrorism situations.

Releasing political prisoners as a sign of appeasement to lower tension is a common tactic used to try to regain the initiative from a revolutionary movement. This was done by Muammar Gaddafi in March 2010[747] , the Tunisian government in January 2011[748] and President Mubarak in Egypt in February 2011[749].

The Syrian government took the same approach in March, May and June 2011, releasing some 1,000 (mostly Islamist) political prisoners as part of a general amnesty demanded by the Islamist opposition[750].It was accompanied by other concessions, such as allowing the wearing of the niqab and closing casinos[751] in an attempt to calm the situation.

In 2017, Jean-Yves Le Drian, then Minister of Foreign Affairs, stated:

> *When you were the first to free the jihadists of Daech, you don't give lessons.*
[752]

---

747. «Libya: 202 Prisoners Released But Hundreds Still Held Arbitrarily", Human Rights Watch, 25 March 2010.

748. «The release of political prisoners in Tunisia is an encouraging first step», Amnesty International, 20 January 2011.

749. Maamoun Youssef, "Egypt recognises moderate Islamic party, promises to release political prisoners", Associated Press, 19 February 2011.

750. Zeina Karam, "Syria offers general amnesty", www.washingtonpost.com, 31 May 2011.

751. "Syria lifts niqab ban, shuts casino, in nod to Sunnis", Reuters, 6 April 2011.

752. «Jean-Yves Le Drian responds to Bashar al-Assad's accusations», AFP/YouTube, 19 December 2017.

But Le Drian is lying. He hides the fact that, on the one hand, the reason why there were so many Islamists among the released prisoners is simply that there was no secular opposition and that, on the other hand, as in Libya[753], once released, these Islamists were quickly «recuperated» and armed by the Western special services[754] to form the backbone of an armed opposition. This is the case of *Ahrar al-Sham* and *Jaish al-Islam*, which John Kerry designates as affiliated with *Jabhat al-Nosra* and the *Islamic State*[755] (and which commit the same atrocities), but which the United States, Great Britain and France refuse to put on the United Nations list of terrorist organisations[756].

The timing of the amnesty must be carefully chosen so that it is seen as a good faith initiative, not as a measure taken under pressure. The decision must be taken before the rebellion reaches a critical threshold, otherwise it will be totally ineffective. It must therefore be used wisely and as part of an overall approach that must lead to a demobilisation of the terrorist will, without putting new terrorists back on the market. It is the role of strategic intelligence to make proposals on timing. In Syria, these measures were taken too late and were overwhelmed by the dynamics of the rebellion.

In Vietnam, amnesty was at the centre of the Chieu Hoï (Open Arms) programme, which was designed to convince terrorists to return to civilian society. It helped bring some 181,000 Viet Cong members into the government forces in the South between 1963 and 1975. The aim was not only to remove fighters from the enemy, but also to use these defections to demonstrate the weaknesses of the communist organisations. The defectors were then - at least some of them - integrated into South Vietnamese counter-guerrilla units[757].

Algeria also offered an amnesty to Islamist fighters in the context of the fight against terrorism in the late 1990s. On 13 July 1999, it adopted the law on civil concord, approved by referendum on 16 September 1999 (98.6% «yes»!)[758] which allows the reintegration into society of persons involved or having been involved in acts of terrorism or subversion, «accused, detained or not detained» on the date of the promulgation of the law and until 13 January 2000. It defines several categories of persons:

---

753. Daniel Iriarte, «Islamistas libios se desplazan a Siria para «ayudar» a la revolución», ABC.es, 17 December 2011; Jomana Karadsheh, «Libya rebels move onto Syrian battlefield», CNN, 18 July 2012.
754. Aron Lund, "Jaish al-Sham: An Ahrar al-Sham Offshoot or Something More?", Carnegie Middle East Center, 16 October 2015.
755. Juan Cole, "Is Kerry Right? Are Freemen of Syria and Army of Islam Radical Terrorists?", Informed Comment, 13 July 2016.
756. "U.S., Britain, France block Russia bid to blacklist Syria rebels", Reuters, 11 May 2016.
757. The Chieu Hoi Program in South Vietnam, 1963-1971, R-1172-ARPA, RAND Corporation, January 1973 (declassified 7 November 2005).
758. «La loi sur la concorde civile du président algérien plébiscitée avec 98,6% de «oui» «, Le Monde, 17 September 1999.

- those who were members of armed organisations but who did not commit acts resulting in death, permanent disability or rape, as well as those who did not use explosives in public places: these persons will be amnestied and the criminal proceedings against them cancelled. Civil liability remains, and to facilitate compensation for victims, the law provides for the subrogation of the State to pay damages, which can then turn against the perpetrator of the damage;

- combatants who have been part of armed organisations without having commanded them: if they have not committed massacres or explosive attacks on public places, if they have surrendered within 3 months of the promulgation of the text and if they have been accepted by the authorities to participate in the fight against terrorism, they will be subject to a probationary period of 3 to 10 years during which legal proceedings will be frozen. This probationary period may be cancelled, particularly in the case of false statements. Otherwise, at the end of the probationary period, «repentant terrorists» will be brought to trial and their sentence should not exceed 5 years in prison. Probation committees have been set up in each prefecture;

-leaders of armed groups and those who created them: provided they have not committed massacres or bombings, their sentence will be reduced to a maximum of 12 years' imprisonment (instead of the death penalty or life imprisonment).

This law made it possible to grant amnesty to some 1,700 Islamists and for certain movements to lay down their arms. Moreover, it was supplemented by a decree of President Bouteflika of 10 January 2000, granting *an amnesty* to *persons who belonged to organisations that voluntarily and spontaneously decided to put an end to acts of violence and placed themselves at the full disposal of the state*, which allowed the dissolution of the Islamic Salvation Army (AIS).

In Israel, amnesties are systematically followed by a resumption of settlements in the occupied territories, and are often nothing but an incitement to terrorism.

3.4.5.5. *The role of special operations forces*

3.4.5.5.1. The hunting war

In operational terms, the 'hunting war' is one of the methods used to track down terrorist groups in order to prevent them from establishing themselves in a given area. It was used in Algeria between 1958 and 1962 by General Challe, with the «hunting commandos» or «harkas».

In Afghanistan, the special operations forces engaged in Operation ENDURING FREEDOM are applying the method of chase warfare. However, the action was conceived as an 'anti-terrorist' operation, not a 'counter-terrorist' one, and therefore neglected to build a popular support base and engaged directly in a real hunt. The result was meagre. Special forces operating in southeast

Afghanistan do not enjoy the full cooperation of the local population, who are willingly bribed to provide information, but who also provide information to Islamist groups. The method of hunting warfare must be carefully mastered.

3.4.5.5.2. Self-defence militias

The training of self-defence militias is also one of the missions of US Special Forces. A US Special Forces sergeant is capable of forming a battalion-sized local force. In Vietnam, village militias were formed to prevent Viet Cong encroachment in several areas of the country along the Laotian and Cambodian borders. One of the main tasks of the US 5ᵉ Special Forces Group (5th SFG) was the training and conduct of *Civilian Irregular Defense Groups (CIDGs)* and *Mobile Guerrilla Forces* (later renamed *Mobile Strike Forces - MSF*). The 5th SFG led local forces totalling up to 45,000 men that were particularly effective in limiting Viet Cong encroachment into rural areas.

3.4.6. Negotiations and concessions

The idea of negotiating or finding compromise solutions with terrorists is generally considered taboo, mainly because it is considered a form of blackmail to try to «exchange» their violence for the fulfilment of their demands. This is correct, but it is only valid from the moment they have decided to embrace terrorism: before they embark on this path, negotiation is possible. So we have to be careful. The experience of the wars in Afghanistan and Iraq shows the limits of solutions aimed at eradicating terrorism by force alone.

Dialogue and negotiation must therefore be part of the range of available instruments of struggle. Negotiations with Yasser Arafat's *Palestine Liberation Organisation* (PLO), the *Irish Republican Army* (IRA) and the *Revolutionary Armed Forces of Colombia* (FARC) are all examples of how the issue can be addressed pragmatically.

This is where identifying the type of terrorism and its purpose is essential. For example, with common law terrorism, which uses violence to gain direct advantage, negotiation is impossible, as giving in to the demands of violence could lead to chaos.

In other cases, however, terrorists are not always in demand of a peace process. This can be the case with Marxist revolutionary processes, where terrorism is used to increment a process of violence with a mobilising effect, and negotiations could then undermine the whole process. It is also important here to understand the de-escalation mechanism. The disappearance of some Marxist terrorist movements was only due to the collapse of communism at the end of the Cold War and was only in very few cases the result of government action.

Those who use terrorism to force an occupying power to leave their country ('Al Qaeda', the Islamic State, the Taliban, etc.) will not be inclined to engage in a negotiation process either, as the objective can only be achieved by the departure of the occupier. Thus, in Afghanistan in 2019-2020, negotiations were not about substantive issues, but only about the modalities of American departure. In the Second World War, no Resistance group would have thought of negotiating with the German occupier.

The principle is that one cannot negotiate under the pressure of attacks. On the other hand, when a party to a conflict seeks to extricate itself from a mechanism of violence and is willing to negotiate without using pressure or threats, an opening should be possible. In this case, the approach is one of violence prevention.

One example, experienced first-hand by the author[759] , is the attempted surrender of the *Lord's Resistance Army* (LRA), a Christian terrorist organisation that operated in northern Uganda and Congo and southern Sudan. Fought in all three countries, its leaders decided to negotiate a surrender in 2005 and sent three messages to the *United Nations Mission in Sudan* (UNMIS). Contact was then established with its leaders, who were ready to surrender their weapons on condition that they be judged according to the laws of the Acholi tribe, from which they come. But at the same time, in October 2005, the *International Criminal Court* (ICC) issued an international arrest warrant for the five main leaders of the group and proved intractable on possible negotiations, thus putting an end to the dialogue. This was a confrontation between «white» international justice and traditional justice. In the end, no agreement was reached and the LRA continued to scour the border area from Southern Sudan to the Central African Republic, causing hundreds of deaths...

The idea of compromising and offering concessions in order to calm public opinion, to reduce the grip of grievances and thus 'pull the rug out' from under violence is a possible strategy. But its consequences can be unpredictable and do not always lead to a peaceful solution. As early as 1905, the Russian government granted amnesty to Bolshevik agitators (including Lenin, who took refuge in Switzerland) to calm the first revolts, which heralded the 1917 revolution. More recently, between 2008 and 2011, the governments of Tunisia, Egypt, Libya and Syria adopted similar measures in the hope of curbing popular discontent. Contrary to what the French government or some journalists claim, Bashar al-Assad did not release Islamists in order to aggravate the situation in Syria (!), but on the contrary to try to defuse a situation.

At first glance, this strategy of 'deconfliction' may seem negative, because in many countries, the desire to calm popular discontent by compromising with extremists has not weakened the insurrectionary process, on the contrary.

---

759. The author was then head of the Joint Mission Analysis Centre (JMAC), the intelligence arm of the United Nations Mission in Sudan (2005-2006).

However, this is the realm of *fake news*, because a second analysis shows that these failures are mainly due to the West, which, in the first instance, took over the freed extremists and armed them, and then, in the second instance, exploited this reversal in the media[760] to accuse the Libyan and Syrian governments of having wanted to add fuel to the fire by granting amnesty to Islamist prisoners at the start of the popular riots. The process is not new, since Germany had already used it in 1917, repatriating Lenin to Russia and financing the Bolshevik revolution, in order to force Russia to ease its pressure on the Eastern Front. In 2011, France and Britain will join forces with the *Libyan Islamic Fighting Group* (LIFG), then listed as a terrorist movement, to overthrow Gaddafi. The same scenario will be repeated in Syria, with the Free Syrian Army (considered «moderate» and close to the Muslim Brotherhood) whose fighters will swell the ranks of the EI.

Negotiation as part of a counter-terrorism strategy aims to reduce the terrorist movement's willingness to find solutions through violent action. This negotiation, which focuses on the strategic objectives of the movement, is however only possible with a certain type of terrorism. Political or guerrilla terrorism, which is committed to a specific revolutionary process, generally offers more scope for negotiation. Marginal and common law terrorism is terrorism that can generally be fought outside of political solutions.

In Colombia, the *19 April Movement (M-19) was* legalised as a political party on 20 November 1983, which led to the signing of a peace agreement in July 1984 with the Betancour government. The movement did not die out overnight, but its influence and military capabilities rapidly declined. Despite a brilliant coup with the seizure of the Bogotá courthouse in November 1985, and a last burst of activity with the kidnapping of Alvaro Gómez Hurtado[761] in May 1988, the M-19 abandoned the armed struggle.

3.5. Counter-terrorism - Pre-emptive and reactive action

Tactics without strategy is only noise before defeat. (Sun Tsu)

Terrorism, as its name suggests, seeks its effect through emotions, and the West has responded emotionally and irrationally. The total lack of analysis of the terrorist phenomenon has led the West to entrench itself behind security walls.

---

760. See Léo Roynette, 'As early as 2011, Bashar al-Assad fanned the jihad in Syria', slate.fr, 18 March 2016; Armin Arefi, 'Syria: how Bashar al-Assad used the Islamic State', lepoint.fr, 28 August 2014.
761. Presidential candidate and leader of the Conservative Party, released two months later in exchange for a meeting between the government and the M-19 at the Nunciature in Bogotá, which led to a final peace agreement.

Counter-terrorism is complementary to counter-terrorism, and comes into play after the failure of the latter, and concerns all measures taken to counter terrorists *downstream of* their decision and prevent them from carrying out their plan. The absence of *upstream* counter-terrorism measures means that the initiative has been left to the terrorists.

Counter-terrorism is divided into two strands, both of which are subject to completely different intelligence work: pre-emptive action and reaction. What both have in common is that they take place *after* the terrorists have decided to commit an attack. In plain English, this means that in both these strands, the terrorists have the initiative.

Counter-terrorism includes a number of technical and legal measures, which we will not detail in this book, designed to protect individuals and society from attack, such as

- a legal framework for the prosecution, trial and conviction of terrorists;
- protection and physical security measures (creation of security perimeters, anti-intrusion measures, reinforcement of vulnerable points, etc.);
- personal protection measures (behavioural adaptation, personal protection staff, etc.);
- detection and warning devices (detection of explosives, weapons, etc.);
- mechanisms and means of intervention (against intruders, hostage-takers, etc.).

To be effective, counter-terrorism measures must be part of a comprehensive plan and be consistent with counter-terrorism measures. For example, Israel's «security fence» around the West Bank has certainly improved security on a tactical level, but at the same time it has reinforced the Palestinians' feeling that their land is being «nibbled away», which is at the root of their struggle and fuels support for radical Palestinian movements.

3.5.1. The role of intelligence

The role of intelligence in a counter-terrorism context is essentially tactical. The risk, in an atmosphere of individual terrorism, is that state surveillance of society as a whole will be greatly increased.

3.5.1.1. The use of torture

Strangely enough, like it or not, Americans understand their security by the yardstick of movies and TV shows and are obsessed with the idea of a bomb that is set off and that can only be defused by the terrorist's confession before it explodes.

In the United States, in addition to fear, there is an almost animal-like sense of revenge, which has resulted mainly in intervention in Afghanistan and Iraq, but also in demonstrations of force with often counterproductive security effects.

This is the case with the torture widely used by the American army and the CIA, but which their own manuals advise against:

> *[...] the use of force is a poor technique, as it produces unreliable results, can be detrimental to subsequent collection efforts, and can encourage the source to say whatever he or she thinks the interviewer wants to hear.*[762]

Yet on 7 February 2002, George W. Bush signed an executive order releasing the United States from its international obligations under the Geneva Conventions:

> *I determine that none of the provisions [of the Geneva Conventions] apply to our conflict with al Qaeda, in Afghanistan or elsewhere in the world, because, among other reasons, al Qaeda is not a contracting party [to the Geneva Conventions] ... I have the authority under the Constitution to suspend [the Geneva Conventions] between the United States and Afghanistan ......] Article 3 [of the Geneva Conventions] does not apply to either Al Qaeda or the Taliban, because, among other reasons, the conflict in question is international in nature and Article 3 «is applicable to non-international armed conflicts» only ... I determine that the Taliban detainees*[763] *are unlawful combatants and therefore do not qualify as prisoners of war under Article 4 [of the Geneva Conventions]. I note that because the Geneva [Conventions] do not apply to our conflict with Al Qaeda, Al Qaeda detainees cannot be considered prisoners of war either.*[764]

On the same day, he decided to set up the CIA's secret prison system, the first of which was operational in March 2002 in Thailand[765].These were prisons in which the CIA subcontracted the torture activities that it could not carry out on American territory. It should be noted here that the PATRIOT Act authorises the use of confessions obtained under torture if they are obtained abroad. Thus, several European countries contributed to the American programme by giving free passage to the CIA planes that transported the prisoners, and others - with

---

762. FM 34-52 - Intelligence Interrogation, Department of the Army, May 1987, p. 1.

763. It should be noted here that the Afghan Taliban have never been considered a terrorist organisation by the White House or the State Department (see http://www.state.gov/j/ct/rls/other/des/123085.htm), although the Treasury Department considers them a group that deserves the same sanctions as a terrorist group.

764. Memorandum of 7 February 2002, to be reaffirmed in Executive Order 13440 of 20 July 2007. See the original document: https://www.gpo.gov/fdsys/pkg/FR-2007-07-24/pdf/07-3656.pdf.

765. John Barry, Michael Hirsh & Michael Isikoff, "The Roots of Torture", Newsweek, 24 May 2004.

their experience from the communist era, such as Poland and Romania - practised torture to please the Americans this time.

There are two basic forms of torture: torture as a punishment and torture to obtain information or action from the victim. In general, and regardless of its purpose, torture is most often carried out by perverted and often mentally disturbed individuals.

The first has nothing to do with intelligence. It is frequently encountered in Latin America and Africa, where it is a means of humiliating the 'defeated' through degrading treatment (often with sexual overtones) and often takes the form of a tragic and stupid sadistic game. In addition to its vengeful nature, it claims to be a deterrent.

The second can have various objectives, including information gathering. It is applied in a «cooler» way and is generally oriented towards an operational result and not towards the satisfaction of personal fantasies.

There are two main methods of torture for obtaining information, which can obviously be combined:

- Coercive methods (use of physical pain) ;

- Sensory deprivation methods (mental torture), developed in the USA and Britain in the 1960s, and used in Northern Ireland by the British Army. Derived from psychological and behavioural science research, these interrogation techniques are based on disorienting the prisoner by manipulating their sensory perceptions, and are very effective. These methods do not use physical violence, but variations in sound and light to destabilise and disorientate the detainee, and make them more cooperative.

An examination of the torture of Afghan and Arab prisoners in American custody shows not only that the techniques used were more primitive and less effective than those used by the British in Northern Ireland forty years earlier, but also that their use of torture was punitive and for personal revenge. This is confirmed by the US Senate Committee of Inquiry into the interrogation and detention programme, which found that torture was even used in cases where it was known to be unnecessary!

The actions revealed by the press in April 2004 about the treatment of Iraqi prisoners by US forces in Abu Ghraib prison in Baghdad were - in reality - intended to «prepare» the prisoners for non-coercive interrogation. However, in spirit and manner, they are more akin to «sadistic» torture as practised in the Third World and which seeks to debase the enemy. The SECRET report by Major General Antonio M. Taguba, published in May 2004, clearly states:

(S) that between October and December 2003, in the Abu Ghraib Isolation Facility, there were numerous incidents of sadistic, flagrant and wanton abuse

of several detainees. This systemic and unlawful abuse of detainees was intentionally perpetrated by several members of the Military Police guards [...].[766]

In Iraq, the non-application of the Geneva Conventions to prisoners and the link established between the intervention and the fight against terrorism have *de facto* generated a 'legitimacy' for practices contrary to international law and to the values defended by the West. In 2015, the Islamic State will also invoke France's failure to respect international law to justify its terrorist acts.

On 7 May 2004, the beheading of Nicholas Berg in Iraq deeply shocked Western public opinion. But little was said about the reasons for such barbarity: published on an Islamist website on 11 May 2004, his execution was a response to American practices, as one of the terrorists explains:

> *For the mothers and wives of American servicemen, please know that we have asked the US administration to exchange these hostages with detainees in Abu Ghraib and they have refused. So the dignity of the Muslim men and women of Abu Ghraib will only be restored by blood [...] Does al-Qaeda need any more excuses? And how can a free Muslim sleep comfortably as he watches Islam being slaughtered and his dignity trampled?*[767]

Amy Goodman, an American interrogator who conducted some 300 interrogations in Iraq in 2006, wrote two years later:

> *It is no exaggeration to say that at least half of our casualties and injuries [in Iraq] were foreign [fighters] who joined the fight because of our prisoner treatment policy. The number of US soldiers who died because of our torture policy will never be definitively known, but it is reasonable to say that it is close to the number of lives lost on 11 September 2001. How can we claim that the use of torture protects Americans - unless we don't consider American soldiers to be Americans?*[768]

For example, the torture techniques used by the US military to humiliate prisoners have only dishonoured the entire US military and the memory of those who fought loyally, stimulated terrorist activity and - for the jihadists - given

---

766. AR 15-6 Investigation of the 800th Military Police Brigade, Investigating Officer MG ANTONIO M. TAGUBA, Deputy Commanding General Support, Coalition Forces Land Component Command, DODD0A-000248, 27.05.2004. (NOA: the (S) means that the paragraph is secret).
767. Statement by one of the terrorists on the Nicolas Berg beheading video (Iraq Occupation Watch Center, San Francisco, California).
768. Mattew Alexander (pseudonym of Amy Goodman), "I'm Still Tortured by What I Saw in Iraq", Washington Post, 30 November 2008.

legitimacy to terrorism! More broadly, Western violations of international law undermine their rhetoric about the defence of values and law. This illustrates not only a lack of strategic vision, but also a failure to tackle terrorism across a broad spectrum.

In Belgium, Fayçal Cheffou, who was suspected - wrongly - of belonging to the group responsible for the attacks of 22 March 2016, was tortured in the same way as the Abu Ghraib detainees. According to his testimony, the purpose of the torture was not to gather intelligence, but was merely punitive (sleep deprivation, insults, etc.). As in the Iraqi case, the problem is the imbecility of the unprofessional guards, who arrogate to themselves the right to punish, which is contrary to the principles of the rule of law. Moreover, in a context of asymmetric terrorism, abusive treatment should be prosecuted as an encouragement to terrorism.

In this type of conflict, where the very notion of victory is different on both sides, the traditional logic of war is no longer applicable. We are at the very heart of the definition of asymmetric warfare: the 'success' of one side feeds the success of the other side. In such a context, the American, Belgian and other torturers have only helped the terrorists by offering them justifications to commit new attacks. In this type of conflict, «collateral damage», miscommunications and injustices feed the opponent's centre of gravity and turn the «patriot» into an objective accomplice of the opponent! In fact, these torturers should have been tried as traitors to their own country...

In the ultimate paradox, Bradley E. Manning, the soldier who exposed some of these crimes - albeit in violation of confidentiality rules - was punished more severely than the criminals themselves with a 35-year sentence in maximum security prison. Among the 700,000 documents handed over by Manning and revealed by Wikileaks is the film[769] of the murder of two Reuters journalists by the crew of an AH-64 Apache helicopter... who were never charged[770]. The officer in charge of the Abu Ghraib prison, Brigadier General Janis Karpinski, was 'simply' relieved of her command (for a reason other than her role in the torture) and demoted to the rank of colonel.

On 9 December 2014, a 500-page document on the CIA's *Detention and Interrogation Programme* was released by the US Congress[771]. It summarises more than 6,000 pages of a classified report, itself based on a review of 6.3 million pages of documents produced on this programme by the CIA. Senator Dianne

---

769. https://www.youtube.com/watch?v=5rXPrfnU3G0 (viewed over 15 million times as of 20 February 2016).

770. "Bradley Manning: a sentence both unjust and unfair", The Guardian, 21 August 2013.

771. Committee Study of the Central Intelligence Agency's Detention and Interrogation Program, Senate Select Committee on Intelligence, 3 December 2014, downloadable from http://fas.org/irp/congress/2014_rpt/ssci-rdi.pdf.

Feinstein, the rapporteur of the enquiry, called the CIA torture programme «a *stain on [US] values and history*" and noted that it had not produced any information that could not have been obtained by other means and that would have enhanced national security. It recalls that in 1990 the US Senate ratified the International Convention on Torture, which states:

> *No exceptional circumstances whatsoever, whether a state of war or threat of war, internal political instability or any other public emergency, may be invoked as a justification of torture.*[772]

The programme was designed by two 'experts' who, in reality, had no experience in interrogation techniques. Not only were they responsible for designing and evaluating the results of the programme, but they also participated in the interrogations themselves, which was a clear conflict of interest. In total, these two experts received $80 million from the CIA! Not only were the techniques advocated by these «experts» shams in terms of the results obtained, but they were marked by sexual perversities similar to what had been observed at Abu Ghraib. Ironically, in designing this programme, they relied on techniques developed in the 1960s to counter interrogations by countries not respecting the Geneva Conventions and reverse engineered[773].

Despite initial claims that the interrogation programme was effective in obtaining information or in getting detainees to co-operate, the Senate Inquiry's report found that the programme as a whole was counterproductive and did not save a single human life. None of the various successes claimed by the CIA to justify its torture programme could be confirmed by the committee:
- because the information leading to an arrest or neutralisation was acquired separately from the interrogation;
- because the information obtained from the interviewee had not played any role in the arrest or neutralisation of terrorists;
- because the terrorist plot in question did not exist or pose any threat to Americans or American interests.

The commission did not find a single example where the use of torture was used to prevent a terrorist plot in progress («*ticking time bomb*») or imminent danger. Most of the time, the use of torture led to fabricated information. For example, Ibn al-Shaykh al-Libi, former head of a training camp in Afghanistan

---

772. Art 2, para 2, «Convention against Torture and Other Cruel, Inhuman or Degrading Treatment or Punishment», adopted and opened for signature, ratification and accession by the UN General Assembly on 10 December 1984, entered into force on 26 June 1987, http://www.ohchr.org/FR/ProfessionalInterest/Pages/CAT.aspx.
773. Philip Ross, "Who Are Jim Mitchell And Bruce Jessen? CIA Torture Psychologists Were Experts In Communist Chinese Interrogation", International Business Time, 10 December 2014.

and suspected al-Qaeda member, was allegedly «interrogated» by CIA and FBI specialists. He revealed preparations for attacks on the American embassy in Yemen and the headquarters of the 5ᵉ Fleet in Bahrain, which could never be proven[774] ; he also «confessed» to links between Iraq and «al-Qaeda»[775] , a false information, as we have seen. One could mention Zain al-Abidin Muhammad Husain (alias Abu Zubaydah), captured in a joint US-Pakistani raid on 28 March 2002, who was subjected to coercive interrogation and whose «confessions» remain highly questionable: «He talks, but the problem is sorting out what is true and what is not, what is reality and what is bluster.»[776] Cited by George Bush in an interview as a successful example of his torture policy, Abu Zubaydah also «confessed» to an attempted «dirty nuclear bomb» attack in Washington, which never took place[777] .

One of the problems pointed out by the Senate Committee was that the CIA acted on the basis of false information obtained under torture, thereby diverting valuable resources to unnecessary actions. Secondly, it was noted that the doubts expressed by some analysts about the validity and veracity of the information acquired were almost systematically ignored.

In order to avoid the wrath of the political establishment, the CIA kept the extent of its programme from President George Bush until April 2006. Similarly, Colin Powell, then Secretary of State, was not informed, as the CIA feared he would «*go* ballistic»[778].Even the CIA's Inspector General was not made aware of the methods used by the CIA. More importantly, the Agency knew that the information gathered through torture was of poor quality and mostly false. The enquiry report notes that the Agency had not even questioned the methods used, despite the bad experiences. Detainees were most often interrogated without supervision by CIA agents who had received no training in interrogation tech-niques and who used methods that were not in the official catalogue of the interrogation programme!

As in the case of Abu Ghraib, the individuals recruited to make prisoners talk often had a personal history that should have automatically ruled them out of such an engagement.

For example, on 11 August 2004, the UK Court of Appeal - the highest court in the UK, just ahead of the House of Lords - ruled that information obtained under torture was admissible in court for counter-terrorism trials, provided that

---

774. Associated Press, 24 April 2002.
775. Richard Norton-Taylor, "Waterboarding is no basis for truth", The Guardian, 9 November 2010.
776. Interview with one of the interrogators, Associated Press, 24 April 2002.
777. Richard Norton-Taylor, op. cit.
778. July 31, 2003 email from John Rizzo, quoted by Ms. Feinstein before Congress on December 9, 2014.

UK officials were not involved[779]. The US PATRIOT Act[780] also allows courts to use information allegedly obtained by methods prohibited in the US. Although the legislature had espionage in mind here (permitted to collect information abroad, but prohibited in US criminal proceedings), it opened the door to the admissibility of information obtained in a manner contrary to international humanitarian law (law of war).

This may also explain the fact that suspected Islamists claim credit for countless - and often unrealistic - attacks. This has been the case in the cases of Khalid Sheikh Mohammed ('KSM'), Zacarias Moussaoui and José Padilla in the United States. KSM has been *waterboarded* 183 times[781], has «confessed» to involvement in over 30 terrorist attacks worldwide (including 9/11, the Reid shoe bombs, the Bali bombing and many others). He was one of the CIA's main «sources», feeding his torturers the answers they wanted to hear... all false[782] ! His confessions of involvement in a multitude of attacks were such that he was dubbed the «*One-Stop Shopping Terrorist Super* Store»[783] .

The management and conduct of the CIA's interrogation programme was almost non-existent. The use of unapproved techniques, by interrogators who were not trained for the task, was commonplace. The CIA even went so far as to torture its own informants... by mistake!

Thus, from a strict intelligence perspective - and leaving aside moral and humanitarian issues - accepting information from coercive interrogations, and without knowing exactly under what conditions the information was obtained, opens the door to intoxication and disinformation. On a more strategic level, the centre of gravity of terrorist movements - and particularly Islamist movements - is very often linked to the legitimacy of the action. The state or authority facing a terrorist situation must take this into account and avoid allowing the adversary to legitimise its violence. Respect for justice and the law thus becomes a strategic imperative, while failure to do so can at best only bring tactical benefits.

The publication of the Senate committee's report has been criticised as potentially provoking violent reactions around the world, as Mike Rogers, chairman of the House Intelligence Committee, points out:

---

779. Audrey Gillan, "Judges in row over torture ruling", The Guardian, 12 August 2004.

780. Its full name is the Uniting and Strengthening America by Providing Appropriate Tools Required to Intercept and Obstruct Terrorism Act of 2001.

781. Often translated as «simulated drowning», waterboarding is the same as the «bathtub» torture once used by the Gestapo.

782. Dexter Filkins, "Khalid Sheikh Mohammed and the C.I.A.", The New Yorker, 31 December 2014.

783. http://mayday.blogsome.com/2007/03/19/khalid-sheikh-mohammed-the-wally-world-of-wickedness/

While it is entirely appropriate for congressional intelligence committees to conduct a rigorous assessment of classified programs, I fear that the release of details of this classified program - which was legal, authorized, and properly presented to the intelligence committees - will only inflame our enemies, risk the lives of those who sacrifice for us, and weaken the very organization we ask to do the hardest work in the most difficult places.[784]

The concern is legitimate, but the problem is turned on its head, because the concern does not come from the report itself, but from activities that are poorly conceived, poorly managed, poorly conducted and ineffective, carried out in defiance of the values that we defend. Beyond the legal aspects, a strategic aspect emerges, as Dr Ayman al-Zawahiri, Osama bin Laden's former right-hand man, testifies in an interview on the Islamist channel Al-Sahab:

The fact that America has neglected what it signed up to in the Geneva Conventions; the prohibition of physical and psychological torture of Muslim prisoners, their detention in clandestine sites leaving their families unaware of their fate, holding them indefinitely without charge, all these crimes give more rights to Muslims to stand up against American aggression and treat America in the same way.[785]

The danger of deviating from the values one defends is that it legitimises the deviations of others.

The ineffectiveness of torture and its counter-productive nature should have been identified before this programme was undertaken. The United States could thus have easily avoided creating new opponents, or even strengthening its own legitimacy (in strategic terms: its centre of gravity) by saving taxpayers' money, without losing its dignity or honour, and by taking away additional reasons for the opponent to commit terrorist acts, all without diminishing the overall efficiency of the fight against this scourge!

The American torturers were therefore nothing but fools, who understood nothing of the asymmetrical context, and only helped the insurgents by giving them justification to commit new attacks. In fact, logically, they should have been tried as traitors to their own country... But those who were convicted were given surprisingly light sentences, thus testifying to the fact that the United States has not really understood the nature of the conflict it is conducting.

---

784. Spencer Ackerman, Dominic Rushe, & Julian Borger, "Senate report on CIA torture claims spy agency lied about 'ineffective' program", The Guardian, 9 December 2014.
785. «Iman Defeats Arrogance», Inspire, n° 12, Spring 2014, p. 11.

3.5.1.2. A deficit analysis

The hijacking of the Italian liner *Achille Lauro* (7 October 1985) illustrates the importance of strategic analysis in a counter-terrorism situation.

From the moment the hijacking was announced, intelligence was a problem: the ship could not be located immediately because of the intense maritime traffic in the Mediterranean and the radio discipline imposed by the terrorists on the crew. In addition, the American, Italian and Israeli services had difficulty identifying the perpetrators and their motives.

Through cross-checking, the terrorists were identified as members of the *Palestine Liberation Front* (PLF). The PLF is now divided into three factions and it is not known which one is responsible for the hijacking:

- The State Department's *Bureau of Intelligence and Research (INR) was* quick to suggest that it was an «accidental» action, due to panic within the terrorist group. It attributed it to the Abu al-Abbas Faction, loyal to Yasser Arafat and opposed to Syrian influence.

- The US *Central Intelligence Agency (CIA)* and *Defense Intelligence Agency (DIA)*, because of the good relations between Italy, Egypt and the PLO, considered it unlikely that the Abu al-Abbas Faction was responsible for the hijacking. They suggest the Tal'at Ya'aqub Faction (based in Damascus since 1981), of Marxist tendency, pro-Syrian and close to the PFLP and the DFLP, or the Abd el-Fatah el-Ghanem Faction (based in Damascus since 1984), also of pro-Syrian tendency. The CIA and the DIA then believe that the action was carried out by a group seeking to ruin the efforts of rapprochement between Arafat and the international community.

Operationally, the INR hypothesis offered the prospect of resolving the incident through negotiation, whereas the CIA and DIA hypothesis led to an uncertain negotiation outcome and armed intervention appeared to be the only option.

Politically, the INR analysis called into question the relationship with Arafat, while the CIA and DIA analysis preserved it. This is why the US *State Department,* anxious to maintain a dialogue with Yasser Arafat, refutes the INR's assessment.

As for the Italian government of Bettino Craxi, which sought to maintain its role in the Arab-Israeli negotiation process, it immediately favoured negotiations with the terrorists, regardless of the faction involved. In terms of intelligence, the Italians were very weak at the time and depended almost exclusively on American and Israeli capabilities[786].But they sought to avoid American action: they knew that the United States would seek to conduct an operation against the ship before it reached the territorial waters of a country that might oppose

---

786. Fulvio Martini, Nome in codice Ulisse, Rizzoli, 1999, p. 116.

intervention and to avoid the possibility that the hostages might be dispersed on land and thus be difficult to locate.

But as the hours passed, Israeli electronic intelligence confirmed the INR hypothesis. Finally, after a brief unsuccessful attempt to negotiate the release of the 413 passengers in exchange for 50 Palestinian prisoners, and then to obtain guarantees against possible American, British and German reprisals, the terrorists surrendered to the Egyptian authorities in Port Said.

In the end, the exact reasons for this act of piracy remain unclear: it seems to be the result of insufficient preparation and haphazard conduct by the group. According to Abu al-Abbas himself[787] , the idea was to use the liner to infiltrate Israel in order to commit an attack. But shortly after leaving Alexandria, a crew member discovered the terrorists' weapons and raised the alarm. In a panic, the terrorists seized the ship and demanded the release of 50 Palestinian prisoners. In the end, only one person was killed, Leon Klinghoffer, a disabled American of Jewish faith, who was shot and thrown into the sea with his wheelchair. According to the testimonies, this murder seems to be more the result of the victim's attitude than of his religion.

In 1985, Westerners were not the protagonists, but merely the «hostages» of the conflict between Palestinians and Israelis. Twenty years later, the West is the direct protagonist of conflicts that it has illegally created through clumsy policies. They are in no position to negotiate with their enemies and no Western country can really play the role of mediator. There is even a fear of dealing with the problem at the political level for electoral and credibility reasons.

The official report of the British Intelligence and Security Committee, in its assessment of the causes of the 7 July 2005 attack in London, focuses on the police aspects and does not mention at any time the Blair government's foreign policy or the lies - already known at the time - that were used to justify the British alignment with the United States in attacking Iraq, thus contributing to the illegitimacy of this war in the eyes of the Islamists[788].Among the thousands of books and articles devoted to terrorism, very few study the genesis of the attacks, as if each event were unique, the result of a sudden and random impulse from some deranged brain. But this is not the case. Jihad is in essence a response, and Islamic attacks are operational expressions of it.

---

787. Arrested in Italy following this event (by the hijacking of his plane by the US Air Force), Abu al-Abbas was released for lack of evidence. The subsequent trial in Italy resulted in his being sentenced in abstentia to life imprisonment (June 1986). The United States put pressure on the PLO to expel him from the Executive Committee (September 1991). The 1993 Oslo Accords granted him amnesty for the Achille Lauro affair. In April 1996, he apologised to the Palestinian National Council for the murder of Leon Klinghoffer. He took refuge in Baghdad in 1995, where he was captured by American forces on 15 April 2003.

788. «Could 7/7 Have Been Prevented? Review of the Intelligence on the London Terrorist Attacks on 7 July 2005", Intelligence and Security Committee, London, May 2009.

One incident will allow the British government to literally stage an Islamist plot in Britain and attempt to establish the credibility of its involvement in Afghanistan and Iraq. This was the discovery, on 9 August 2006, of a 'plot' to blow up seven aircraft simultaneously in flight using liquid explosives. As a first step, the United Kingdom closed all its airports, including Heathrow (Great Britain), and banned all liquids on board aircraft taking off from the country.

This plot was uncovered through the «confession» under torture of a prisoner in Pakistan, as part of the CIA's torture programme. 24 people were arrested, including a baby, of whom 14 were almost immediately released and 8 were indicted. A first trial is held in April 2008 to try the 8 accused of terrorist conspiracy and attempted murder of thousands of passengers on flights to North America. On 9 September 2008, the court convicted three of them of attempted murder, but failed to reach a verdict on the most important charge, that of blowing up planes. On 17 February 2009, a second trial opened to retry the eight defendants. As the second trial failed to reach a verdict, a third trial was held in 2010. In the end, of the eight defendants, five were found innocent and three were charged and tried for terrorism, for acts that had nothing to do with the destruction of planes.

The headlines were about the Islamist mothers who were planning to use their babies' bottles to blow up planes! In fact, it turned out that the chemicals found in the bottles were sterilisation products available in pharmacies. It should be noted that none of the protagonists of this «imminent attack» had bought a plane ticket. Moreover, some of them did not even have passports and could not fly out of the country[789] ...

The plot 'imagined' by British intelligence services envisaged the use of binary explosives, i.e. made of two harmless components which, when combined, become highly explosive. A film-maker's fantasy, because although this type of explosive has been seen in many films, it is not feasible in the current state of knowledge[790] , under improvised conditions, for example on board an aircraft, as explosives experts from the British army have stated[791] .

The scenario was therefore unfeasible, and none of the protagonists were found guilty of an explosive plot against aircraft. Yet security measures were put in place and remained in place at airports around the world, including a ban on carrying liquids above a certain volume in the cabin. But these measures have

---

789. Craig Murray, "Liquid Lies Revisited", 3 July 2014, https://www.craigmurray.org.uk/archives/2014/07/liquid-lies-revisited/

790. Thomas C Greene, "Mass murder in the skies: was the plot feasible?", The Register, 17 August 2006.

791. Nafeez Ahmed, "Source: August terror plot is a 'fiction' underscoring police failures", rawstory.com, 18 September 2006, http://www.rawstory.com/news/2006/Sources_August_Terror_Plot_Fiction_Underscoring_0918.html.

failed to detect a single bottle of explosives in the nearly 35 billion passengers who have flown since 2006.

The threat was therefore completely imaginary and was 'hyped up'. The question - and one that will be asked many times in other countries - is to assess the extent to which the intelligence services suffer from an analytical deficit and the extent to which threat analysis is simply a flight to safety to assert the authority of governments that are not in control of the situation.

3.5.2. Pre-emptive action

3.5.2.1. Protective measures

Protective measures include all passive measures aimed at preventing the execution of an attack and limiting its effects. They can have a preventive effect as part of a deterrence strategy in symmetrical forms of terrorism (common or marginal terrorism). In asymmetric forms of terrorism, and contrary to common rhetoric, protective measures do not have a preventive effect, but only a «pre-emptive» one. In other words, they do not influence the decision of the terrorists, but only the execution of the attack.

They include the physical protection of people, facilities and buildings, the security and integrity of information (both in the physical domain and in cyberspace) and can extend to border control.

They are only truly effective (i.e. they achieve their purpose) and efficient (i.e. they achieve their purpose with a reasonable expenditure of energy) if the nature of the terrorists' objectives is known and understood.

Thus, in December 2015, a few months after the attempted attack on the Thalys (21 August 2015), the Hollande government inaugurated metal detection gates at the Gare du Nord on the line between Paris and Brussels with great fanfare[792].In fact, this is a unilateral measure, which is not coordinated with Belgium and the Netherlands (where Thalys passengers bound for Paris are not subject to controls), and only concerns this line. Clearly, this is a poorly thought-out protection measure, useless because it is not applied on any other TGV/Thalys line, and costly because no real analysis of the threat was ever carried out. Moreover, at this stage, we don't even know the criminal's motives.

What we have seen in Belgium and France in 2015-2016 shows that thinking is based on preconceived ideas and without even trying to understand what the enemy is looking for. In January 2015, after the incident in Verviers (Belgium) and the arrest of a terrorist cell, which specifically targeted the police in Brussels and Molenbeek, the response was to deploy more police on the streets. Thus, in a way, the designated 'targets' were placed in the heart of the population,

---

792. «Security gates for Thalys: it will be like for the London Eurostar», RTBF, 25 November 2015.

instead of being made less visible. The attack on four soldiers in the Louvre on 3 February 2017 brings the same observation[793].The problem is that we respond to terrorism as if it were ordinary crime, without taking into account its strategic objectives or its asymmetric nature.

3.5.2.2. *The role of special operations forces*

Counter-terrorism units are engaged in ad hoc intervention and direct action missions. They can neutralise terrorists and control the effect and impact of terrorist action, but they do not tackle terrorism itself. It was really the taking of Israeli athletes hostage at the 1972 Munich Olympics, and the disaster caused by the clumsy intervention of the German police, that demonstrated the need for special forces specially trained for this type of action. Thus was born the idea of a specialised intervention group, the GSG-9, which has been followed by many units around the world.

Intervention units are mainly devoted to solving difficult situations, such as hostage-taking, hijacking, maritime piracy, commando actions, etc. They therefore intervene at best just before the terrorist action (pre-emptive action), and generally after the terrorist action has been triggered (reactive action). They intervene at best just *before* the terrorist action (pre-emptive action), and generally *after the* terrorist action has been triggered (reactive action). Their intervention is characterised by great speed, precise teamwork and meticulous preparation.

Intervention units are not 'special forces' in the strict sense, but 'special operations' forces. They can be engaged in terrorist situations or, more often, to neutralise the insurgents. They may be military or police, depending on the country.

3.5.2.3. *Cyberwarfare*

Today, while the EI has defined its main battlefield in the Near and Middle East region, its external operations in the West are very much dependent on the knowledge that its supporters have of the situation in Iraq and Syria. The videos showing the casualties and destruction caused by the international coalition are, in fact, the main material that motivates European jihadists.

It is therefore tempting to cut off this source of information through cyberwarfare and censorship. Such operations are carried out with the help of service providers such as Twitter, Facebook, Microsoft, Google, etc., with two major consequences.

---

793. Eugénie Bastié, 'Avec Sentinelle, les militaires sont devenus des magnants à terroristes', lefigaro.fr, 3 February 2017.

Firstly, insofar as terrorism and the Internet are two means of communicating a message, cutting off the Internet encourages jihadists to use only terrorism as a means of communication.

Second, because most of the intelligence on terrorists comes from monitoring computer networks, locking them down will drive terrorists to alternative means of communication that will be beyond the reach of our «cyber-police». This is what happened in Afghanistan, where Afghan resistance fighters reactivated old methods of communication, using carrier pigeons or messengers that are totally beyond the reach of Western technology. In the West, this has had the consequence of tightening the networks on siblings or families. This is what the theorists of individual jihad recommend.

Thus, the fight against terrorism cannot be reduced to censorship measures on the Internet and should include real communication strategies towards communities likely to have sympathies for jihadists. The problem is that terrorism is the result of Western actions that are often illegal and that we find difficult to explain and justify...

3.5.3. Reactive action

The reaction to an event is the final step in the counter-terrorism process. In essence, it means that all other phases have failed. Often presented as a success, it (sometimes) saves lives, but more often than not it is already a political success for the terrorists, especially in an asymmetric context.

3.5.4. Judicial treatment

In a state governed by the rule of law, crime is dealt with within the framework of the law. When the tools provided by normal legislation are no longer sufficient, a state of emergency allows the law to be temporarily extended to deal with an exceptional situation.

It should be noted, however, that entering a judicial phase means that preventive measures have failed and that one is unable to deal with the problem strategically.

In France, justice - often ideological and dogmatic - is not really part of the solution and tends to create new problems.

In fact, in France, the notion of apology for terrorism - punishable under criminal law since November 2014 - gives rise to the most diverse and fanciful interpretations. As the press has reported, children are arrested and severely punished for remarks that are probably more akin to a spanking than a prison sentence[794]. The problem here is that French justice has not realised that it operates

---

794. Louise Tourret, «Apologie du terrorisme, la justice doit protéger les mineurs», slate.fr, 30 January 2015.

in an asymmetric context and that hasty, spectacular judgements that are more attached to the letter than to the spirit tend to contribute to the development of terrorism. Just as the noisy campaign against the comedian Dieudonné has probably contributed more to the development of anti-Semitism than his jokes, which are not always in the best taste. The measures taken to fight terrorism are mostly counterproductive.

The conviction of individuals who consulted websites that offer Islamist material to researchers, as mentioned above, tends to prevent any understanding of the jihadist terrorist phenomenon. In fact, the judiciary has followed the lead of politicians, who - as Belgian expert Rik Coolsaet notes - *'share the view that trying to explain terrorism means in a way excusing it'*[795].

Our inability to understand and explain terrorism in any other way than by fate leads us to see it as a strictly criminal phenomenon. In an asymmetric context, this tends to focus on tactics and exclude strategic action:

> *Conceptually, terrorism is, and in my view must continue to be, seen as an international crime, albeit in a very dangerous and heinous form. International cooperation to combat it is therefore not a military matter, but basically follows the methods and procedures of police and judicial cooperation in criminal cases.*[796]

This legal approach, which is supposed to have a deterrent function, originated in the fight against organised crime. It is totally outdated for dealing with asymmetric phenomena and, in fact, helps to promote terrorism.

Democracy is criticised for allowing the emergence of individuals or organisations that seek to destroy it. The result is a strong temptation to restrict democratic freedoms and to infiltrate the privacy of citizens in order to better control opposition forces. Moreover, as we have seen, jihadist terrorism does not seek to «destroy our democracies», but only to make us reconsider unwise decisions.

The conversion of emergency measures into ordinary legislation is a sleight of hand that reflects the inability of the authorities to overcome the terrorist crisis. It reflects the lack of a coherent strategy to deal with the problem in depth and perpetuates superficial measures that essentially affect the vast majority of honest citizens.

One of the key difficulties in dealing with clandestine forces is to strike the right balance between the necessary and legitimate need for security and control

---

795. Rik Coolsaet, Anticipating the Post-DAESH Landscape, Egmont Paper 97, October 2017.
796. Seger Paul, "Fighting terrorism while respecting international law and human rights", Workshop on Combating the Financing of Terrorism, CISP Proceedings, Geneva, 27-28 November 2003.

and respect for the values one seeks to defend. During the parliamentary enquiry into the events of 11 September 2001, General Michael Hayden, Director of the NSA, was to end his statement with the following words

> *Let me finish by telling you what I hope will come out of the national dialogue that these commissions are creating. I am not really helped by being reminded that I need more Arab linguists or by someone trying to interpret yet another obscure intercept in our files that might make more sense today than it did two years ago. What I really need is for you to talk to your constituents and find out where the American people want to draw the line between security and freedom.*[797]

The problem with counter-terrorism measures - especially preventive measures - is that they almost inevitably require an adjustment of the legal basis, in order to have instruments for intrusive surveillance before a terrorist act takes place. The question is how to minimise the effects of such measures by adopting upstream measures (counter-terrorism).

Americans understand their security by the yardstick of films and television series, and are obsessed with the idea of a *ticking* bomb ([798]) that can only be neutralised by a prisoner's confession. This rather simplistic perception is at the origin of the legalisation of the use of torture by the American government, and of the special status of Guantanamo detainees, as explained by Donald Rumsfeld, Secretary of Defense:

> *Detaining enemy combatants [...] can help us prevent future acts of terrorism. It can save lives and I am convinced that it can accelerate [our] victory.*
> [799]

... and the legend continues. On 11 September 2021, during a RTBF programme directed by Sasha Daoud, a journalist justified the existence of the Guantanamo detention camp by the permanent threat of Islamism[800].A paradox for a profession whose lies and distortions of information are at the root of our lack of understanding of the problem.

---

797. Testimony of Lieutenant General Michael V. Hayden (USAF), Director of the National Security Agency (NSA) and Chief of the Central Security Service before the Joint Inquiry of the Senate Select Committee on Intelligence and the House Permanent Select Committee on Intelligence, October 17, 2002, pp. 11-12.

798. Defusing the Ticking Bomb Scenario: Why we must say No to torture, always, Association for the Prevention of Torture, Geneva, 2007.

799. Martin Bright, "Guantanamo has 'failed to prevent terror attacks'", The Guardian, 3 October 2004.

800. Special edition, RTBF, 11 September 2021.

The status of prisoners captured in Afghanistan and held at Guantanamo Bay is an example of the inadequacy of the legal basis for counter-terrorism, the lack of separation of powers in the United States, and its failure to respect international and humanitarian law by denying POW treatment to captives[801].

In the context of an asymmetric conflict, where legitimacy is often a centre of gravity, such treatment - like torture - can fuel the legitimacy of terrorists.

However, these detentions do not appear to have prevented any terrorist action[802].Since the camp opened on 11 January 2002, a total of 779 prisoners have been held at Guantanamo, the youngest of whom was 13 years old and the oldest 89 years old. According to US government data, 92% of them were not linked to «al-Qaeda», 21 were children, and 9 died in detention. In fact, only 5% of the detainees were captured by US forces and 86% were handed over by US allies, Afghan warlords and Pakistani bounty hunters for payment. Virtually all were released after years of detention, without regard to international law, and without any charges being brought against them. For example, Abdullah Kamel Al-Kandari was arrested and imprisoned for the sole «crime» of owning a Casio F91W digital watch (a reputed favourite of «Al Qaeda» bombers), only to be released after several years without any other charges being brought against him!

As of January 2018, 41 are still incarcerated there, including 3 who have been convicted of a crime, 23 who are «considered dangerous and unreleasable», even though they have no charges or evidence, and 5 who are releasable... but are not released[803] , because the Americans are too afraid that these individuals, innocent but tortured and deprived of freedom for nothing, will turn against them... According to a confidential report of the Department of Defense, about one out of seven released prisoners has taken up arms against Americans[804].Their story continues to fuel Islamist propaganda for the recruitment of new fighters.

Special courts for terrorism cases

Right to/from	Courts Northern Ireland	South African courts (Apartheid)	US Courts	American courts-martial	US Military Commissions
Civil judge				-	-
Choice of lawyer					-

---

801. According to the Geneva Conventions, when there is doubt about the status of prisoners captured in combat, they must be treated as prisoners of war, pending the determination of their status by a competent tribunal (Geneva Convention relative to the Treatment of Prisoners of War of 12 August 1949, Article 5).
802. Martin Bright, op. cit.
803. https://www.aclu.org/feature/close-guantanamo?redirect=closegitmo.
804. Elizabeth Bumiller, "Later Terror Link Cited for 1 in 7 Freed Detainees", The New York Times, 20 May 2009.

Remaining silent		-		
Open trial			-	-
Jury	-	-	-	-
Privacy				-
Knowledge of the file				-
Appeal to an independent judge				-

Table 22 (check number) - Comparison of different special courts for the treatment of terrorism.

[Sources: US Department of Defense, Diplock Commission Report, Cape Town Legal Resources Centre, Human Rights Watch, Amnesty International, The Economist]

Guantanamo is a symbol of the abandonment of our values and the rules of law that were established after the sad experiences of the Second World War. To justify its existence is to justify the crimes of the Second World War.

3.5.5. The use of force

The use of force means that we have failed to dissuade the adversary from engaging in terrorism, and therefore that the counter-terrorism strategy has failed because of our inability to understand the mechanics of jihadist terrorism.

The main reason for this failure is a belief that terrorism is an inescapable and inherent phenomenon of Islam[805]. This reading originates from Israel, where the authorities link Palestinian resistance to religious objectives (which are by definition difficult to negotiate) in order to rule out any negotiation with the Palestinians on territorial issues. As a result, the solution can only be found in the use of force. This vision is widespread in France and Belgium and is conveyed by some whose concern is not only to inform. It is extremely dangerous because it presents terrorism as a phenomenon that cannot be fought upstream by a holistic strategy, but only in a reactive manner by force. Its effect is to 'de-pluralise' the causes of terrorism and to favour communitarianism. As we have seen, it is at the root of the intensification of terrorism and our inability to deal with it.

In fact, the use of force is only really effective against terrorism of a symmetrical nature. Asymmetrical terrorism (jihadist or Marxist terrorism) feeds on the use of force: avoiding the use of force thus contributes to «suffocating» the terrorist movement. But, in more than sixty years, Israel has still not understood this...

---

805. Antoine Hasday, «La pensée djihadiste décryptée», slate.fr, 6 November 2017.

The use of force in counter-terrorism is double-edged: it must achieve its objective without providing additional motivation for the terrorists. In 1990, a Vietnam War veteran said:

> *The longer we stayed in Vietnam, the more Viet Cong there were, because we created them; we produced them... The Vietnamese hated me and I gave them every reason to hate me.*[806]

This is the same discourse that we hear today about Operation BARKHANE. On 6 July 2009, the High Command of the NATO force in Afghanistan (ISAF), recognising - somewhat belatedly - the asymmetrical nature of the conflict, issued a directive stating

> *We must avoid the trap of winning tactical victories - but suffering strategic defeats - by generating excessive civilian casualties or damage and thus alienating the population.*[807]

There is no rule to determine the «optimal level» of force to be used to be effective against terrorism. Instead, the upper limit is given by the three basic principles of international humanitarian law[808] for the planning and execution of military operations:
- the principle of distinction, which requires a distinction between civilians and combatants. It prohibits indiscriminate attacks that are not aimed at a specific military objective, using a method or means of combat whose effects cannot be contained;
- the principle of proportionality, which requires that the damage caused must be in proportion to the direct and concrete military benefit;
- the precautionary principle, which obliges the attacker to take all possible precautions to protect the civilian population and property from the effects of its attacks.

Israel is frequently singled out for its failure to respect these three basic principles. For example, in May 2021, during the fighting in Jerusalem and Gaza, Jonathan Conricus, spokesman for the Israeli army, justified the number of Palestinian civilians killed by the intermingling of combatants and civilians in

---

806. "Magnificent Storyteller Soldier Reveals What He Saw In Vietnam," YouTube, July 19, 2018, https://youtu.be/tixOyiR8B-8.

807. Jim Garamone, "Directive re-emphasizes protecting Afghan civilians", American Forces Press Service, 6 July 2009, www.af.mil/News/Article-Display/Article/119831/directive-re-emphasizes-protecting-afghan-civilians/

808. Protocol Additional to the Geneva Conventions of 12 August 1949, and relating to the Protection of Victims of International Armed Conflicts (Protocol I), 8 June 1977.

382

Gaza. But this is fallacious, because the principle of distinction clearly prohibits opening fire when one is not able to discriminate between military and civilian targets.

The problem with Western forces is that they seek to achieve victory through *firepower superiority*. This is the way war was fought in 1914-1918, in a very symmetrical situation with virtually no strategy. Today, in an asymmetric conflict, it often leads to transgressing the rules of the law of war, without leading to victory.

Of course, Western armies and the Israeli army are by far not the only ones to violate international humanitarian law. The problem is that, unlike these 'renegade' armies, Westerners justify their interventions by defending 'our values': the fact that the EI does not apply international law justifies fighting it, but if we do not respect this law either, then we justify the EI's existence and fight.

For example, in July 2017, with the recapture of Mosul by the Western coalition, the Islamic State published an infographic on social networks under the title «Who won in Mosul? « which compared the capture of the city in 2016 by the Islamic State (by 300-400 mujahideen equipped with small arms, in 4 days, without destruction by bombing, pushing 60,000 Iraqi fighters to flee, and capturing 2,700 vehicles with weapons and ammunition) and the recapture of the city by the coalition (with more than 100,000 fighters, after a 9-month battle, killing or wounding 60,000 people, destroying part of the city, with the support of 60 countries, while the city was defended by 3,000 mujahideen with no outside support) and concluded: «Who really won and who really lost? « This is a perfect illustration of how Islamists think. But it also shows the inability of Westerners to respond to such reasoning, which contributes to the mobilisation mechanism of the militants.

The problem is often more the disproportion between the means engaged by the Westerners or the Israelis and those of the combatants (resistance fighters, terrorists, insurgents and others). This is why figures are often cheated. For example, during the May 2021 incidents in Jerusalem and Gaza, an attempt was made to explain the 10:1 ratio of Palestinian to Israeli casualties by explaining that Israel had intercepted 90% of Palestinian rockets with its IRON DOME system. The balance is thus apparently restored. But this is not true. In reality, the IRON DOME is not as effective. According to CNN, in May 2021, the system would have intercepted only 1,200 out of 2,650 missiles, or 45%[809].This is in line with estimates of the system's actual effectiveness. Moreover, the system is only deployed around certain sensitive sites and is not, for example, deployed in the Sderot sector, near the Gaza Strip. In other words, this shows that the

---

809. Tim Lister, "Israel's Iron Dome doesn't chase every rocket it sees", CNN, 18 May 2021.

Palestinian rockets are not aimed at killing as many people as possible, and that there is a real disproportion in the means used on both sides.

For example, in May 2021, according to the Israeli media *Channel 12*, Israeli pilots confessed to shooting down buildings in Gaza to *'vent their* frustration'[810]. In the fight against terrorism, the use of force must be rigorously supervised to prevent it from being carried away by emotion and turning into violence.

3.5.5.1. The Cheney doctrine

In fact, this definition stems from a doctrine enunciated by Vice President Dick Cheney in 2001, better known as the «*Cheney Doctrine*» or «*1% Doctrine*»:

> *If there is a 1% probability that Pakistani scientists are helping terrorists develop or build weapons of mass destruction, we must treat that as a certainty in terms of response.*[811]

It is a bit like the modern version of the Wild West «hip shot». It is symptomatic of our way of understanding the law and our way of waging war: without values and without honour. Now we see that the United States, after 20 years of war in Afghanistan, is only losing ground to the Taliban, to the point where they no longer dare leave the country...

3.5.5.2. The Bethlehem doctrine

For Americans, the use of lethal force against terrorists - let alone US nationals - is justified by the «imminent» nature of the threat. This notion suggests two things: that the terrorist action is close in time and that there is a body of evidence to support it. Despite their considerable resources, US intelligence services are not able to detect an imminent attack, which implies that the elimination of a terrorist in Pakistan would be legally virtually impossible. But of course, President Obama is a lawyer! In February 2013, NBC News released a Department of Justice 'White Paper', which provides the necessary interpretations for the use of 'lethal force' against US citizens associated with 'Al Qaeda', and redefines the word 'imminent'. As a result,

> *the imminent threat of a violent attack against the United States does not require the United States to have evidence that a specific attack against US persons or interests will take place in the immediate future.*[812]

---

810. https://www.mako.co.il/pzm-magazine/Article-90031632ea98971027.htm?Partner=rss.

811. Ron Suskind, The One Percent Doctrine: Deep Inside America's Pursuit of Its Enemies Since 9/11, Simon & Schuster, 15 May 2007.

812. Lawfulness of a Lethal Operation Directed Against a U.S. Citizen Who Is a Senior Operational Leader of Al-Qa'ida or an Associated Force, Department of Justice White Paper, 4 February 2013.

This doctrine was developed by Daniel Bethlehem[813] , legal advisor to Benjamin Netanyahu and then to British Prime Minister Tony Blair. It postulates that states have a right to *preventive self-defence* against an 'imminent' attack.

While the principle appears legitimate, it is the interpretation of the word 'imminent' that is problematic. In intelligence matters, the «imminence» of an attack is defined according to indications of its proximity in time and the probability that it will take place. But this is no longer the case here:

> *It must be right that states should be able to act in self-defence in circumstances where there is evidence of imminent attacks by terrorist groups, even if there is no specific evidence of where such an attack will take place or the precise nature of the attack.*[814]

Thus, a terrorist attack can be considered «imminent» even if the details and timing of the attack are unknown. This makes it possible, for example, to launch an air strike based on the mere suspicion of an upcoming attack.

In its February 2018 report, the *Human Rights Council* (HRC) reports that during the Gaza border protests (Return Marches), the Israeli army shot 183 civilians, including 154 who were unarmed and 35 children[815].In February 2019, he reports that the Israeli army *intentionally* shot children, medical personnel (wearing badges and shot in the back[816] !), journalists and disabled people[817].The Palestinian children shot by Israeli snipers with fragmentation bullets[818] , while simply standing in front of the border in Gaza in 2018[819] or the handcuffed and blindfolded Palestinian youth shot in the back in April 2019[820] are war crimes.

---

813. Daniel Bethlehem, "Principles Relevant to the Scope of a State's Right of Self-Defense against an Imminent or Actual Armed Attack by Non-state Actors", The American Journal of International Law, volume 106, 2012.

814. Daniel Bethlehem QC, "Written evidence submitted by Daniel Bethlehem QC, Director of Lauterpacht Research Centre for International Law, University of Cambridge, International Law And The Use Of Force: The Law As It Is And As It Should Be", Lauterpacht Research Centre for International Law, 7 June 2004, https://publications.parliament.uk/pa/cm200304/cmselect/cmfaff/441/4060808.htm.

815. Report of the UN Commission of Inquiry on the 2018 protests in the OPT, www.ohchr.org /EN/HRBodies/HRC/CoIOPT/Pages/Report2018OPT.aspx.

816. Ali Abunimah, «Gaza nurse killed by Israel was shot in the back», www.aurdip.org, 3 June 2018.

817. Report of the independent international commission of inquiry on the protests in the Occupied Palestinian Territory, (A/HRC/40/74), Human Rights Council, 25 February 2019.

818. Pierre Stambul, 'Gaza: silence, on tue', French Jewish Union for Peace, 23 April 2018; 'Over 100 bullet fragments in brain of Palestinian child shot by Israel soldier', Middle East Monitor, 15 July 2019.

819. Noa Landau, "UN Council: Israel Intentionally Shot Children and Journalists in Gaza", Haaretz, 28 February 2019.

820. Tamar Pileggi, "IDF shoots handcuffed, blindfolded Palestinian suspect during escape attempt", The Times of Israel, 22 April 2019.

Israel's supporters claim *self-defence*[821] , but this is fallacious, as the videos published by the United Nations show[822].Firstly, because the victims were in a 150m security strip within Gaza[823] , separated from Israel by a fence and a wide berm, from which Israeli snipers fire.

The IDF, which built its successes - and its reputation for bravery - on audacity in the 1960s and 1970s, is now building them on brutality and war crimes. This poses several problems for Israel.

The first is a growing disaffection on the part of American Jews who see a growing divergence between their values and those of the Jewish state. Thus, while the Trump administration has been the most openly pro-Israel in decades[824] and while in Israel 70% of the Israeli population had a preference for Donald Trump[825] , 77% of American Jews voted for Joe Biden in the 2020 presidential election[826].

The second is that the Palestinians enjoy increasing support from international opinion, to the detriment of the legitimacy of the Israeli government's action[827].

The third is that the disproportionate use of force tends to justify terrorism and encourage militants to become activists. The likelihood of hitting innocent people corresponds to the risk of creating new volunteers for terrorist action. Thus, beyond the purely humanitarian issue, it is a problem of strategy. It is for this very reason that Operation BARKHANE is meeting with growing opposition among the Sahelian populations: it is a war already lost.

3.5.5.3. *The Dahiya doctrine*

The Israeli army deliberately ignores the principles of international humanitarian law and applies the «*Dahiya doctrine*», developed by General Gadi Eisenkot,

---

821. Ibid.

822. "COI on Gaza Protests: Lethal force against demonstrators not posing imminent threat", UN Human Rights Council/YouTube, 3 April 2019.

823. Initially 50m wide, according to the Oslo Accords, it has varied between 100m and 500m over the years, without the Israeli authorities explicitly defining or marking it; OCHA, 'The humanitarian impact of restrictions on access to land near the perimeter fence in the Gaza Strip', 3 August 2018 cited in Human rights situation in Palestine and other occupied Arab territories - Report of the detailed findings of the independent international Commission of inquiry on the protests in the Occupied Palestinian Territory, Human Rights Council, Document A/HRC/40/CRP.2, 18 March 2019.

824. Tracy Wilkinson, "Trump administration support for Israel goes beyond its predecessors and isolates U.S. internationally", Los Angeles Times, 17 May 2018.

825. "By 70% to 13%, Israeli Jews say Trump is better candidate than Biden for Israel", The Times of Israel, 3 November 2020.

826. Danielle Ziri, "Over Three-quarters of U.S. Jews Voted for Biden in Election, Poll Finds", Haaretz, 4 November 2020.

827. Jonathan Freedland, "Israel should take note: the weight of opinion is turning against it", The Guardian, 21 May 2021.

now Chief of the General Staff. It advocates the use of «*disproportionate force*» in order to create maximum damage and destruction[828] , and considers that there are «*no civilian villages, these are military bases [...] This is not a recommendation. This is a* plan»[829].

Contrary to *Wikipedia*[830] , it is a tactic that can only work in a symmetrical context, i.e. when the action has a linear effect on weakening the opponent. In an asymmetrical context, where determination is a function of the brutality of the adversary, such destruction only serves to stimulate the will to resist and the determination to use a terrorist approach.

In fact, the very existence of this doctrine shows that the Israelis have not understood the nature of the threat. Israel is the only country in the world that has not been able to control terrorism in more than 70 years... This is the consequence of an intellectual incapacity to understand conflicts that can be seen in the way intelligence services understand their environment. Israeli intelligence services are masters at locating terrorists, but have always been unable to understand their logic.

3.5.5.4. The Hannibal Directive

Also rarely mentioned is the «HANNIBAL directive», in force from 1986 to 2016 in the Israeli army, designed to prevent Israeli prisoners from being used as bargaining chips by the Palestinians. It stipulated that those holding the prisoner should be destroyed by all means (including at the cost of the prisoner's own life and that of civilians in the area). Implemented during Operation PROTECTIVE BORDER, it was responsible for the total destruction of a neighbourhood in Rafah on 1ᵉʳ August 2014, an event known in Palestine as *Black Friday*[831].

3.5.6. Negotiations and concessions

Most Western countries have a stated policy of 'non-negotiation'. In reality, however, they are more like 'quiet negotiation' policies, often carried out by private negotiators. In 1985, Ronald Reagan's Republican administration did not hesitate to secretly sell arms to Iran in exchange for a deal on American hostages held by pro-Iranian terrorist movements in Lebanon. This scandal,

828. Gabi Siboni, "Disproportionate Force: Israel's Concept of Response in Light of the Second Lebanon War", Institute for National Security Studies (INSS), Insight n° 74, 2 October 2008; https://wikileaks.org/plusd/cables/08TELAVIV2329_a.html.
829. «Israel warns Hezbollah war would invite destruction", Reuters, 3 October 2008.
830. Wikipedia, article "Dahiya doctrine".
831. Raf Sanchez, "Israel ends the 'Hannibal Directive' - military policy to kill your own troops rather than let them be captured", The Telegraph, 29 June 2016; https://blackfriday.amnesty.org/report.php; The Hannibal Directive - Featured Documentary, Al Jazeera/YouTube, 8 October 2016.

which became known as *Irangate*, was a major political setback for President Reagan.

In fact, this false firmness reflects a very poor understanding of terrorist movements.

In the context of counter-terrorism (i.e. *downstream of* the terrorist decision), a negotiation process is de *facto* carried out under the threat of violence. In counter-terrorism, negotiations and concessions are usually about resolving tactical situations, such as hostage-taking or threats of destruction. Unlike a strategic objective, which is more difficult to negotiate and make recursive concessions on, a tactical objective has the particularity of being infinitely «reproducible». Thus, any negotiation mechanism has to be initiated with the risk that the blackmail will be repeated. However, there is a difference between a policy of 'non-negotiations' and a policy of 'non-concessions'.

Some countries, such as the United States, have a declared policy of non-concession with terrorist movements. This policy has a dual purpose: a) to prevent blackmail from being repeated over and over again, and b) as a deterrent by making it clear that any blackmail is hopeless for the terrorist movement. It does not mean that the US government will not negotiate, but simply that it will not make concessions. For symmetrical terrorism, this policy is effective. In an asymmetric context, however, it immediately places us in a no-win situation where, a priori, the solution can only be found in the execution of the terrorist threat. It therefore works in favour of the terrorists.

However tenuous, the possibility of a positive outcome for the terrorists must be maintained. Non-negotiation policies are inappropriate in asymmetric situations.

In the case of hostage-taking, for example, the primary objective of a negotiation process is to gain control of the initiative and prevent it from remaining in the hands of the terrorists. In addition to the fact that in a negotiation process it is usually possible to obtain a softening of the terrorist demands or the conditions of the hostages' detention, maintaining a dialogue allows the security forces to «manage» the terrorists' nervousness and to choose the optimal moment for an intervention. In particular, it was the unpreparedness of the Russian security forces' negotiation mechanisms that led them to lose control of the situation in Beslan (3 September 2004) and forced them to intervene at an unfavourable time.

The bungling of negotiations for the release of journalists Christian Chesnot and Georges Malbrunot in September-October 2004 illustrates the problems of hostage-taking situations. The state - in this case France - is divided between two attitudes: the humanitarian dimension (freeing the hostages) and a dimension that is both moral and strategic (not satisfying a demand under duress). For the terrorists, hostage-taking is seen as the only way to make themselves heard and the 'game' with the lives of the hostages is legitimised by the cause being defended.

At the strategic level, refusing to negotiate often means closing a door to the conflict. In Afghanistan, the Americans had the (very unexpected) skill of not considering the Taliban as terrorists, so as not to deny themselves a path to negotiation. Conversely, France refuses any negotiation with the Sahel rebels: when President Emmanuel Macron decides to close the BARKHANE mission in June 2021, it must withdraw 'under enemy fire'. Contrary to popular belief, intransigence does not help solve the issue of terrorism.

In such a situation, at least one of the parties, the state, has little alternative but to want to 'have its cake and eat it too'. A possible concession - such as the payment of a ransom - would have both a moral (legitimising the violence) and a strategic (setting a precedent) impact. The margin of manoeuvre of the state involved in such a negotiation is very narrow and requires the creation of a climate of trust which takes time. Such a process must be carefully controlled and coordinated: there must be unity of doctrine in the approach, unity of language with the terrorists, and a clear purpose to the negotiation. When a state engages in this process, it usually puts one structure in place. This structure may change when an unforeseen event occurs, and other actors are engaged. It is also possible to engage in parallel negotiations through different channels that look promising.

3.6. Conclusions

The ineffectiveness of the fight against terrorism is largely due to the emotional perception of states. The inability to rationally define terrorist acts has made a coherent strategy impossible. The use of the term 'terrorist', more for punitive purposes than for strategic purposes, has only served to increase terrorism. In France, the United States and Britain, as well as in less affected countries such as Germany, Sweden and Finland, every civilian death can be attributed to irrational government policies.

Organisations of victims of terrorism are guided more by the desire for revenge than by the desire to find solutions to terrorism. As a result, they unfortunately (and curiously) do not contribute to the fight against terrorism and tend - on the contrary - to favour it.

The idea of merging strategic/external intelligence and security (or domestic) intelligence services is just another temptation to confuse the tactical and strategic levels. In France, the fact that the DGSE devotes a large part of its activities to special operations tends to push it towards the tactical level, which no doubt explains the 'breakdowns' in the fight against terrorism.

Western European countries have failed to adapt their intelligence apparatus to the specificity of the jihadist threat. This conceptual deficit is largely due to the fact that they have simply copied the work of the Americans, who had copied that of the Israelis, the only country in the world that had never solved its terrorism problem.

The intelligence services of countries such as the Eastern European countries have retained a strong security tradition from the communist period that affects their ability to run effective strategic intelligence services. The result is a complete inability to look rationally at their Russian neighbour and thus a deep dependence on the United States.

In France, the fight against terrorism is «thought» primarily at the level of the gut, rarely at the level of the head, and almost never at the level of the heart. The experiences of the past have not been adapted to meet modern circumstances and intelligence has gradually slipped into a police intelligence that allows for a lot of punishment, but not for solutions.

In Belgium, there are two fundamental problems: a police approach to the terrorist problem and a lack of imagination and creativity. The procedures become a screen for the lack of efficiency. The domestic intelligence is quite good, but it is not supported by an efficient strategic intelligence.

In Switzerland, the decline of strategic intelligence in the 1990s-2010, due in particular to a leadership that had no experience of intelligence analysis, led to a merger between domestic and foreign (or strategic) intelligence. From analysis-oriented intelligence during the Cold War, the focus has shifted to police-oriented intelligence, which works to arrest individuals but not to prevent. The fact that Switzerland does not get involved in foreign conflicts makes its intelligence - which has become essentially domestic - appear effective, but its strategic intelligence is very poor. The Netherlands had already made the same experience in the 1990s.

Clearly, we are ill-equipped to deal with jihadist terrorism in a strategic and preventive manner. That is why we suffer it, although - paradoxically - we create the conditions for its emergence.

As Sun Tsu said 2500 years ago:

Tactics without strategy is just noise before defeat.

www.ingramcontent.com/pod-product-compliance
Lightning Source LLC
LaVergne TN
LVHW050419060726
842526LV00008B/2678